ATTACK ON TITAN
33
HAJIME ISAYAMA

THE CHARACTERS OF ATTACK ON TITAN

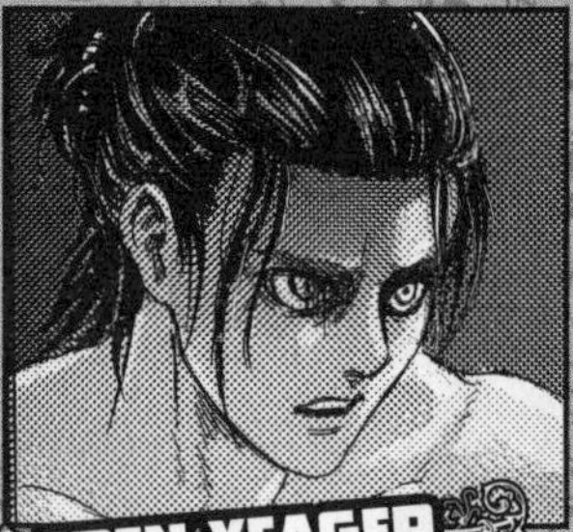

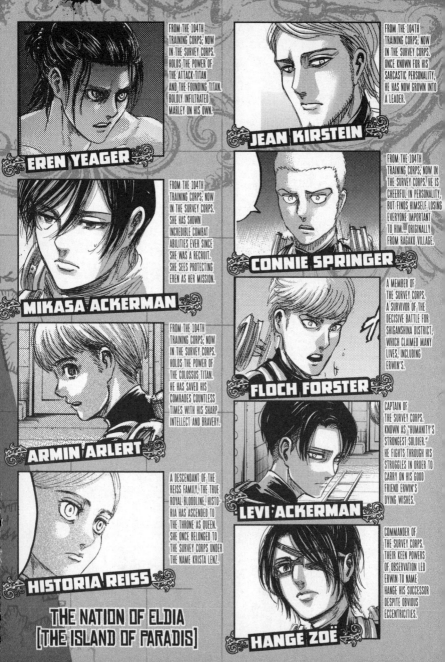

EREN YEAGER

FROM THE 104TH TRAINING CORPS; NOW IN THE SURVEY CORPS. HOLDS THE POWER OF THE ATTACK TITAN AND THE FOUNDING TITAN. BOLDLY INFILTRATED MARLEY ON HIS OWN.

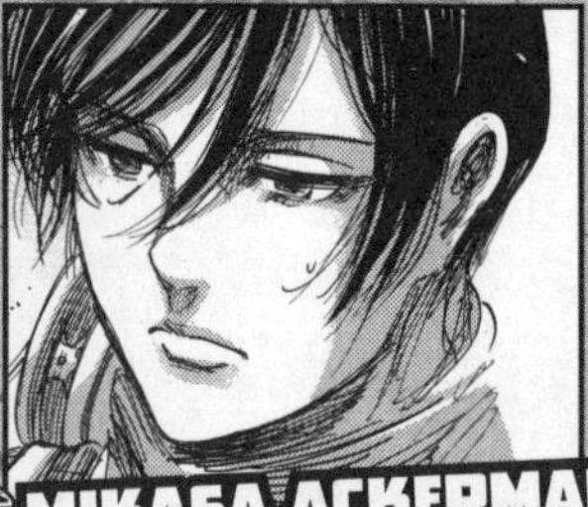

MIKASA ACKERMAN

FROM THE 104TH TRAINING CORPS; NOW IN THE SURVEY CORPS. SHE HAS SHOWN INCREDIBLE COMBAT ABILITIES EVER SINCE SHE WAS A RECRUIT. SHE SEES PROTECTING EREN AS HER MISSION.

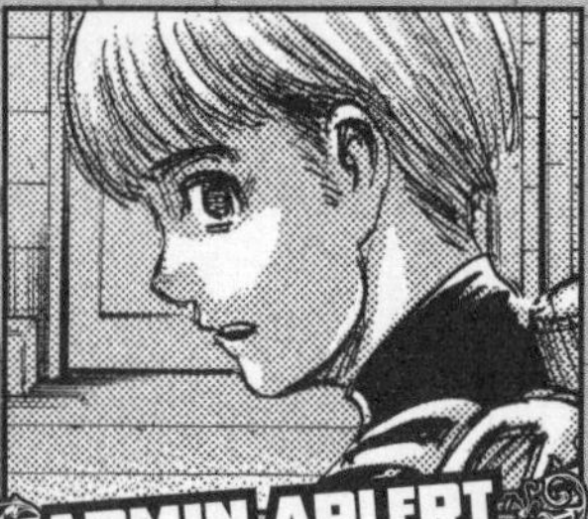

ARMIN ARLERT

FROM THE 104TH TRAINING CORPS; NOW IN THE SURVEY CORPS. HOLDS THE POWER OF THE COLOSSUS TITAN. HE HAS SAVED HIS COMRADES COUNTLESS TIMES WITH HIS SHARP INTELLECT AND BRAVERY.

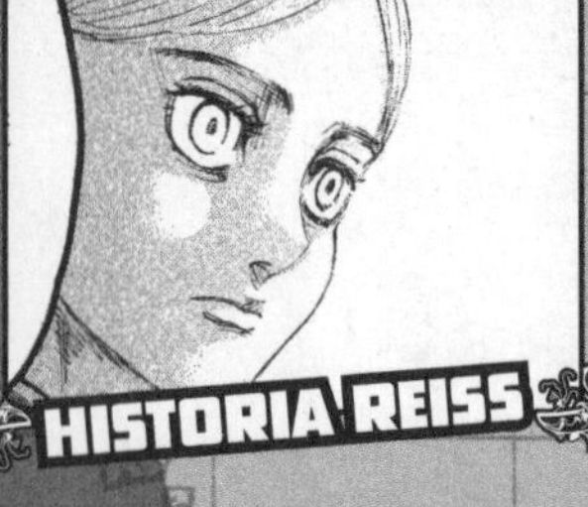

HISTORIA REISS

A DESCENDANT OF THE REISS FAMILY, THE TRUE ROYAL BLOODLINE, HISTORIA HAS ASCENDED TO THE THRONE AS QUEEN. SHE ONCE BELONGED TO THE SURVEY CORPS UNDER THE NAME KRISTA LENZ.

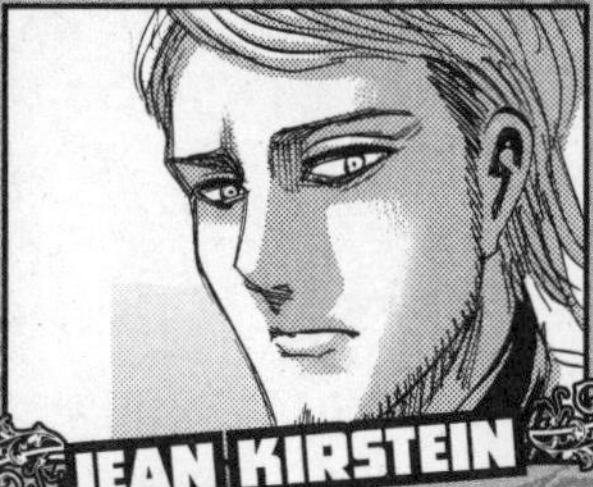

JEAN KIRSTEIN

FROM THE 104TH TRAINING CORPS; NOW IN THE SURVEY CORPS. ONCE KNOWN FOR HIS SARCASTIC PERSONALITY, HE HAS NOW GROWN INTO A LEADER.

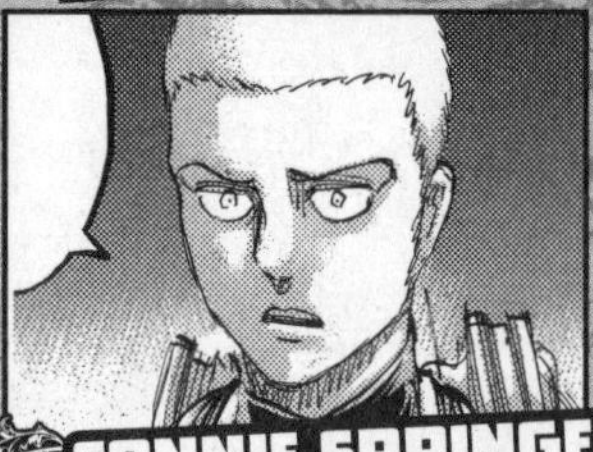

CONNIE SPRINGER

FROM THE 104TH TRAINING CORPS; NOW IN THE SURVEY CORPS. HE IS CHEERFUL IN PERSONALITY, BUT FINDS HIMSELF LOSING EVERYONE IMPORTANT TO HIM... ORIGINALLY FROM RAGAKO VILLAGE.

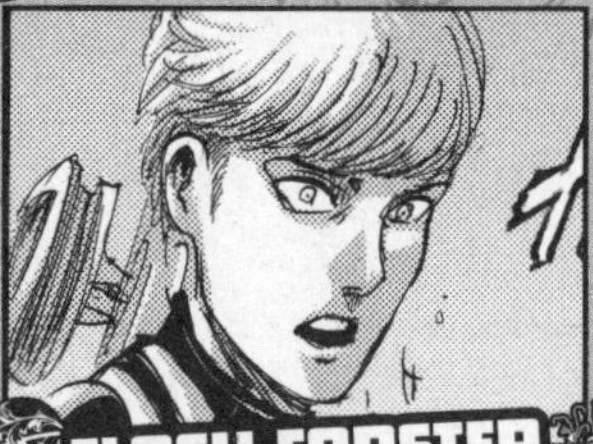

FLOCH FORSTER

A MEMBER OF THE SURVEY CORPS. A SURVIVOR OF THE DECISIVE BATTLE FOR SHIGANSHINA DISTRICT, WHICH CLAIMED MANY LIVES, INCLUDING ERWIN'S.

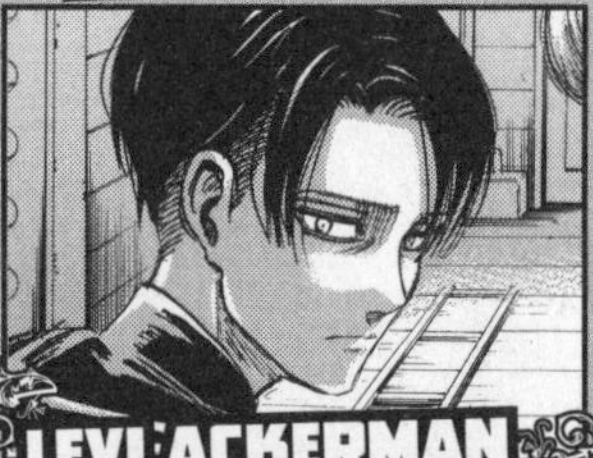

LEVI ACKERMAN

CAPTAIN OF THE SURVEY CORPS. KNOWN AS "HUMANITY'S STRONGEST SOLDIER." HE FIGHTS THROUGH HIS STRUGGLES IN ORDER TO CARRY ON HIS GOOD FRIEND ERWIN'S DYING WISHES.

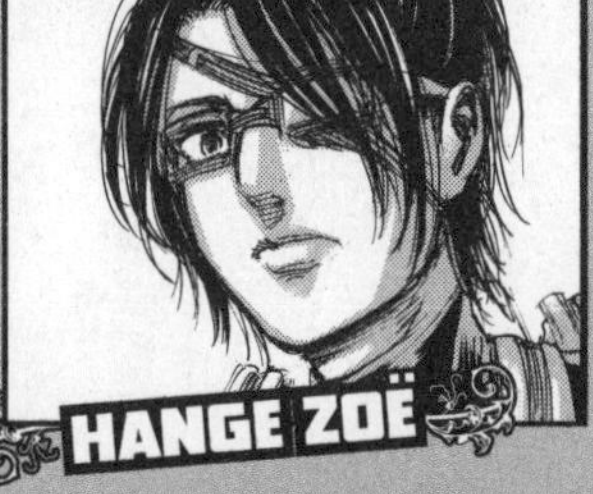

HANGE ZOË

COMMANDER OF THE SURVEY CORPS. THEIR KEEN POWERS OF OBSERVATION LED ERWIN TO NAME HANGE HIS SUCCESSOR DESPITE OBVIOUS ECCENTRICITIES.

THE NATION OF ELDIA [THE ISLAND OF PARADIS]

A Kodansha Comics Trade Paperback Original
Attack on Titan 33 copyright © 2021 Hajime Isayama
English translation copyright © 2021 Hajime Isayama

Published in the United States by Kodansha Comics, an imprint of
Kodansha USA Publishing, LLC, New York.

Publication rights for this English edition arranged through
Kodansha Ltd., Tokyo.

First published in Japan in 2021 by Kodansha Ltd., Tokyo
as *Shingeki no kyojin*, volume 33.

ISBN 978-1-64651-026-9

Original cover design by Takashi Shimoyama/Manami Fukunaga (Red Rooster)

Printed in Mexico.

www.kodanshacomics.com

9 8 7 6 5 4
Translation: Ko Ransom
Lettering: Dezi Sienty
Editing: Ben Applegate, Tiff Joshua TJ Ferentini
Kodansha Comics edition cover design by Phil Balsman

Publisher: Kiichiro Sugawara

Director of publishing services: Ben Applegate
Associate director of operations: Stephen Pakula
Publishing services managing editors: Alanna Ruse, Madison Salters
Assistant production managers: Emi Lotto, Angela Zurlo

FINAL VOLUME COMING FALL 2021!

THE GIRL DREAMS. SHE DREAMS OF A WORLD FREE OF BONDS, AND OF FATE.

THE ELDIAN WARRIORS OF THE MARLEYAN ARMY

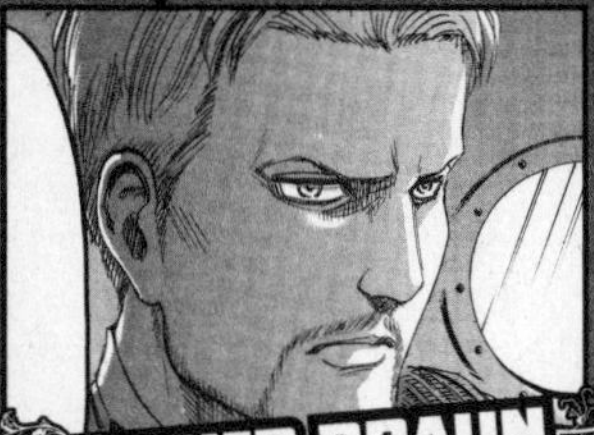

HOLDS THE ARMORED TITAN WITHIN HIM. SINCE HE WAS THE ONLY ONE TO MAKE IT BACK FROM THE MISSION ON PARADIS, HE SUFFERS FROM A GUILTY CONSCIENCE.

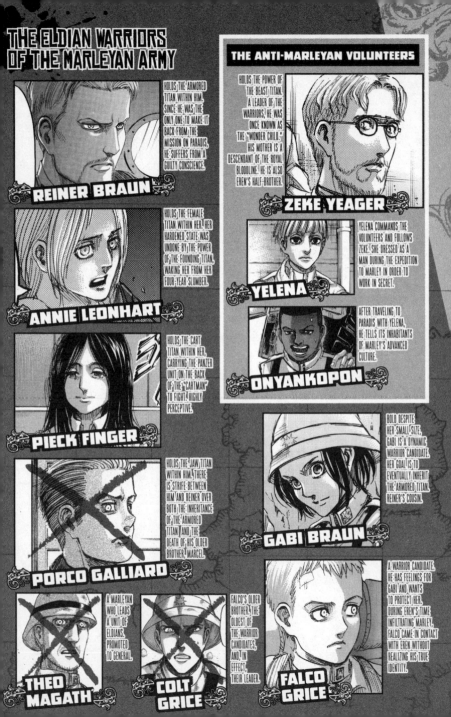

REINER BRAUN

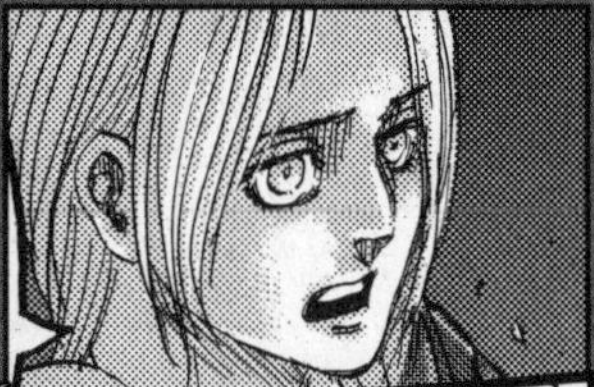

HOLDS THE FEMALE TITAN WITHIN HER. HER HARDENED STATE WAS UNDONE BY THE POWER OF THE FOUNDING TITAN, WAKING HER FROM HER FOUR-YEAR SLUMBER.

ANNIE LEONHART

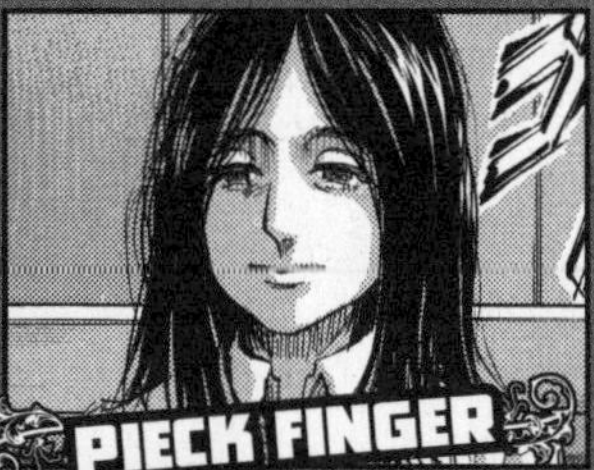

HOLDS THE CART TITAN WITHIN HER, CARRYING THE PANZER UNIT ON THE BACK OF THE "CARTMAN" TO FIGHT. HIGHLY PERCEPTIVE.

PIECK FINGER

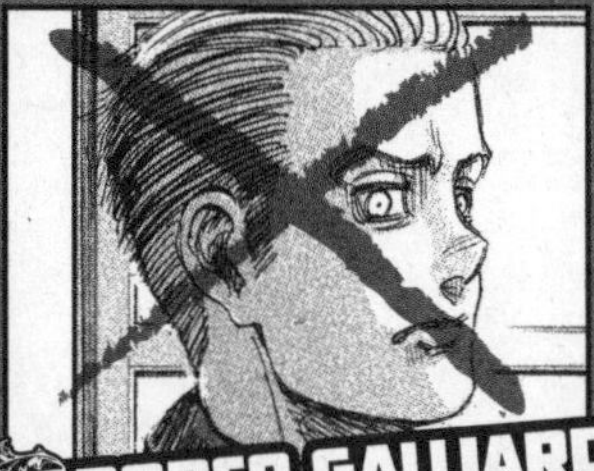

HOLDS THE JAW TITAN WITHIN HIM. THERE IS STRIFE BETWEEN HIM AND REINER OVER BOTH THE INHERITANCE OF THE ARMORED TITAN AND THE DEATH OF HIS OLDER BROTHER, MARCEL.

PORCO GALLIARD

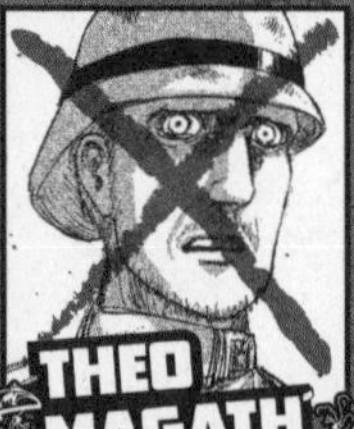

A MARLEYAN WHO LEADS A UNIT OF ELDIANS. PROMOTED TO GENERAL.

THEO MAGATH

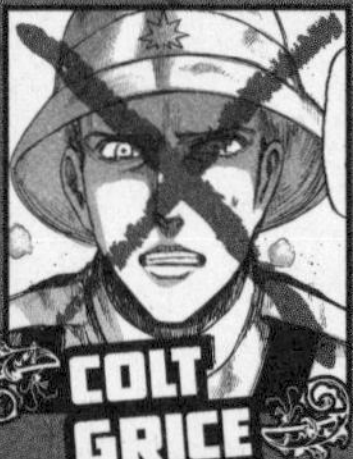

FALCO'S OLDER BROTHER, THE OLDEST OF THE WARRIOR CANDIDATES, AND, IN EFFECT, THEIR LEADER.

COLT GRICE

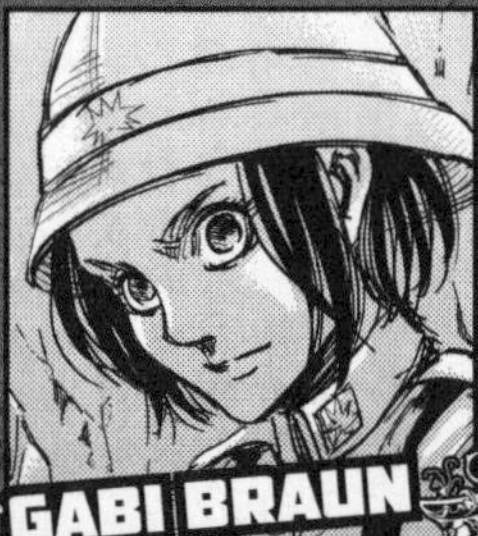

BOLD DESPITE HER SMALL SIZE, GABI IS A DYNAMIC WARRIOR CANDIDATE. HER GOAL IS TO EVENTUALLY INHERIT THE ARMORED TITAN. REINER'S COUSIN.

GABI BRAUN

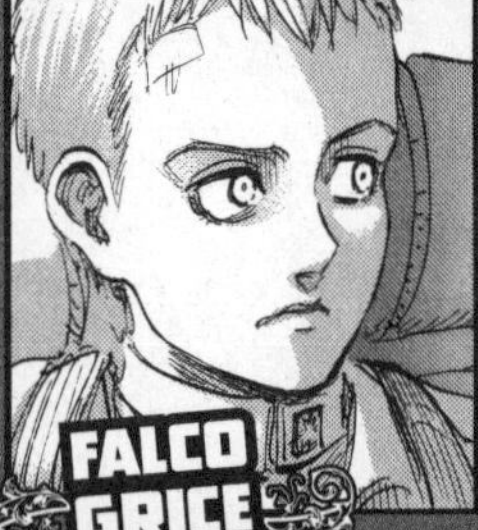

A WARRIOR CANDIDATE. HE HAS FEELINGS FOR GABI AND WANTS TO PROTECT HER. DURING EREN'S TIME INFILTRATING MARLEY, FALCO CAME IN CONTACT WITH EREN WITHOUT REALIZING HIS TRUE IDENTITY.

FALCO GRICE

THE ANTI-MARLEYAN VOLUNTEERS

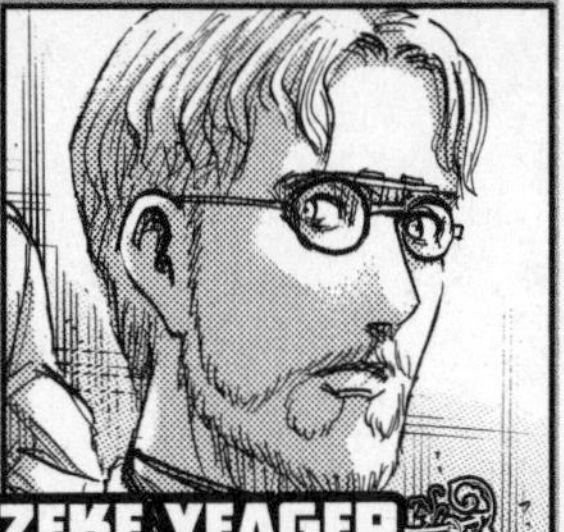

HOLDS THE POWER OF THE BEAST TITAN. A LEADER OF THE WARRIORS, HE WAS ONCE KNOWN AS THE "WONDER CHILD." HIS MOTHER IS A DESCENDANT OF THE ROYAL BLOODLINE. HE IS ALSO EREN'S HALF-BROTHER.

ZEKE YEAGER

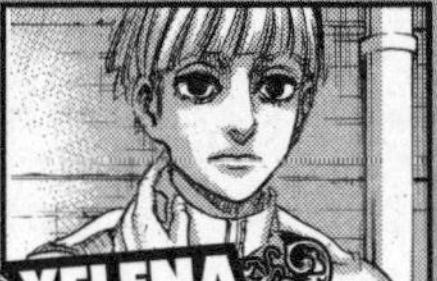

YELENA COMMANDS THE VOLUNTEERS AND FOLLOWS ZEKE. SHE DRESSED AS A MAN DURING THE EXPEDITION TO MARLEY IN ORDER TO WORK IN SECRET.

YELENA

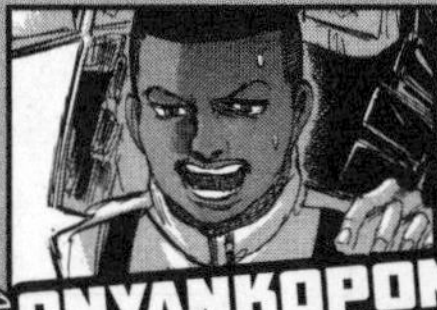

AFTER TRAVELING TO PARADIS WITH YELENA, HE TELLS ITS INHABITANTS OF MARLEY'S ADVANCED CULTURE.

ONYANKOPON

ATTACK on TITAN

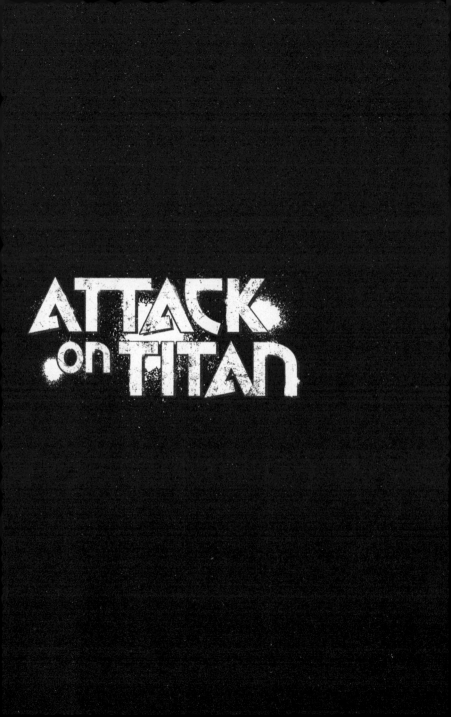

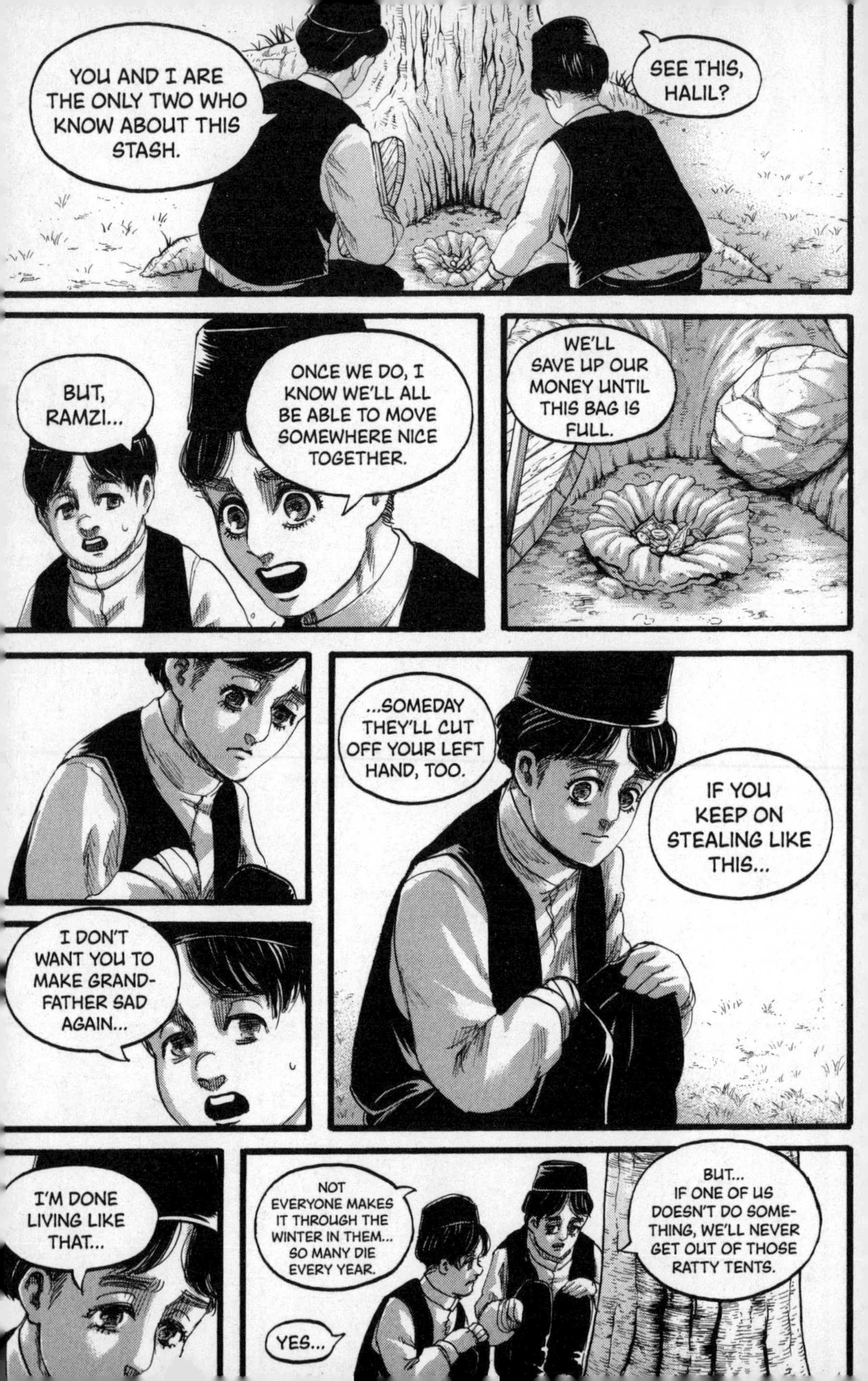
SEE THIS, HALIL?
YOU AND I ARE THE ONLY TWO WHO KNOW ABOUT THIS STASH.
WE'LL SAVE UP OUR MONEY UNTIL THIS BAG IS FULL.
ONCE WE DO, I KNOW WE'LL ALL BE ABLE TO MOVE SOMEWHERE NICE TOGETHER.
BUT, RAMZI...
IF YOU KEEP ON STEALING LIKE THIS...
...SOMEDAY THEY'LL CUT OFF YOUR LEFT HAND, TOO.
I DON'T WANT YOU TO MAKE GRAND-FATHER SAD AGAIN...
BUT... IF ONE OF US DOESN'T DO SOME-THING, WE'LL NEVER GET OUT OF THOSE RATTY TENTS.
NOT EVERYONE MAKES IT THROUGH THE WINTER IN THEM... SO MANY DIE EVERY YEAR.
YES...
I'M DONE LIVING LIKE THAT...

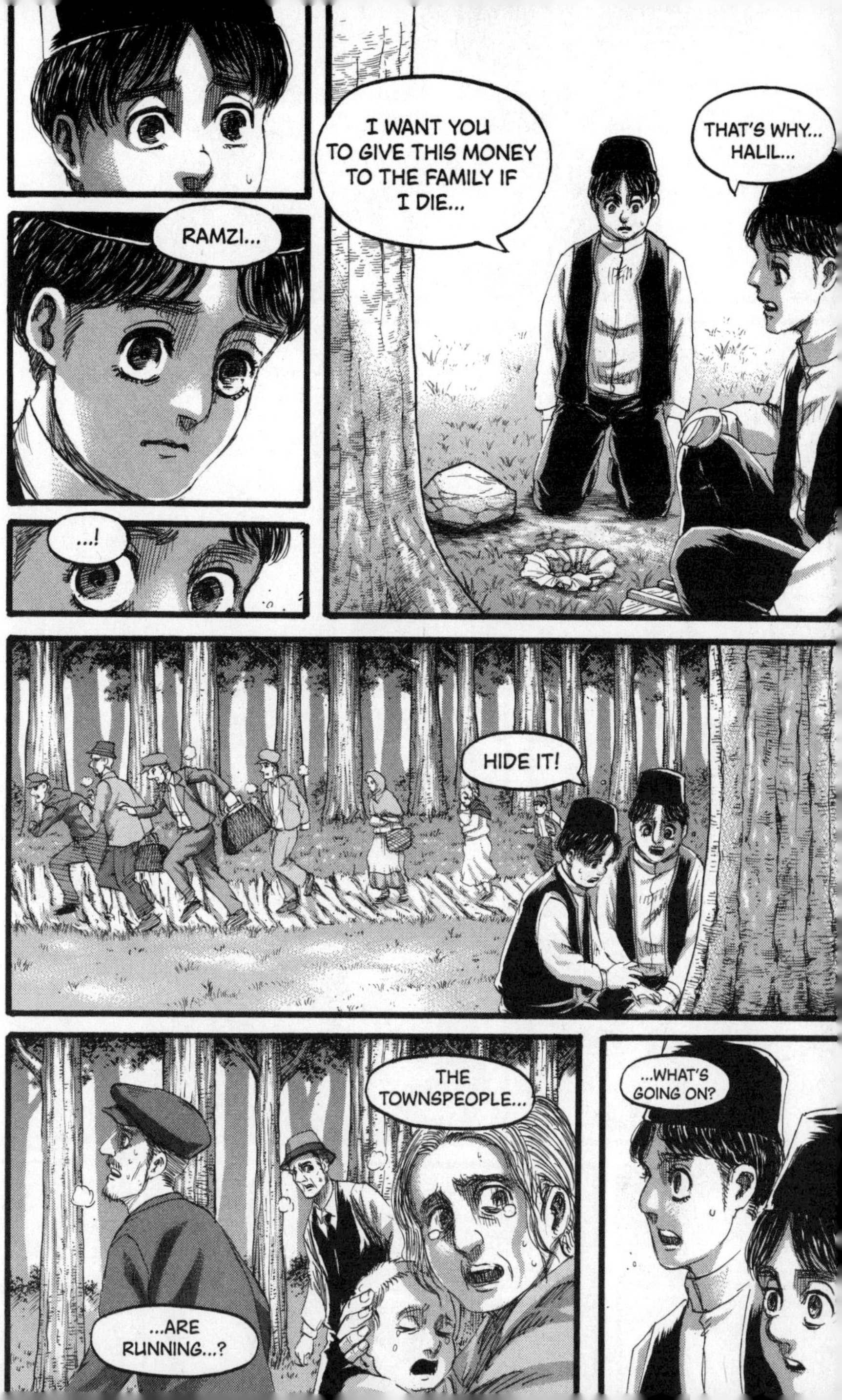
THAT'S WHY... HALIL...
I WANT YOU TO GIVE THIS MONEY TO THE FAMILY IF I DIE...
RAMZI...
...!
HIDE IT!
...WHAT'S GOING ON?
THE TOWNSPEOPLE...
...ARE RUNNING...?

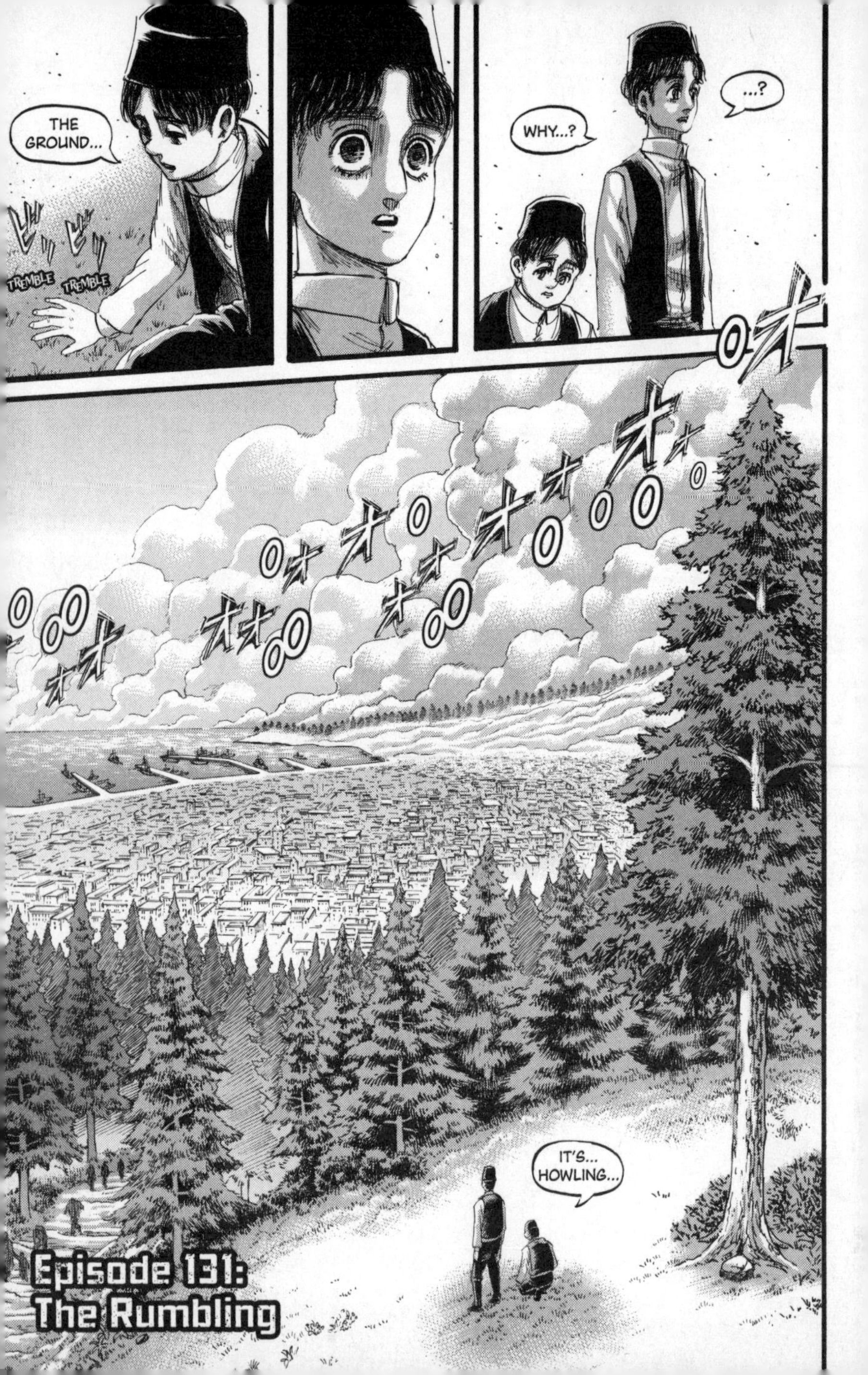

...?
WHY...?
THE GROUND...
TREMBLE
TREMBLE
IT'S... HOWLING...
Episode 131: The Rumbling

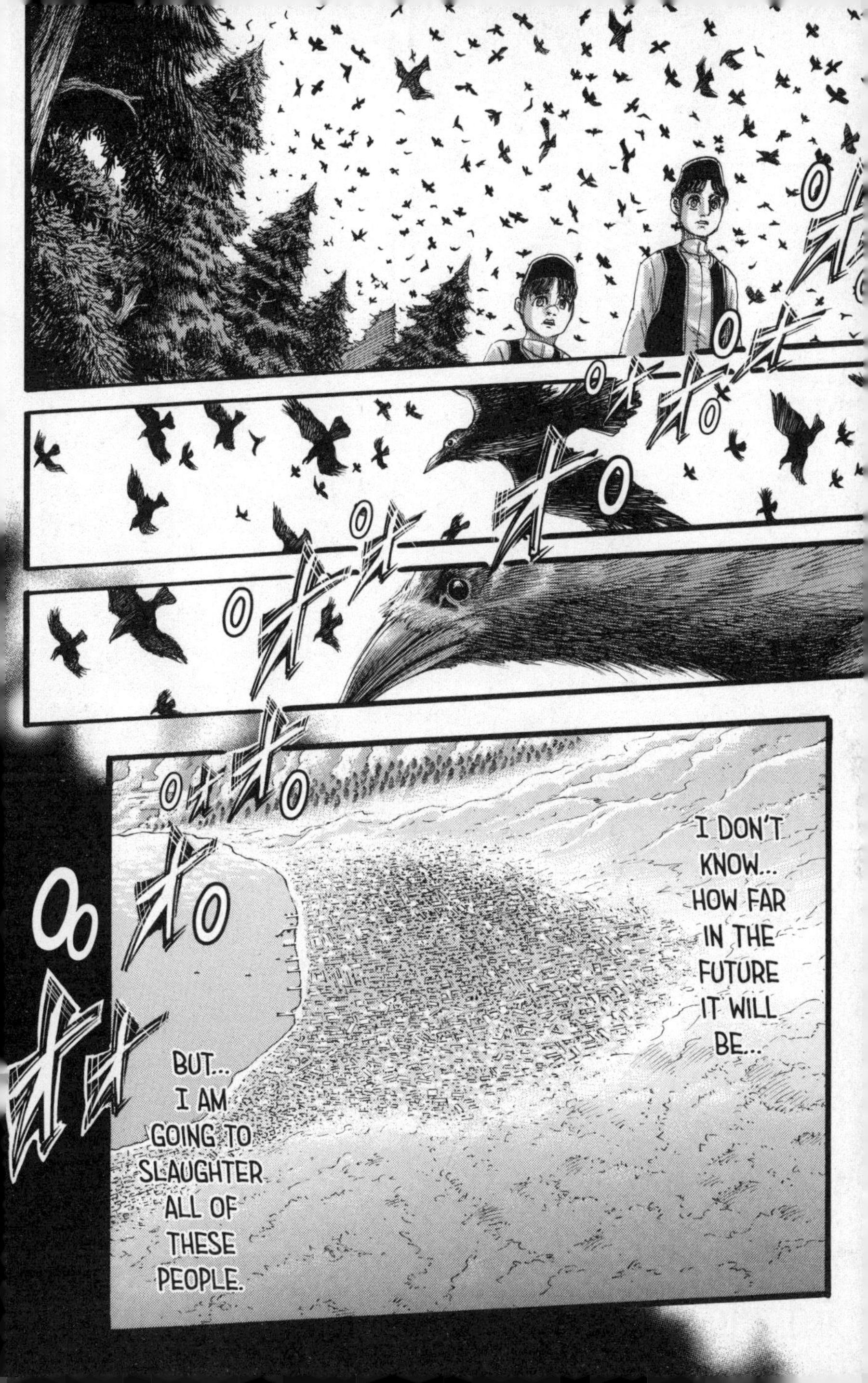
I DON'T KNOW... HOW FAR IN THE FUTURE IT WILL BE...
BUT... I AM GOING TO SLAUGHTER ALL OF THESE PEOPLE.

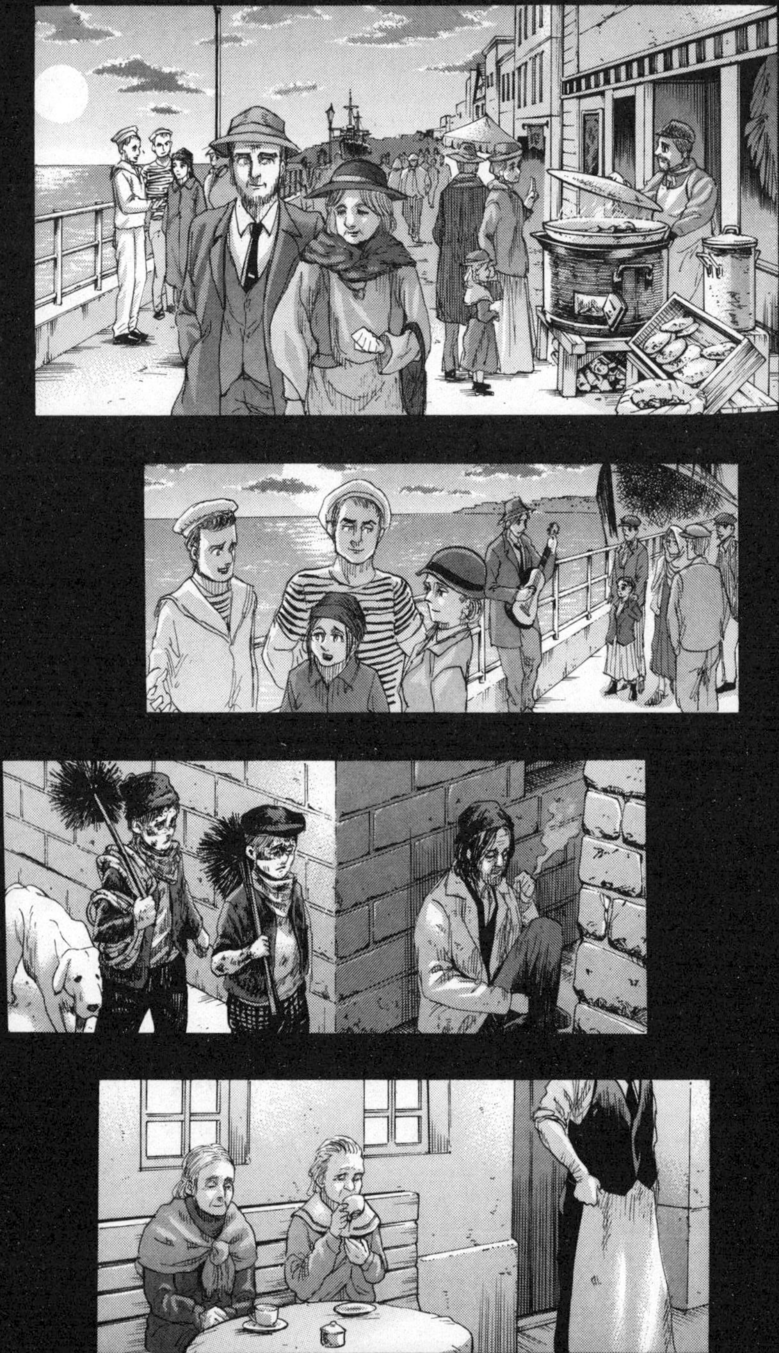

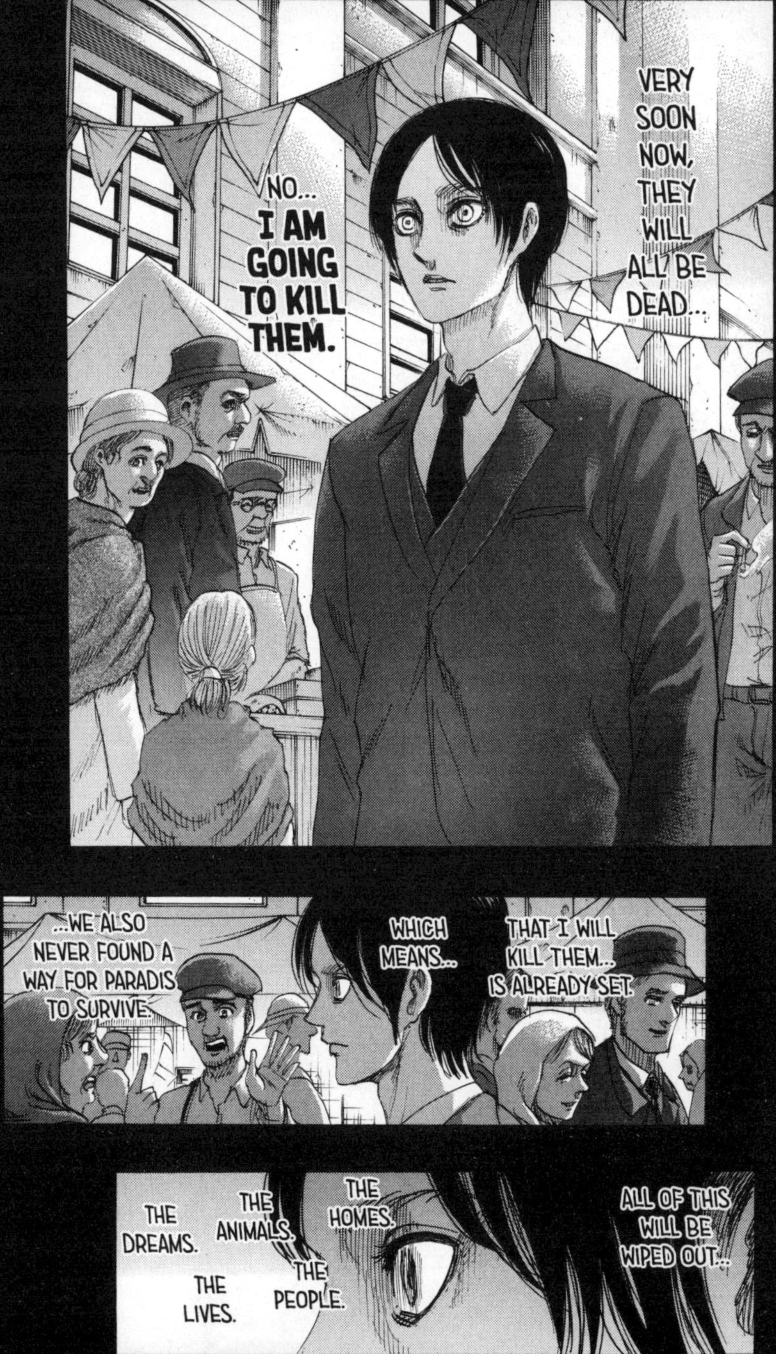
VERY SOON NOW, THEY WILL ALL BE DEAD...
NO... I AM GOING TO KILL THEM.
...WE ALSO NEVER FOUND A WAY FOR PARADIS TO SURVIVE.
WHICH MEANS...
THAT I WILL KILL THEM... IS ALREADY SET.
ALL OF THIS WILL BE WIPED OUT...
THE HOMES.
THE ANIMALS.
THE DREAMS.
THE PEOPLE.
THE LIVES.

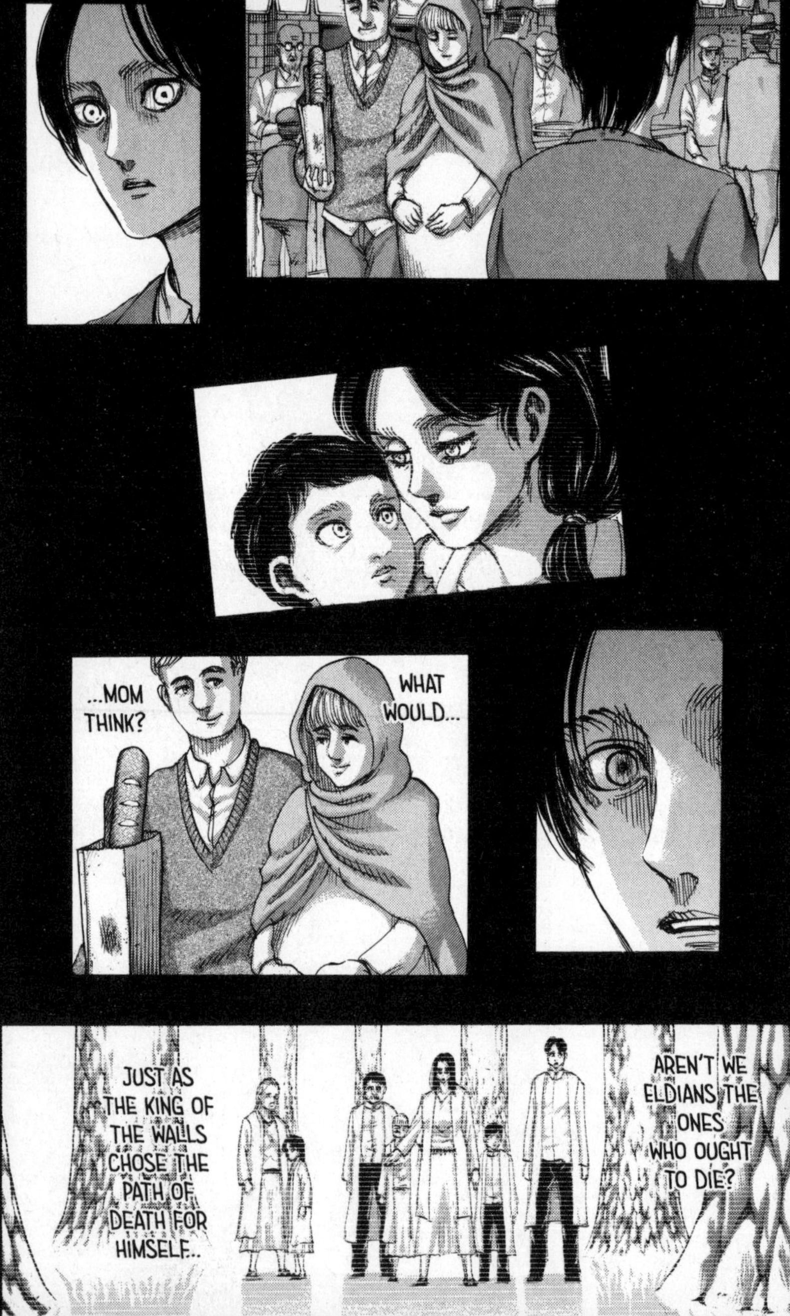
WHAT WOULD...
...MOM THINK?
AREN'T WE ELDIANS THE ONES WHO OUGHT TO DIE?
JUST AS THE KING OF THE WALLS CHOSE THE PATH OF DEATH FOR HIMSELF...

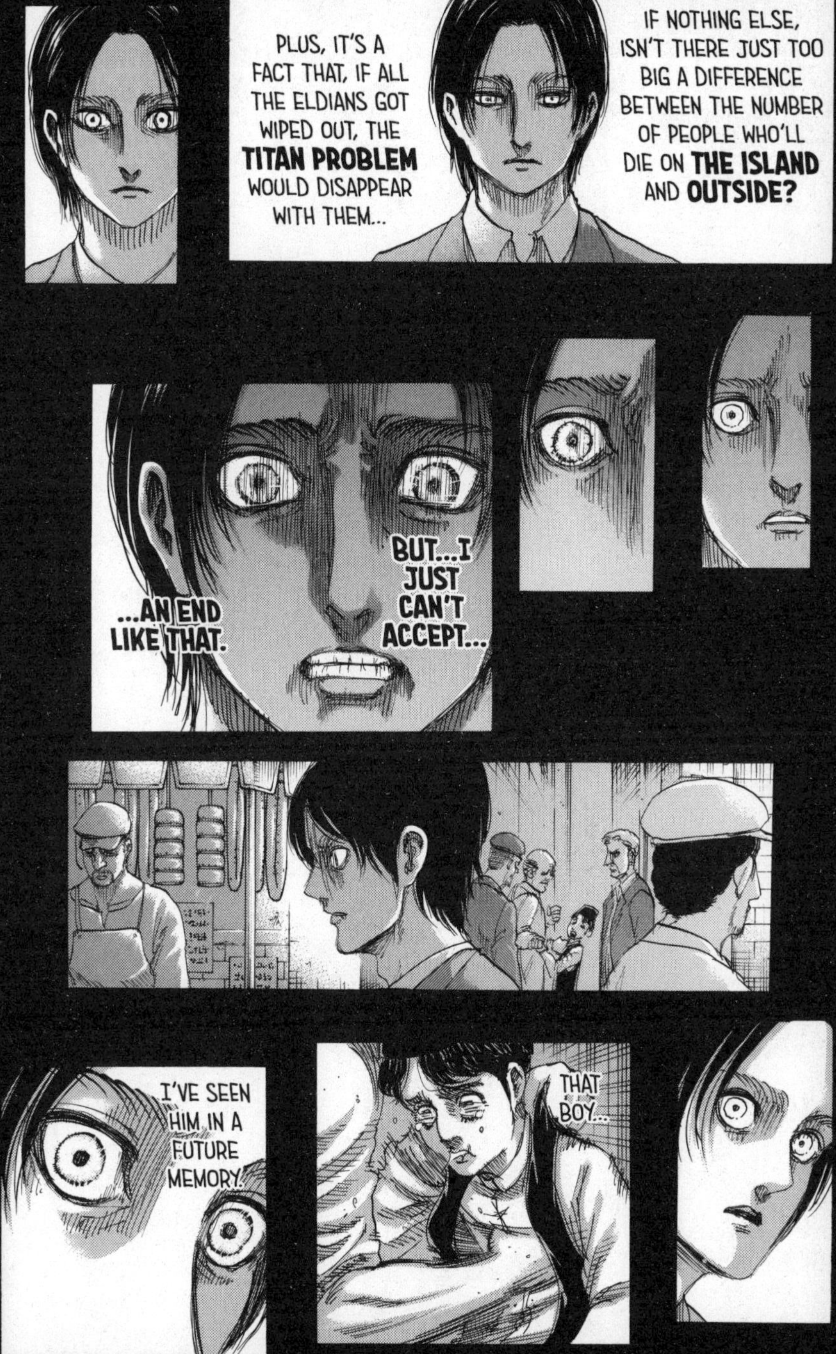
IF NOTHING ELSE, ISN'T THERE JUST TOO BIG A DIFFERENCE BETWEEN THE NUMBER OF PEOPLE WHO'LL DIE ON **THE ISLAND** AND **OUTSIDE?**
PLUS, IT'S A FACT THAT, IF ALL THE ELDIANS GOT WIPED OUT, THE **TITAN PROBLEM** WOULD DISAPPEAR WITH THEM...
BUT...I JUST CAN'T ACCEPT...
...AN END LIKE THAT.
THAT BOY...
I'VE SEEN HIM IN A FUTURE MEMORY.

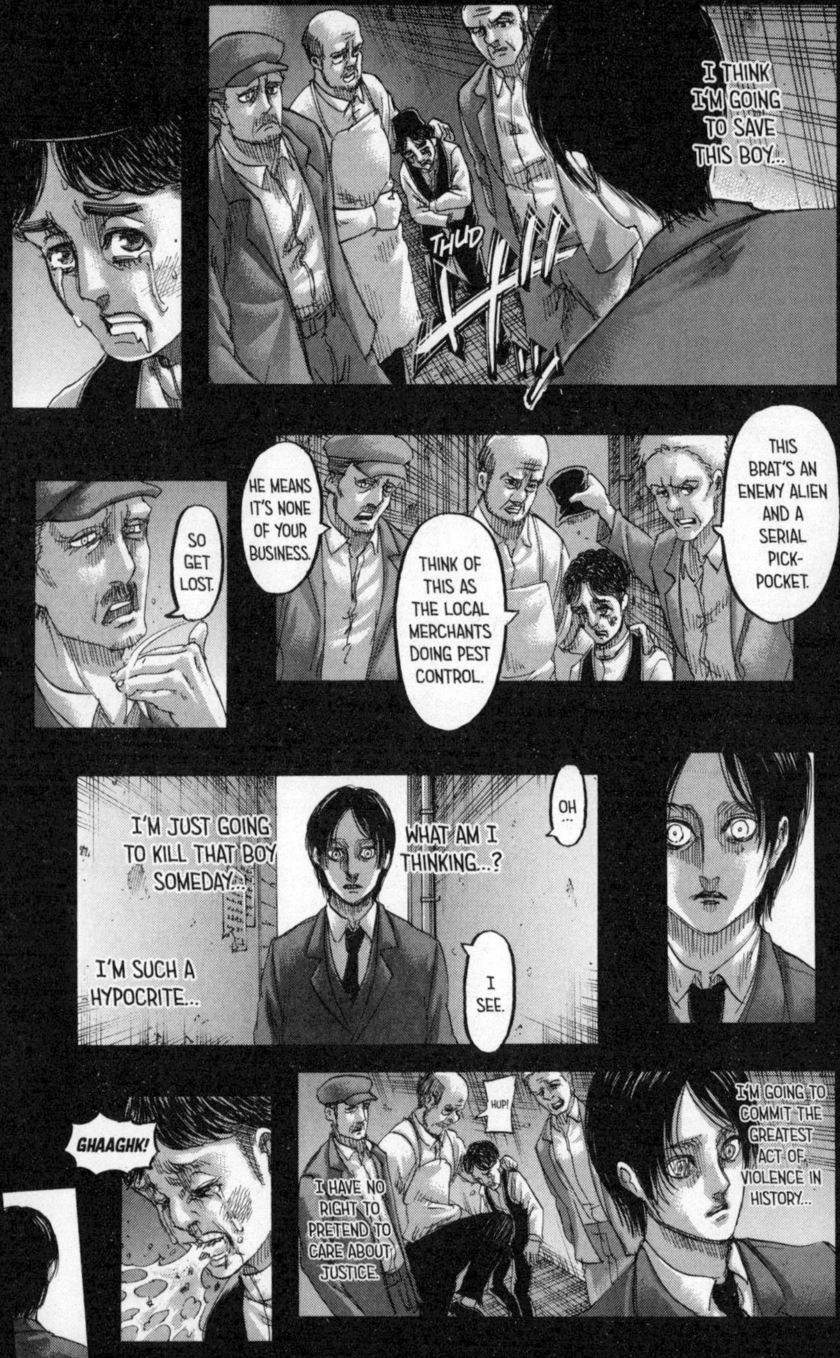
I THINK I'M GOING TO SAVE THIS BOY...
THUD
THIS BRAT'S AN ENEMY ALIEN AND A SERIAL PICK-POCKET.
THINK OF THIS AS THE LOCAL MERCHANTS DOING PEST CONTROL.
HE MEANS IT'S NONE OF YOUR BUSINESS.
SO GET LOST.
OH...
WHAT AM I THINKING...?
I'M JUST GOING TO KILL THAT BOY SOMEDAY...
I SEE.
I'M SUCH A HYPOCRITE...
I'M GOING TO COMMIT THE GREATEST ACT OF VIOLENCE IN HISTORY...
HUP!
I HAVE NO RIGHT TO PRETEND TO CARE ABOUT JUSTICE.
GHAAGHK!

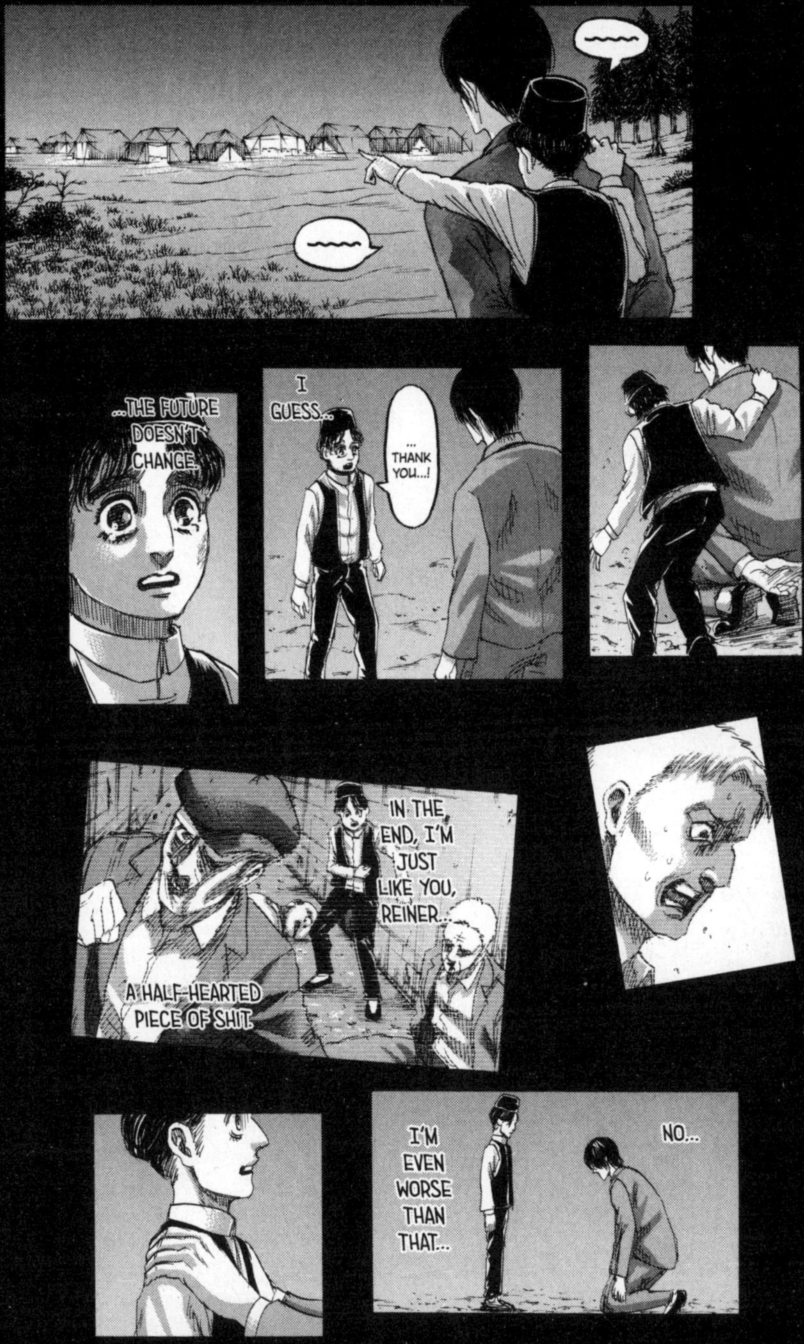
...THANK YOU...!
I GUESS...
...THE FUTURE DOESN'T CHANGE.
IN THE END, I'M JUST LIKE YOU, REINER...
A HALF-HEARTED PIECE OF SHIT.
NO...
I'M EVEN WORSE THAN THAT...

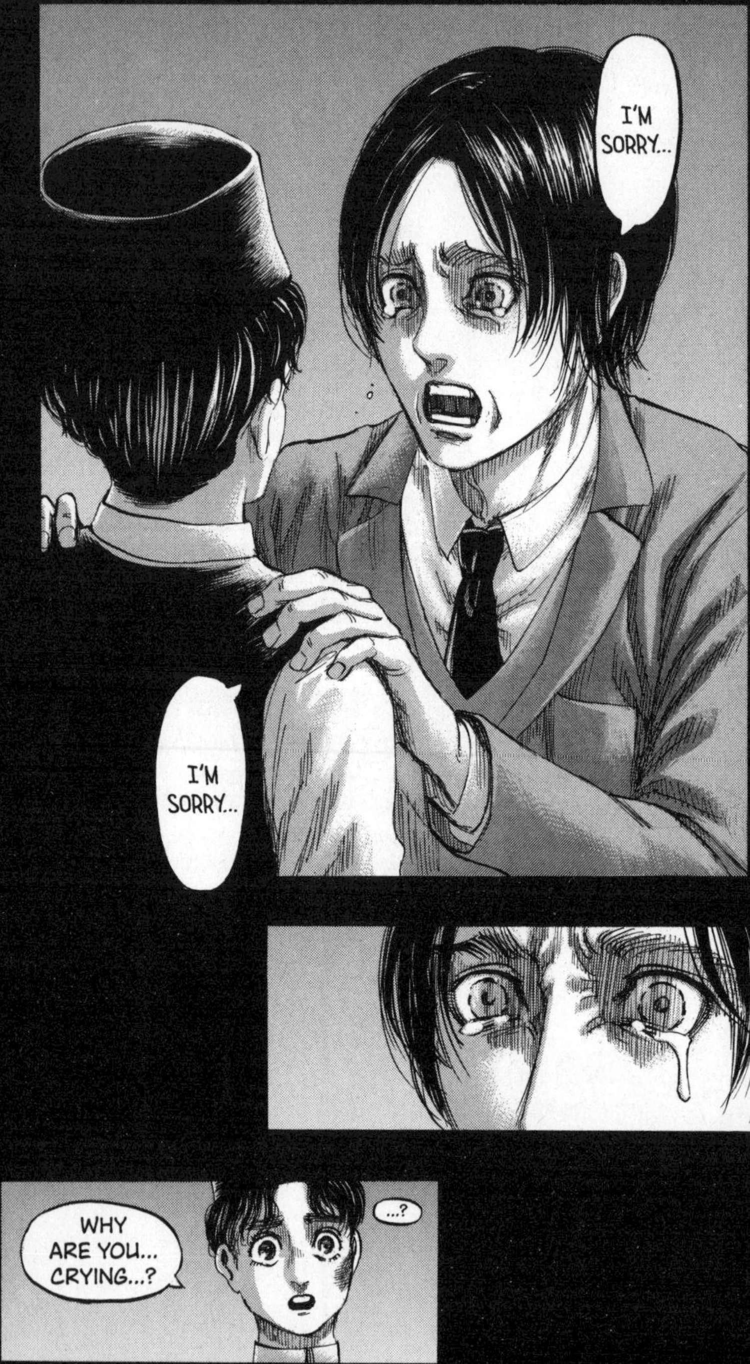
I'M SORRY...
I'M SORRY...
...?
WHY ARE YOU... CRYING...?

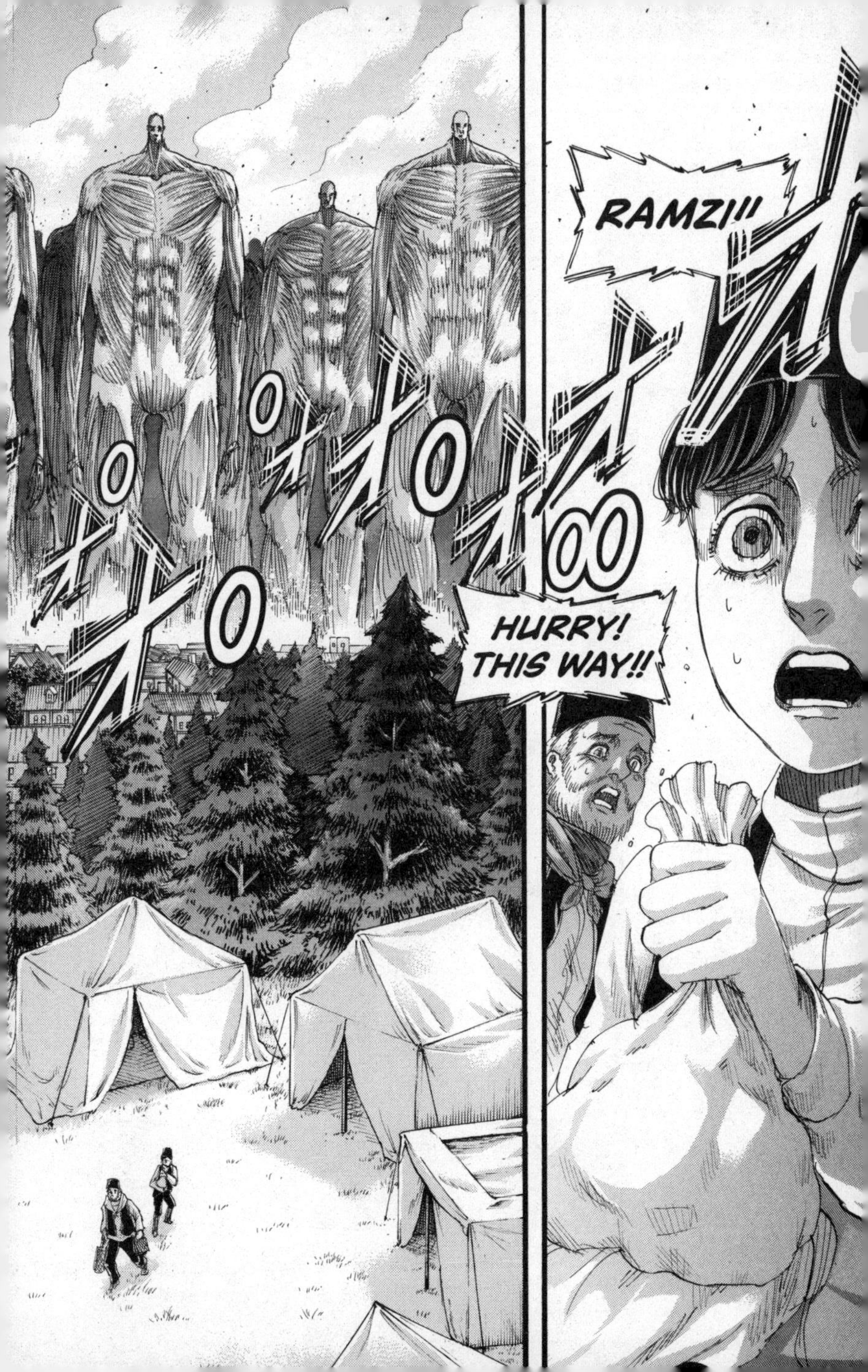
RAMZI!!!
HURRY! THIS WAY!!

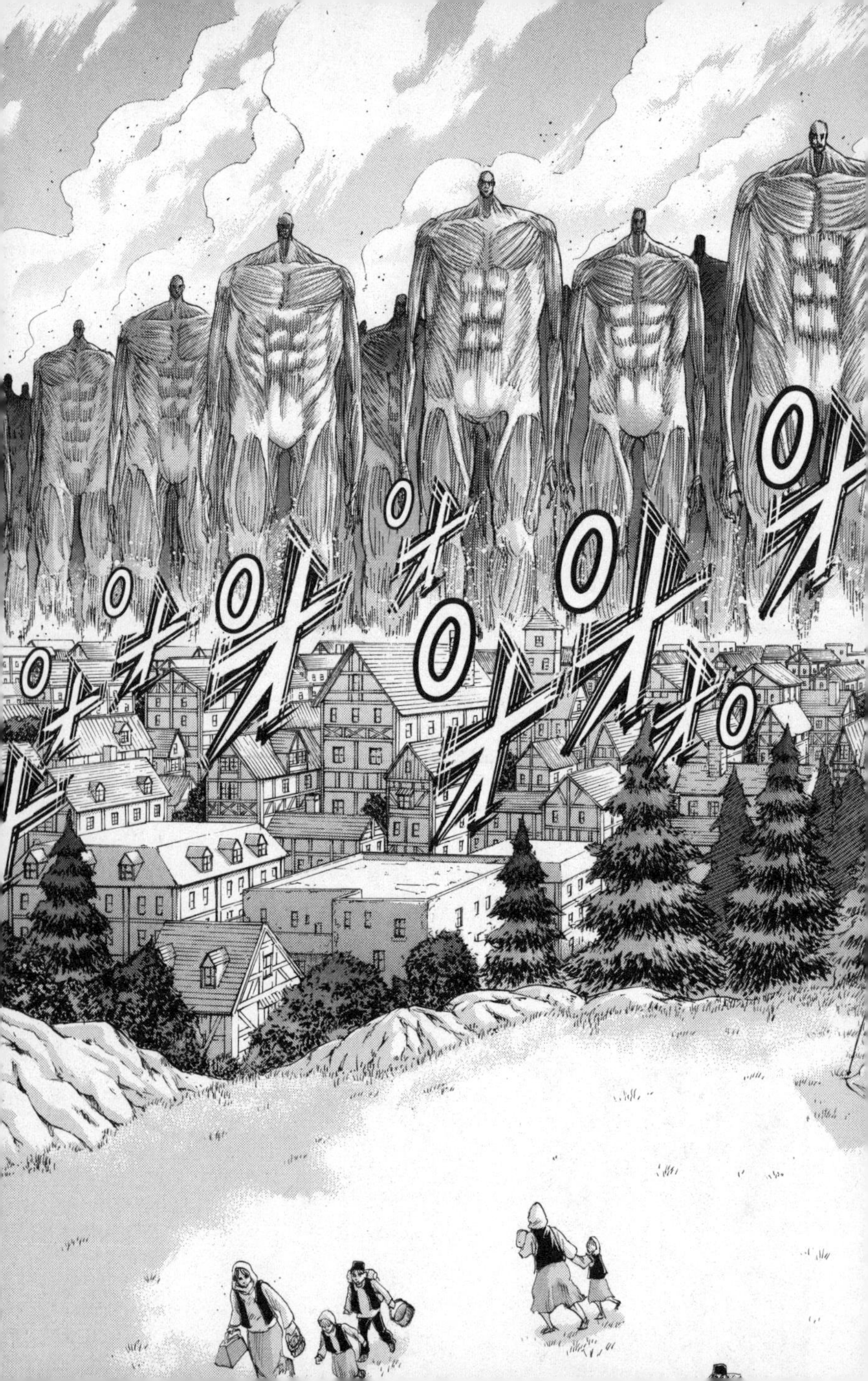
ォォオォオオォオ

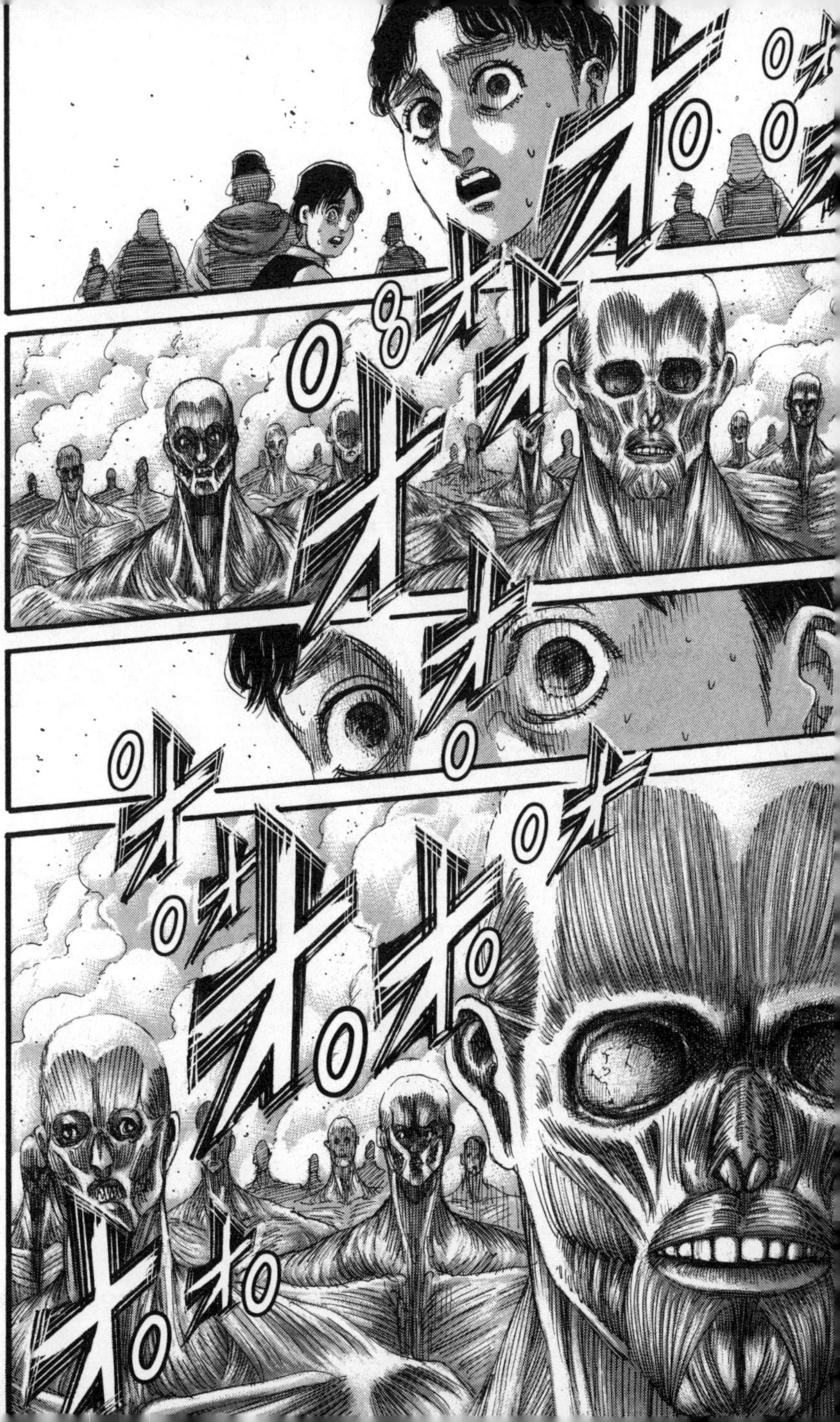

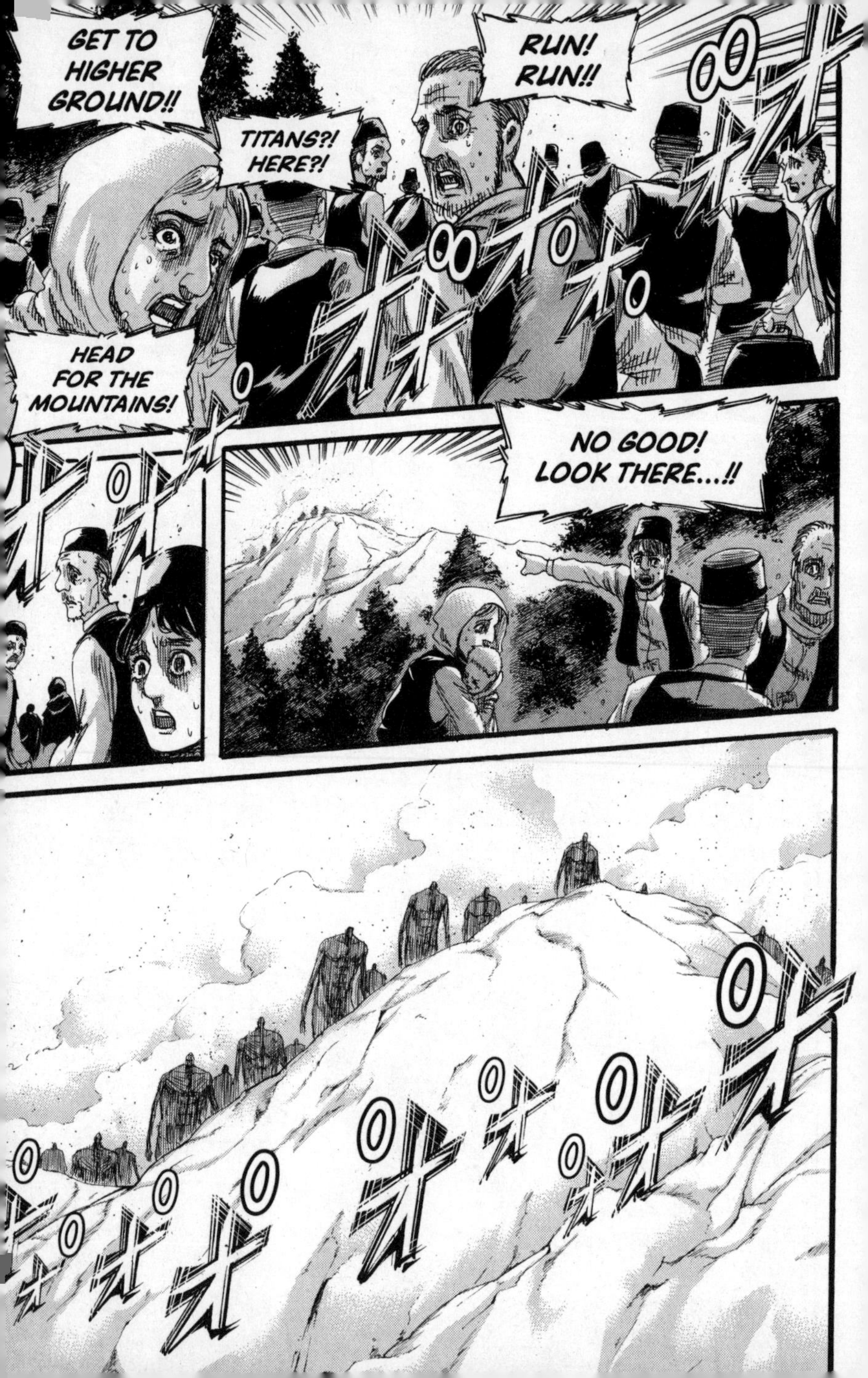
RUN! RUN!!
GET TO HIGHER GROUND!!
TITANS?! HERE?!
HEAD FOR THE MOUNTAINS!
NO GOOD! LOOK THERE...!!

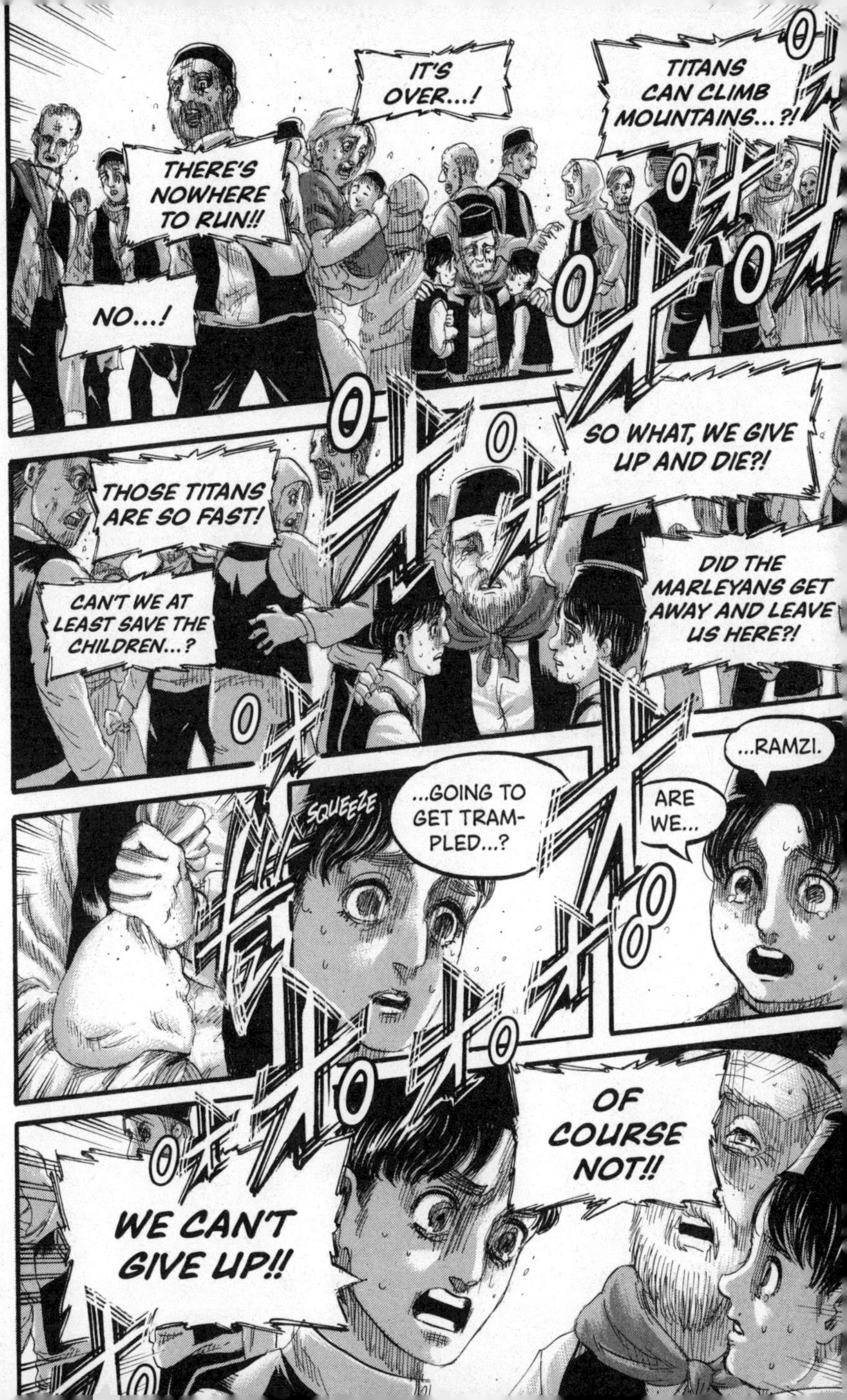
TITANS CAN CLIMB MOUNTAINS...?!
IT'S OVER...!
THERE'S NOWHERE TO RUN!!
NO...!
SO WHAT, WE GIVE UP AND DIE?!
DID THE MARLEYANS GET AWAY AND LEAVE US HERE?!
THOSE TITANS ARE SO FAST!
CAN'T WE AT LEAST SAVE THE CHILDREN...?
...RAMZI.
ARE WE...
...GOING TO GET TRAM-PLED...?
SQUEEZE
OF COURSE NOT!!
WE CAN'T GIVE UP!!

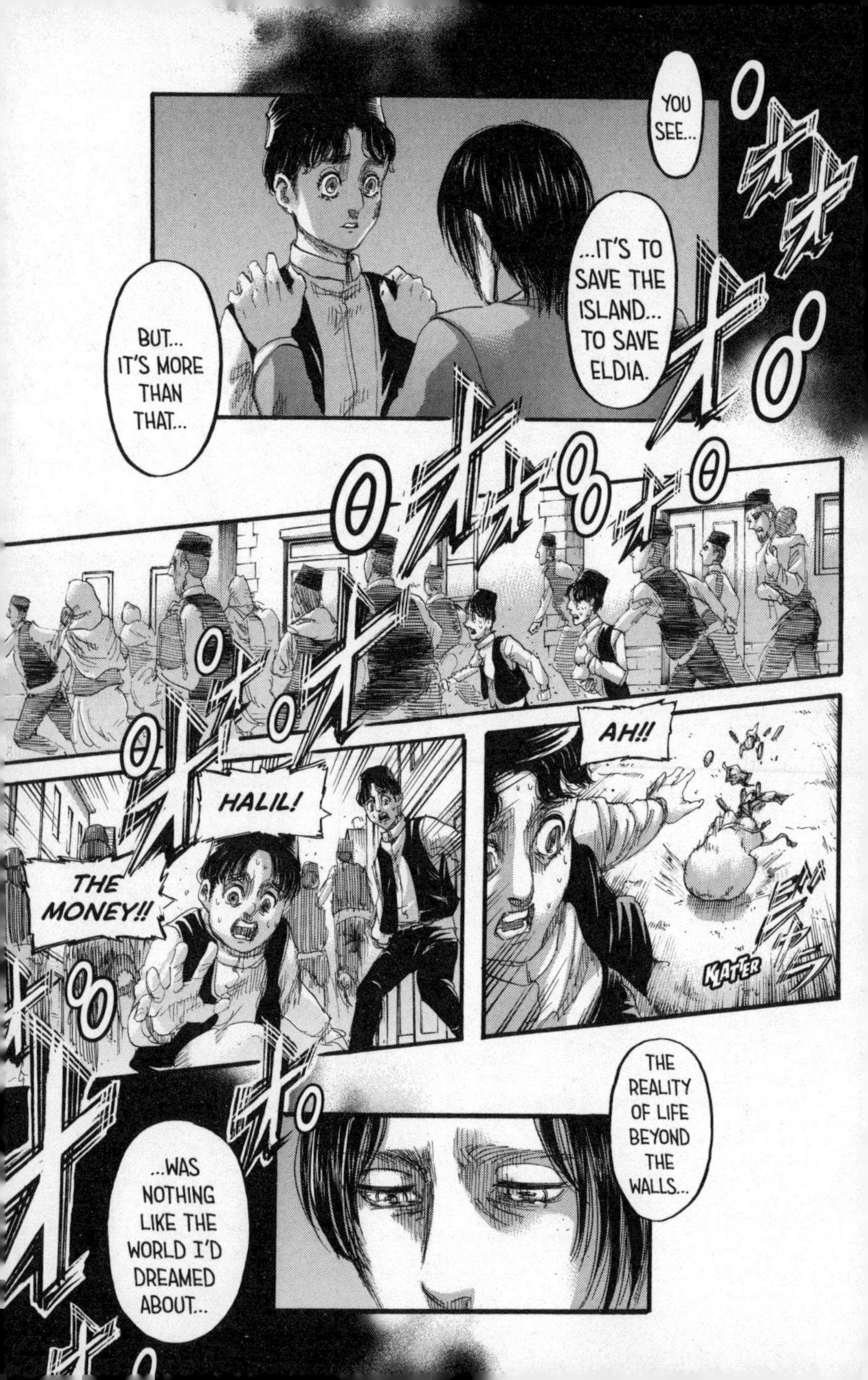
YOU SEE...
...IT'S TO SAVE THE ISLAND... TO SAVE ELDIA.
BUT... IT'S MORE THAN THAT...
AH!!
KLATTER
HALIL!
THE MONEY!!
THE REALITY OF LIFE BEYOND THE WALLS...
...WAS NOTHING LIKE THE WORLD I'D DREAMED ABOUT...

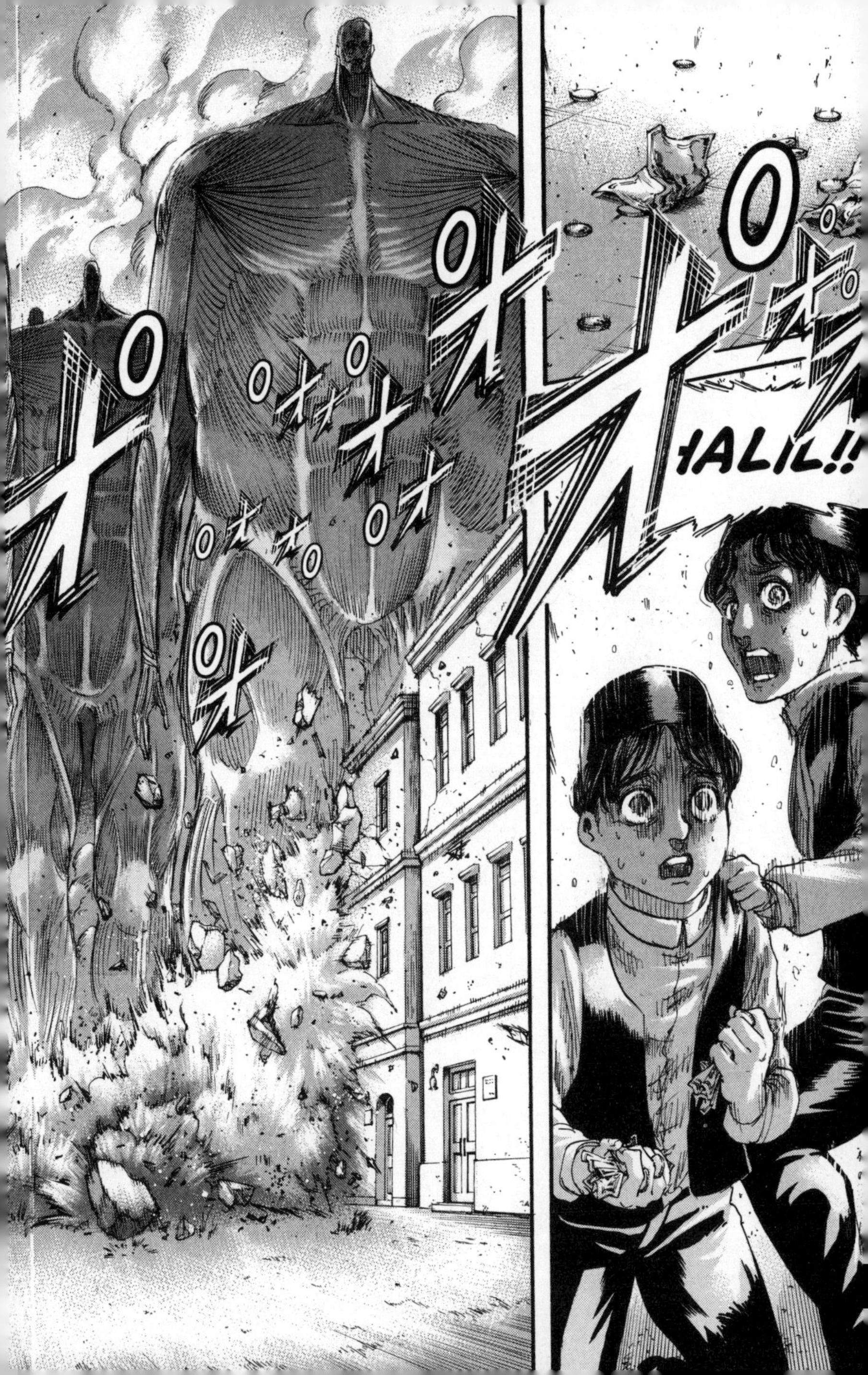
HALIL!!

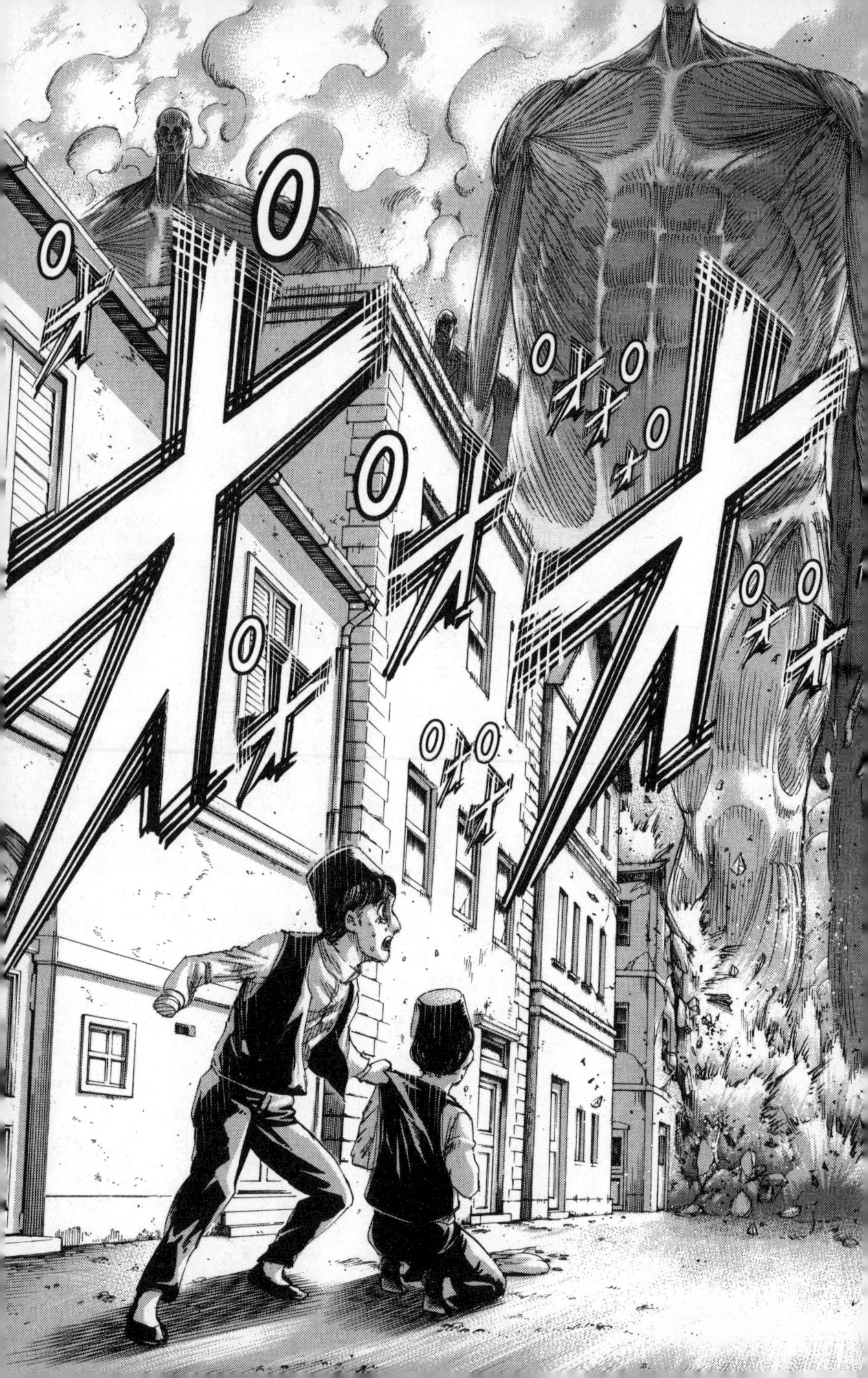

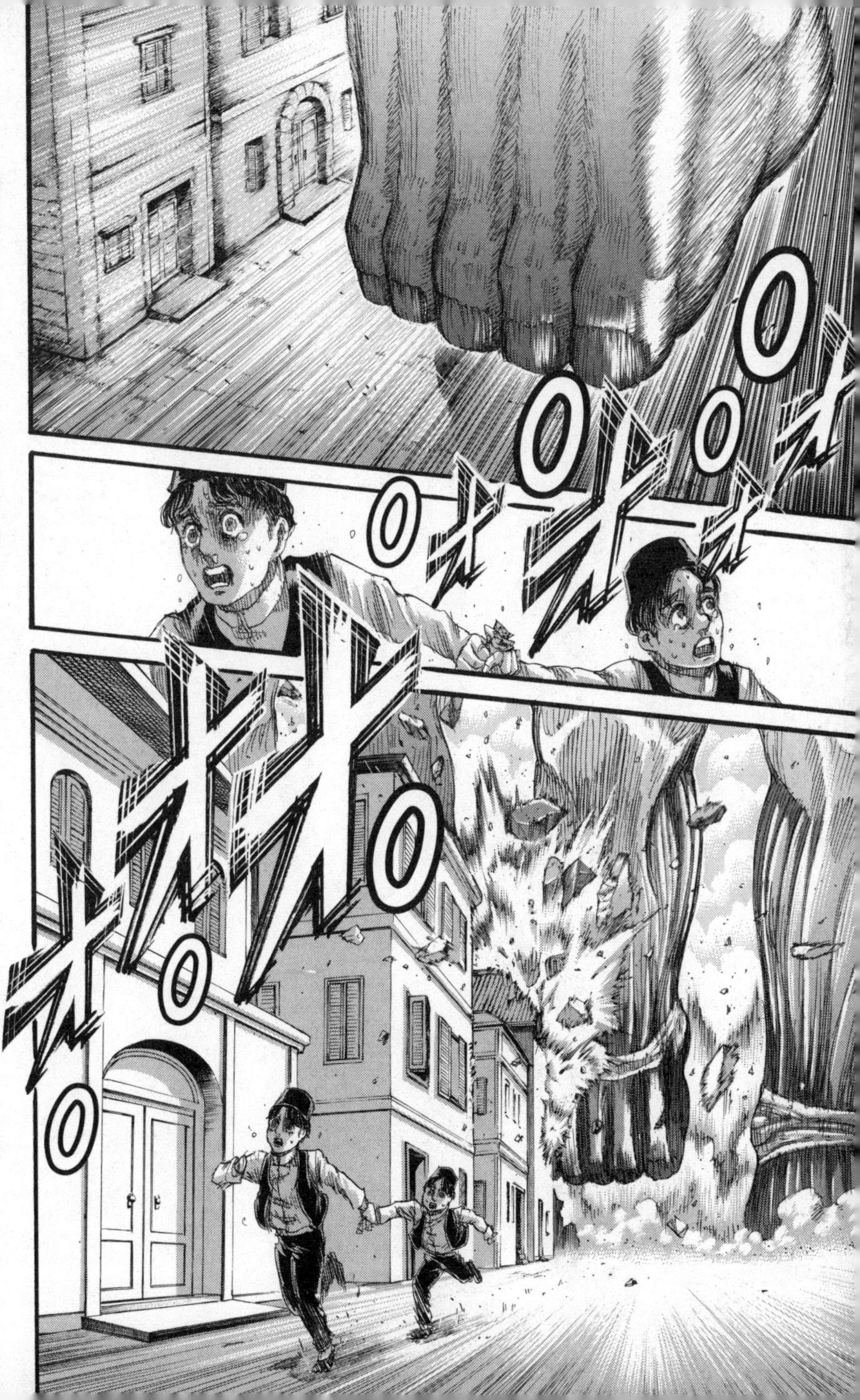

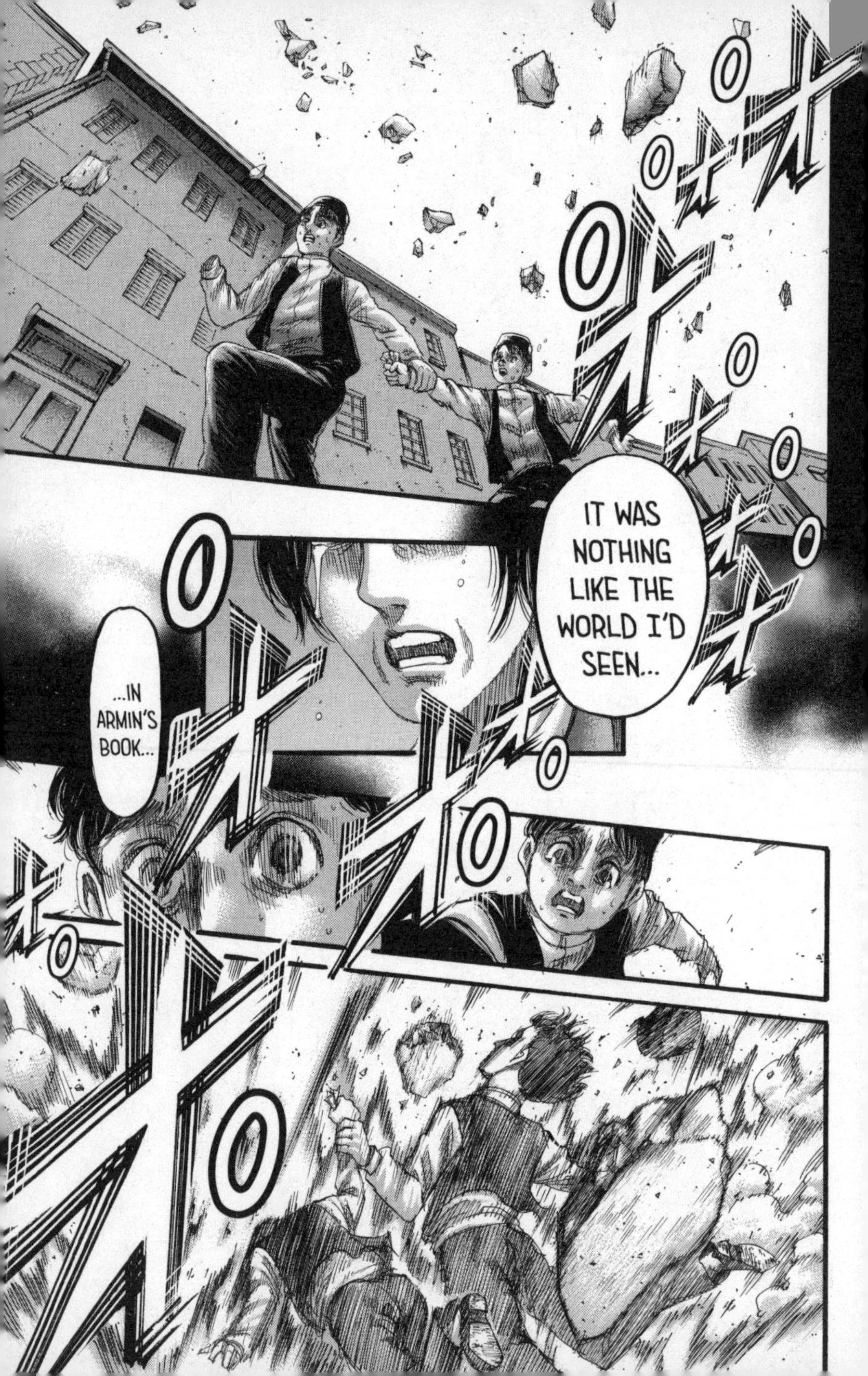
IT WAS NOTHING LIKE THE WORLD I'D SEEN...
...IN ARMIN'S BOOK...

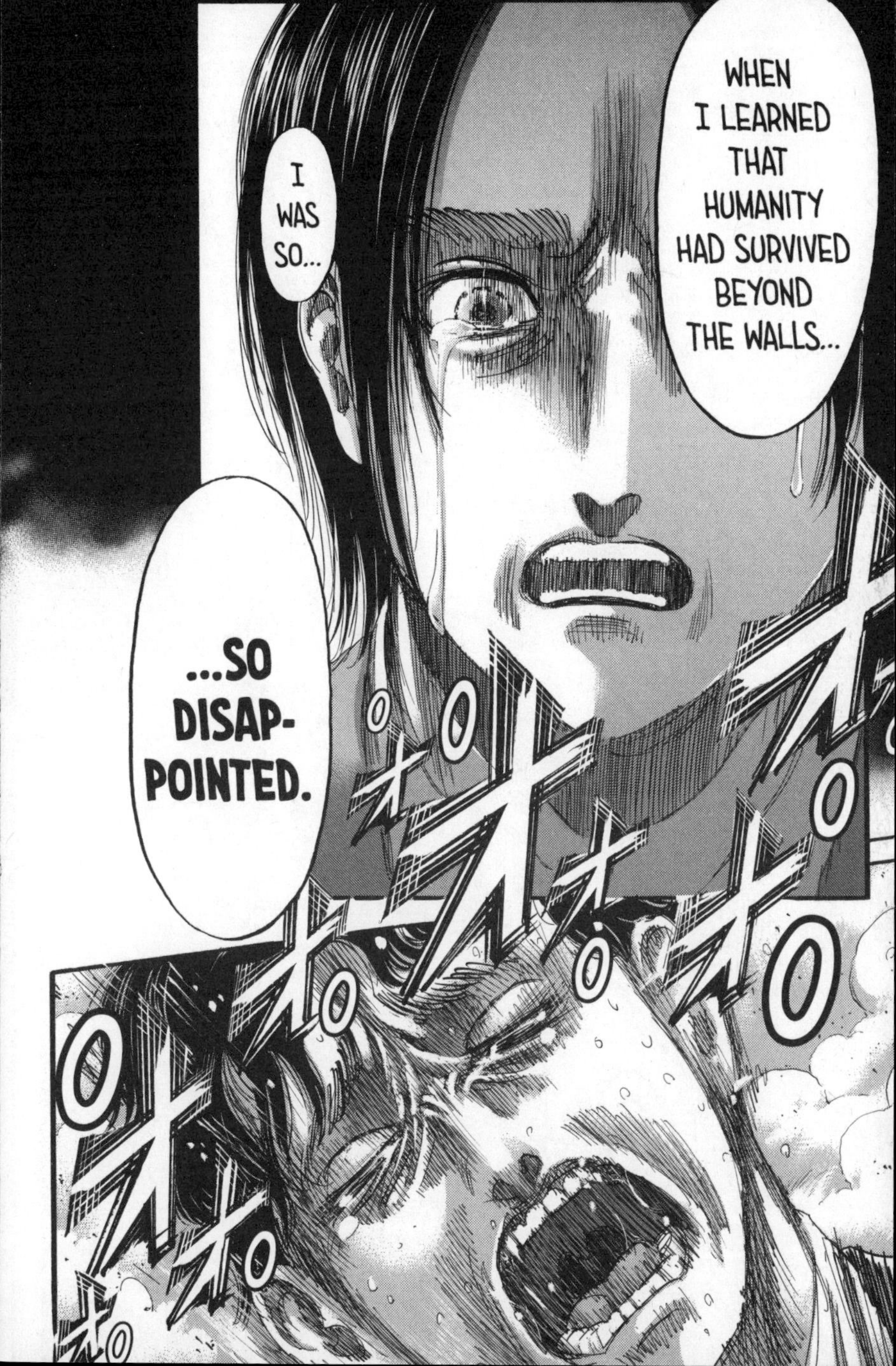
WHEN I LEARNED THAT HUMANITY HAD SURVIVED BEYOND THE WALLS...
I WAS SO...
...SO DISAPPOINTED.

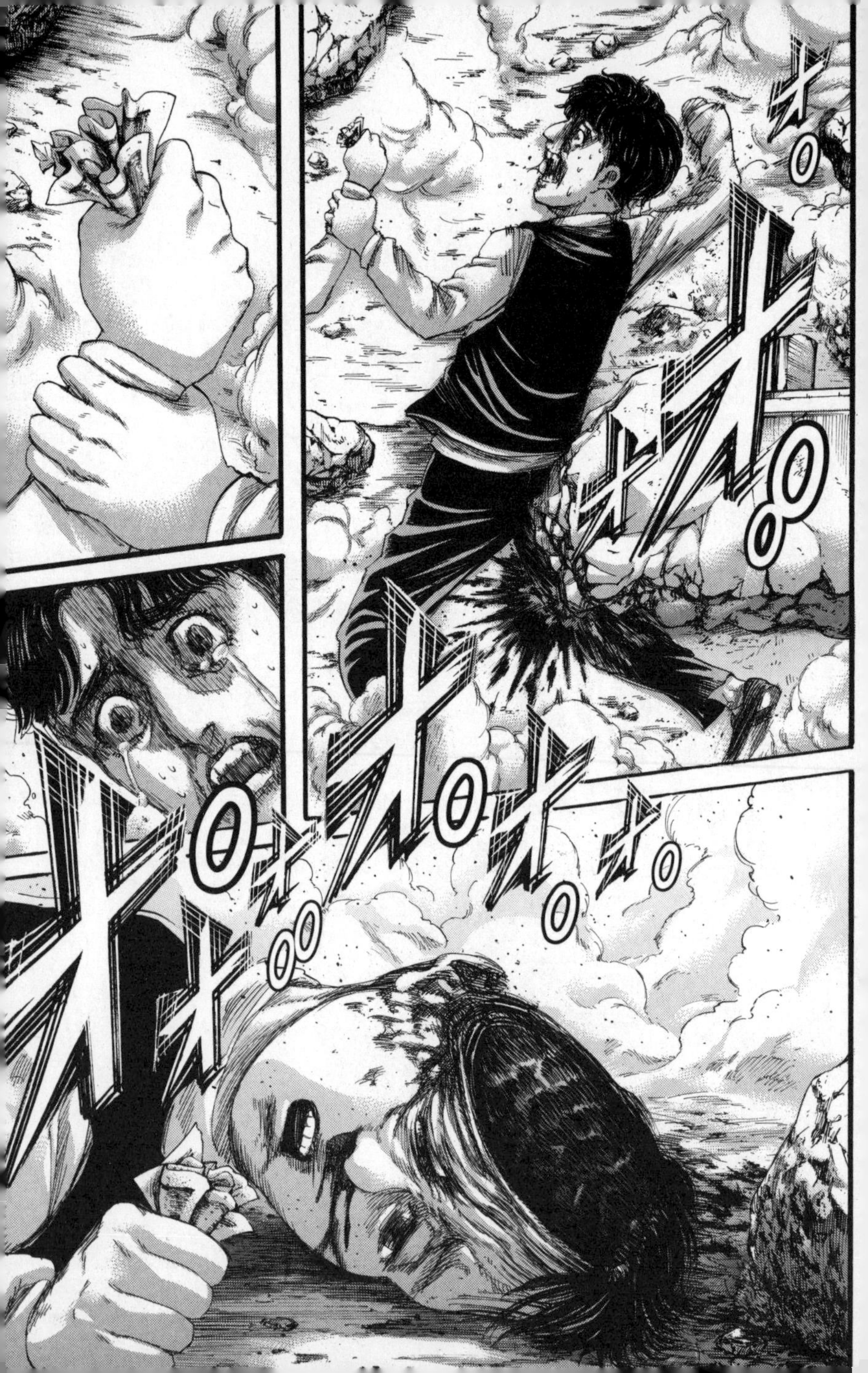

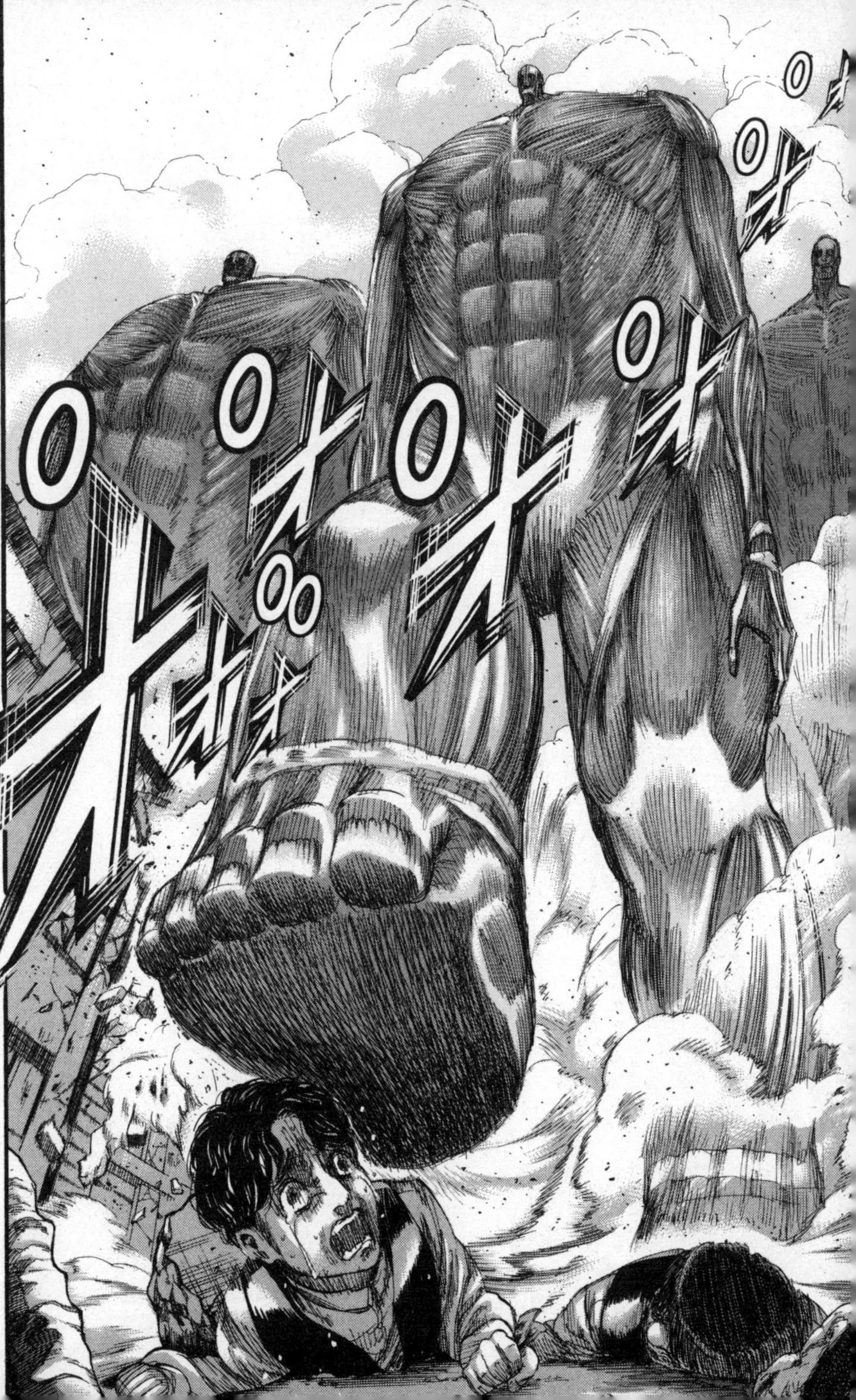

ォ゜ォ゜オ゜オ゜オ゜オ゜オォォオ゜

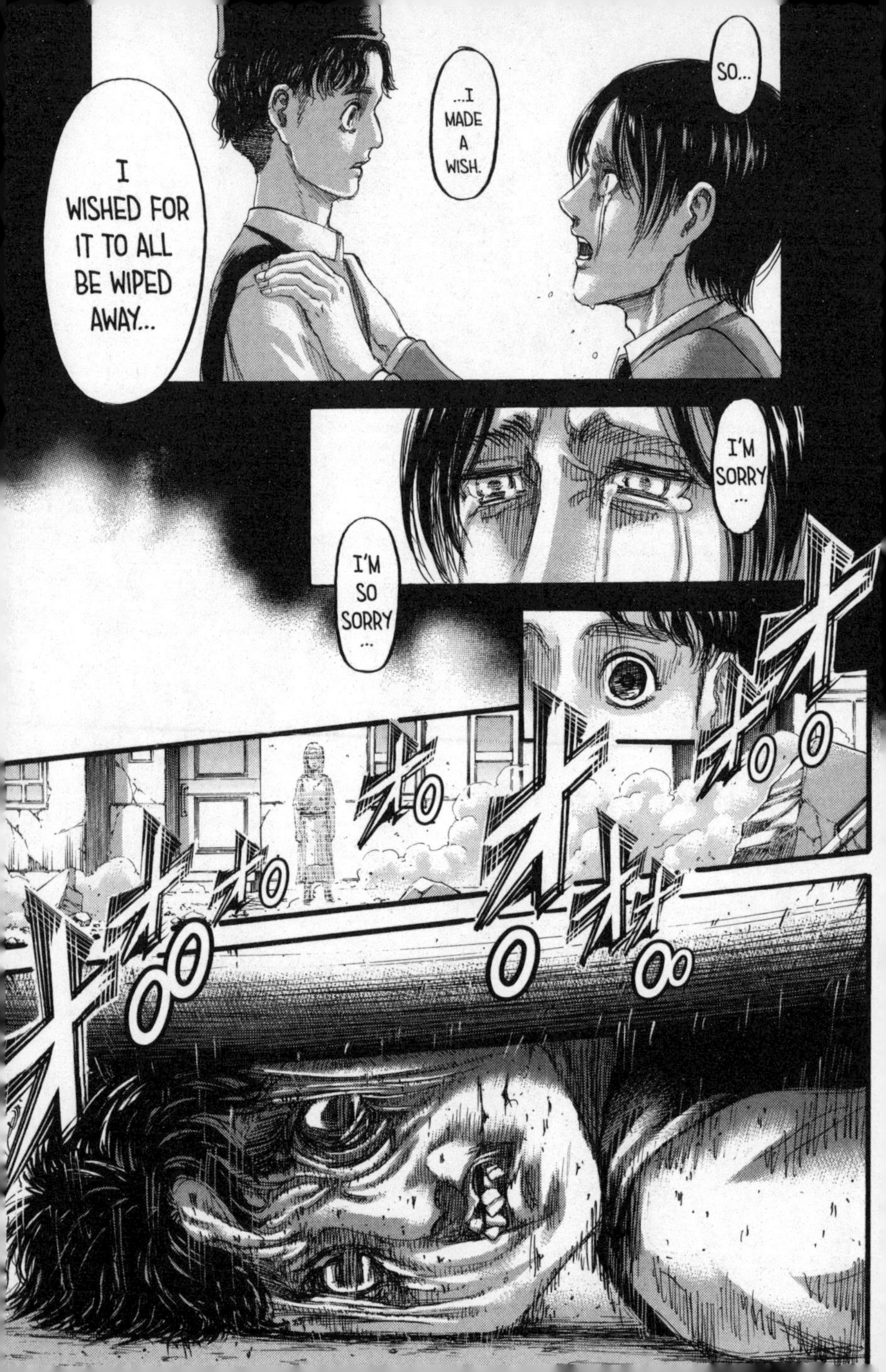
SO...
...I MADE A WISH.
I WISHED FOR IT TO ALL BE WIPED AWAY...
I'M SORRY...
I'M SO SORRY...

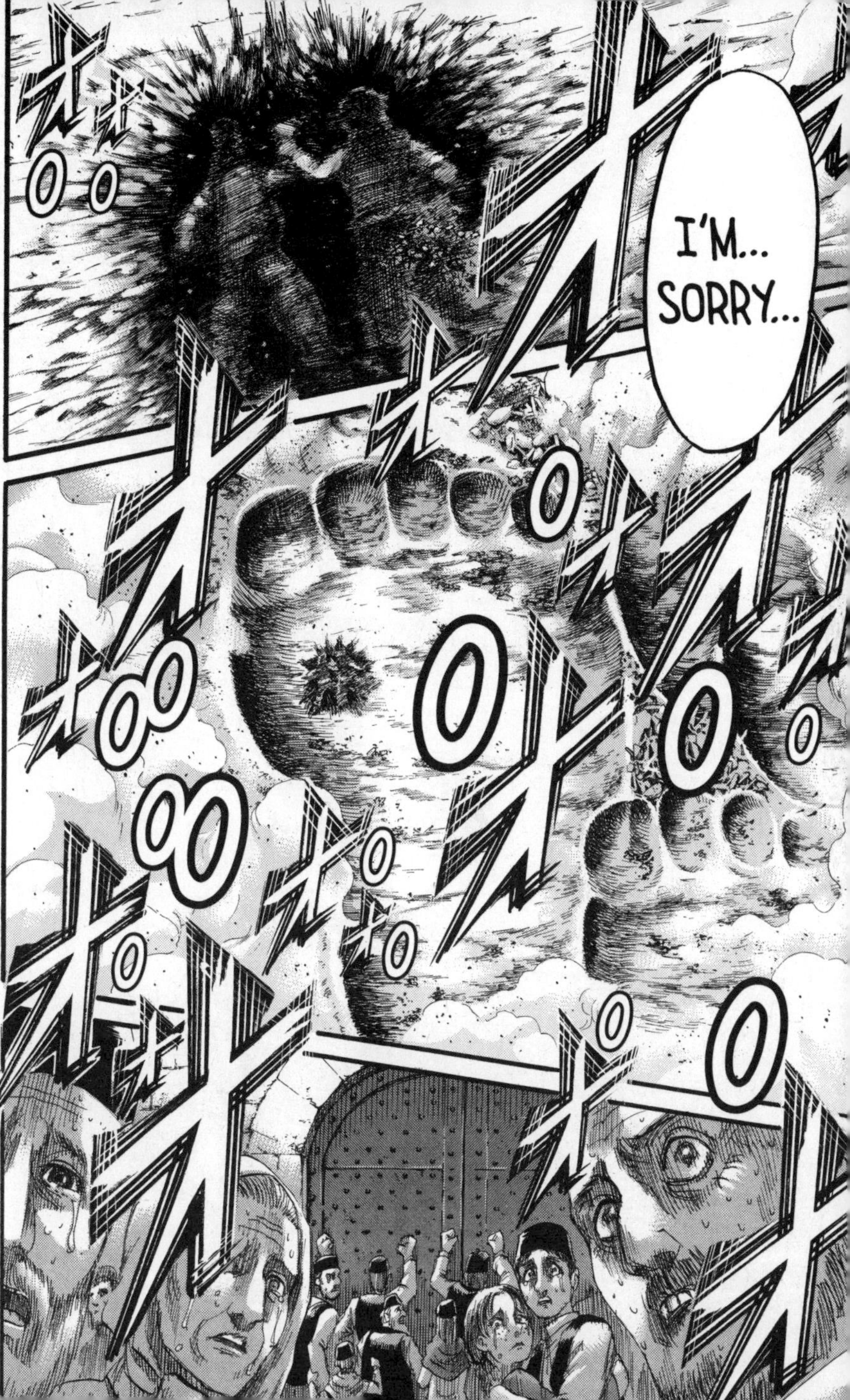
I'M... SORRY...

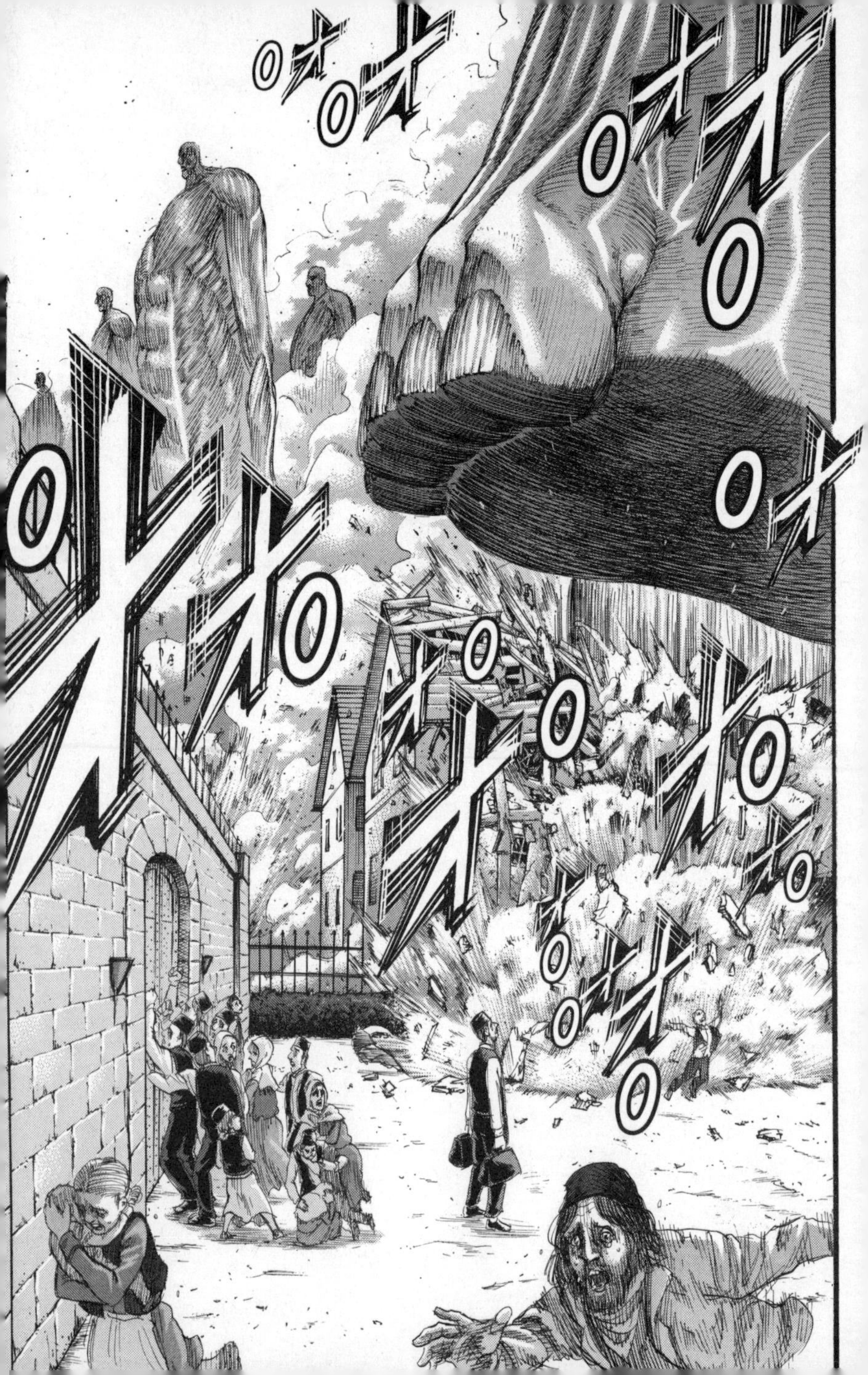

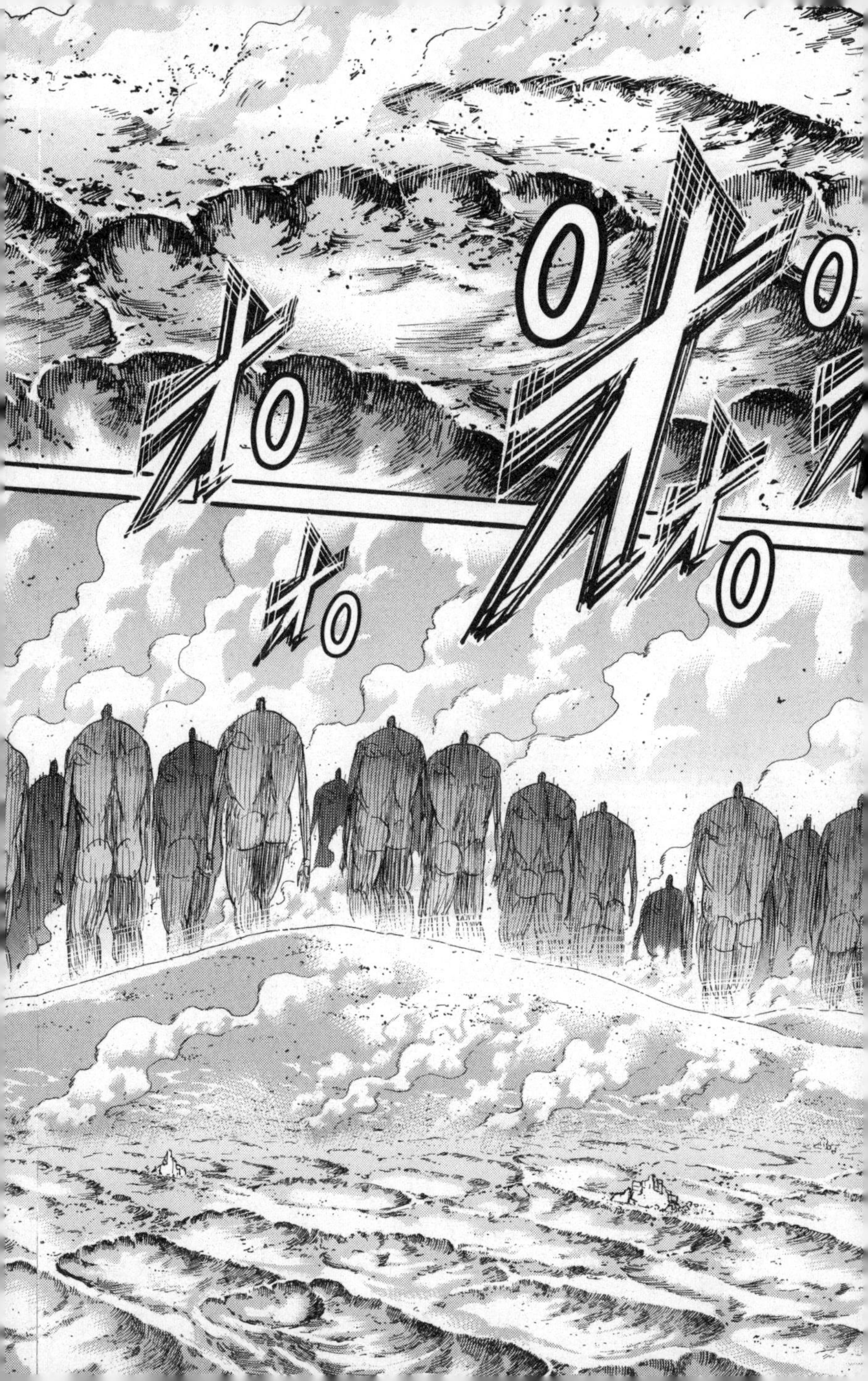

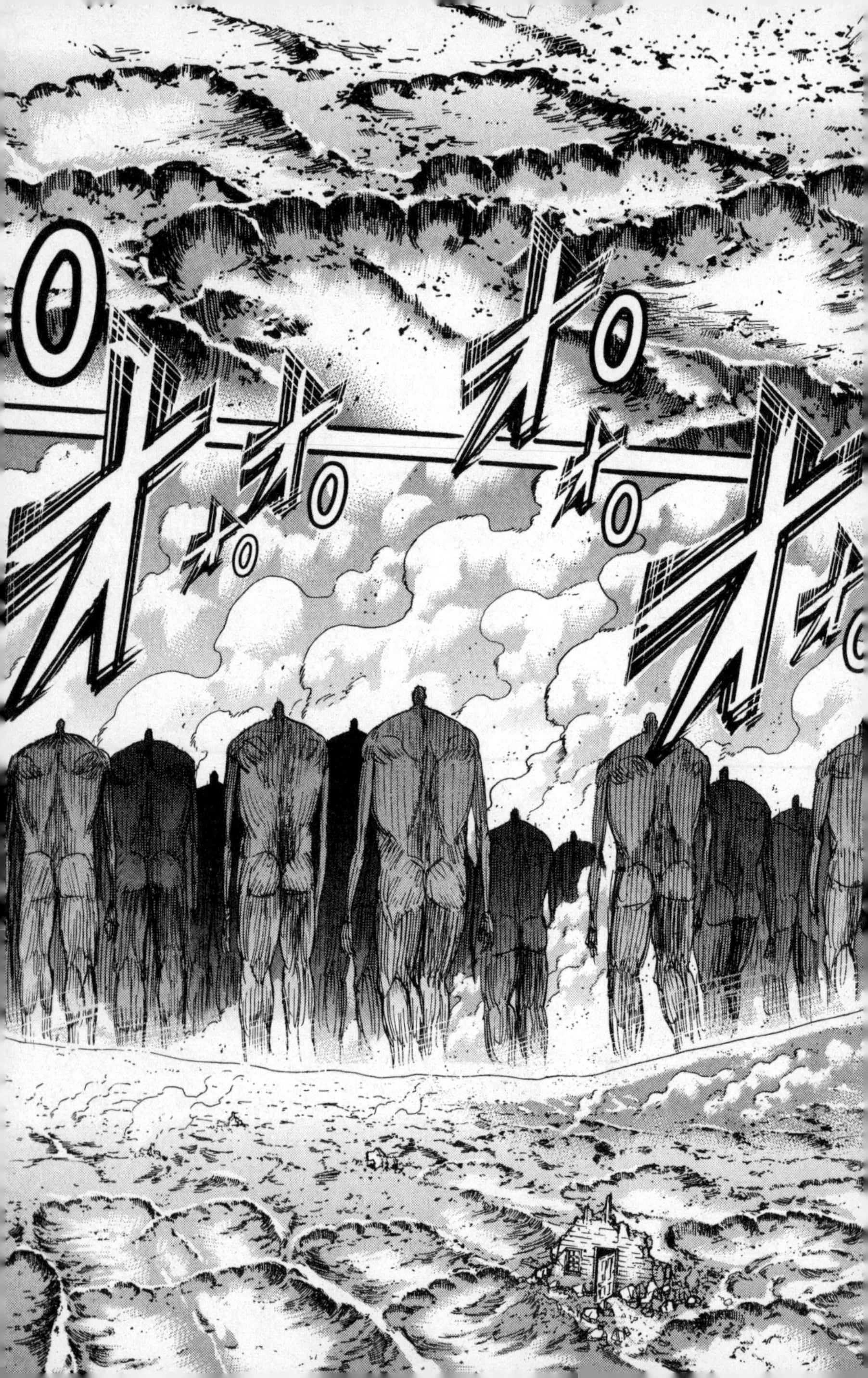
オ゜ォ゜ォ゜
オ゜ォ゜
オォ゜

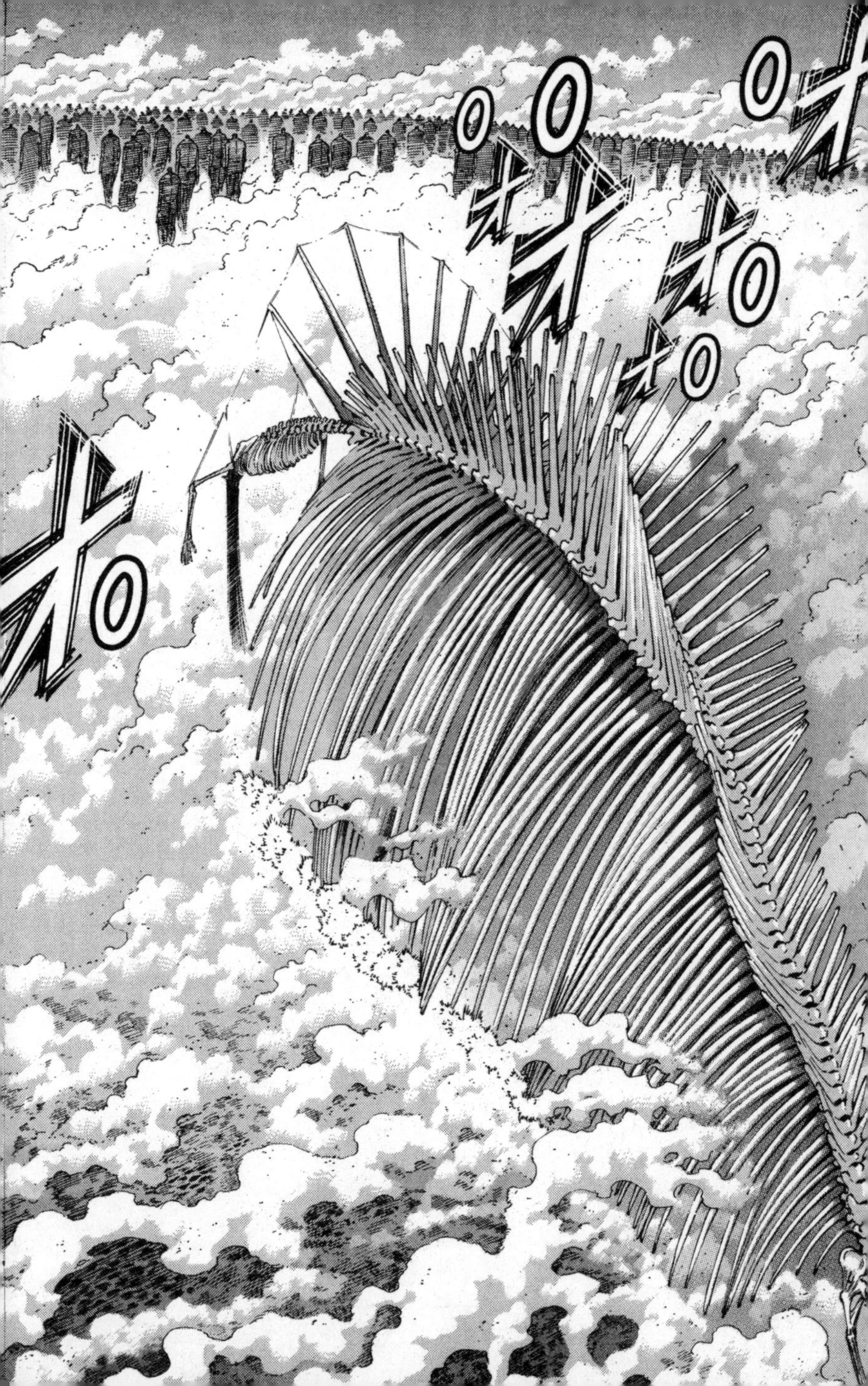
オオオオ
オ

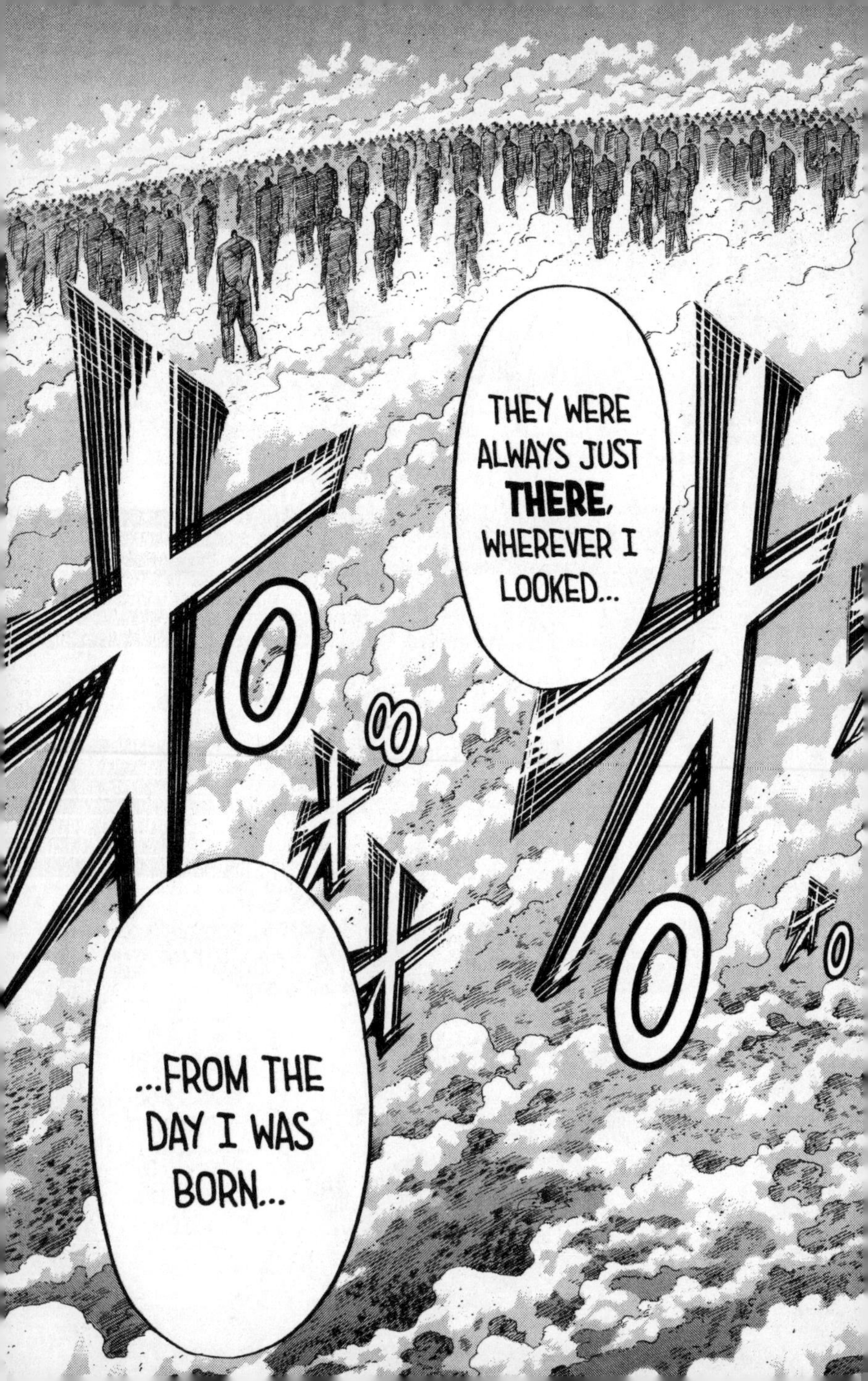
THEY WERE ALWAYS JUST **THERE**, WHEREVER I LOOKED...
...FROM THE DAY I WAS BORN...

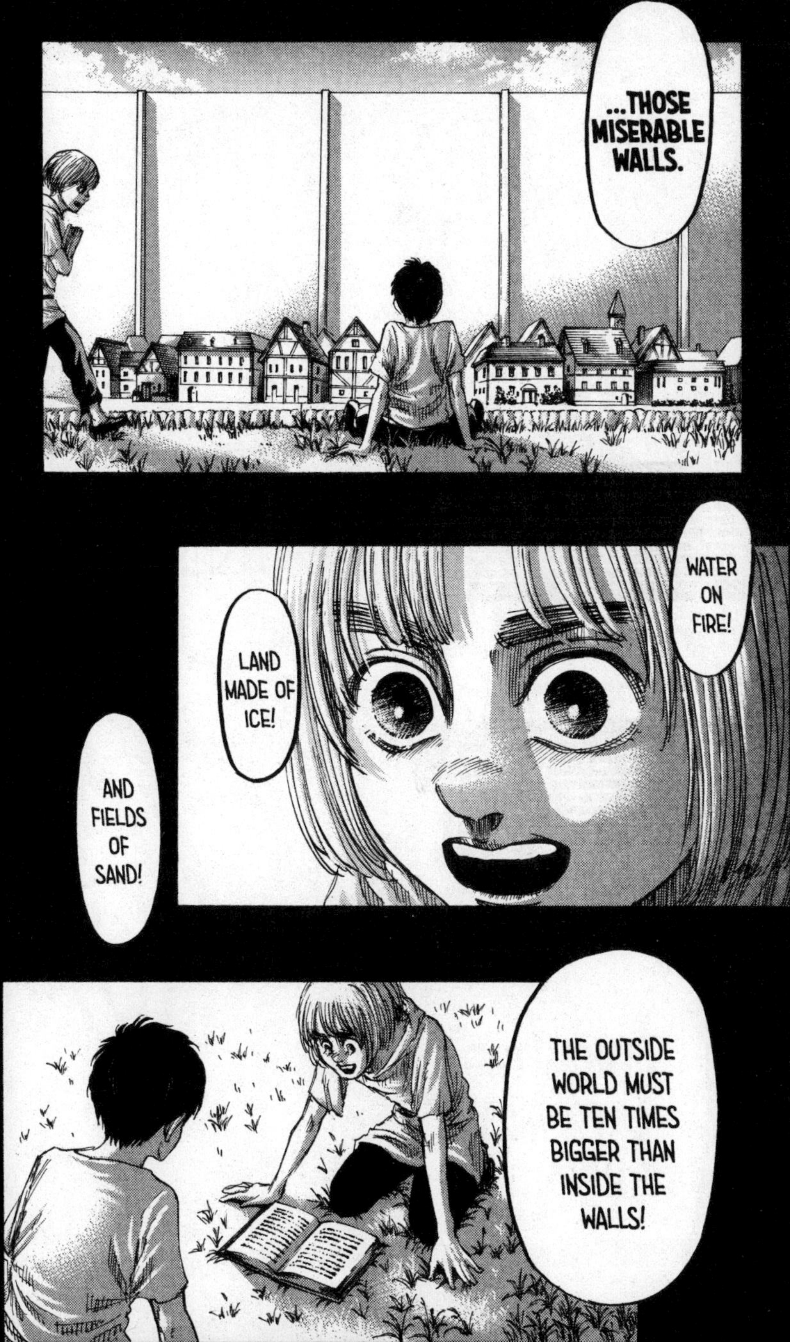
...THOSE MISERABLE WALLS.
WATER ON FIRE!
LAND MADE OF ICE!
AND FIELDS OF SAND!
THE OUTSIDE WORLD MUST BE TEN TIMES BIGGER THAN INSIDE THE WALLS!

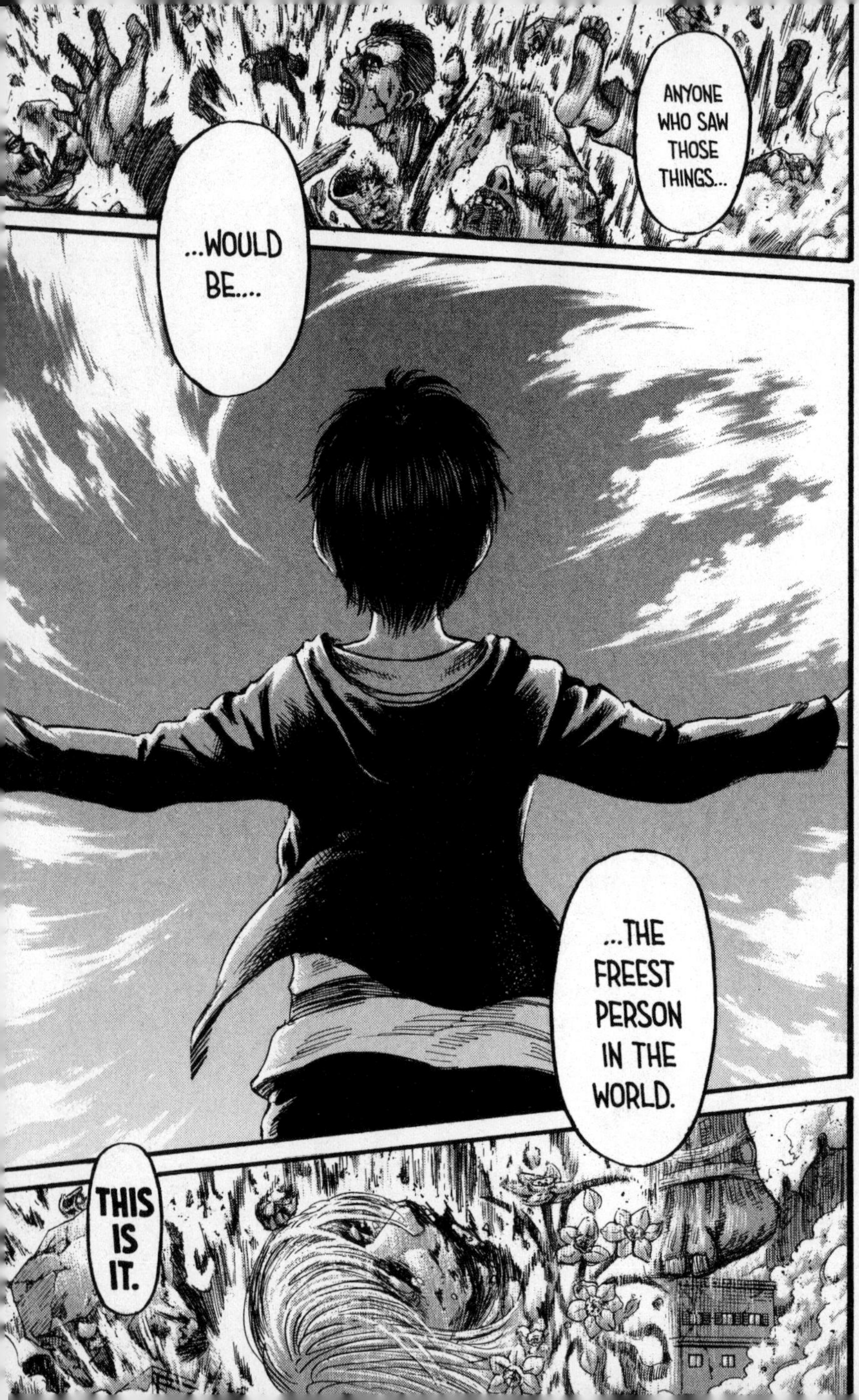
ANYONE WHO SAW THOSE THINGS...
...WOULD BE....
...THE FREEST PERSON IN THE WORLD.
THIS IS IT.

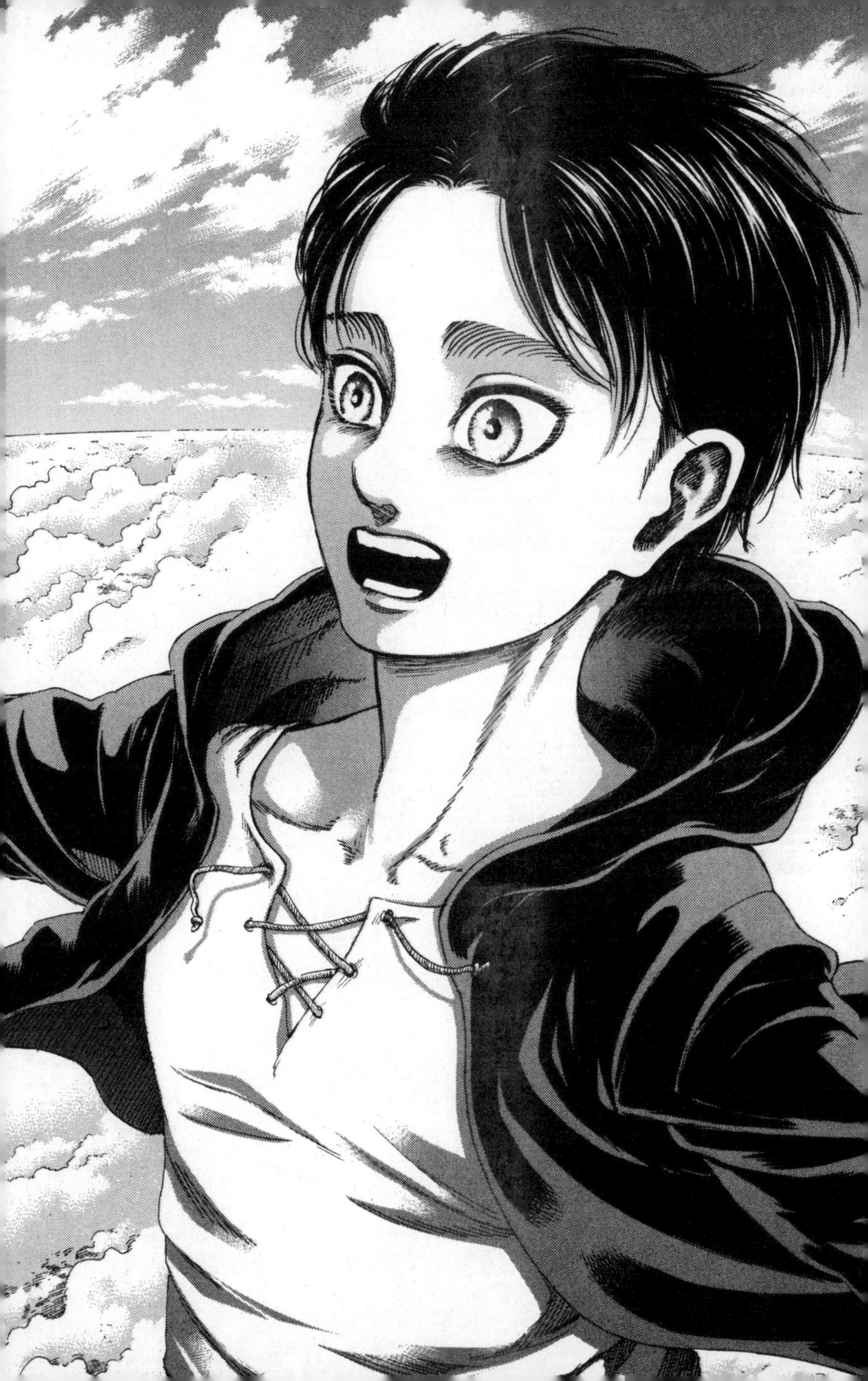

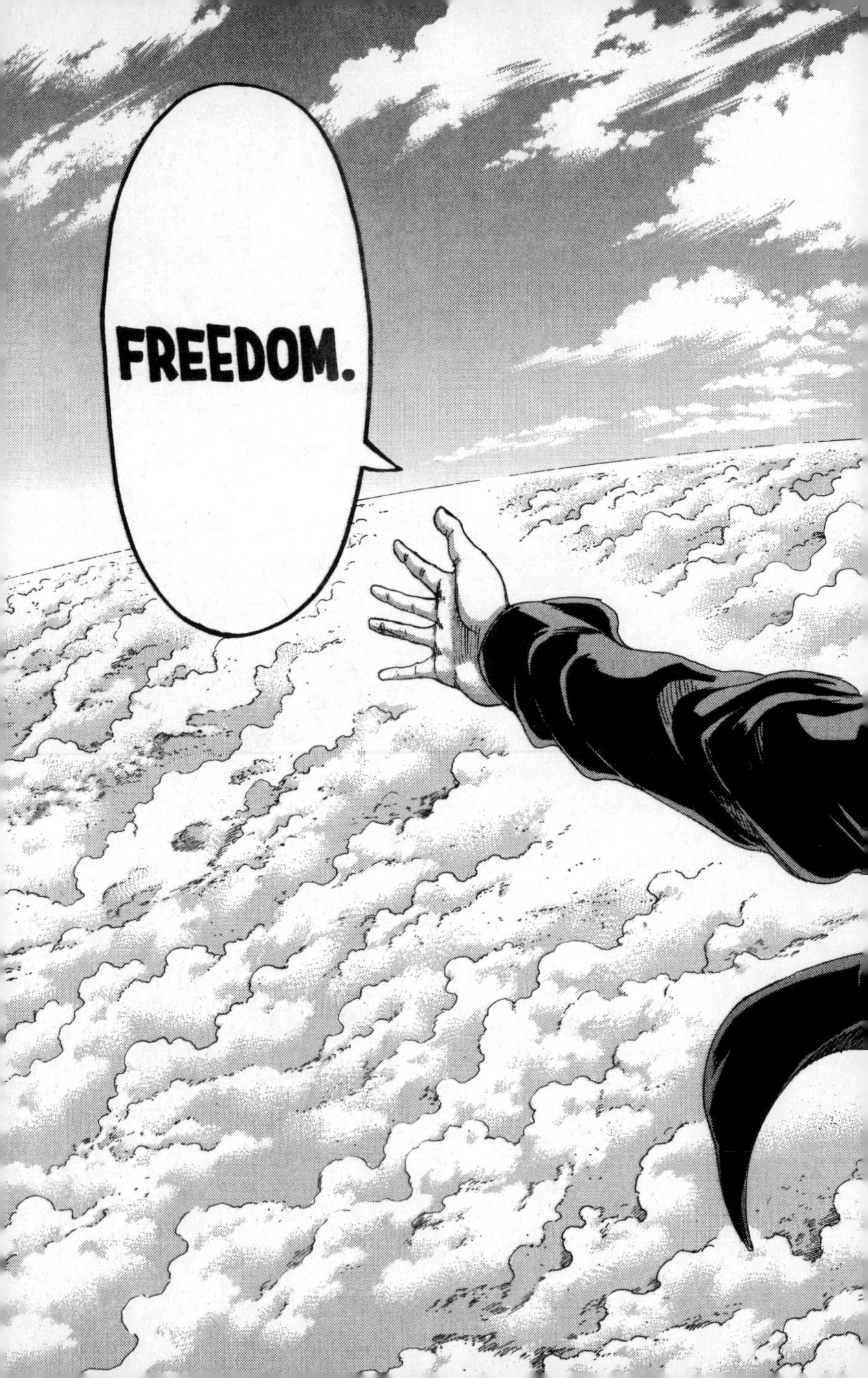
FREEDOM.

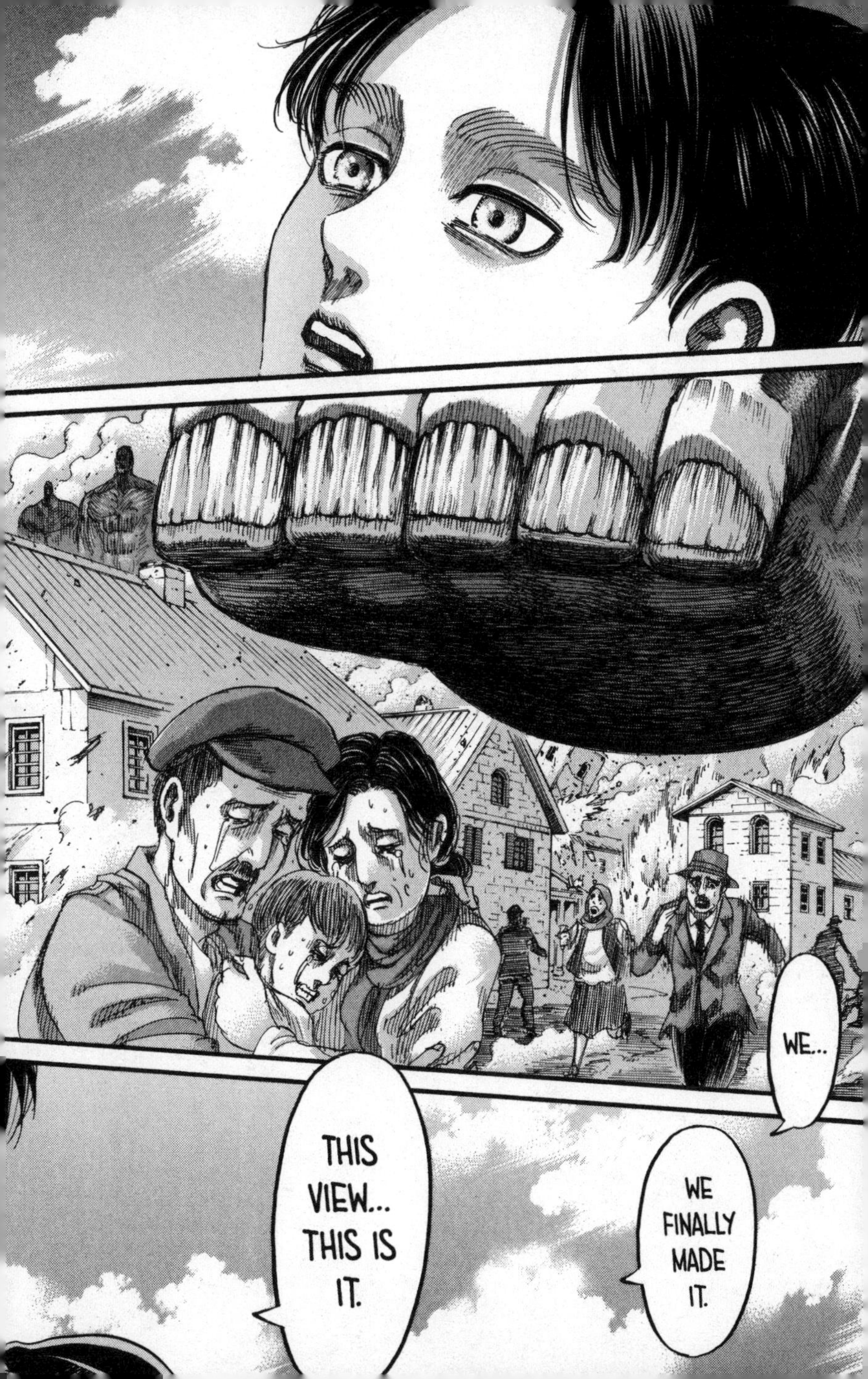
WE...
WE FINALLY MADE IT.
THIS VIEW... THIS IS IT.

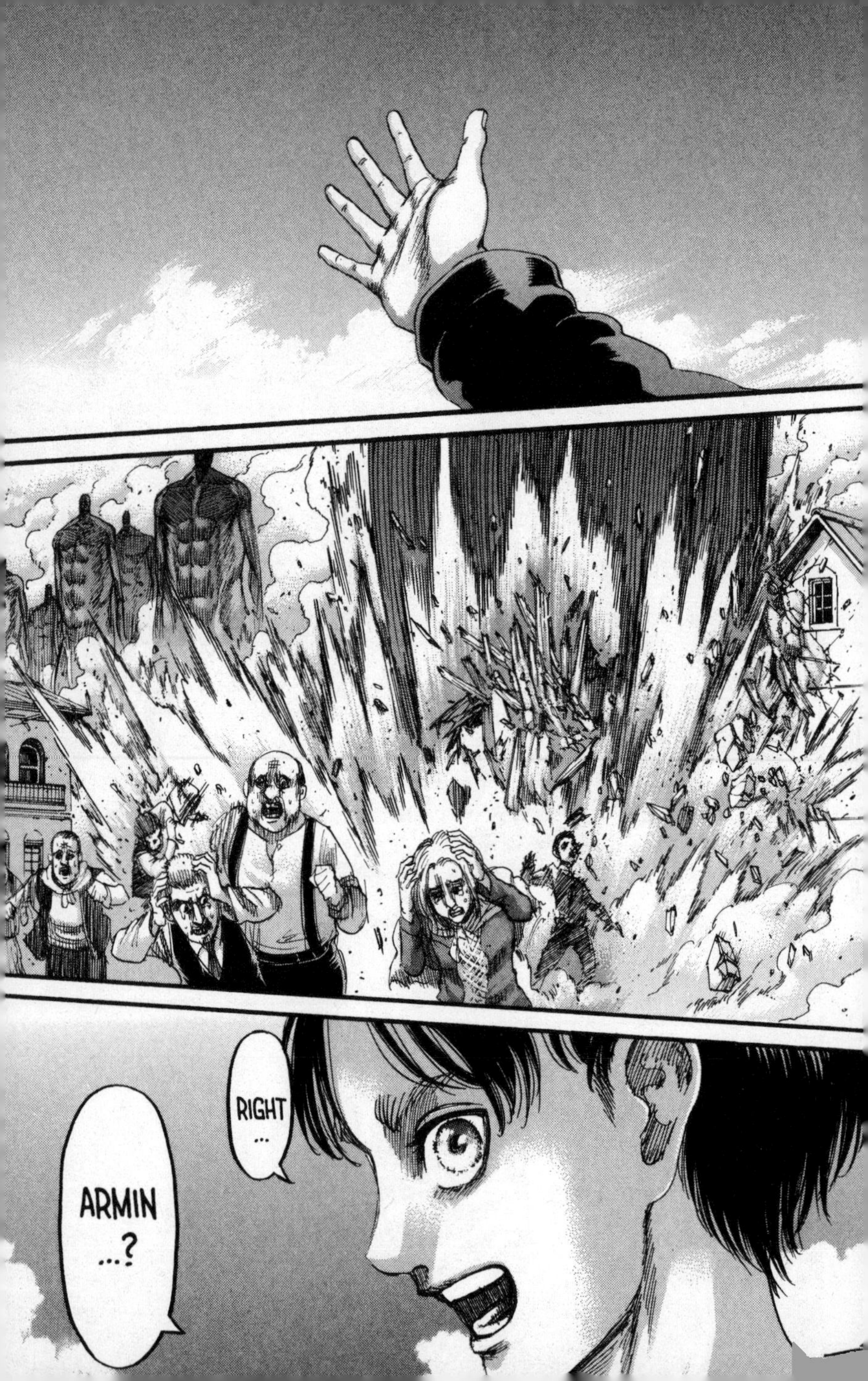
RIGHT ...
ARMIN ...?

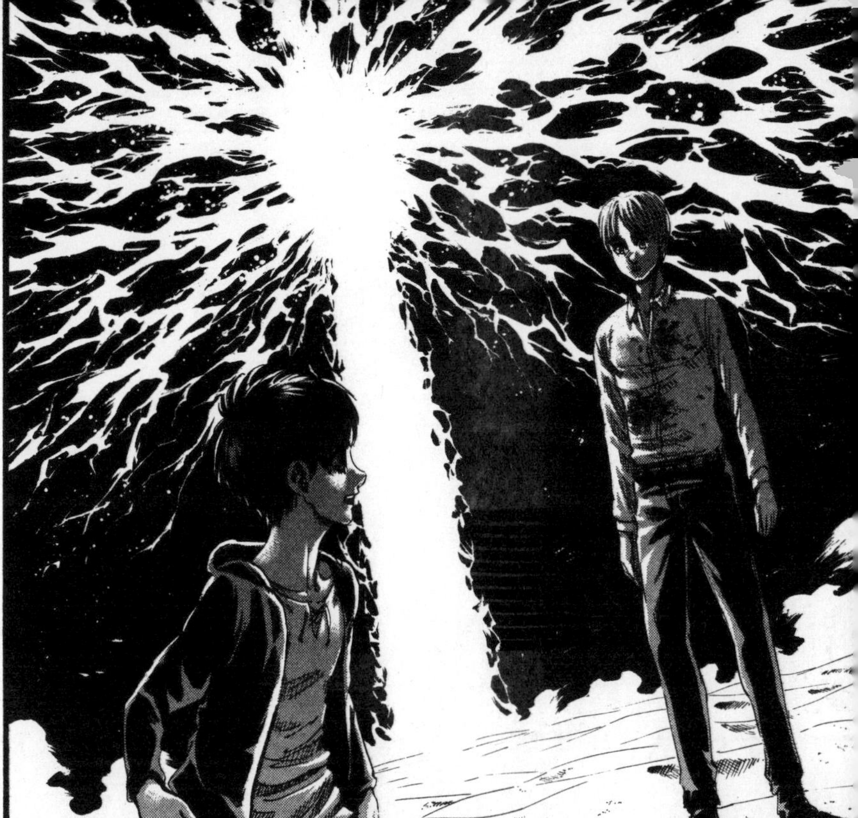
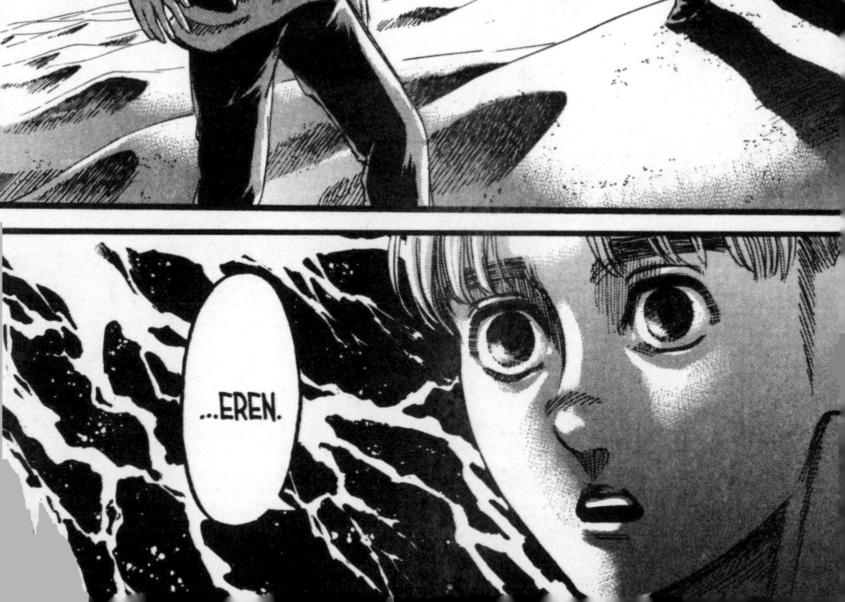
...EREN.

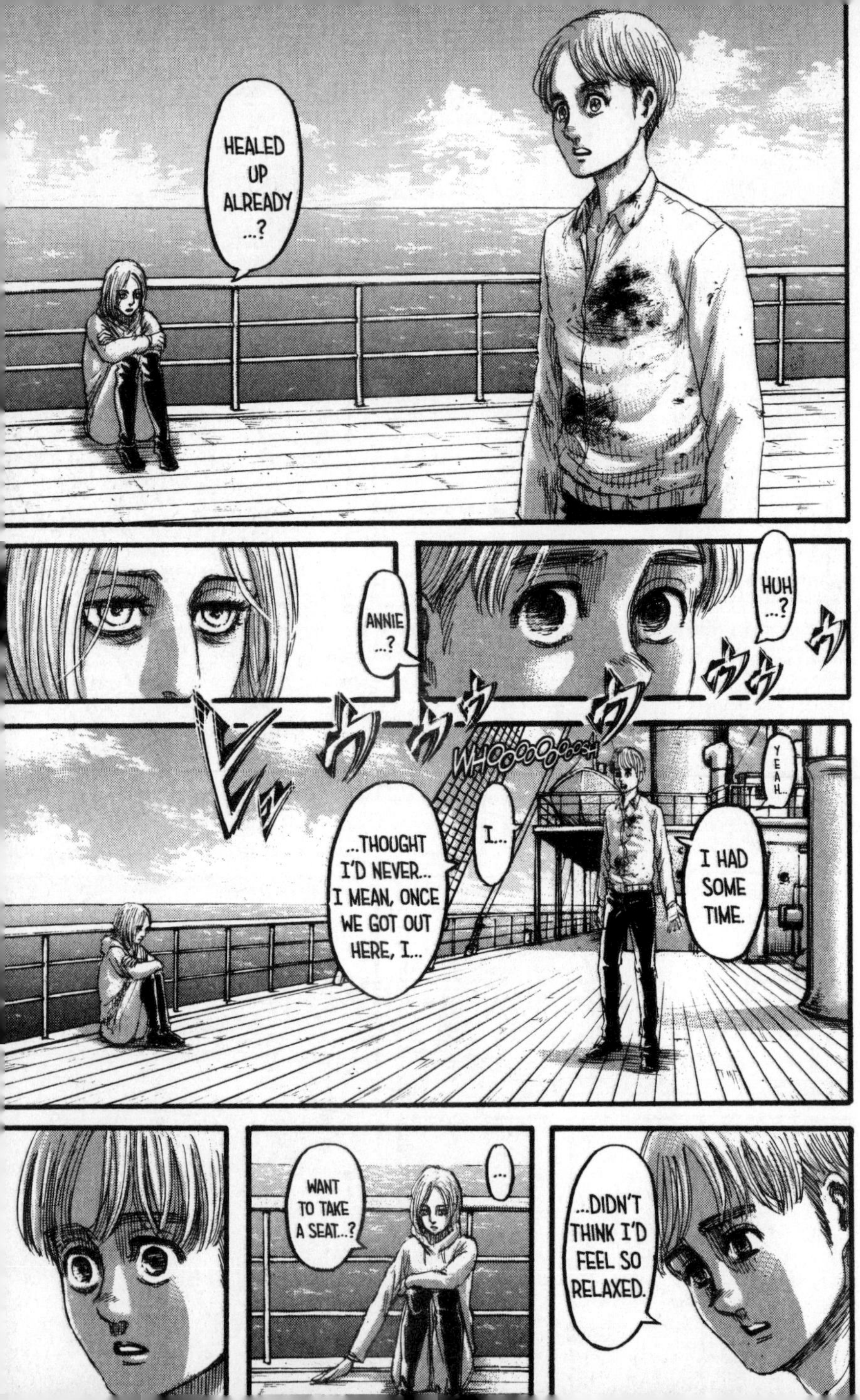
HEALED UP ALREADY ...?
HUH ...?
ANNIE ...?
YEAH...
I HAD SOME TIME.
I...
...THOUGHT I'D NEVER... I MEAN, ONCE WE GOT OUT HERE, I...
WHOOOOOOOSH
...DIDN'T THINK I'D FEEL SO RELAXED.
...
WANT TO TAKE A SEAT...?

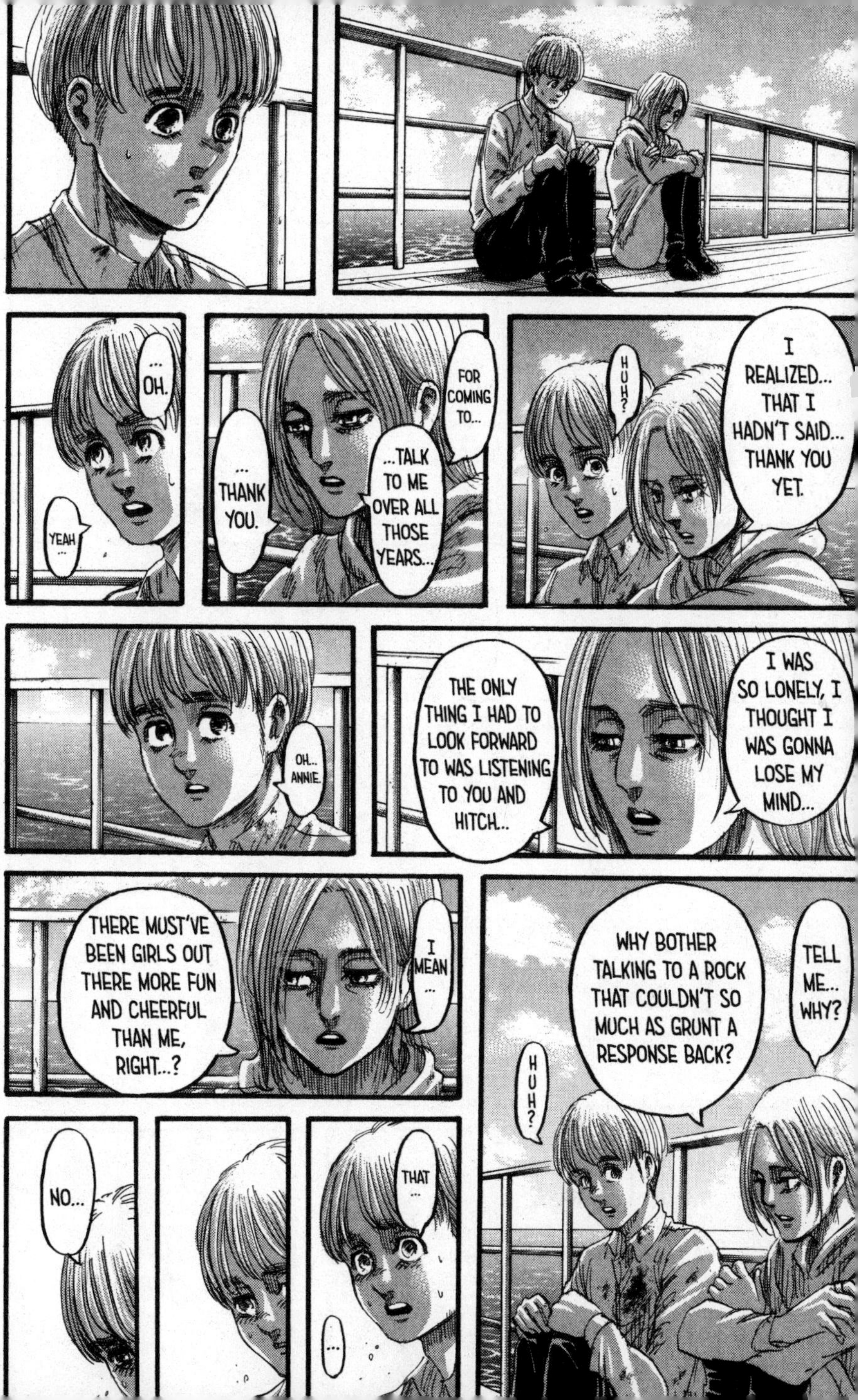
I REALIZED... THAT I HADN'T SAID... THANK YOU YET.
HUH?
FOR COMING TO...
...TALK TO ME OVER ALL THOSE YEARS...
...THANK YOU.
...OH.
YEAH...
I WAS SO LONELY, I THOUGHT I WAS GONNA LOSE MY MIND...
THE ONLY THING I HAD TO LOOK FORWARD TO WAS LISTENING TO YOU AND HITCH..
OH.. ANNIE.
TELL ME... WHY?
WHY BOTHER TALKING TO A ROCK THAT COULDN'T SO MUCH AS GRUNT A RESPONSE BACK?
HUH?
I MEAN...
THERE MUST'VE BEEN GIRLS OUT THERE MORE FUN AND CHEERFUL THAN ME, RIGHT...?
THAT...
...
NO...

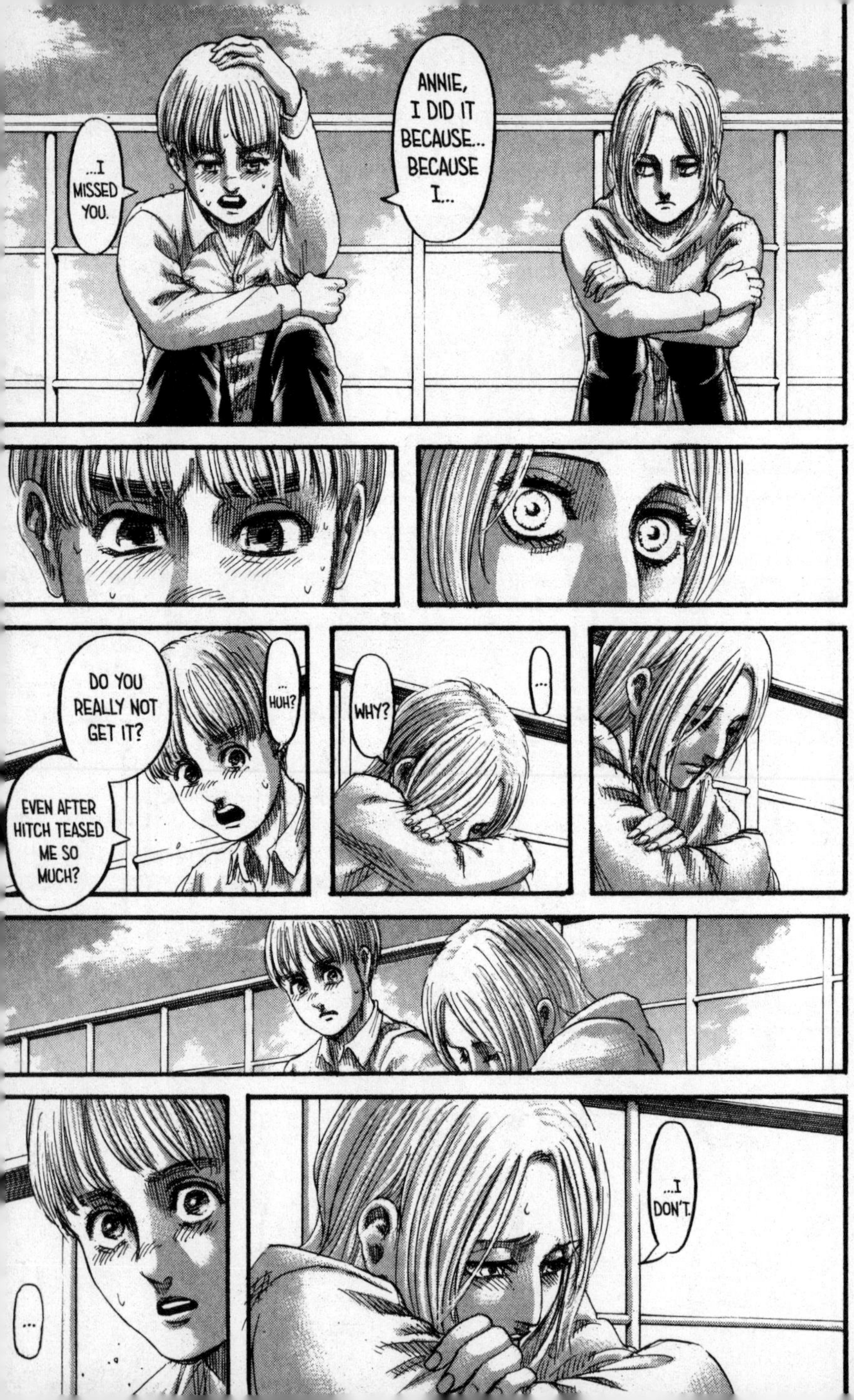
ANNIE, I DID IT BECAUSE... BECAUSE I...
...I MISSED YOU.
...
WHY?
... HUH?
DO YOU REALLY NOT GET IT?
EVEN AFTER HITCH TEASED ME SO MUCH?
...I DON'T.
...

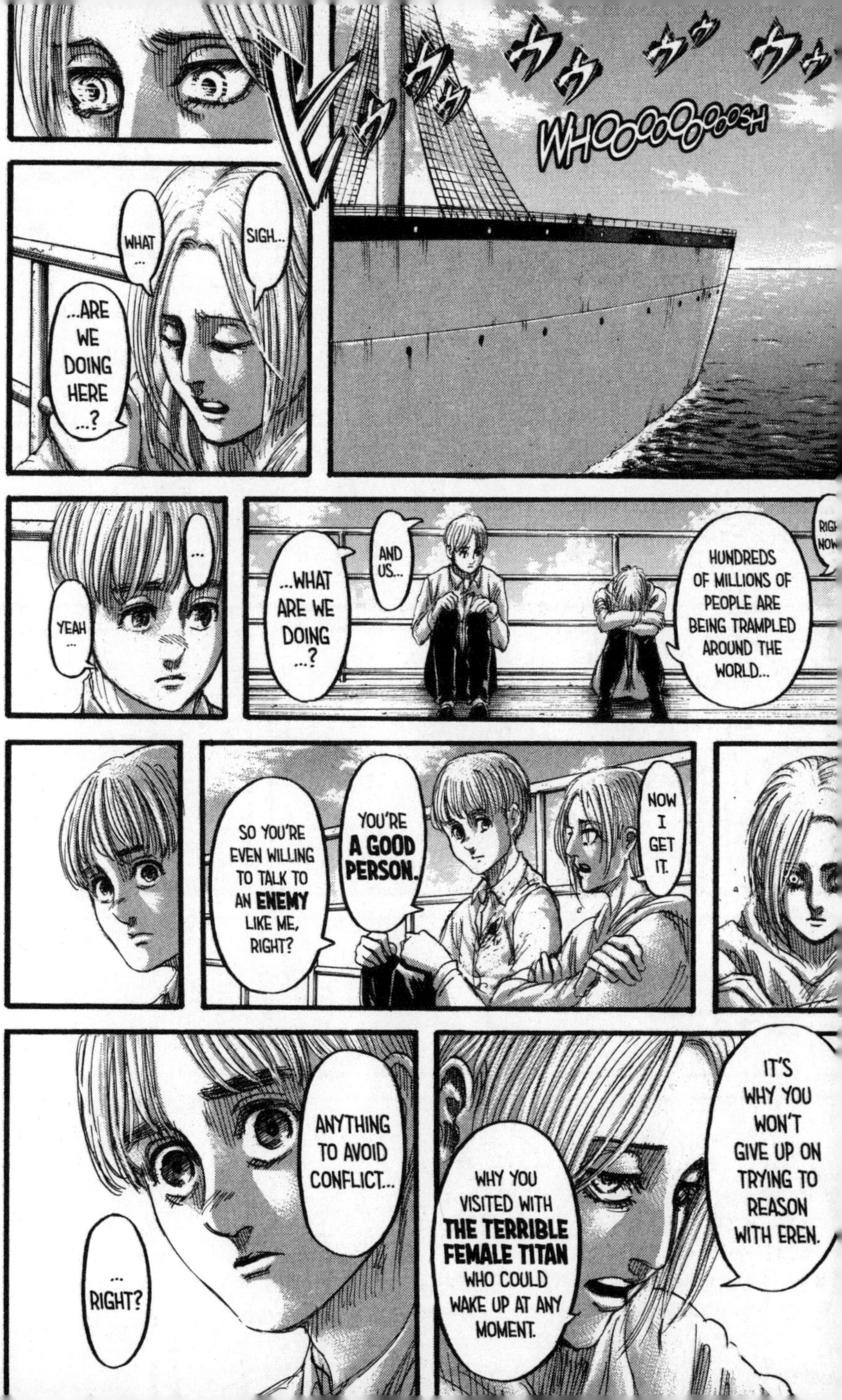

WHOOOOOOOOSH
SIGH...
WHAT...
...ARE WE DOING HERE...?
RIGH NOW
HUNDREDS OF MILLIONS OF PEOPLE ARE BEING TRAMPLED AROUND THE WORLD...
AND US...
...WHAT ARE WE DOING...?
...
YEAH...
NOW I GET IT.
YOU'RE **A GOOD PERSON.**
SO YOU'RE EVEN WILLING TO TALK TO AN **ENEMY** LIKE ME, RIGHT?
IT'S WHY YOU WON'T GIVE UP ON TRYING TO REASON WITH EREN.
WHY YOU VISITED WITH **THE TERRIBLE FEMALE TITAN** WHO COULD WAKE UP AT ANY MOMENT.
ANYTHING TO AVOID CONFLICT...
...RIGHT?

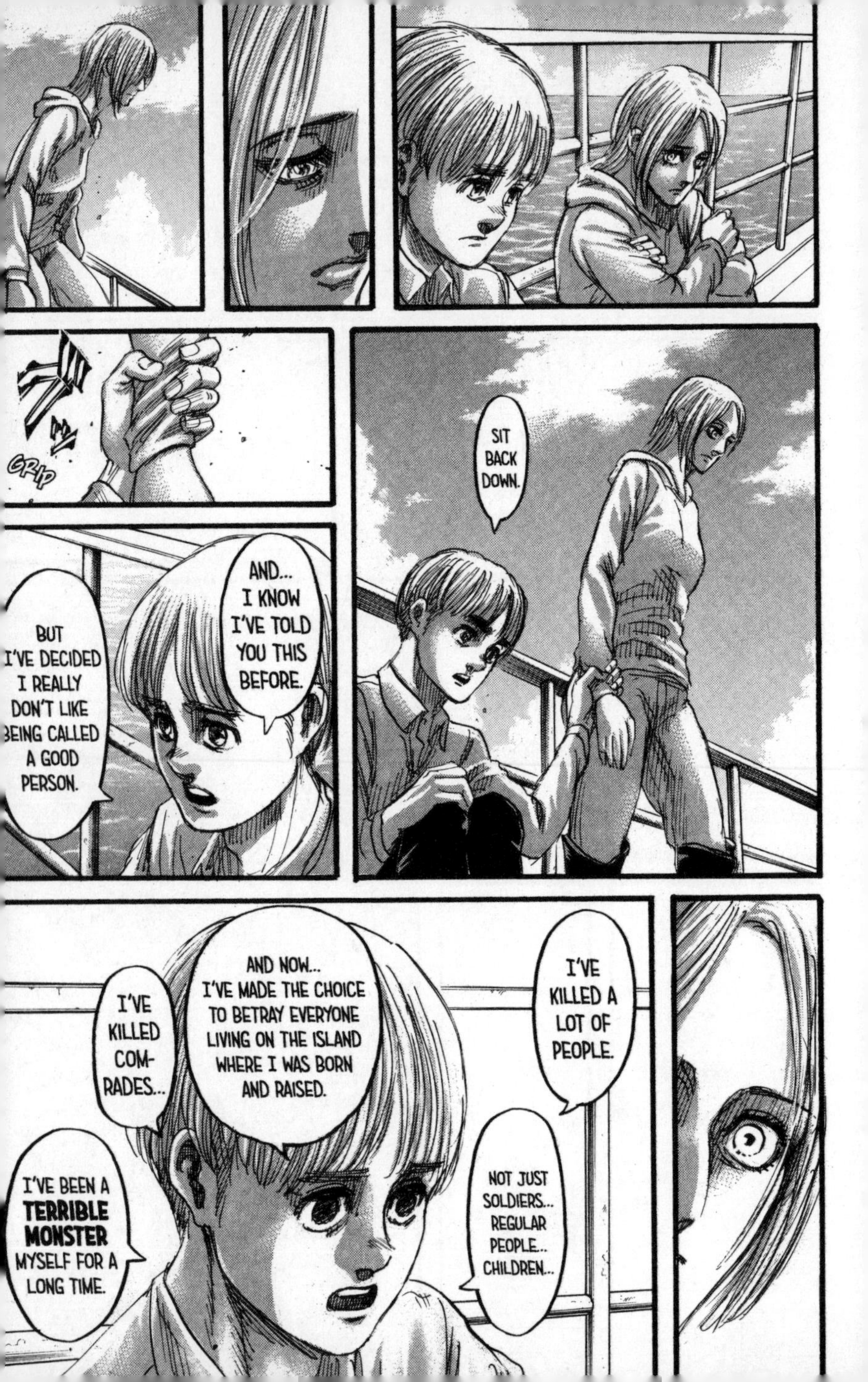
SIT BACK DOWN.
GRIP
AND... I KNOW I'VE TOLD YOU THIS BEFORE.
BUT I'VE DECIDED I REALLY DON'T LIKE BEING CALLED A GOOD PERSON.
I'VE KILLED A LOT OF PEOPLE.
NOT JUST SOLDIERS... REGULAR PEOPLE... CHILDREN...
I'VE KILLED COM-RADES...
AND NOW... I'VE MADE THE CHOICE TO BETRAY EVERYONE LIVING ON THE ISLAND WHERE I WAS BORN AND RAISED.
I'VE BEEN A **TERRIBLE MONSTER** MYSELF FOR A LONG TIME.

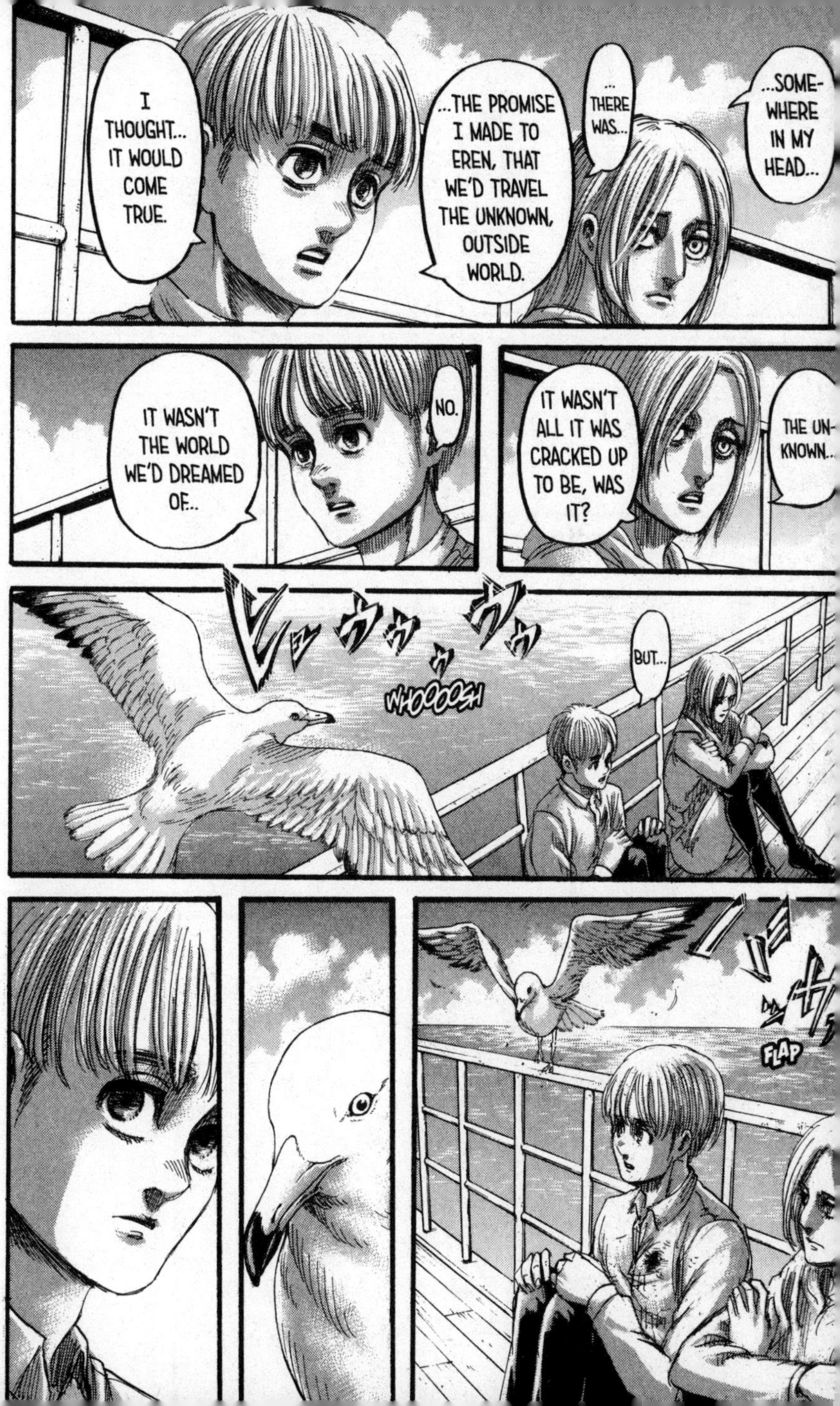

...SOMEWHERE IN MY HEAD...
...THERE WAS...
...THE PROMISE I MADE TO EREN, THAT WE'D TRAVEL THE UNKNOWN, OUTSIDE WORLD.
I THOUGHT... IT WOULD COME TRUE.
THE UNKNOWN...
IT WASN'T ALL IT WAS CRACKED UP TO BE, WAS IT?
NO.
IT WASN'T THE WORLD WE'D DREAMED OF...
BUT...
WHOOOOSH
FLAP

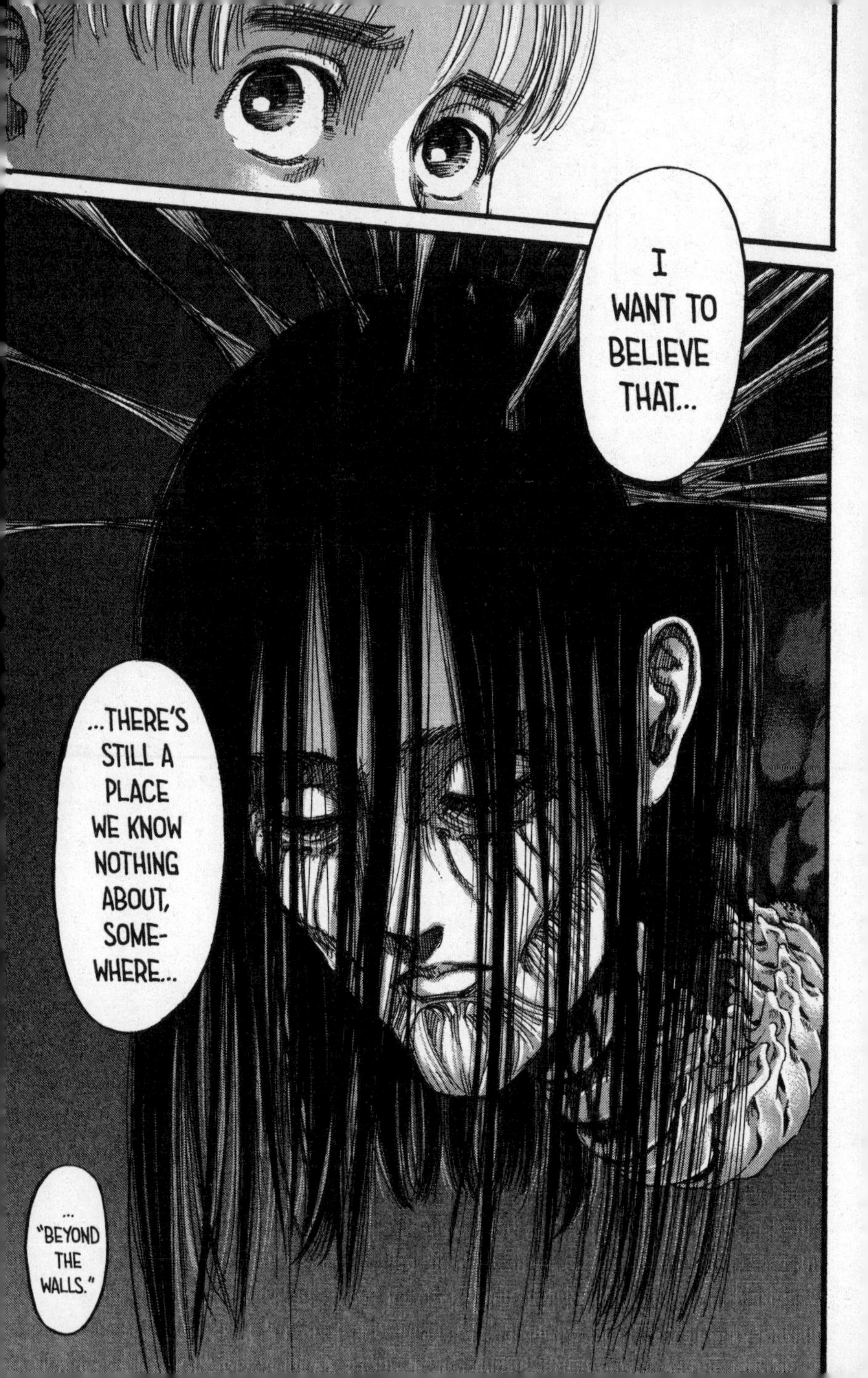
I WANT TO BELIEVE THAT...
...THERE'S STILL A PLACE WE KNOW NOTHING ABOUT, SOME-WHERE...
... "BEYOND THE WALLS."

ATTACK on TITAN

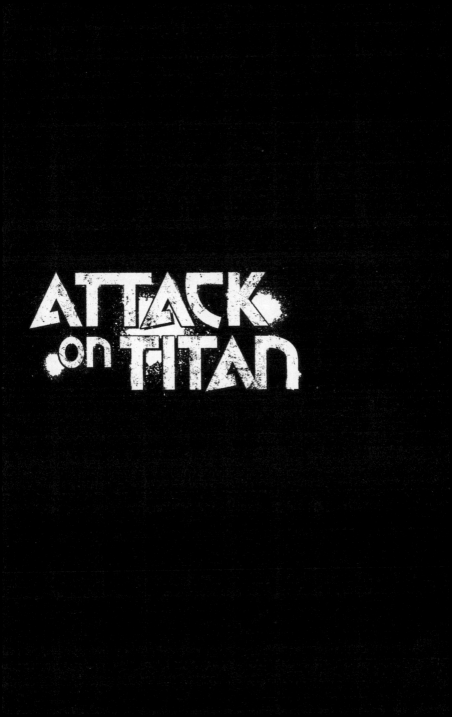

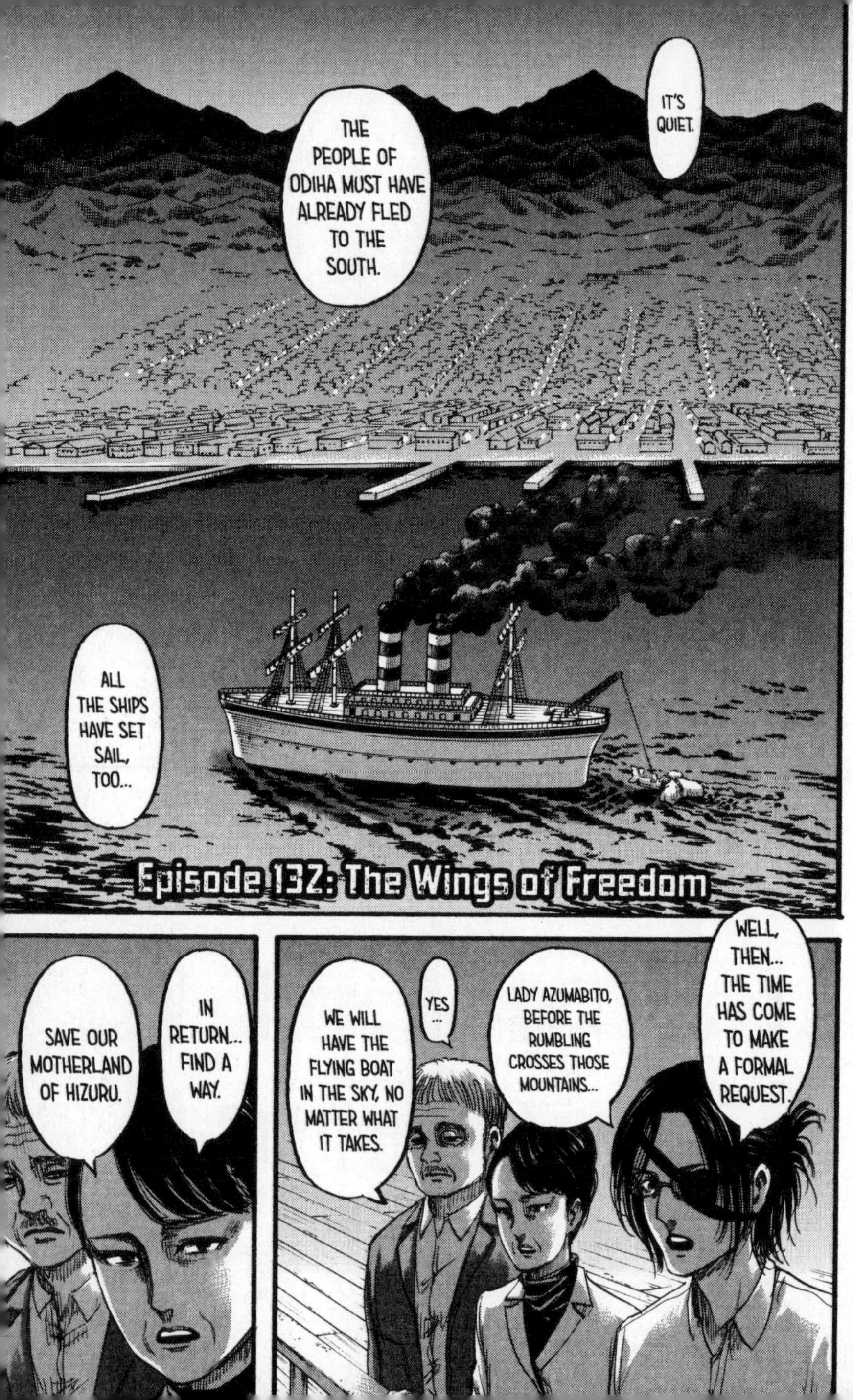
IT'S QUIET.
THE PEOPLE OF ODIHA MUST HAVE ALREADY FLED TO THE SOUTH.
ALL THE SHIPS HAVE SET SAIL, TOO...
Episode 132: The Wings of Freedom
WELL, THEN... THE TIME HAS COME TO MAKE A FORMAL REQUEST.
LADY AZUMABITO, BEFORE THE RUMBLING CROSSES THOSE MOUNTAINS...
YES...
WE WILL HAVE THE FLYING BOAT IN THE SKY, NO MATTER WHAT IT TAKES.
IN RETURN... FIND A WAY.
SAVE OUR MOTHERLAND OF HIZURU.

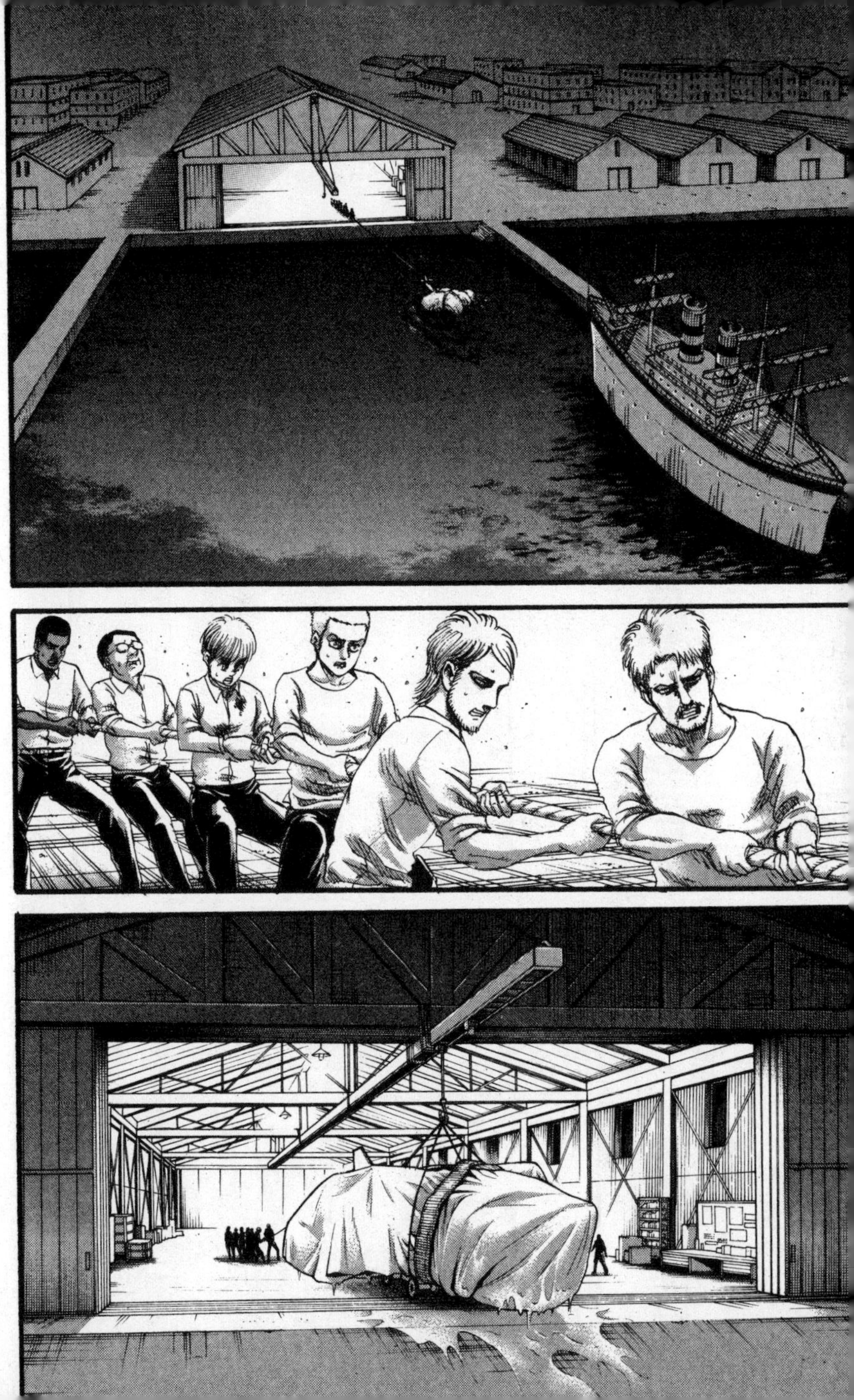

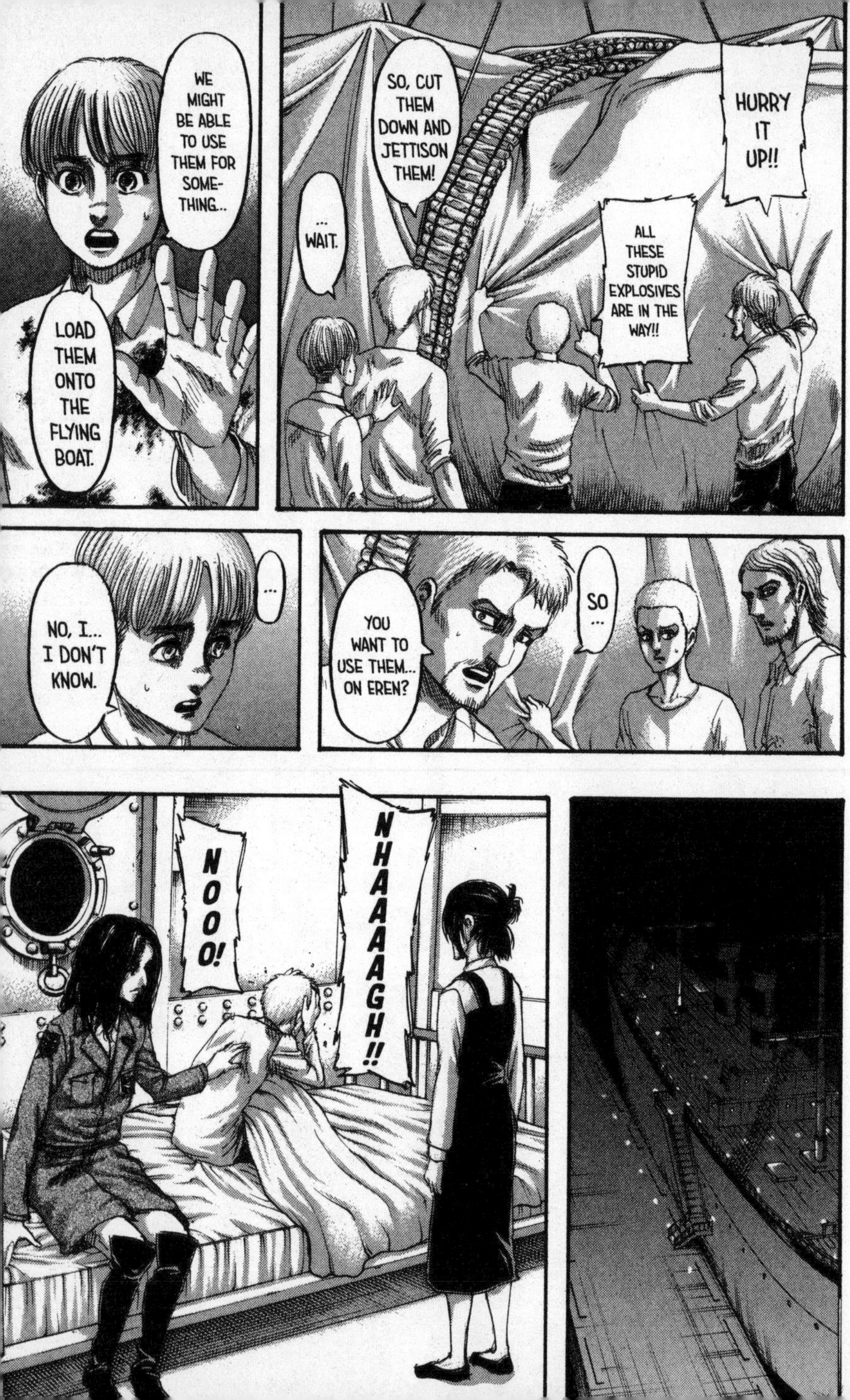
HURRY IT UP!!
ALL THESE STUPID EXPLOSIVES ARE IN THE WAY!!
SO, CUT THEM DOWN AND JETTISON THEM!
... WAIT.
WE MIGHT BE ABLE TO USE THEM FOR SOME-THING...
LOAD THEM ONTO THE FLYING BOAT.
SO ...
YOU WANT TO USE THEM... ON EREN?
...
NO, I... I DON'T KNOW.
NHAAAAGH!!
NOOOO!

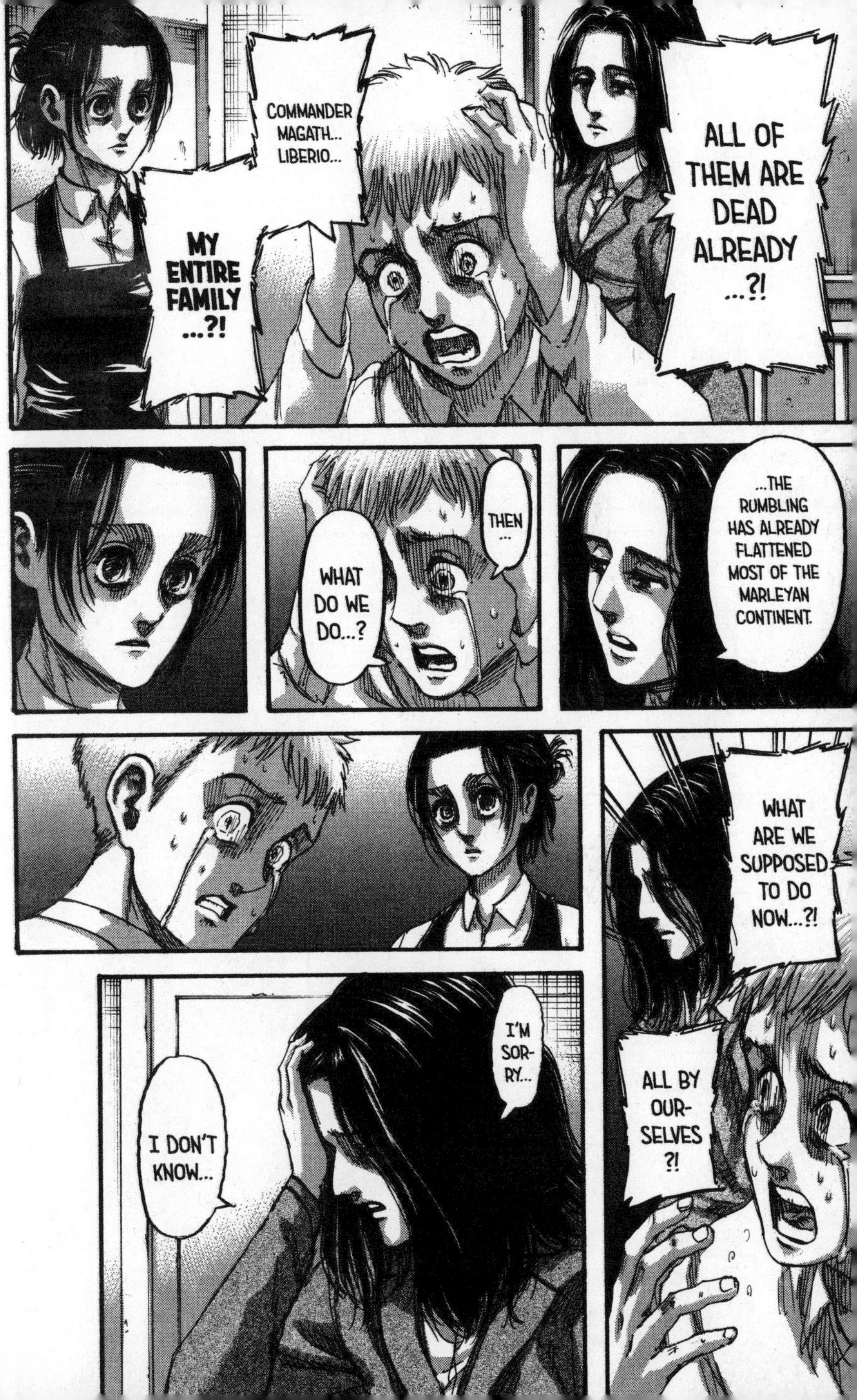
ALL OF THEM ARE DEAD ALREADY ...?!
COMMANDER MAGATH... LIBERIO...
MY ENTIRE FAMILY ...?!
...THE RUMBLING HAS ALREADY FLATTENED MOST OF THE MARLEYAN CONTINENT.
THEN ...
WHAT DO WE DO...?
WHAT ARE WE SUPPOSED TO DO NOW...?!
ALL BY OUR-SELVES ?!
I'M SOR-RY...
I DON'T KNOW...

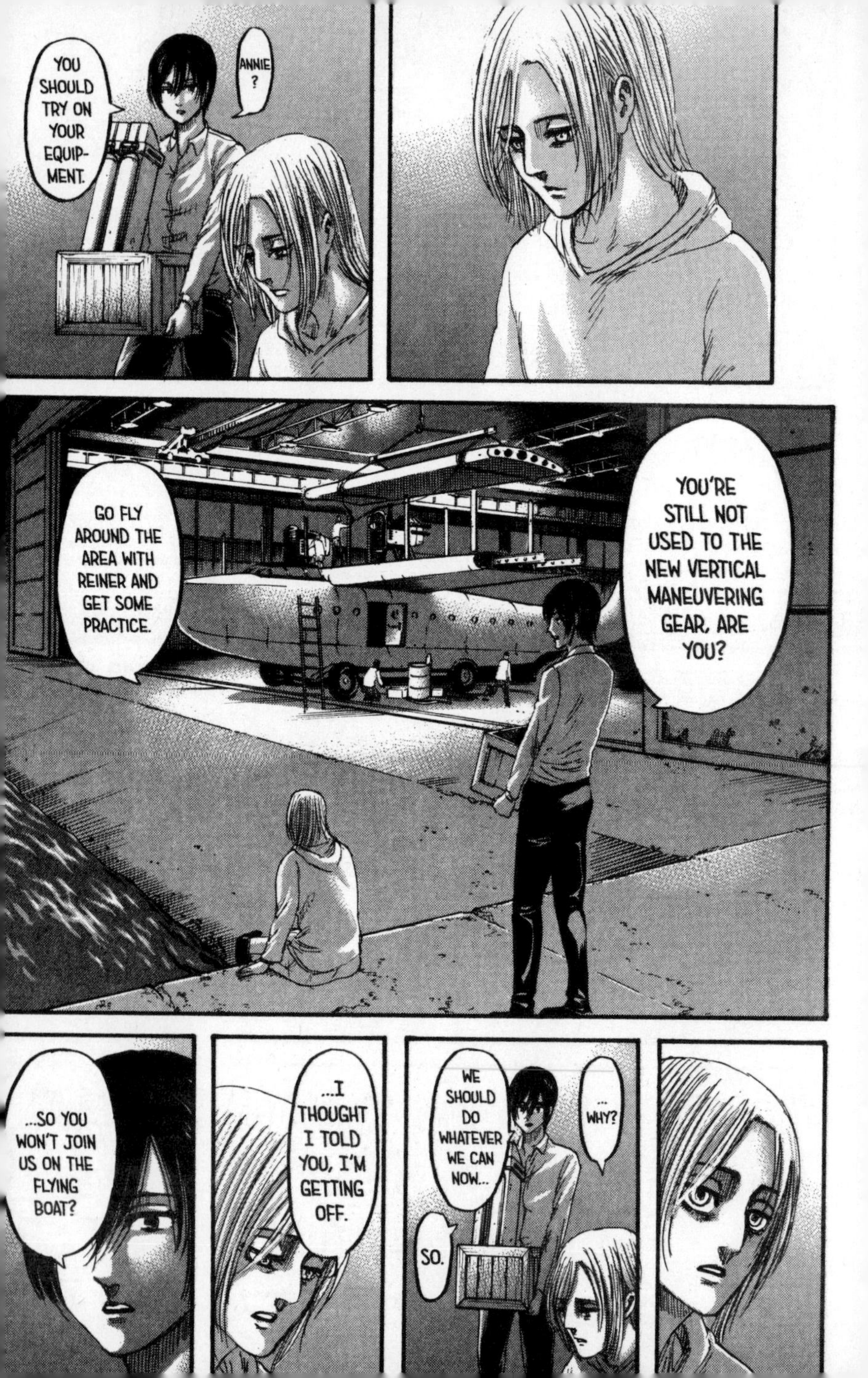
ANNIE ?
YOU SHOULD TRY ON YOUR EQUIPMENT.
YOU'RE STILL NOT USED TO THE NEW VERTICAL MANEUVERING GEAR, ARE YOU?
GO FLY AROUND THE AREA WITH REINER AND GET SOME PRACTICE.
...WHY?
WE SHOULD DO WHATEVER WE CAN NOW...
SO.
...I THOUGHT I TOLD YOU, I'M GETTING OFF.
...SO YOU WON'T JOIN US ON THE FLYING BOAT?

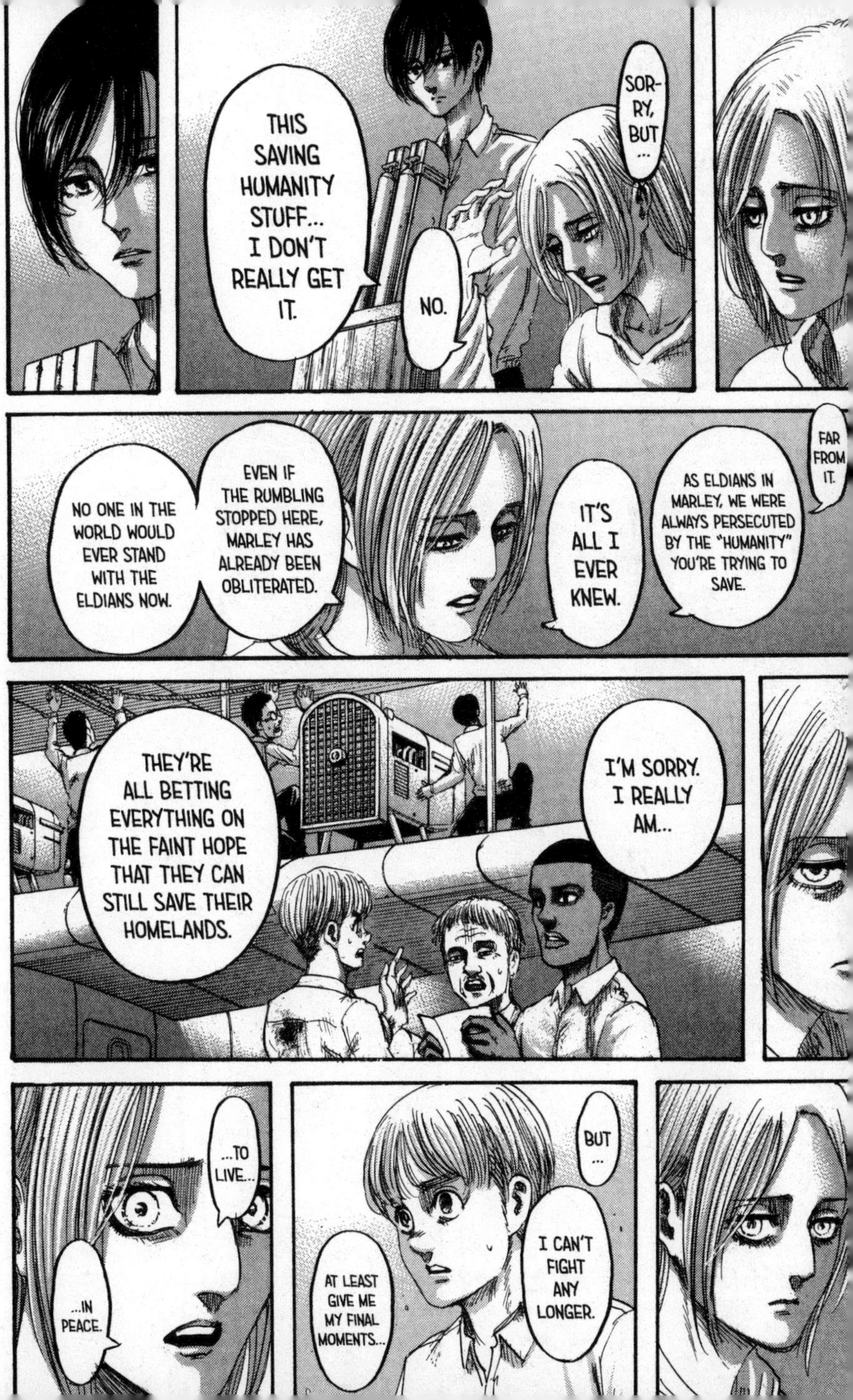
SOR-RY, BUT ...
NO.
THIS SAVING HUMANITY STUFF... I DON'T REALLY GET IT.
FAR FROM IT.
AS ELDIANS IN MARLEY, WE WERE ALWAYS PERSECUTED BY THE "HUMANITY" YOU'RE TRYING TO SAVE.
IT'S ALL I EVER KNEW.
EVEN IF THE RUMBLING STOPPED HERE, MARLEY HAS ALREADY BEEN OBLITERATED.
NO ONE IN THE WORLD WOULD EVER STAND WITH THE ELDIANS NOW.
I'M SORRY. I REALLY AM...
THEY'RE ALL BETTING EVERYTHING ON THE FAINT HOPE THAT THEY CAN STILL SAVE THEIR HOMELANDS.
BUT ...
I CAN'T FIGHT ANY LONGER.
AT LEAST GIVE ME MY FINAL MOMENTS...
...TO LIVE...
...IN PEACE.

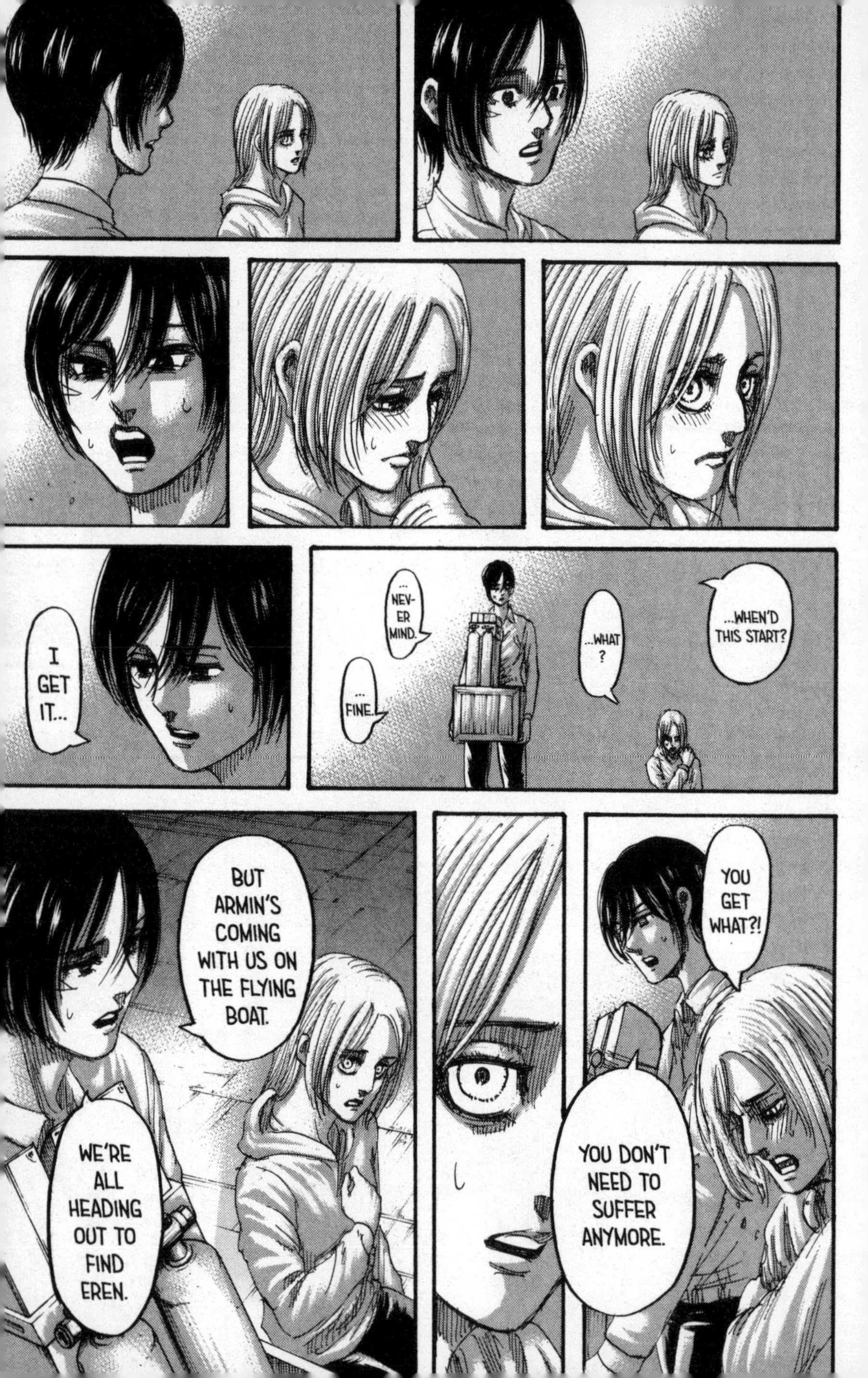
...WHEN'D THIS START?
...WHAT?
...NEVER MIND.
...FINE.
I GET IT...
YOU GET WHAT?!
YOU DON'T NEED TO SUFFER ANYMORE.
BUT ARMIN'S COMING WITH US ON THE FLYING BOAT.
WE'RE ALL HEADING OUT TO FIND EREN.

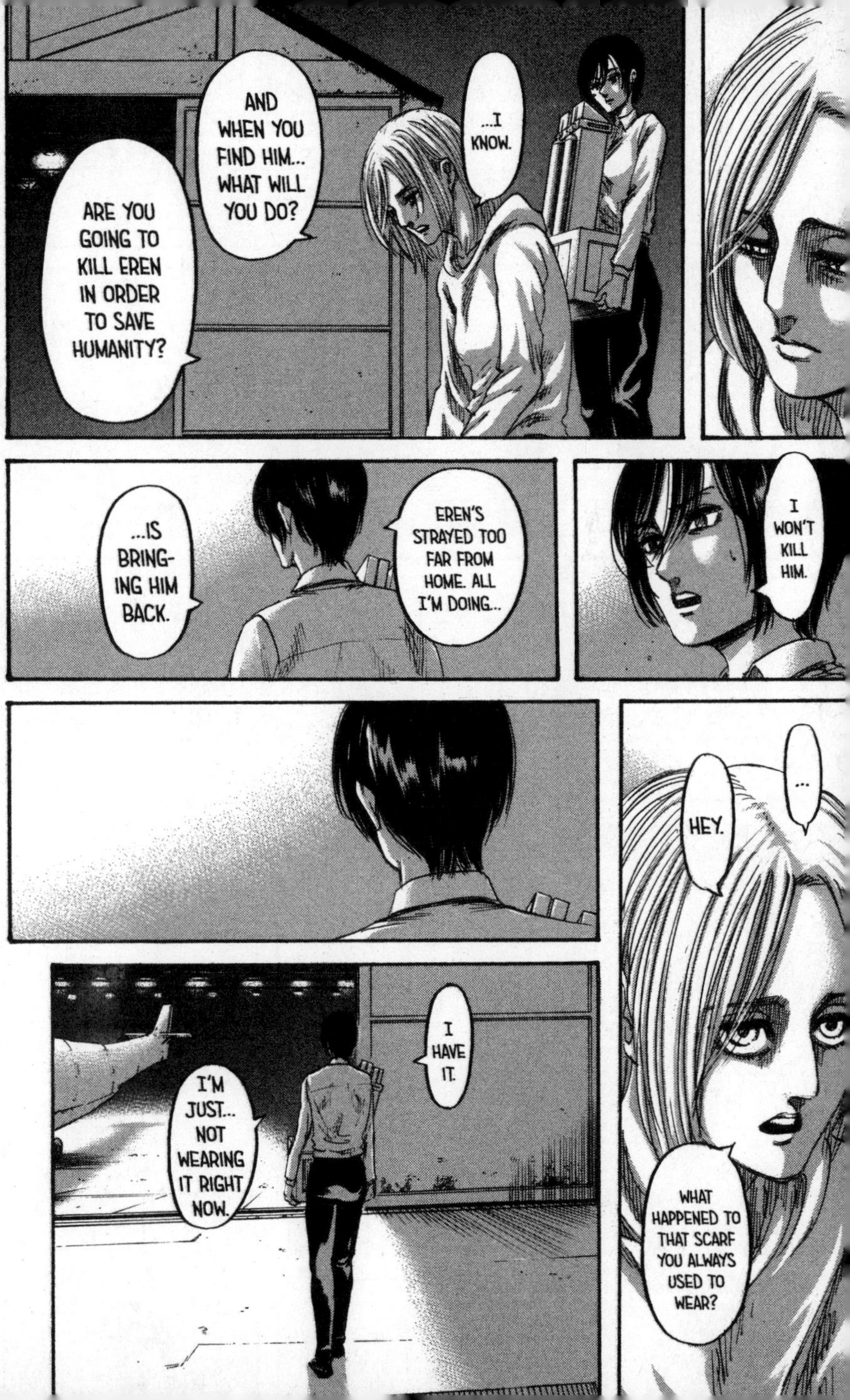
...I KNOW.
AND WHEN YOU FIND HIM... WHAT WILL YOU DO?
ARE YOU GOING TO KILL EREN IN ORDER TO SAVE HUMANITY?
I WON'T KILL HIM.
EREN'S STRAYED TOO FAR FROM HOME. ALL I'M DOING...
...IS BRING-ING HIM BACK.
...
HEY.
WHAT HAPPENED TO THAT SCARF YOU ALWAYS USED TO WEAR?
I HAVE IT.
I'M JUST... NOT WEARING IT RIGHT NOW.

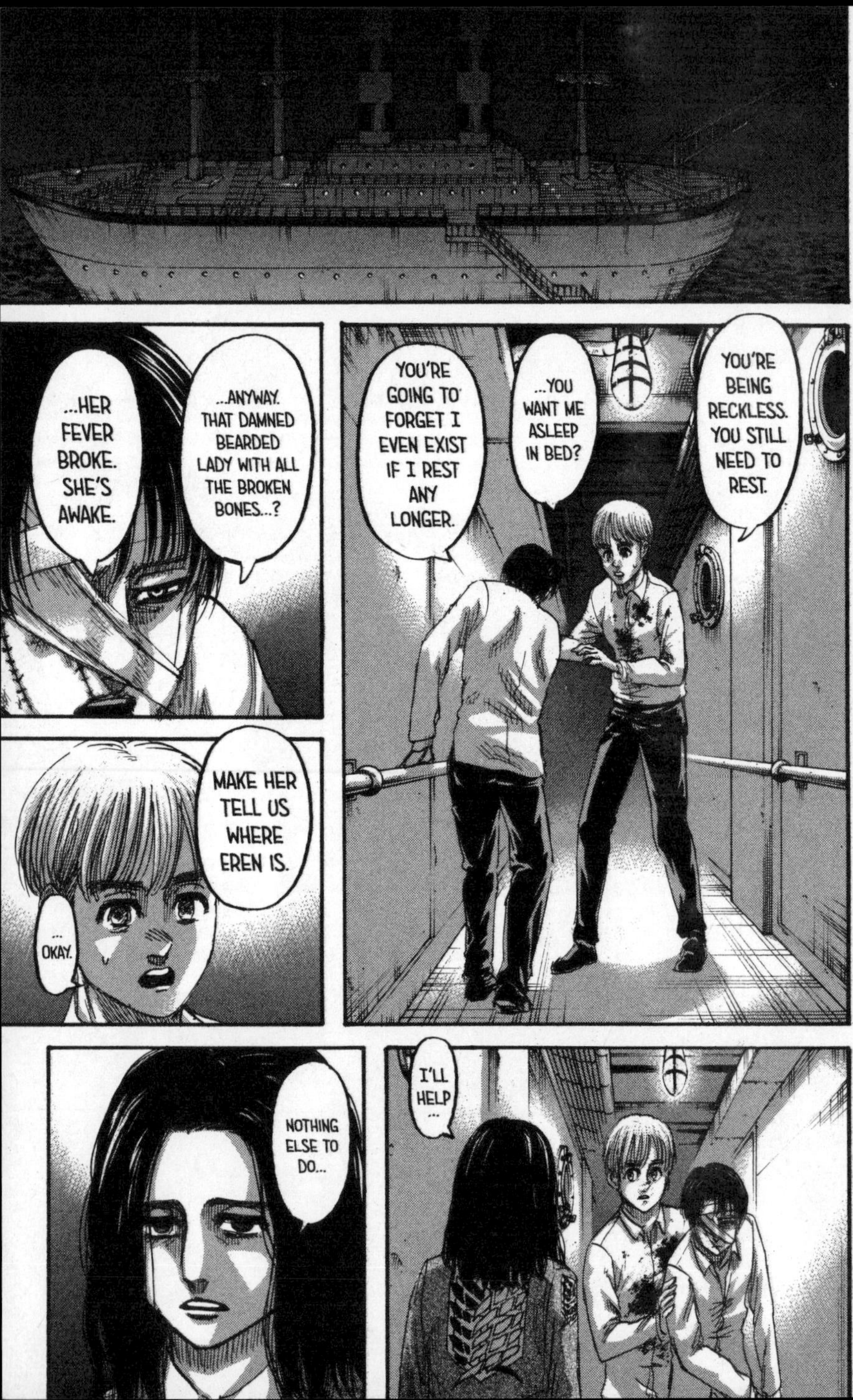
YOU'RE BEING RECKLESS. YOU STILL NEED TO REST.
...YOU WANT ME ASLEEP IN BED?
YOU'RE GOING TO FORGET I EVEN EXIST IF I REST ANY LONGER.
...ANYWAY. THAT DAMNED BEARDED LADY WITH ALL THE BROKEN BONES...?
...HER FEVER BROKE. SHE'S AWAKE.
MAKE HER TELL US WHERE EREN IS.
... OKAY.
I'LL HELP...
NOTHING ELSE TO DO...

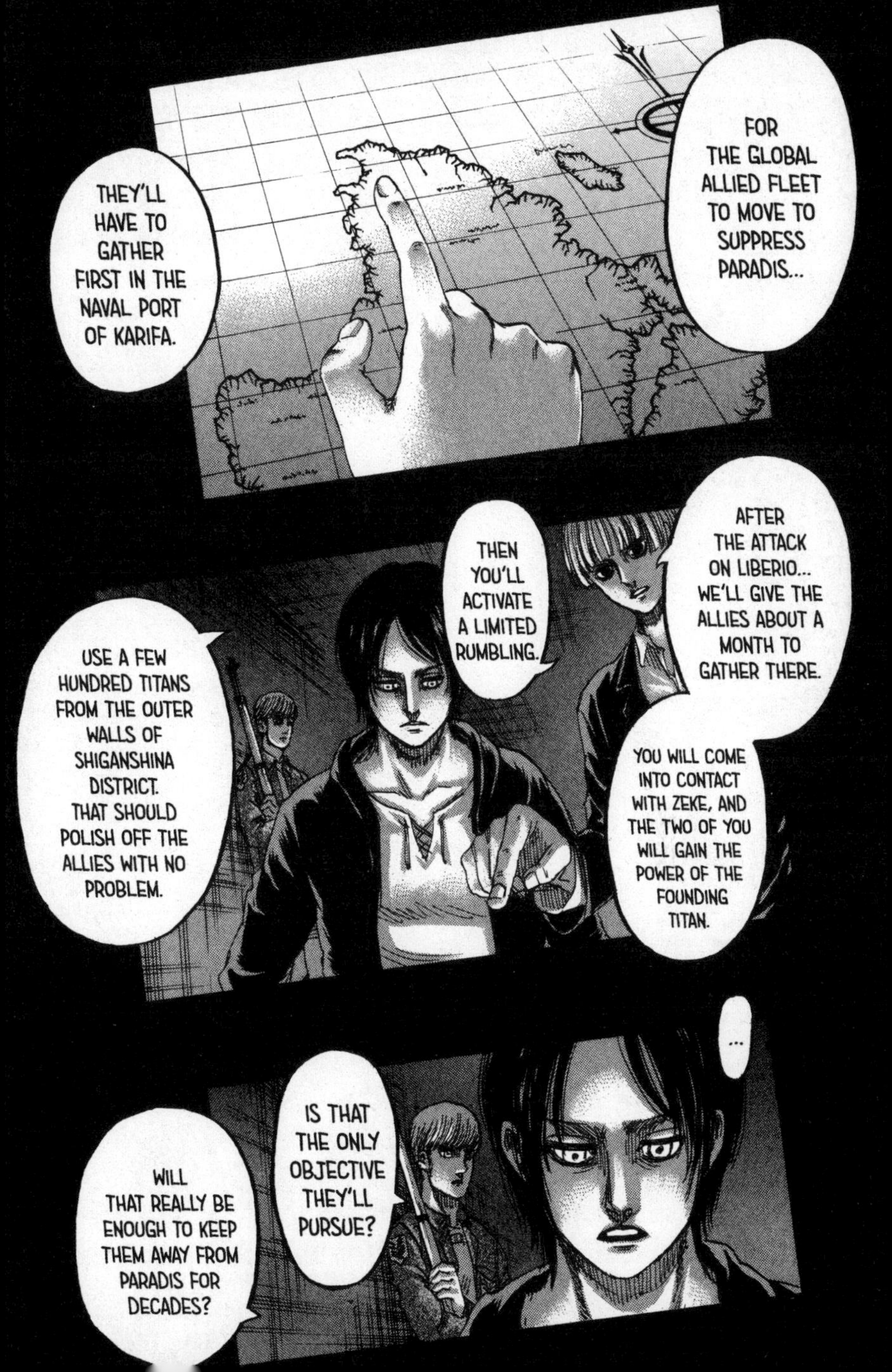
FOR THE GLOBAL ALLIED FLEET TO MOVE TO SUPPRESS PARADIS...
THEY'LL HAVE TO GATHER FIRST IN THE NAVAL PORT OF KARIFA.
AFTER THE ATTACK ON LIBERIO... WE'LL GIVE THE ALLIES ABOUT A MONTH TO GATHER THERE.
THEN YOU'LL ACTIVATE A LIMITED RUMBLING.
USE A FEW HUNDRED TITANS FROM THE OUTER WALLS OF SHIGANSHINA DISTRICT. THAT SHOULD POLISH OFF THE ALLIES WITH NO PROBLEM.
YOU WILL COME INTO CONTACT WITH ZEKE, AND THE TWO OF YOU WILL GAIN THE POWER OF THE FOUNDING TITAN.
...
IS THAT THE ONLY OBJECTIVE THEY'LL PURSUE?
WILL THAT REALLY BE ENOUGH TO KEEP THEM AWAY FROM PARADIS FOR DECADES?

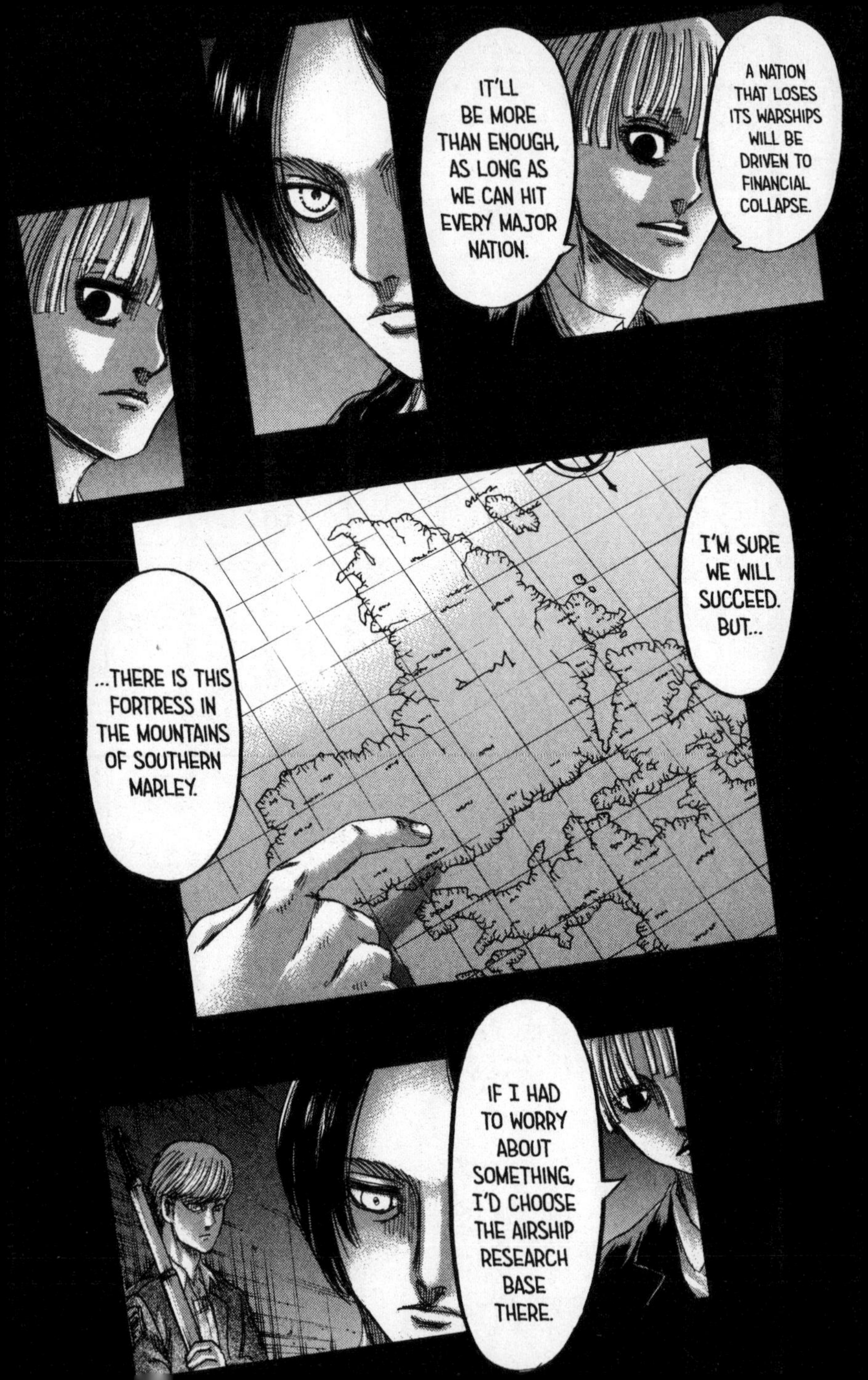
A NATION THAT LOSES ITS WARSHIPS WILL BE DRIVEN TO FINANCIAL COLLAPSE.
IT'LL BE MORE THAN ENOUGH, AS LONG AS WE CAN HIT EVERY MAJOR NATION.
I'M SURE WE WILL SUCCEED. BUT...
...THERE IS THIS FORTRESS IN THE MOUNTAINS OF SOUTHERN MARLEY.
IF I HAD TO WORRY ABOUT SOMETHING, I'D CHOOSE THE AIRSHIP RESEARCH BASE THERE.

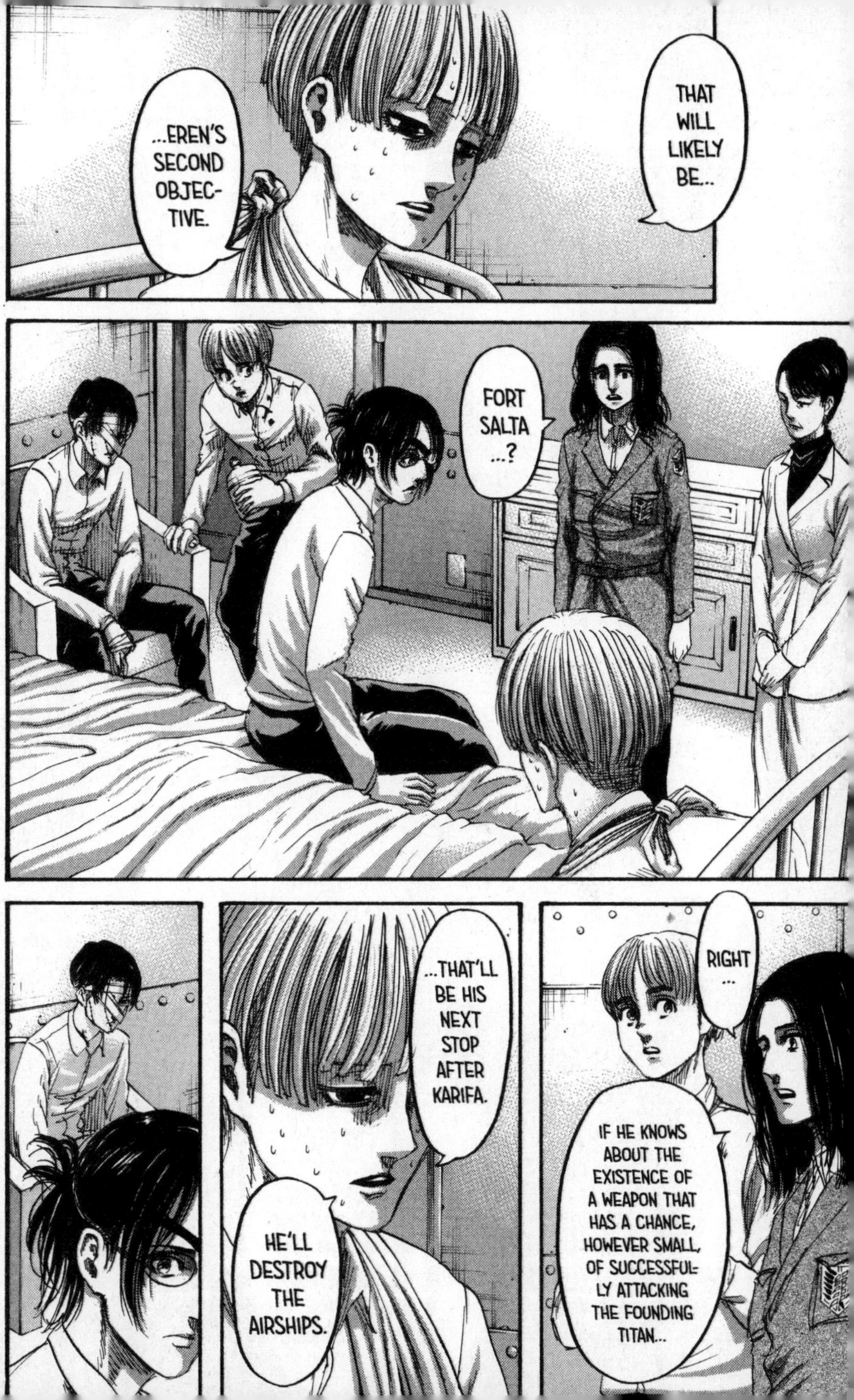
THAT WILL LIKELY BE...
...EREN'S SECOND OBJECTIVE.
FORT SALTA ...?
RIGHT ...
IF HE KNOWS ABOUT THE EXISTENCE OF A WEAPON THAT HAS A CHANCE, HOWEVER SMALL, OF SUCCESSFULLY ATTACKING THE FOUNDING TITAN...
...THAT'LL BE HIS NEXT STOP AFTER KARIFA.
HE'LL DESTROY THE AIRSHIPS.

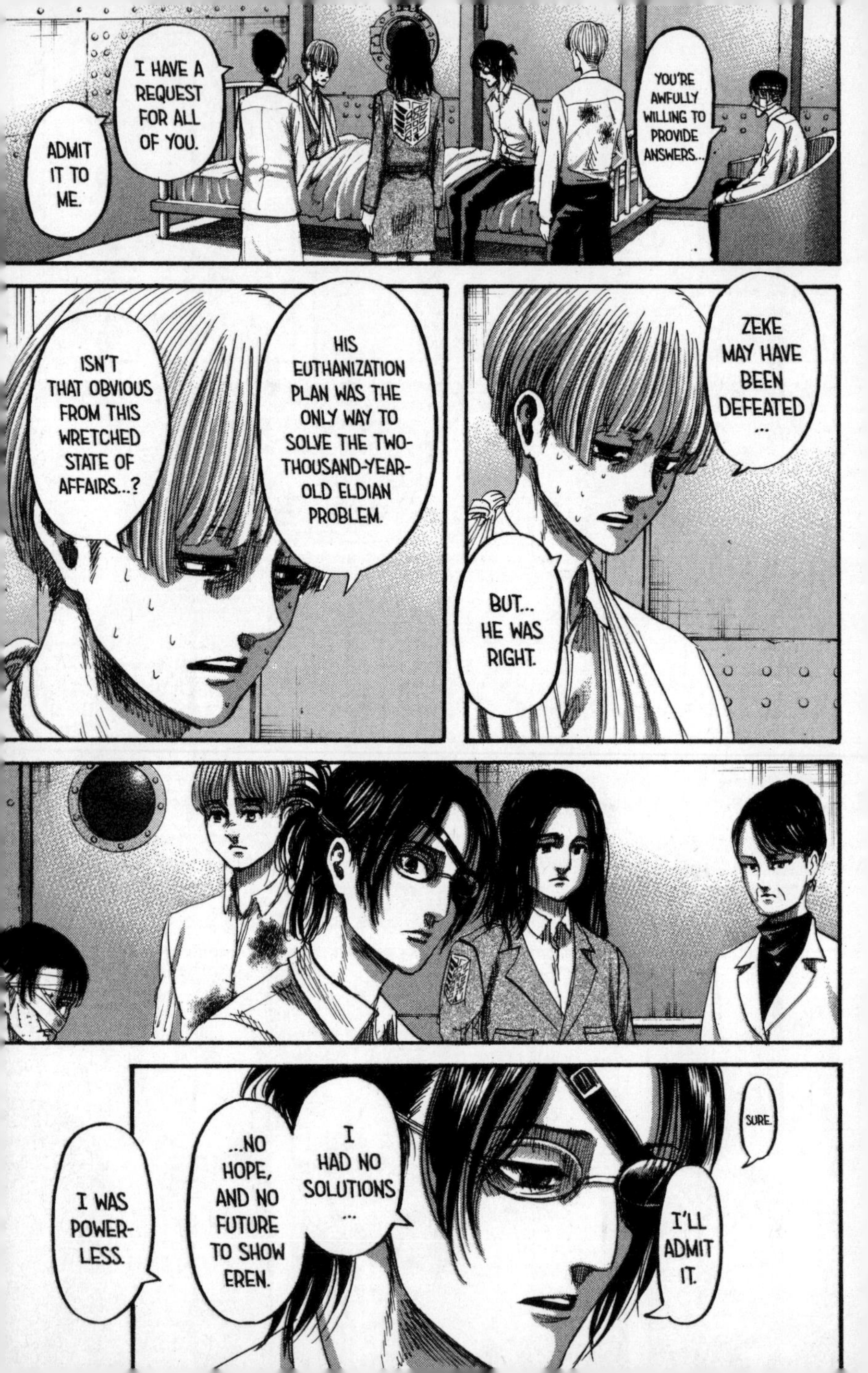
YOU'RE AWFULLY WILLING TO PROVIDE ANSWERS...
I HAVE A REQUEST FOR ALL OF YOU.
ADMIT IT TO ME.
ZEKE MAY HAVE BEEN DEFEATED...
BUT... HE WAS RIGHT.
HIS EUTHANIZATION PLAN WAS THE ONLY WAY TO SOLVE THE TWO-THOUSAND-YEAR-OLD ELDIAN PROBLEM.
ISN'T THAT OBVIOUS FROM THIS WRETCHED STATE OF AFFAIRS...?
SURE.
I'LL ADMIT IT.
I HAD NO SOLUTIONS...
...NO HOPE, AND NO FUTURE TO SHOW EREN.
I WAS POWER-LESS.

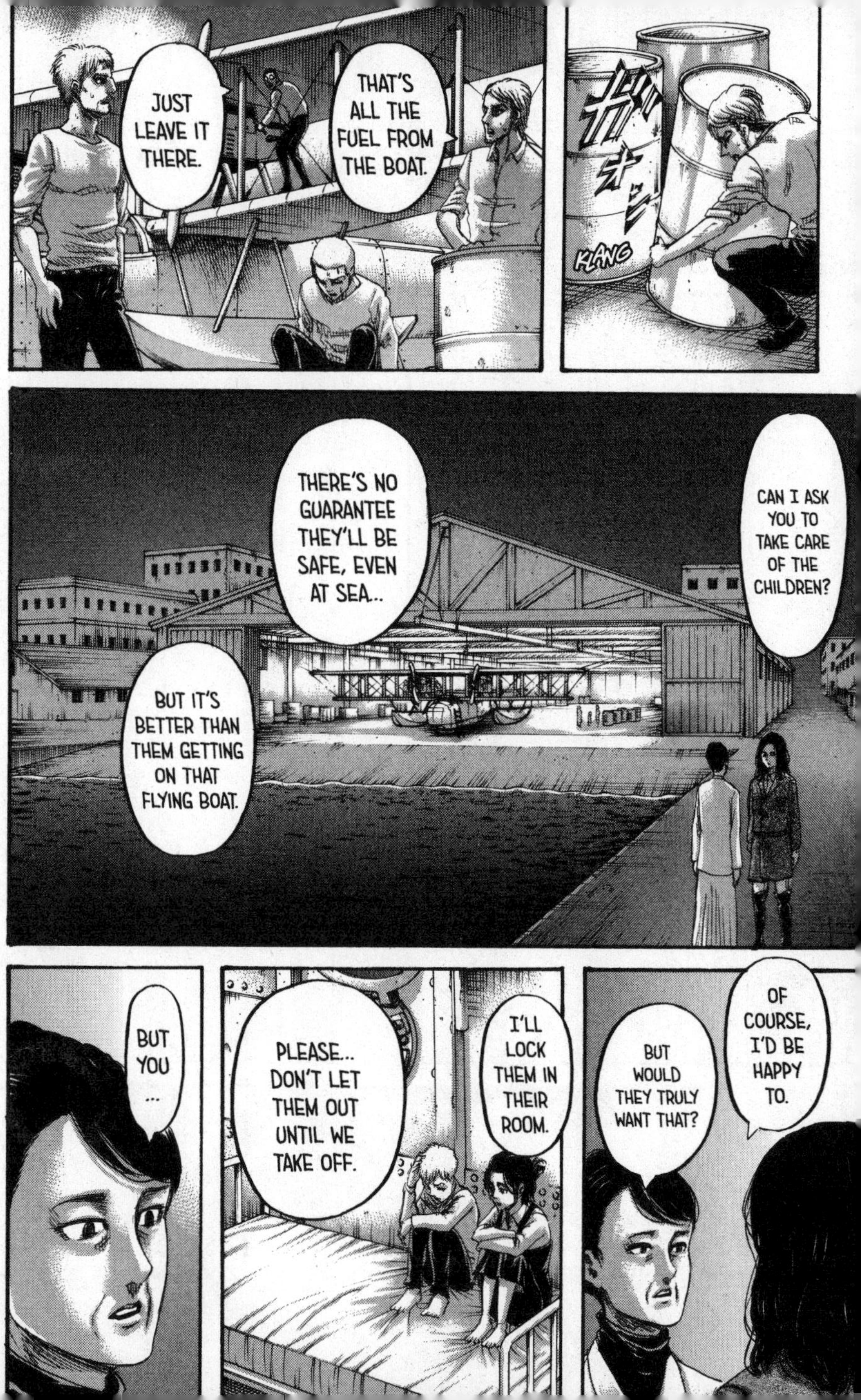
KLANG
THAT'S ALL THE FUEL FROM THE BOAT.
JUST LEAVE IT THERE.
CAN I ASK YOU TO TAKE CARE OF THE CHILDREN?
THERE'S NO GUARANTEE THEY'LL BE SAFE, EVEN AT SEA...
BUT IT'S BETTER THAN THEM GETTING ON THAT FLYING BOAT.
OF COURSE, I'D BE HAPPY TO.
BUT WOULD THEY TRULY WANT THAT?
I'LL LOCK THEM IN THEIR ROOM.
PLEASE... DON'T LET THEM OUT UNTIL WE TAKE OFF.
BUT YOU ...

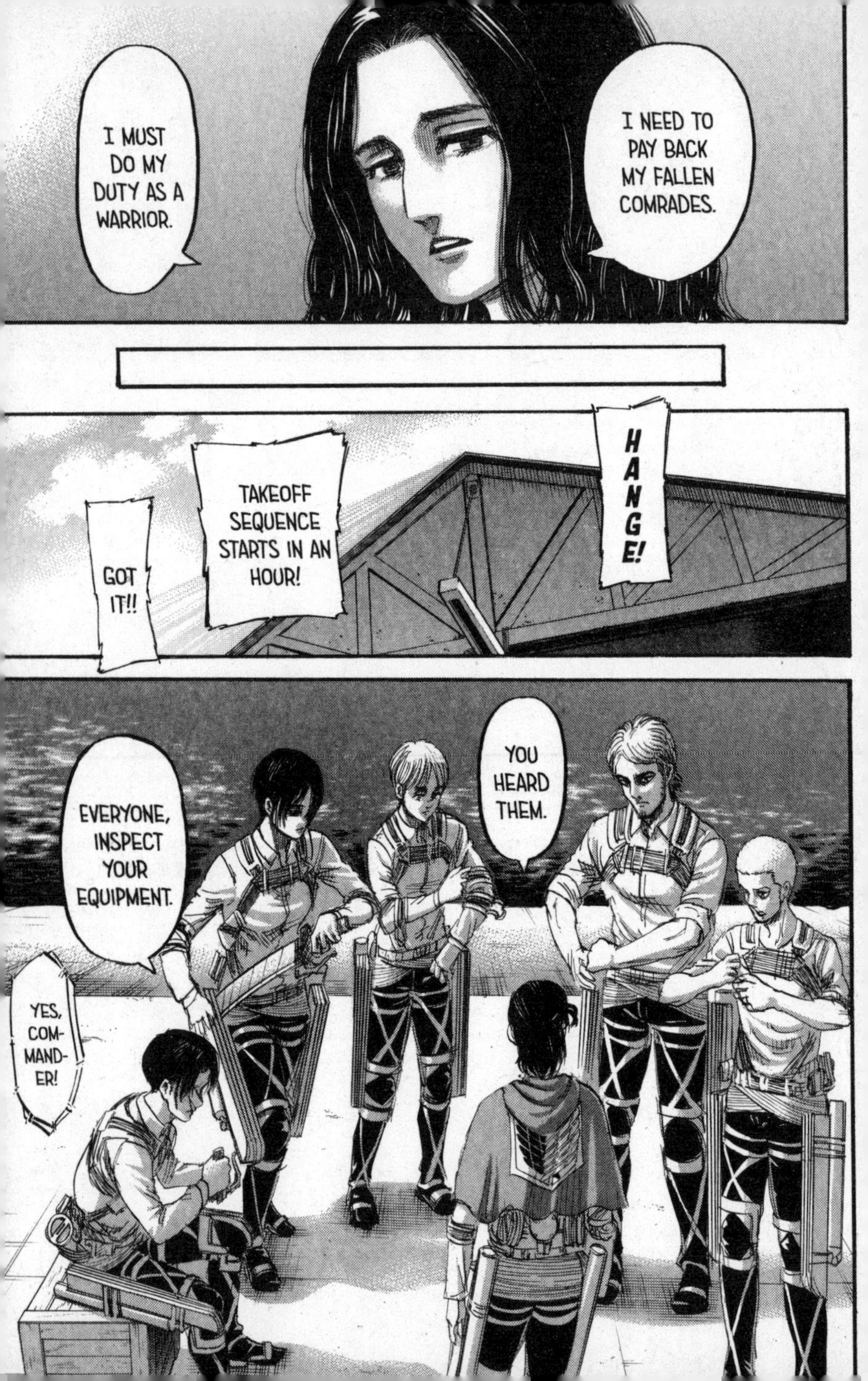
I NEED TO PAY BACK MY FALLEN COMRADES.
I MUST DO MY DUTY AS A WARRIOR.
HANGE!
TAKEOFF SEQUENCE STARTS IN AN HOUR!
GOT IT!!
YOU HEARD THEM.
EVERYONE, INSPECT YOUR EQUIPMENT.
YES, COM- MAND- ER!

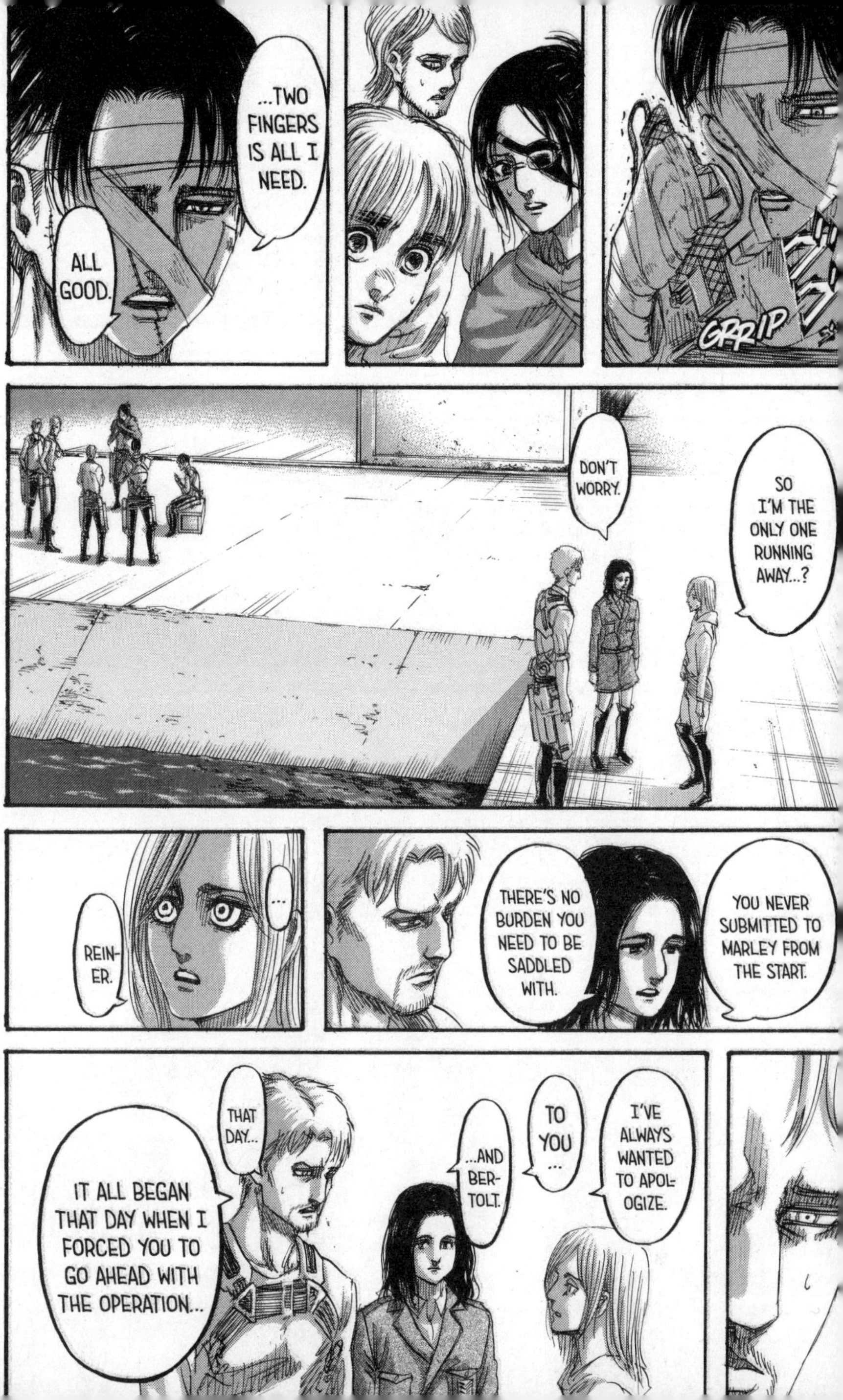
GRRIP
...TWO FINGERS IS ALL I NEED.
ALL GOOD.
SO I'M THE ONLY ONE RUNNING AWAY...?
DON'T WORRY.
YOU NEVER SUBMITTED TO MARLEY FROM THE START.
THERE'S NO BURDEN YOU NEED TO BE SADDLED WITH.
...
REIN-ER.
I'VE ALWAYS WANTED TO APOL-OGIZE.
TO YOU ...
...AND BER-TOLT.
THAT DAY...
IT ALL BEGAN THAT DAY WHEN I FORCED YOU TO GO AHEAD WITH THE OPERATION...

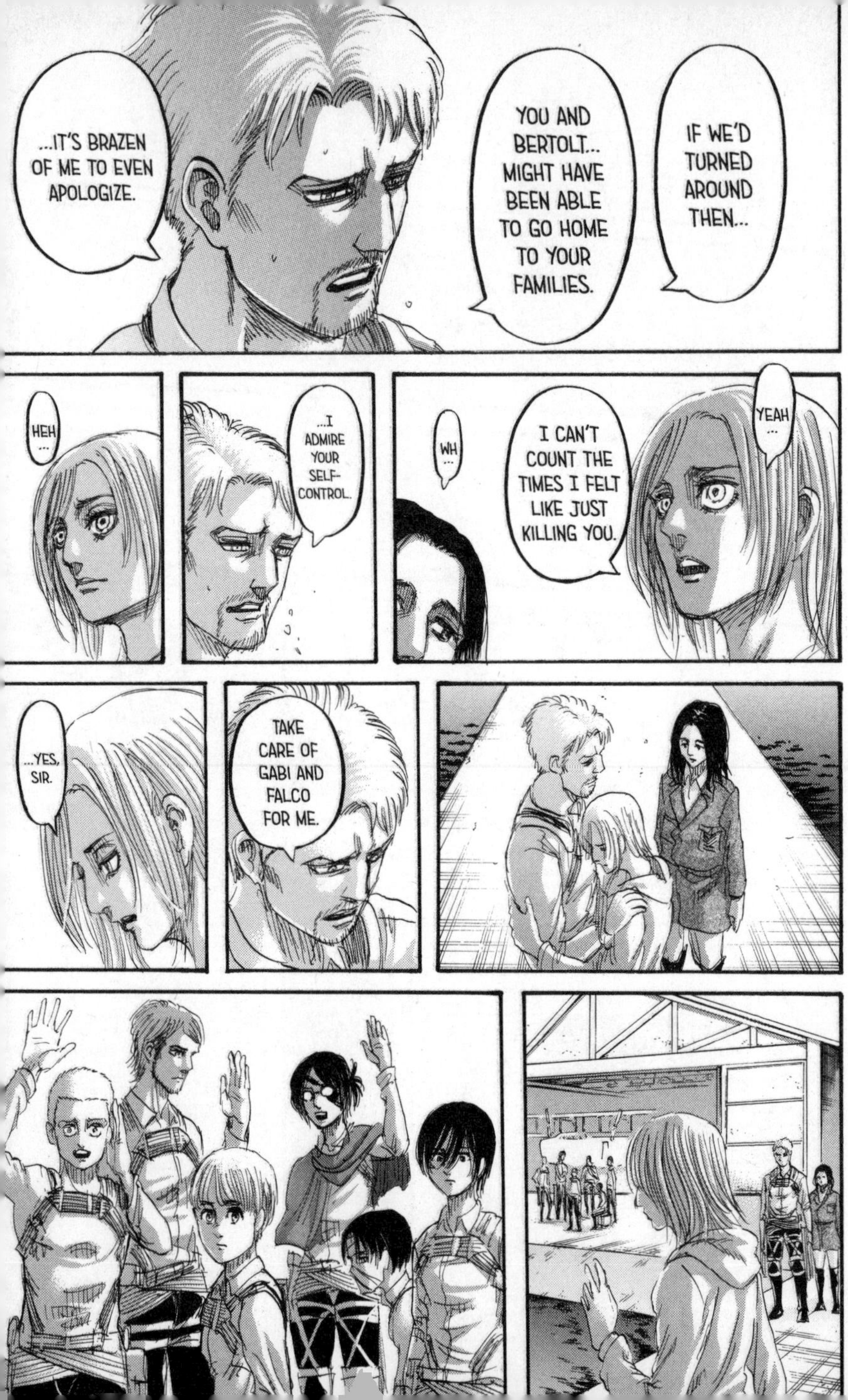
IF WE'D TURNED AROUND THEN...
YOU AND BERTOLT... MIGHT HAVE BEEN ABLE TO GO HOME TO YOUR FAMILIES.
...IT'S BRAZEN OF ME TO EVEN APOLOGIZE.
YEAH ...
I CAN'T COUNT THE TIMES I FELT LIKE JUST KILLING YOU.
WH ...
...I ADMIRE YOUR SELF-CONTROL.
HEH ...
TAKE CARE OF GABI AND FALCO FOR ME.
...YES, SIR.

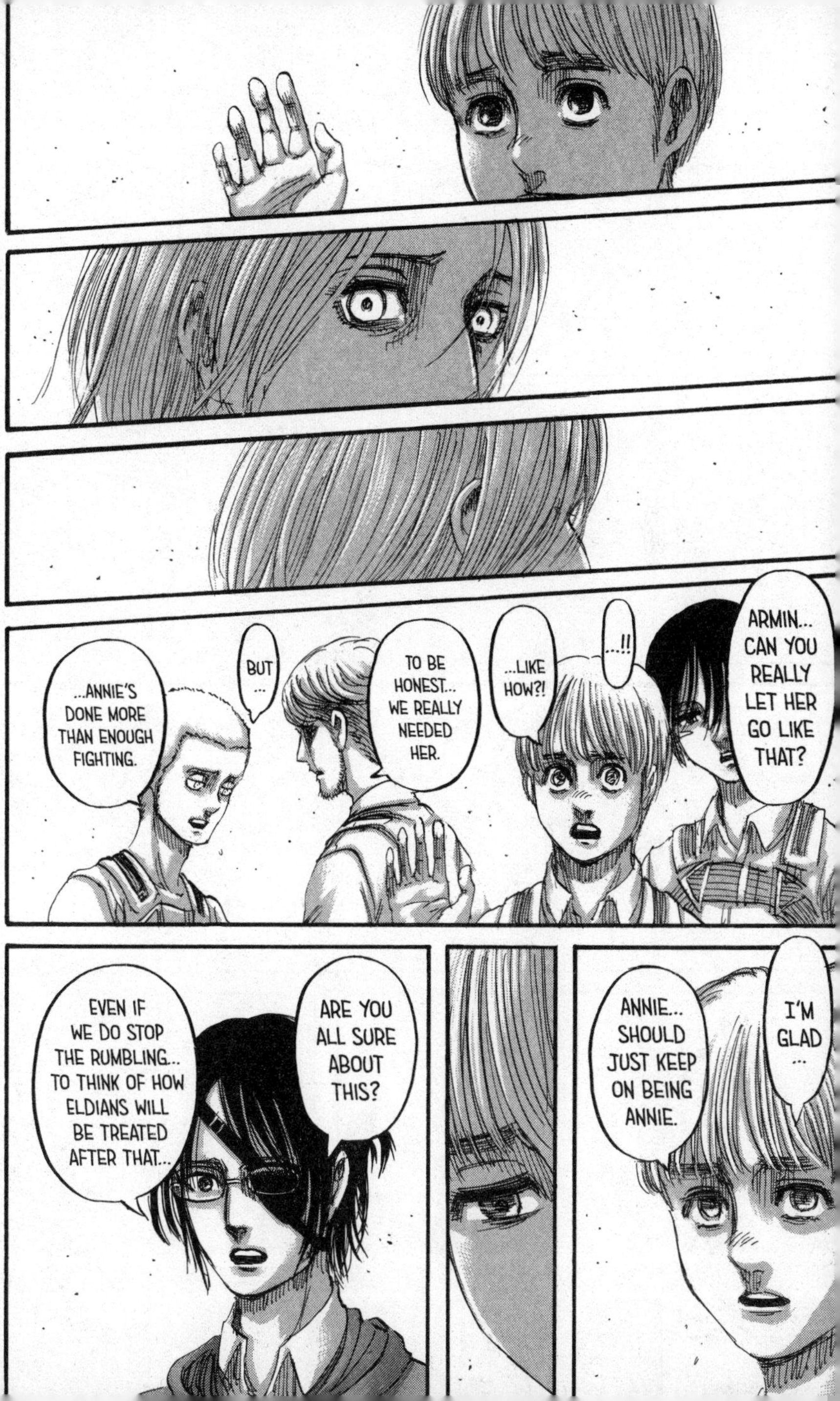
ARMIN... CAN YOU REALLY LET HER GO LIKE THAT?
...!!
...LIKE HOW?!
TO BE HONEST... WE REALLY NEEDED HER.
BUT ...
...ANNIE'S DONE MORE THAN ENOUGH FIGHTING.
I'M GLAD ...
ANNIE... SHOULD JUST KEEP ON BEING ANNIE.
ARE YOU ALL SURE ABOUT THIS?
EVEN IF WE DO STOP THE RUMBLING... TO THINK OF HOW ELDIANS WILL BE TREATED AFTER THAT...

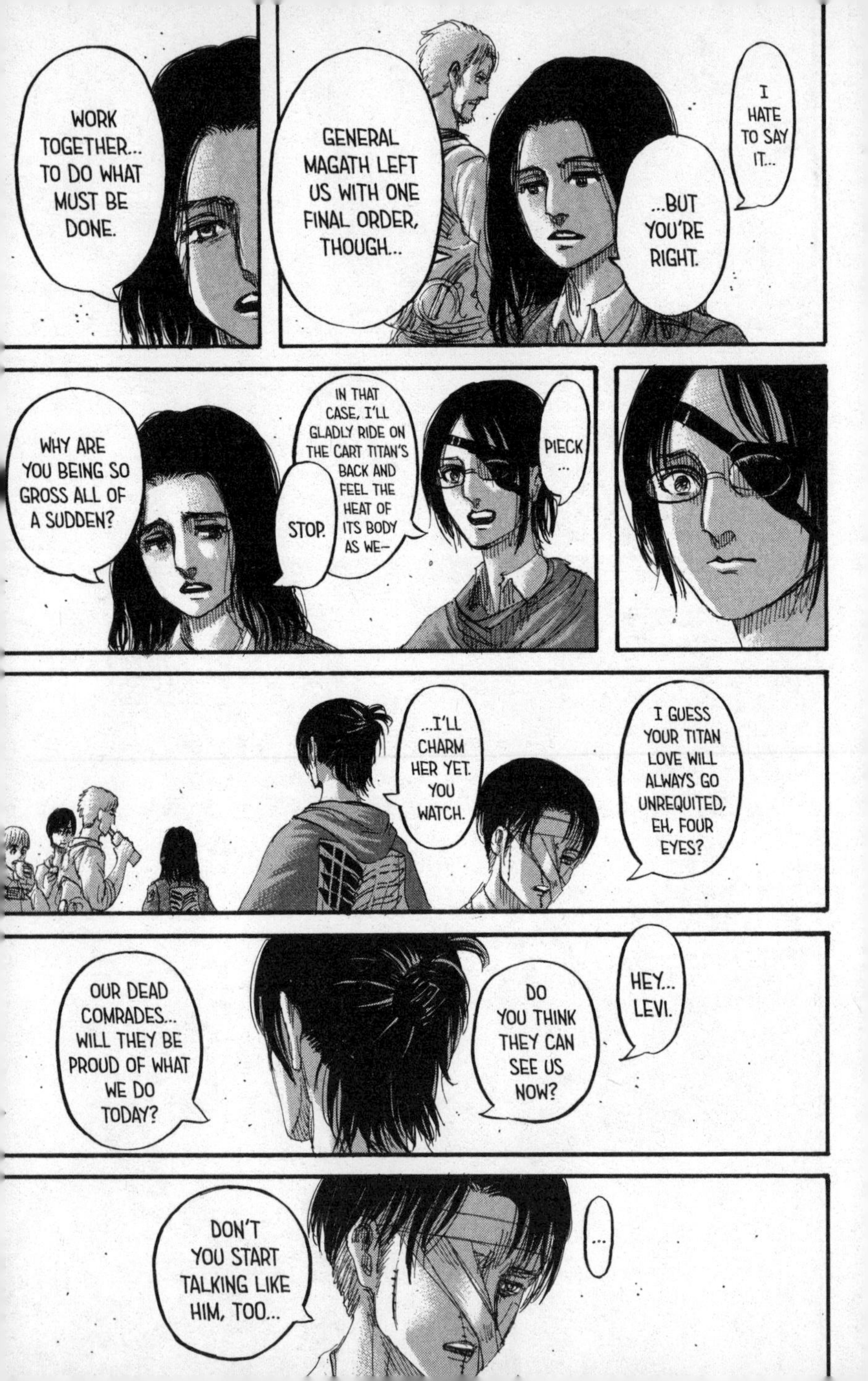
I HATE TO SAY IT...
...BUT YOU'RE RIGHT.
GENERAL MAGATH LEFT US WITH ONE FINAL ORDER, THOUGH...
WORK TOGETHER... TO DO WHAT MUST BE DONE.
PIECK...
IN THAT CASE, I'LL GLADLY RIDE ON THE CART TITAN'S BACK AND FEEL THE HEAT OF ITS BODY AS WE–
STOP.
WHY ARE YOU BEING SO GROSS ALL OF A SUDDEN?
I GUESS YOUR TITAN LOVE WILL ALWAYS GO UNREQUITED, EH, FOUR EYES?
...I'LL CHARM HER YET. YOU WATCH.
HEY... LEVI.
DO YOU THINK THEY CAN SEE US NOW?
OUR DEAD COMRADES... WILL THEY BE PROUD OF WHAT WE DO TODAY?
...
DON'T YOU START TALKING LIKE HIM, TOO...

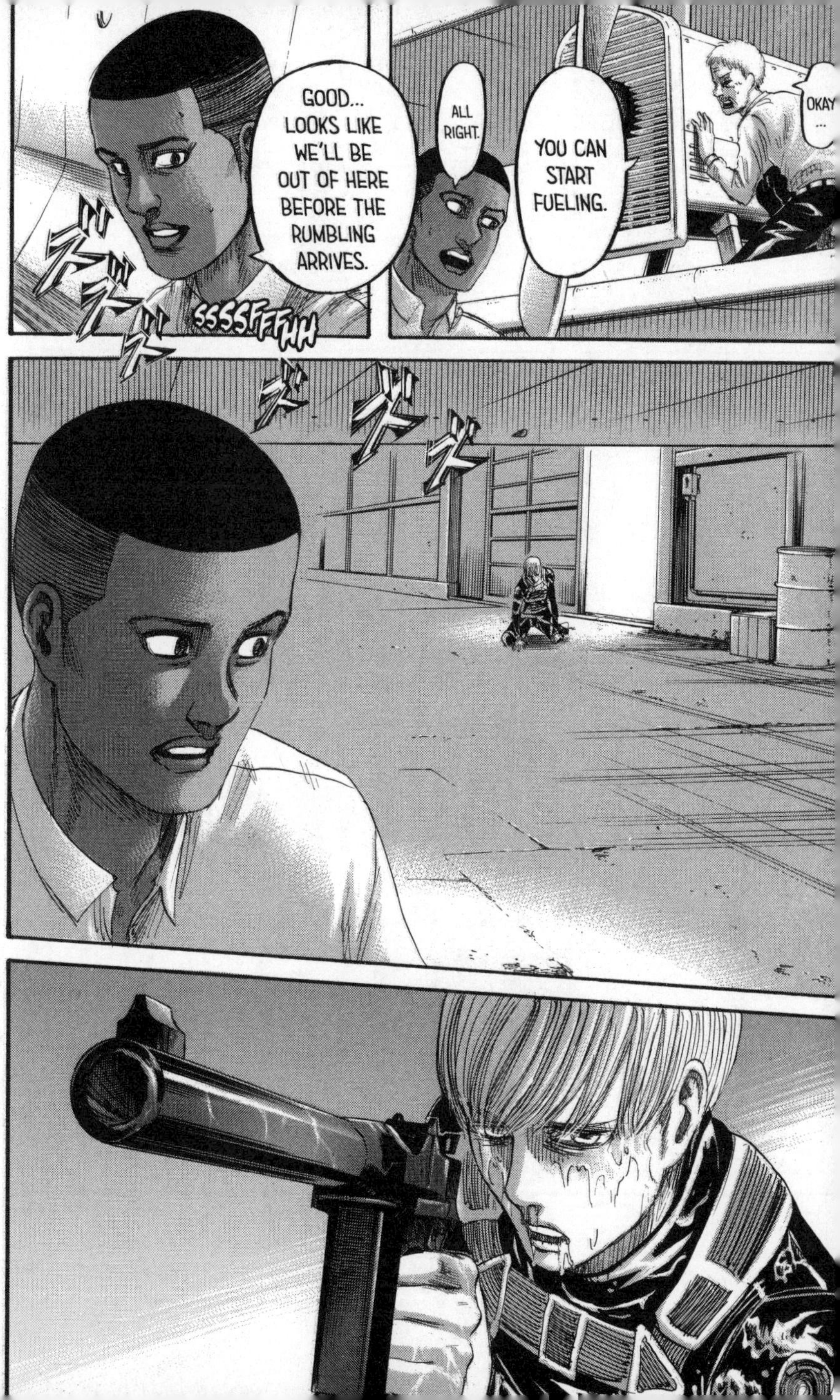
OKAY...
YOU CAN START FUELING.
ALL RIGHT.
GOOD... LOOKS LIKE WE'LL BE OUT OF HERE BEFORE THE RUMBLING ARRIVES.
SSSSFFFHH

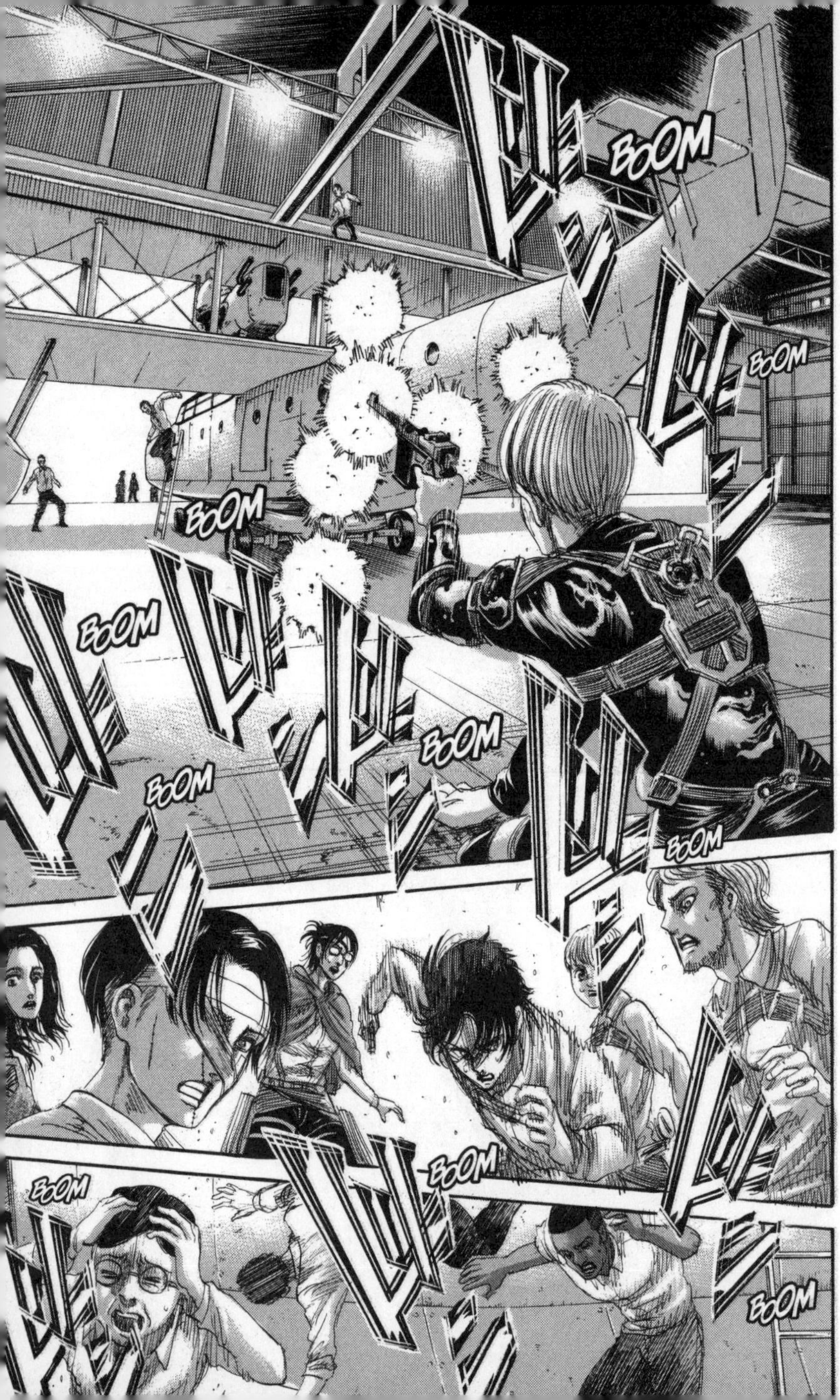
BOOM
BOOM
BOOM
BOOM
BOOM
BOOM
BOOM
BOOM
BOOM
BOOM

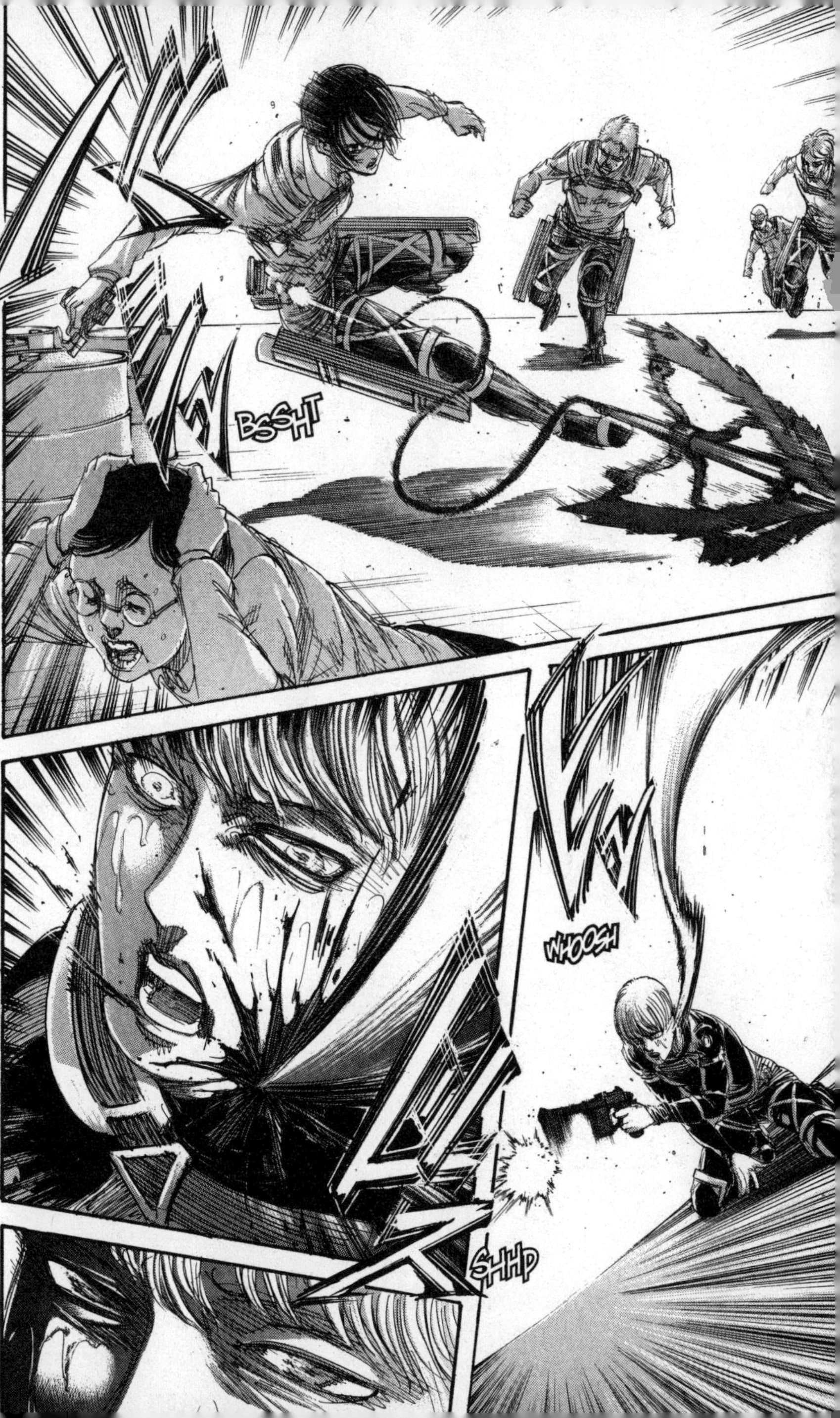
BSSHT
WHOOSH
SHHP

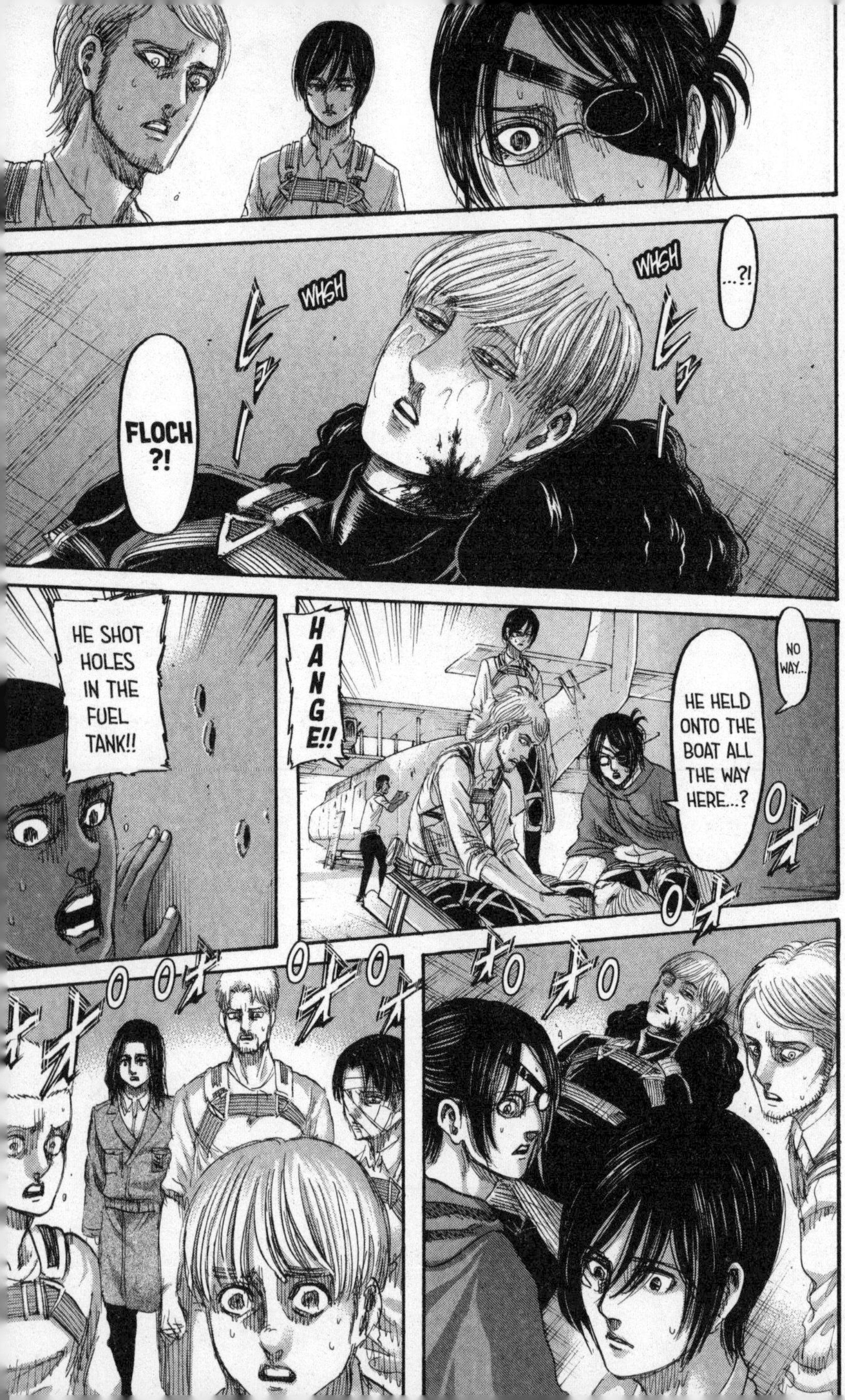
...?!
WHSH
WHSH
FLOCH ?!
NO WAY...
HE HELD ONTO THE BOAT ALL THE WAY HERE...?
HANGE!!
HE SHOT HOLES IN THE FUEL TANK!!

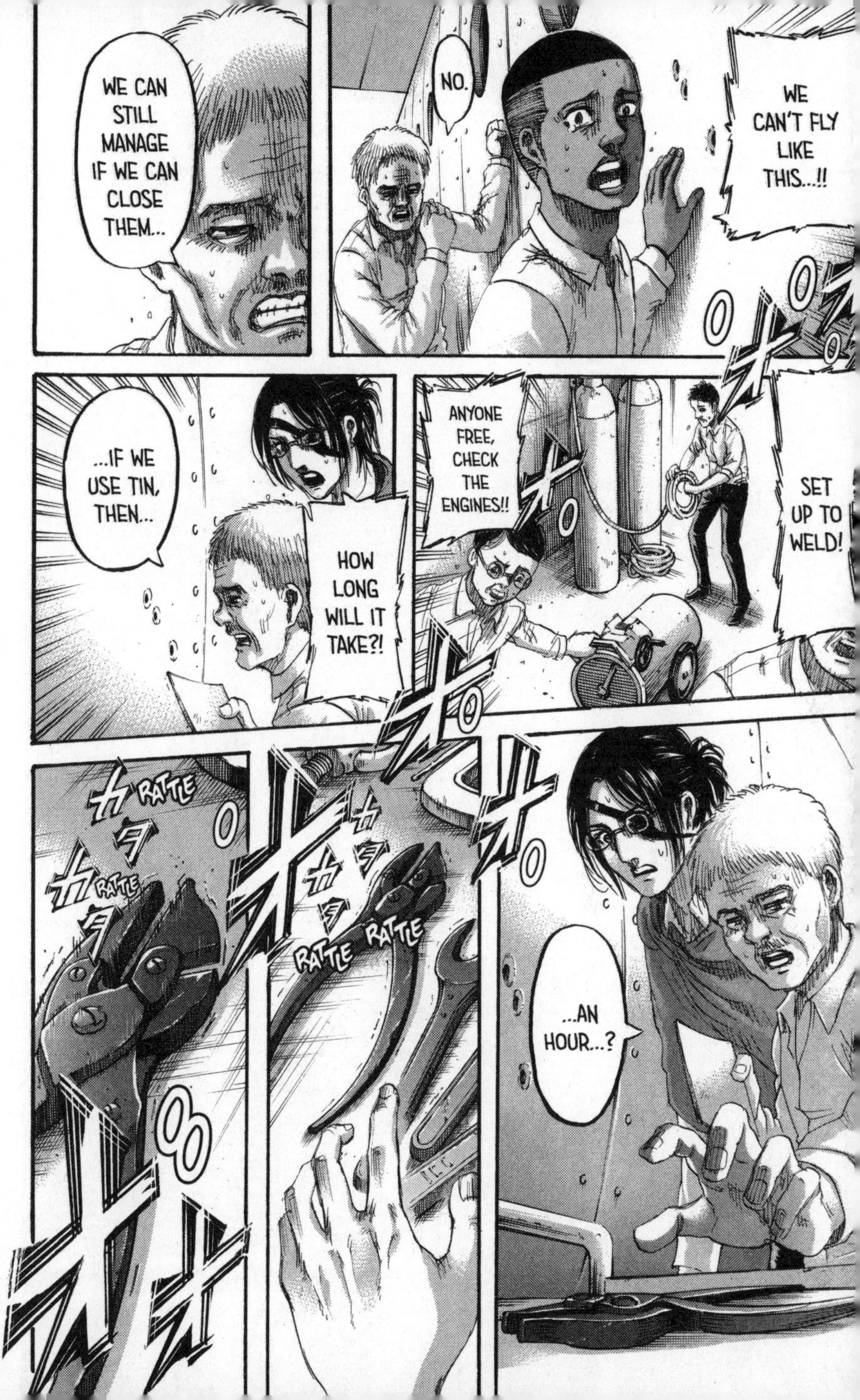
WE CAN'T FLY LIKE THIS...!!
NO.
WE CAN STILL MANAGE IF WE CAN CLOSE THEM...
SET UP TO WELD!
ANYONE FREE, CHECK THE ENGINES!!
...IF WE USE TIN, THEN...
HOW LONG WILL IT TAKE?!
...AN HOUR...?
RATTLE RATTLE
RATTLE RATTLE

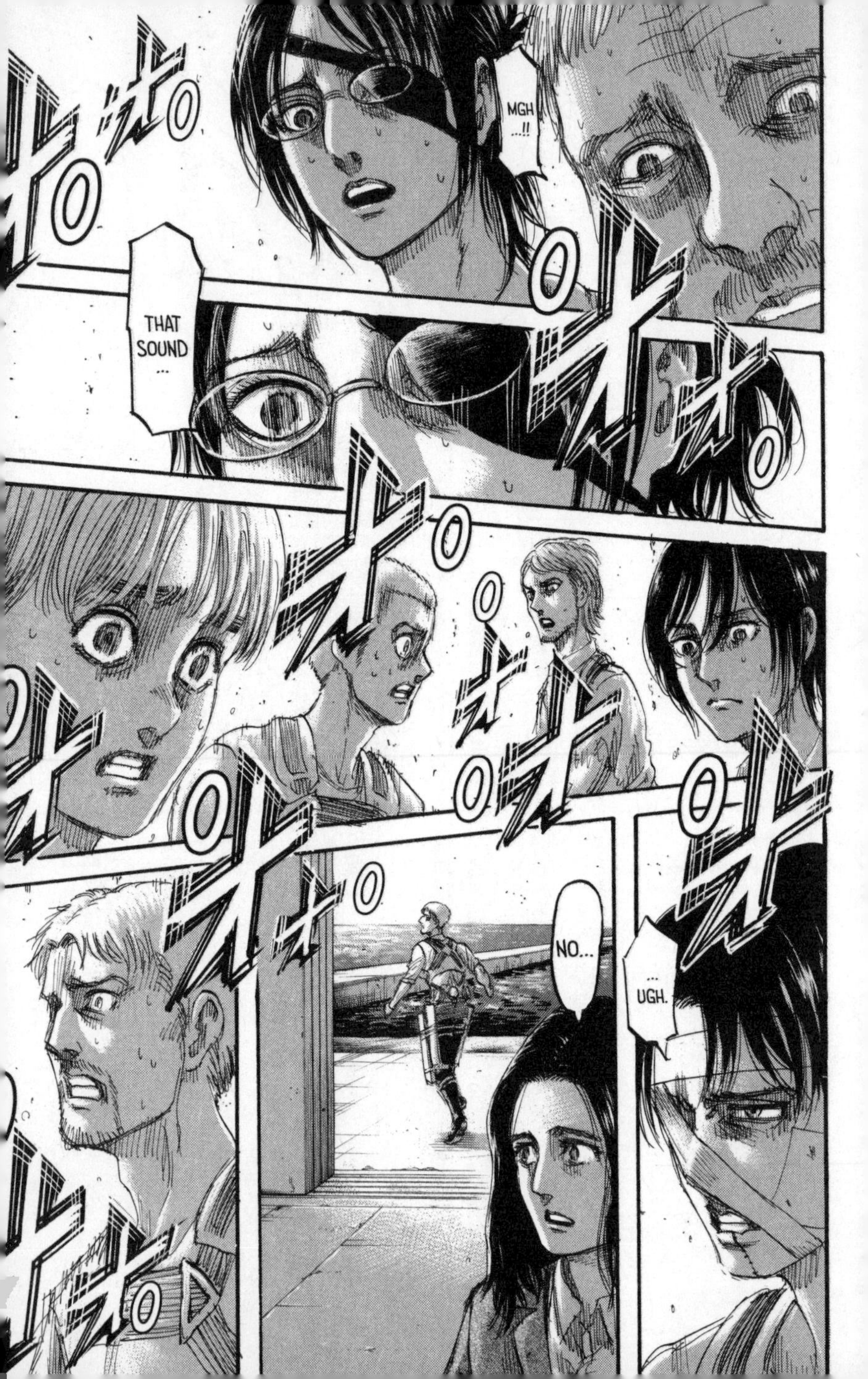
MGH ...!!
THAT SOUND ...
... UGH.
NO...

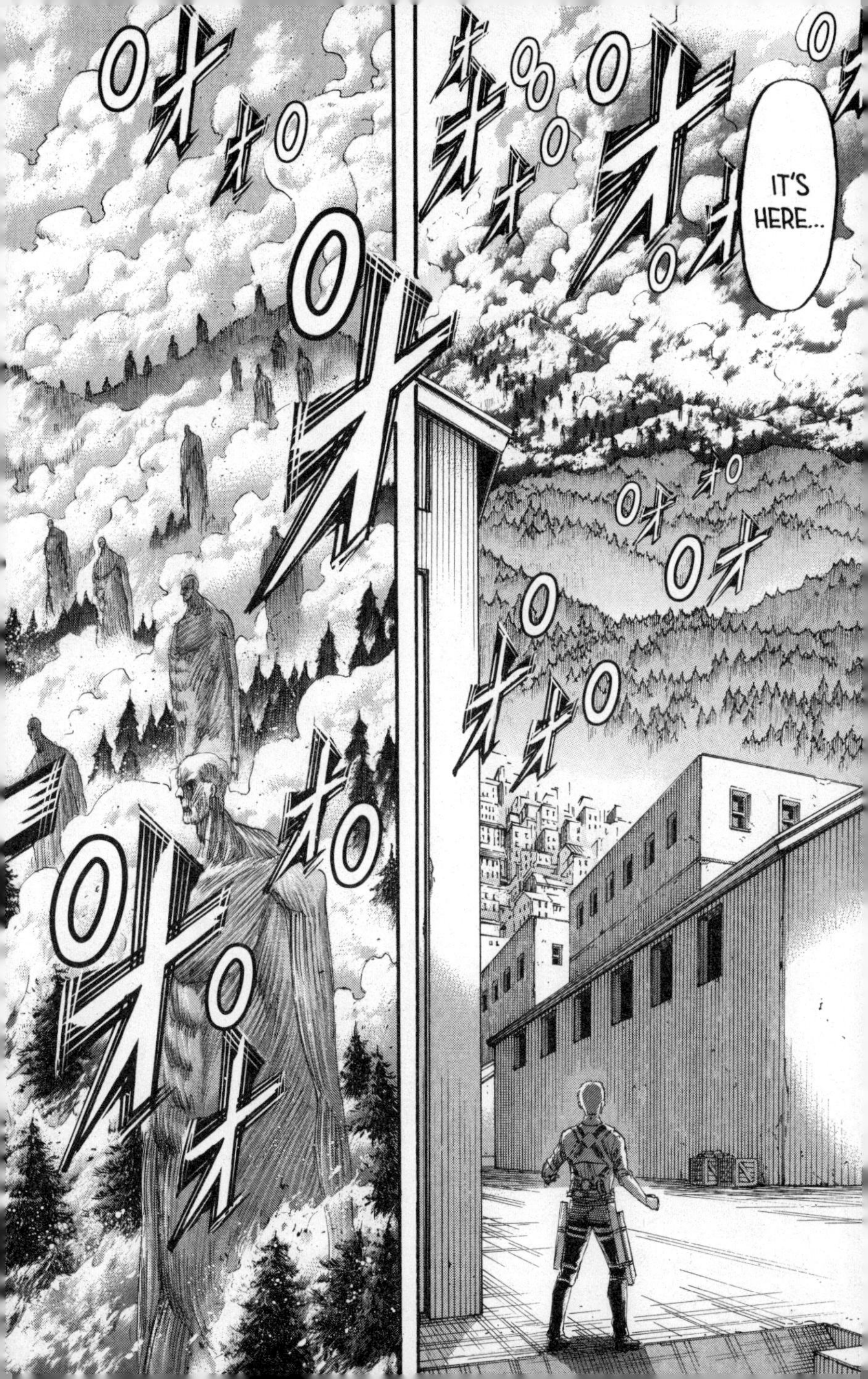
IT'S HERE...

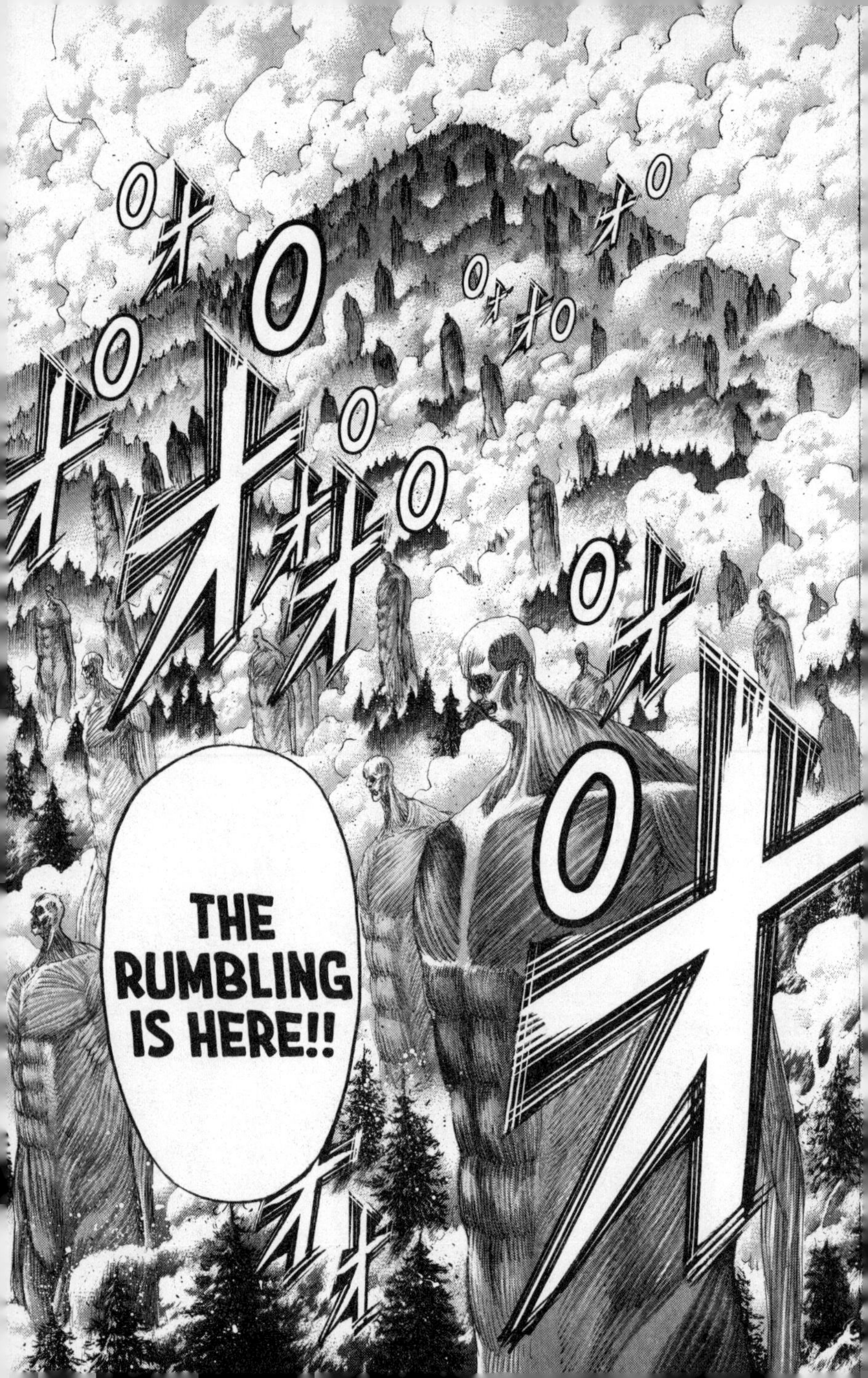
THE RUMBLING IS HERE!!

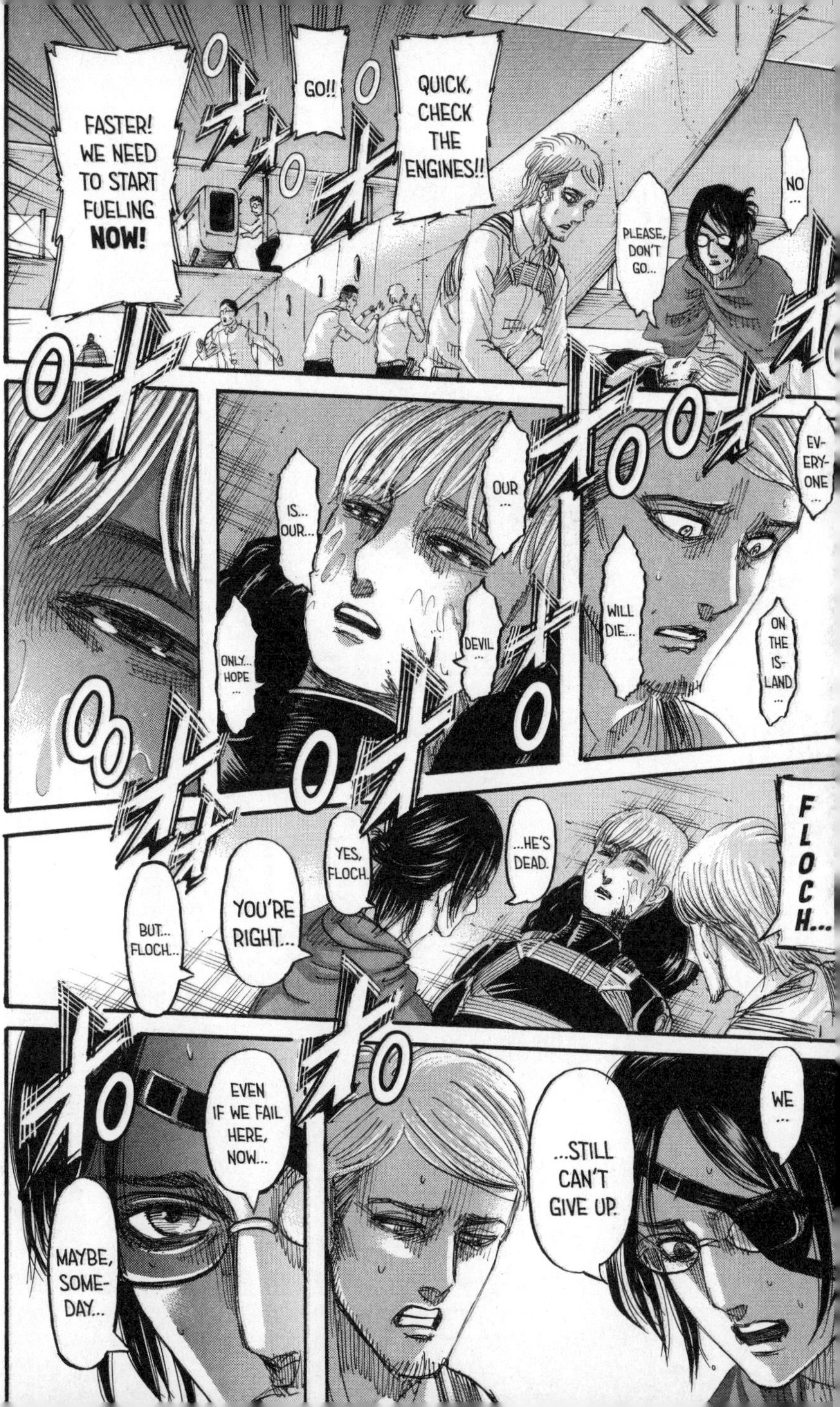
NO ...
PLEASE, DON'T GO...
QUICK, CHECK THE ENGINES!!
GO!!
FASTER! WE NEED TO START FUELING **NOW!**
EV-ERY-ONE ...
ON THE IS-LAND ...
WILL DIE...
OUR ...
IS... OUR...
DEVIL ...
ONLY... HOPE ...
FLOCH...
...HE'S DEAD.
YES, FLOCH.
YOU'RE RIGHT...
BUT... FLOCH...
WE ...
...STILL CAN'T GIVE UP.
EVEN IF WE FAIL HERE, NOW...
MAYBE, SOME-DAY...

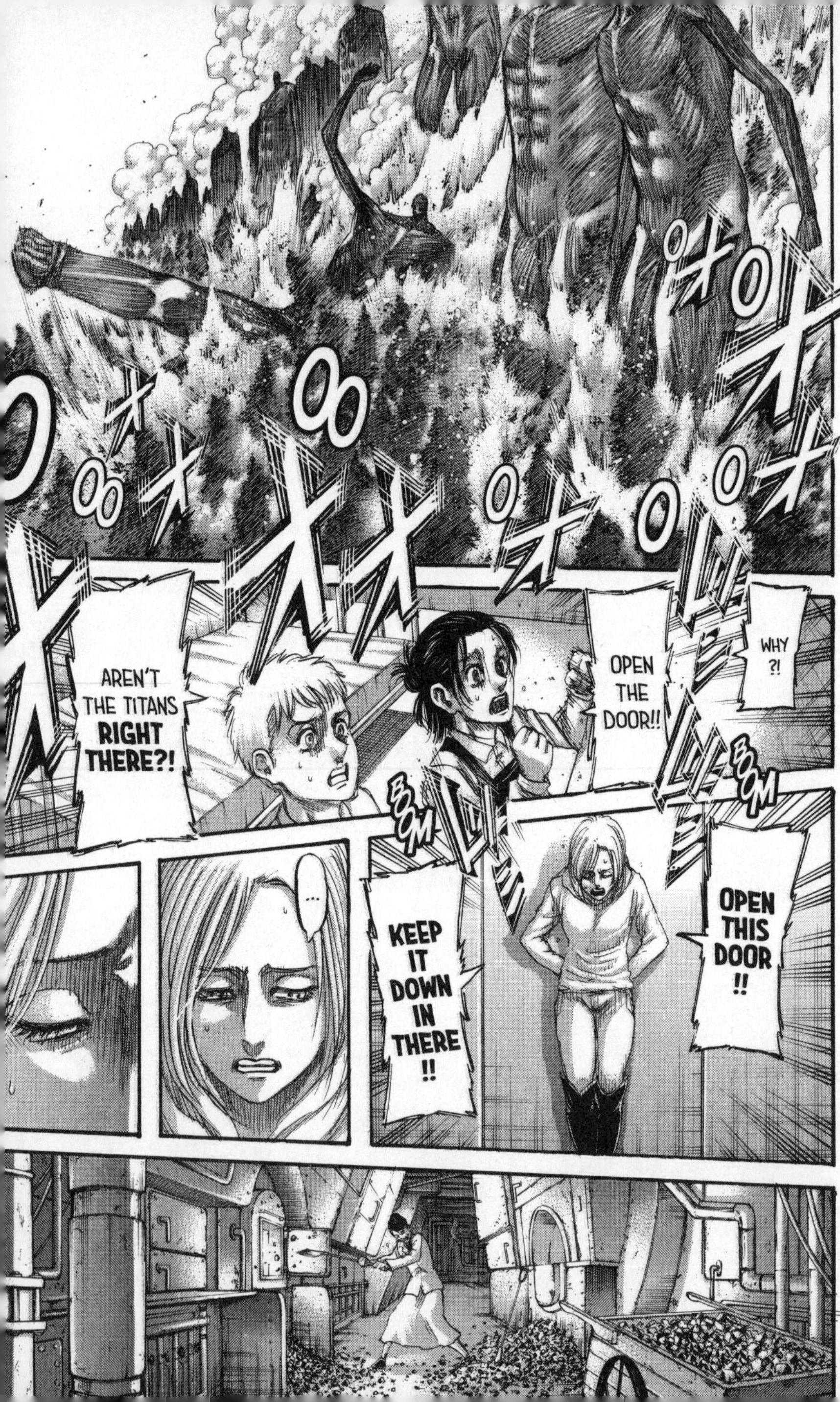
WHY ?!
OPEN THE DOOR!!
AREN'T THE TITANS RIGHT THERE?!
BOOM
BOOM
OPEN THIS DOOR !!
KEEP IT DOWN IN THERE !!
...

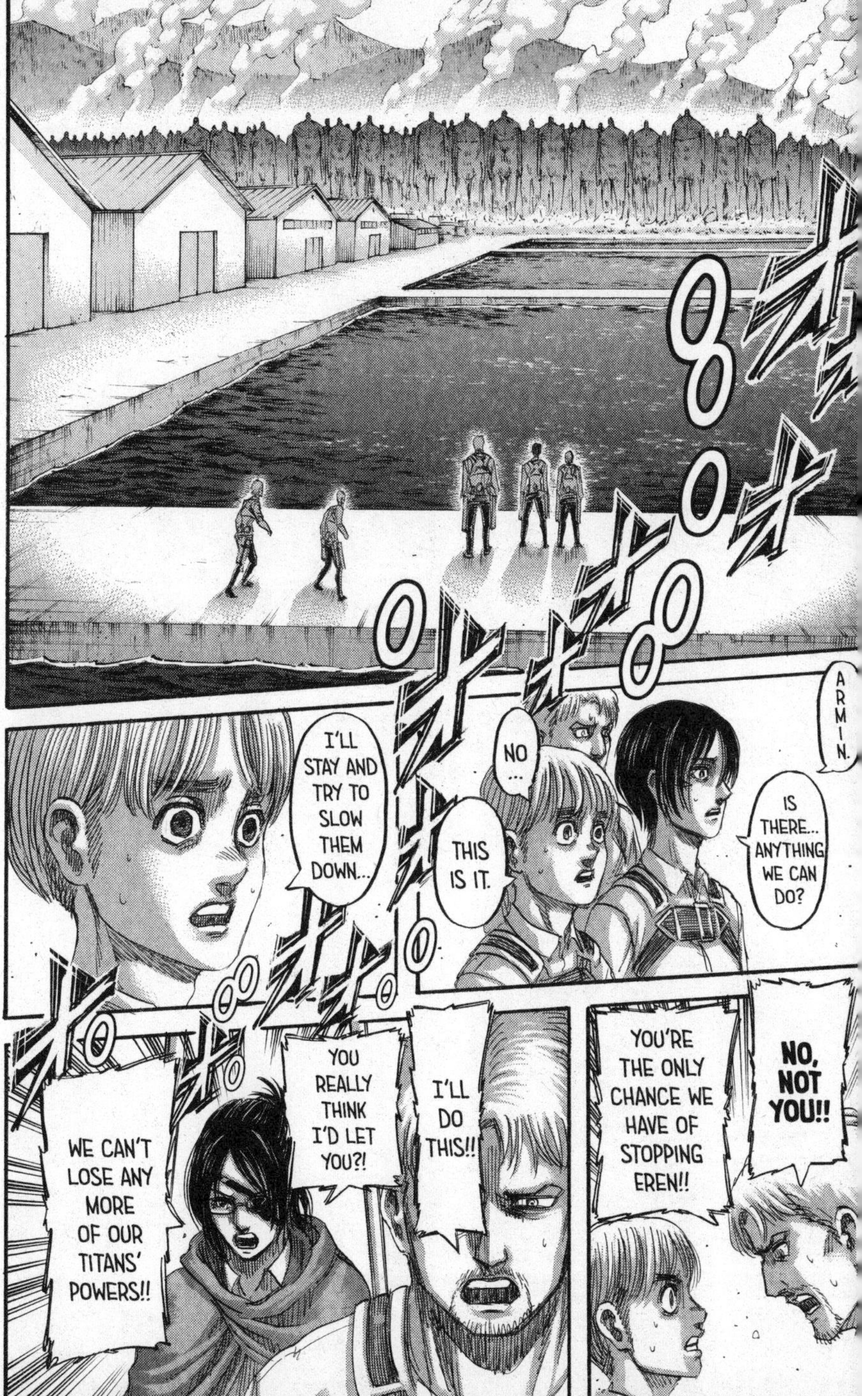
ARMIN.
IS THERE... ANYTHING WE CAN DO?
NO...
THIS IS IT.
I'LL STAY AND TRY TO SLOW THEM DOWN...
NO, NOT YOU!!
YOU'RE THE ONLY CHANCE WE HAVE OF STOPPING EREN!!
I'LL DO THIS!!
YOU REALLY THINK I'D LET YOU?!
WE CAN'T LOSE ANY MORE OF OUR TITANS' POWERS!!

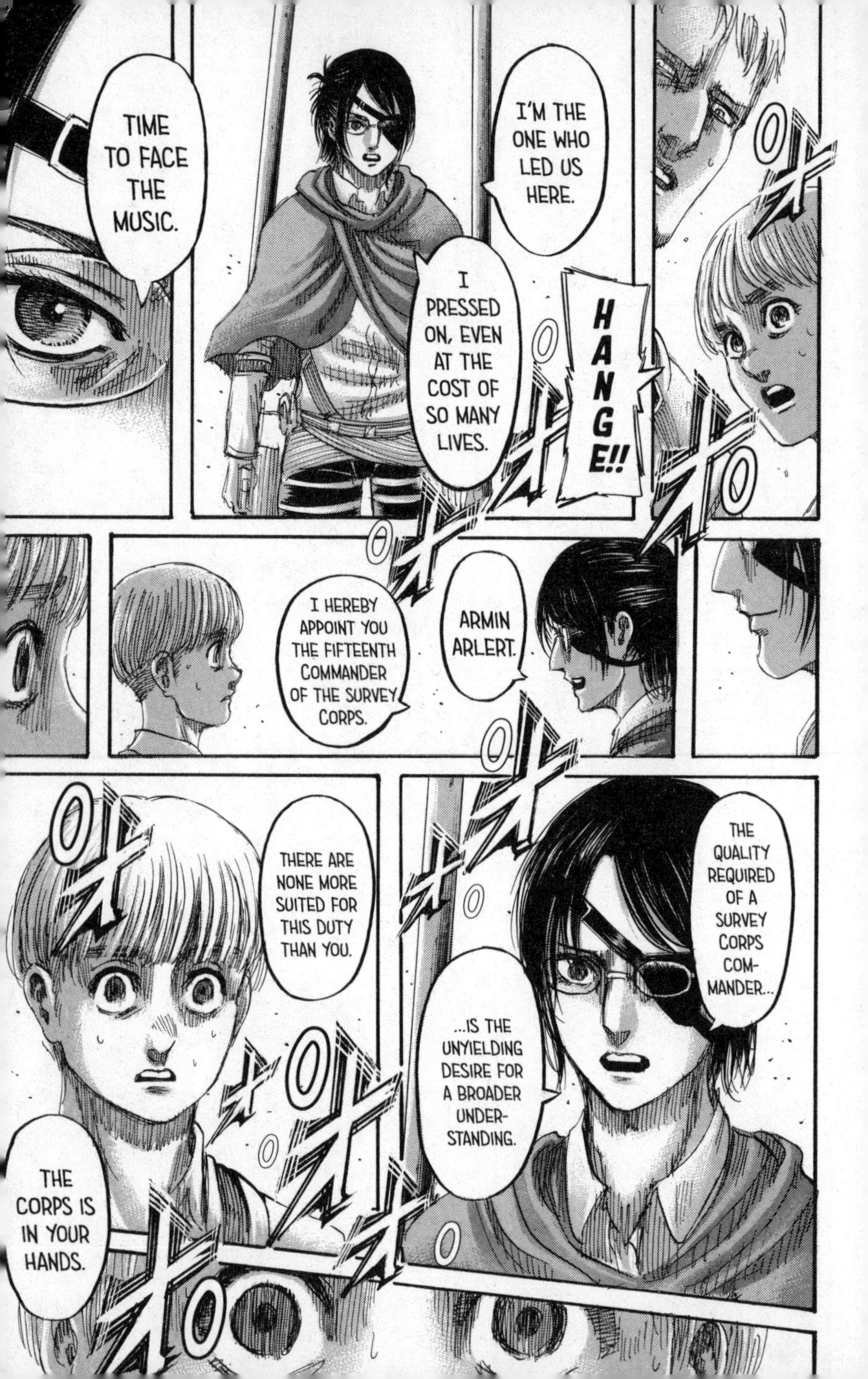
HANGE!!
I'M THE ONE WHO LED US HERE.
I PRESSED ON, EVEN AT THE COST OF SO MANY LIVES.
TIME TO FACE THE MUSIC.
ARMIN ARLERT.
I HEREBY APPOINT YOU THE FIFTEENTH COMMANDER OF THE SURVEY CORPS.
THE QUALITY REQUIRED OF A SURVEY CORPS COM-MANDER...
...IS THE UNYIELDING DESIRE FOR A BROADER UNDER-STANDING.
THERE ARE NONE MORE SUITED FOR THIS DUTY THAN YOU.
THE CORPS IS IN YOUR HANDS.

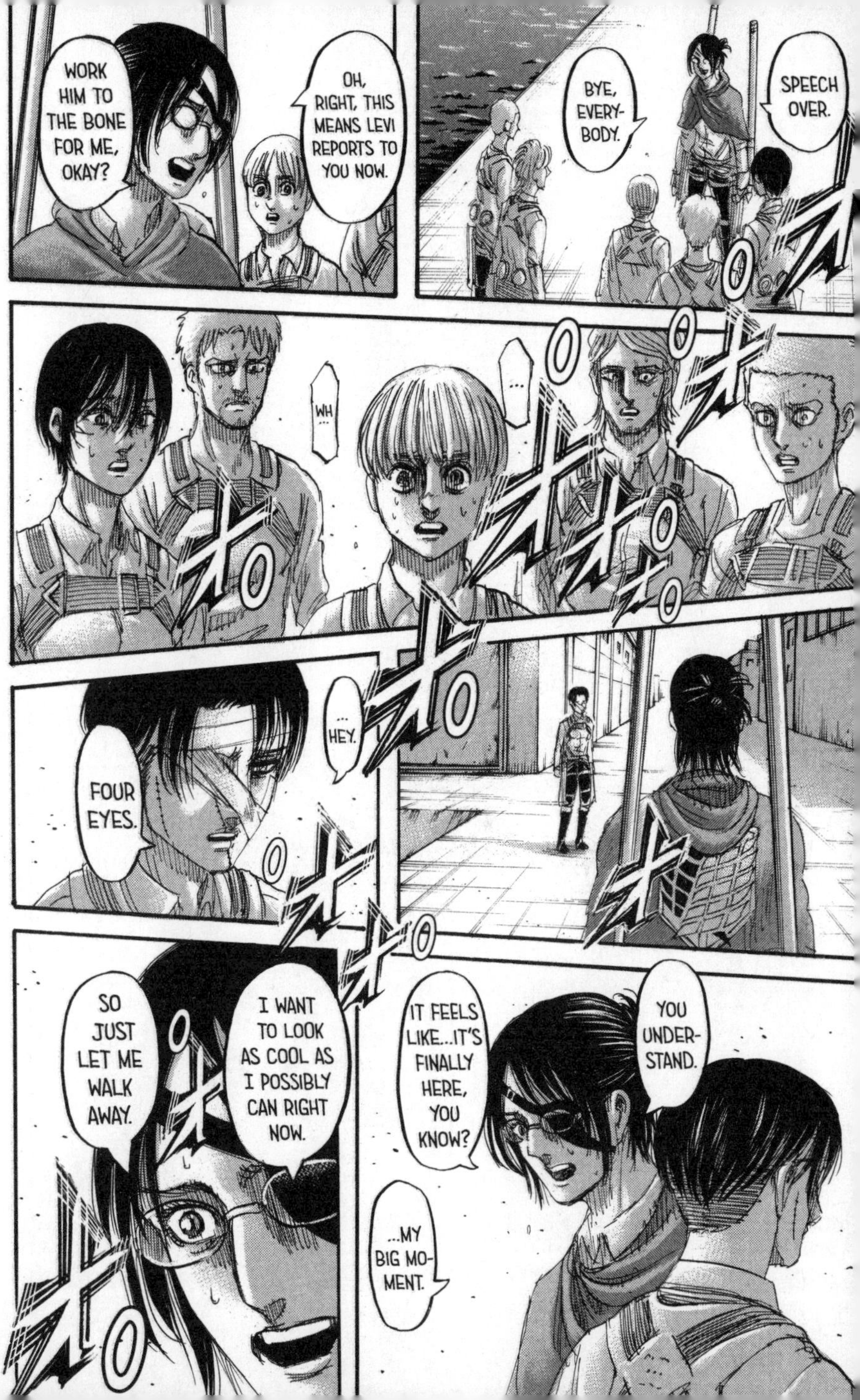
SPEECH OVER.
BYE, EVERY-BODY.
OH, RIGHT, THIS MEANS LEVI REPORTS TO YOU NOW.
WORK HIM TO THE BONE FOR ME, OKAY?
...
WH...
...HEY.
FOUR EYES.
YOU UNDER-STAND.
IT FEELS LIKE...IT'S FINALLY HERE, YOU KNOW?
...MY BIG MO-MENT.
I WANT TO LOOK AS COOL AS I POSSIBLY CAN RIGHT NOW.
SO JUST LET ME WALK AWAY.

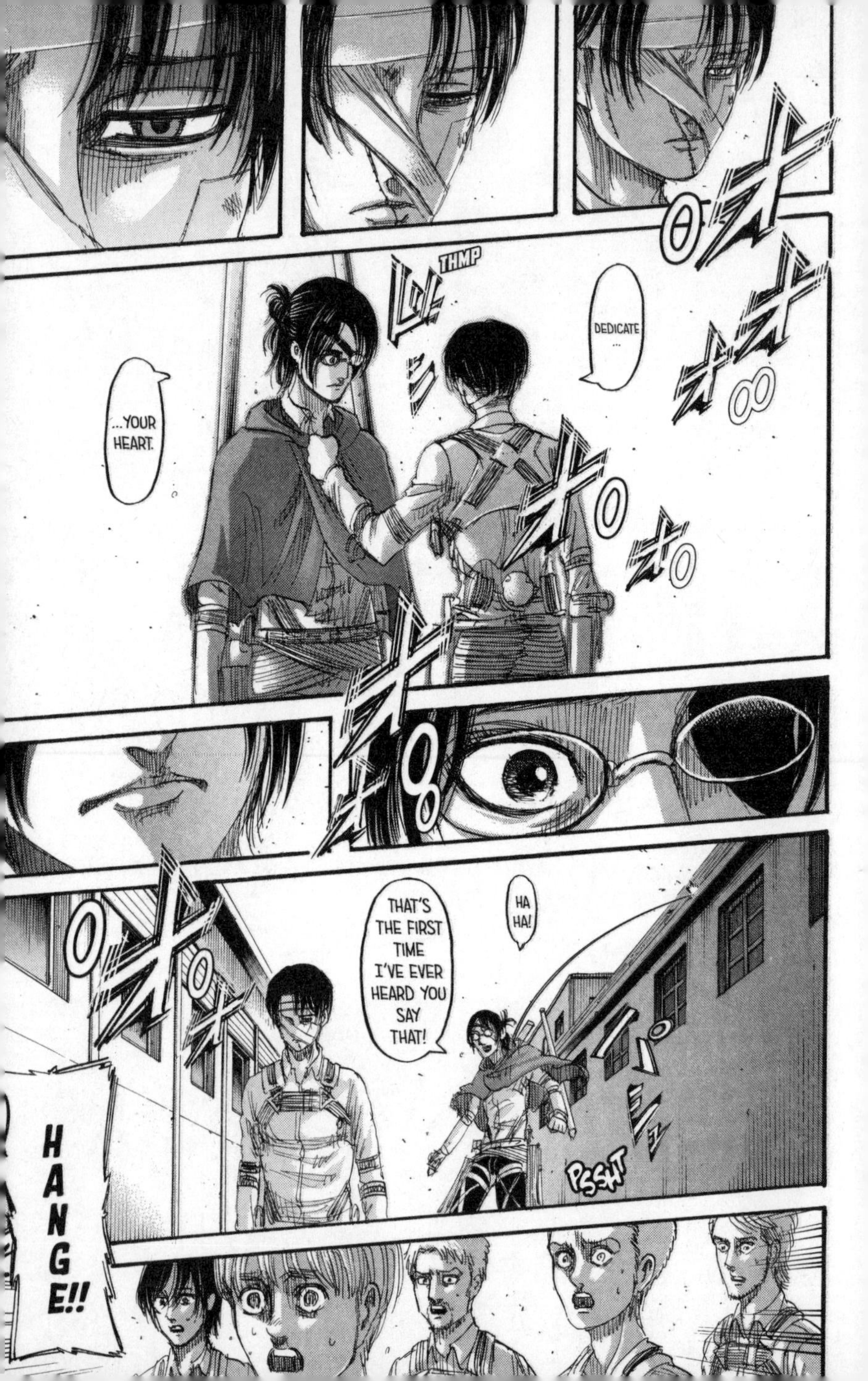
DEDICATE ...
THMP
...YOUR HEART.
HA HA!
THAT'S THE FIRST TIME I'VE EVER HEARD YOU SAY THAT!
PSSHT
HANGE!!

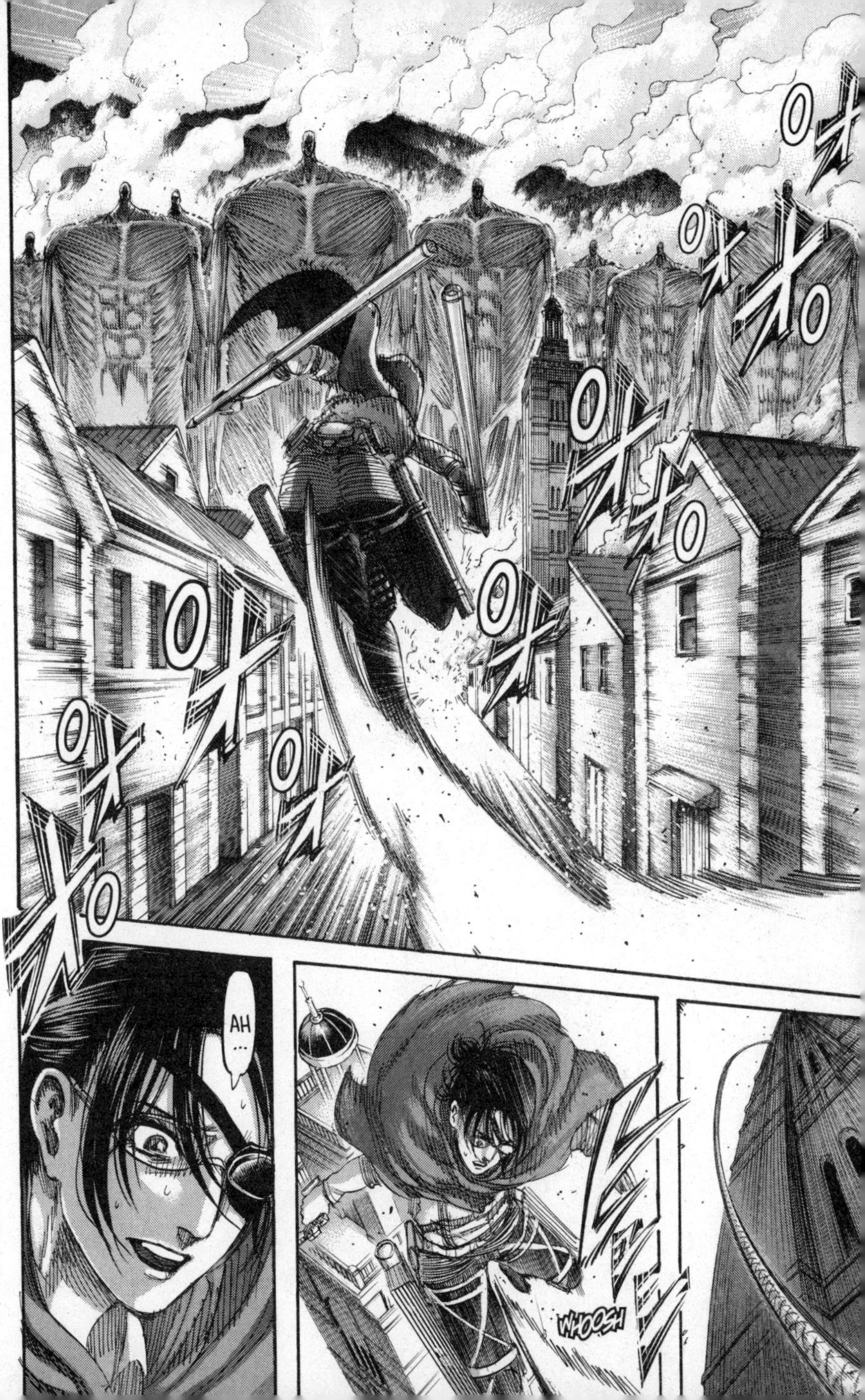
WHOOSH
AH ...

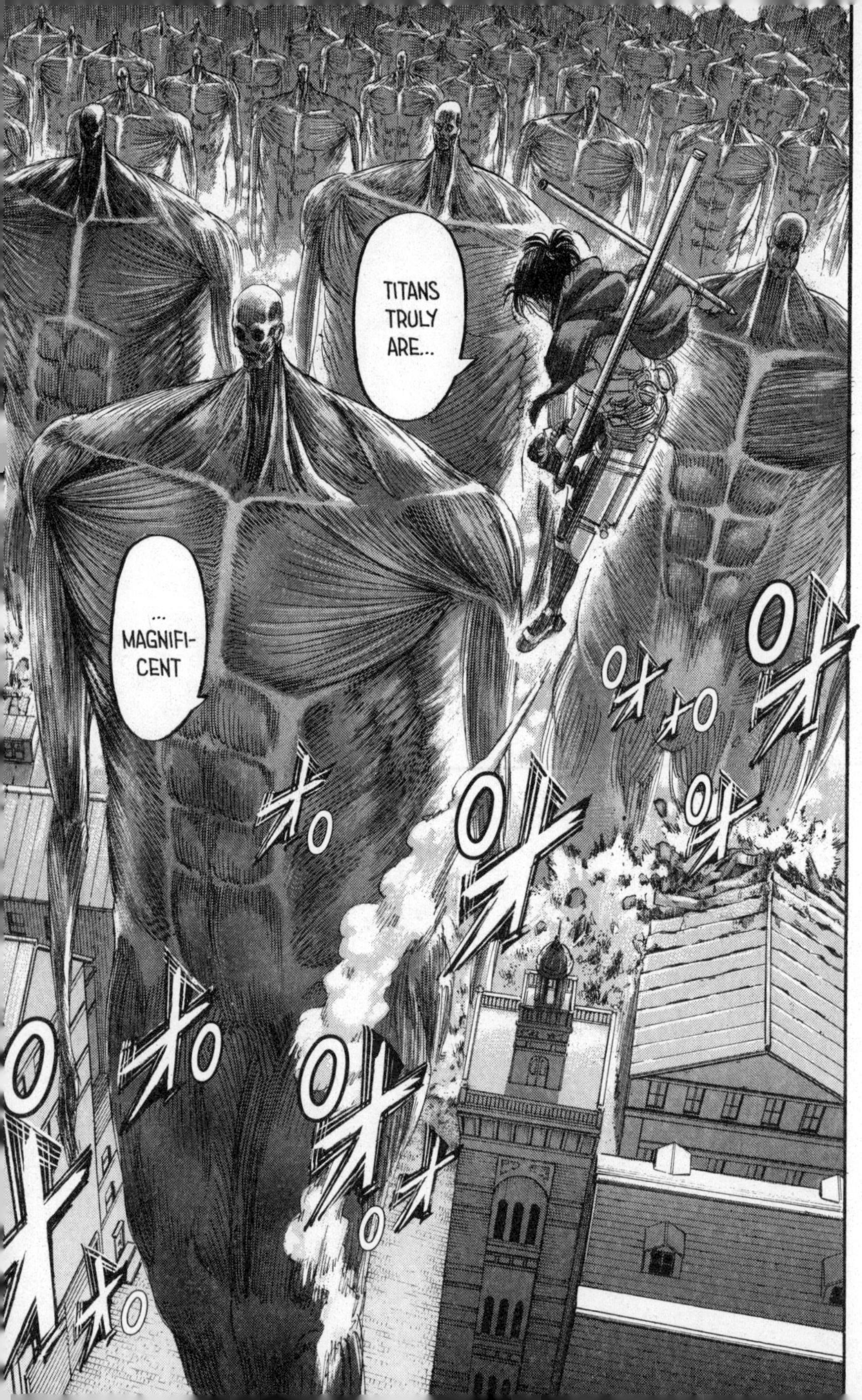
TITANS TRULY ARE...
...MAGNIFICENT

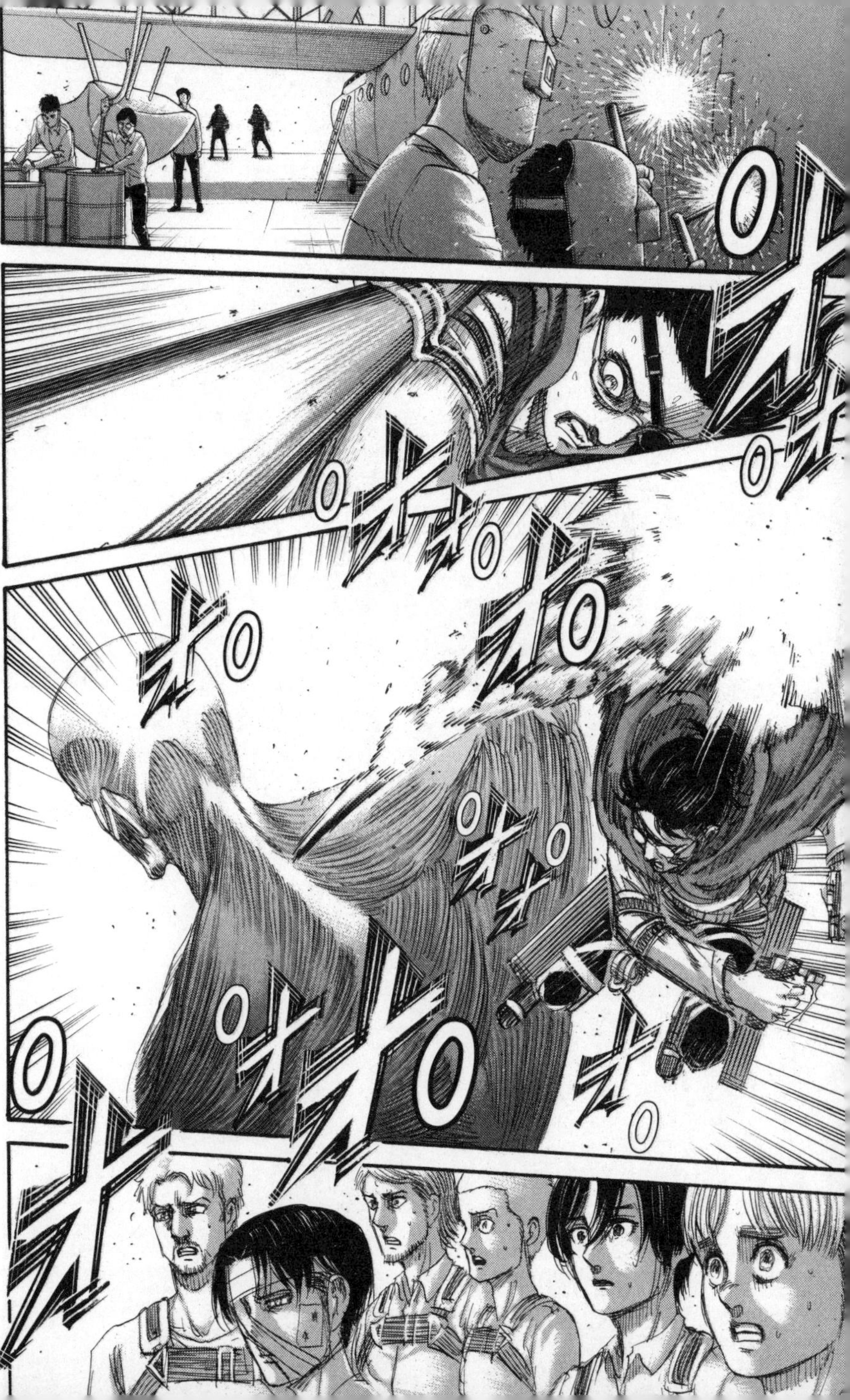

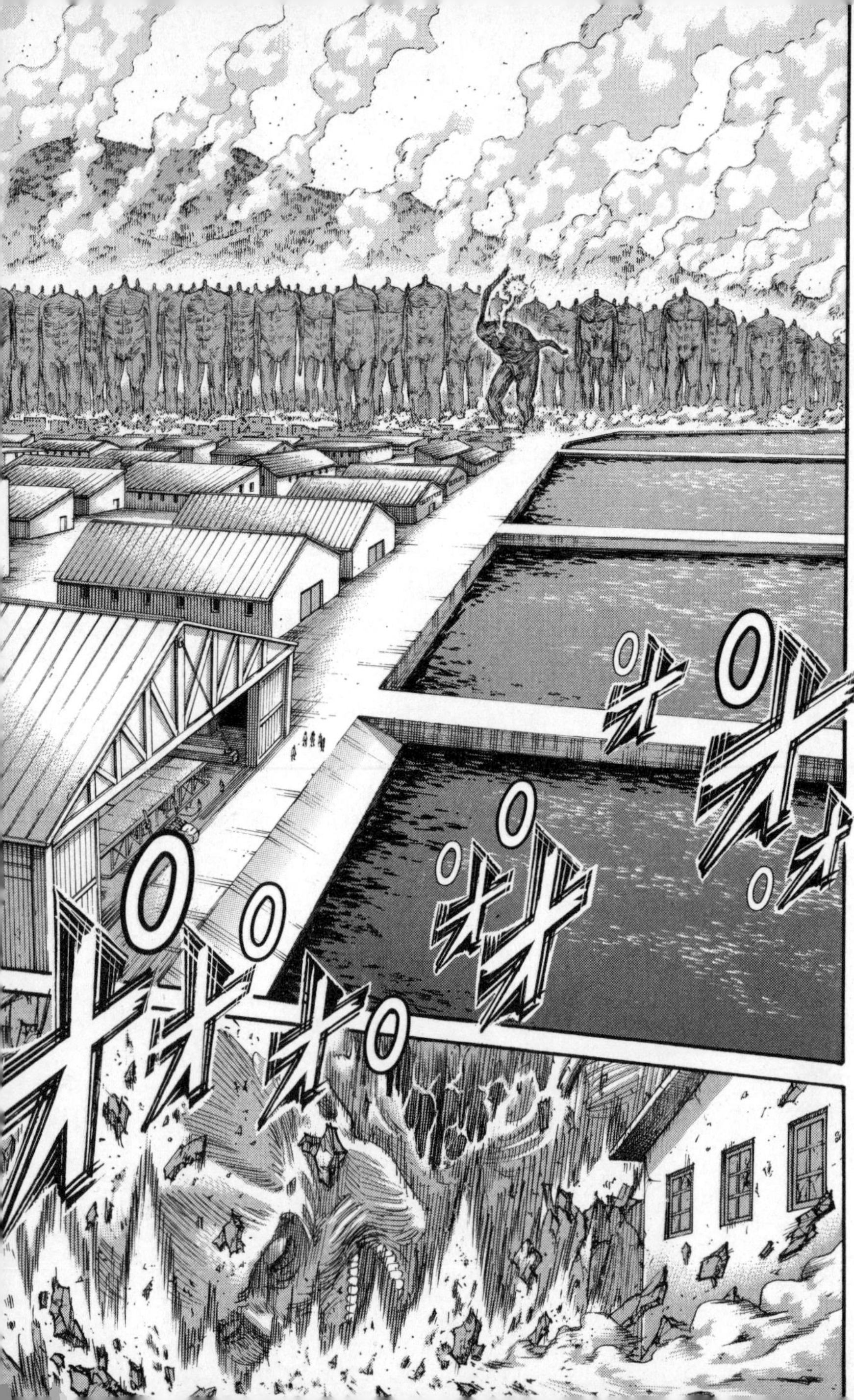
ォオォ
ォオ
オォオ

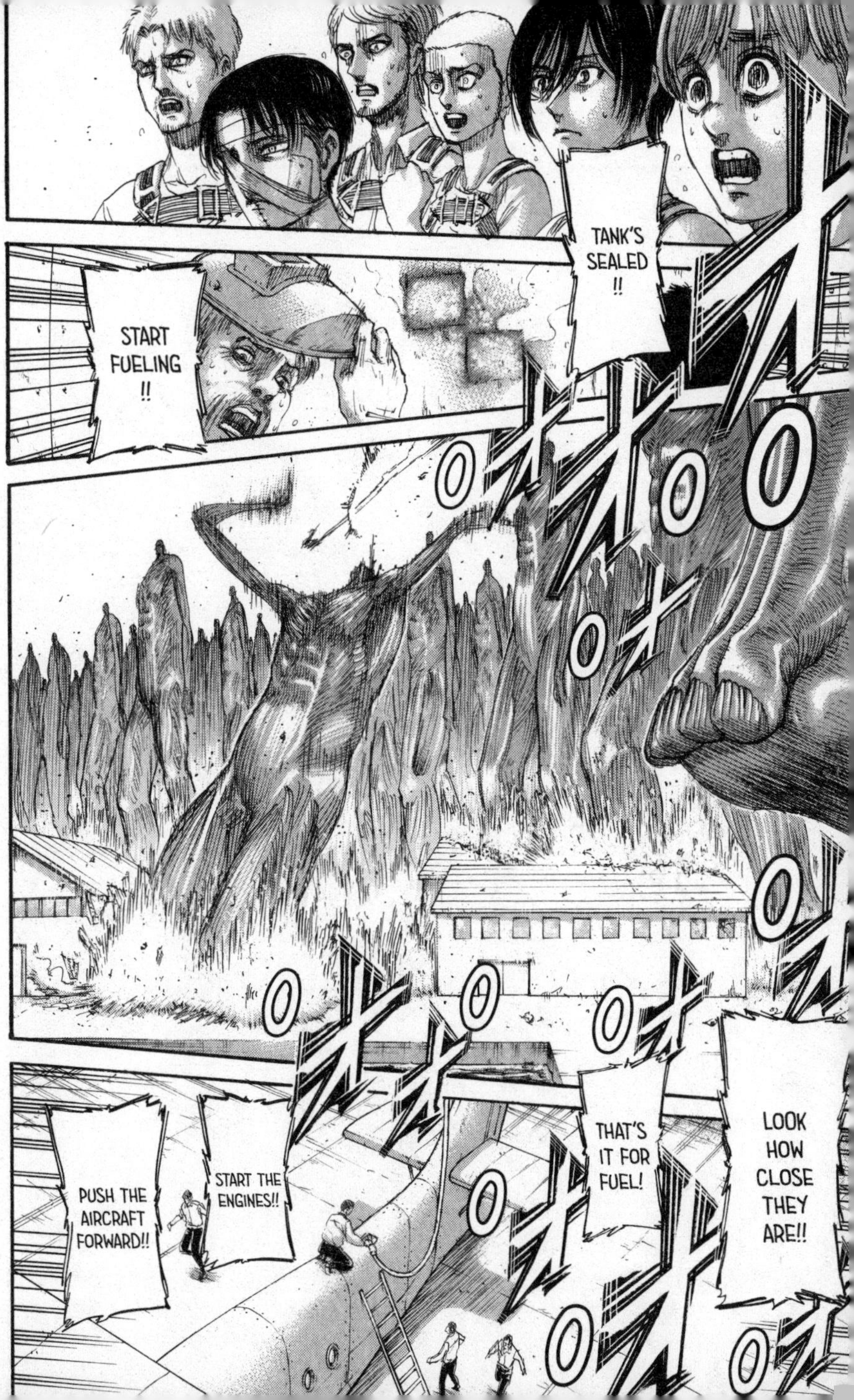
TANK'S SEALED !!
START FUELING !!
LOOK HOW CLOSE THEY ARE!!
THAT'S IT FOR FUEL!
START THE ENGINES!!
PUSH THE AIRCRAFT FORWARD!!

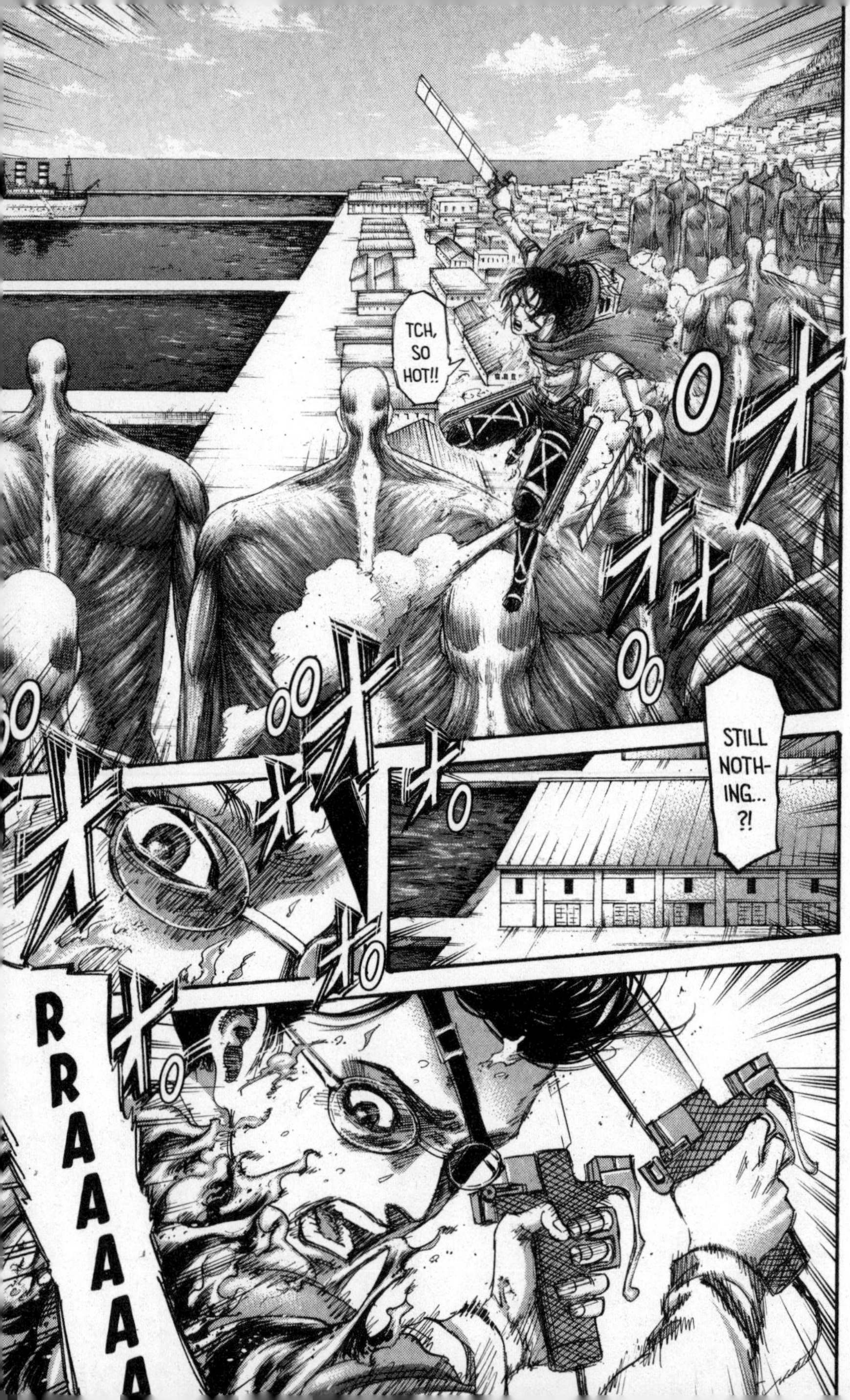
TCH, SO HOT!!
STILL NOTH-ING...?!
RRAAAA

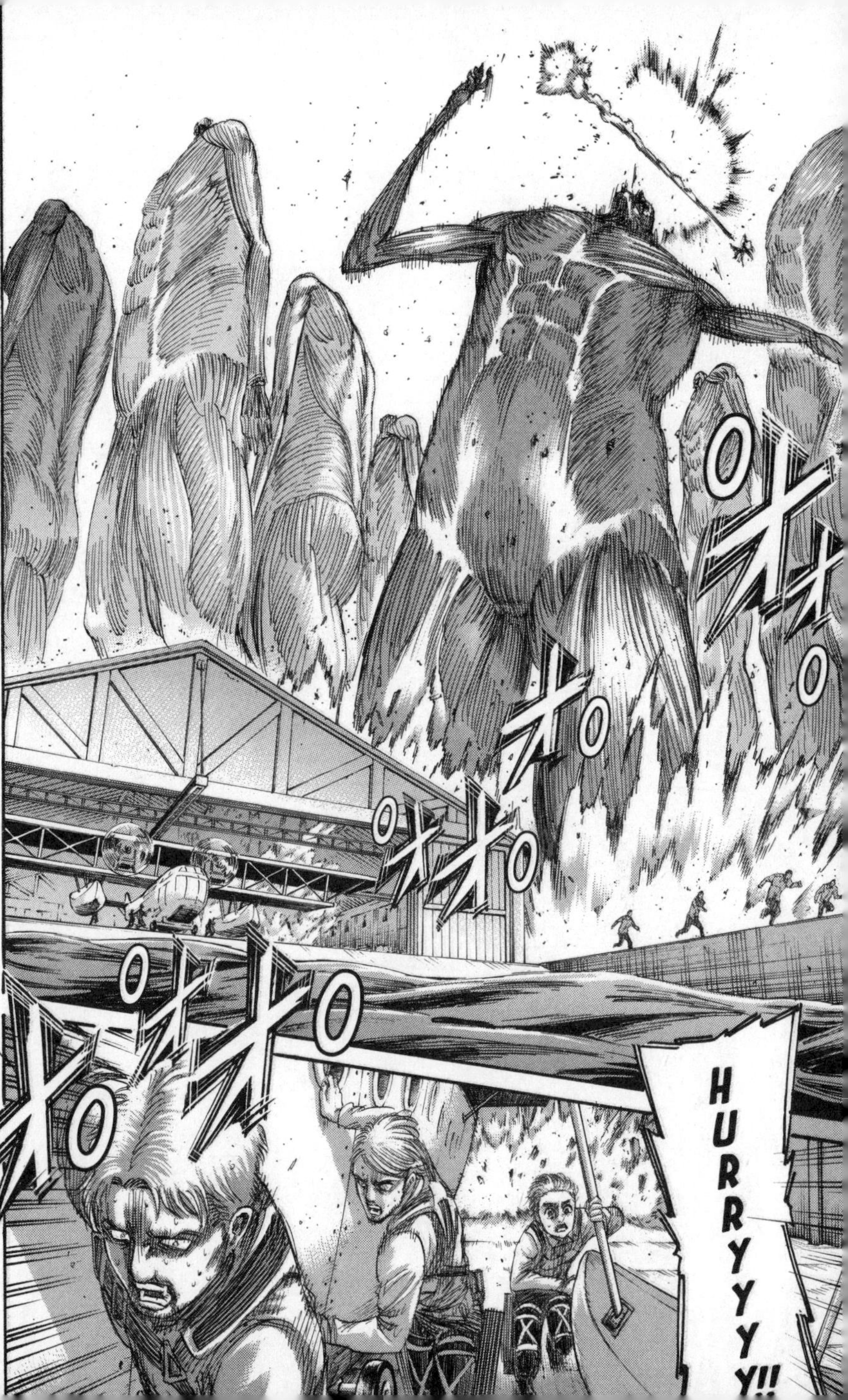
HURRYYYY!!

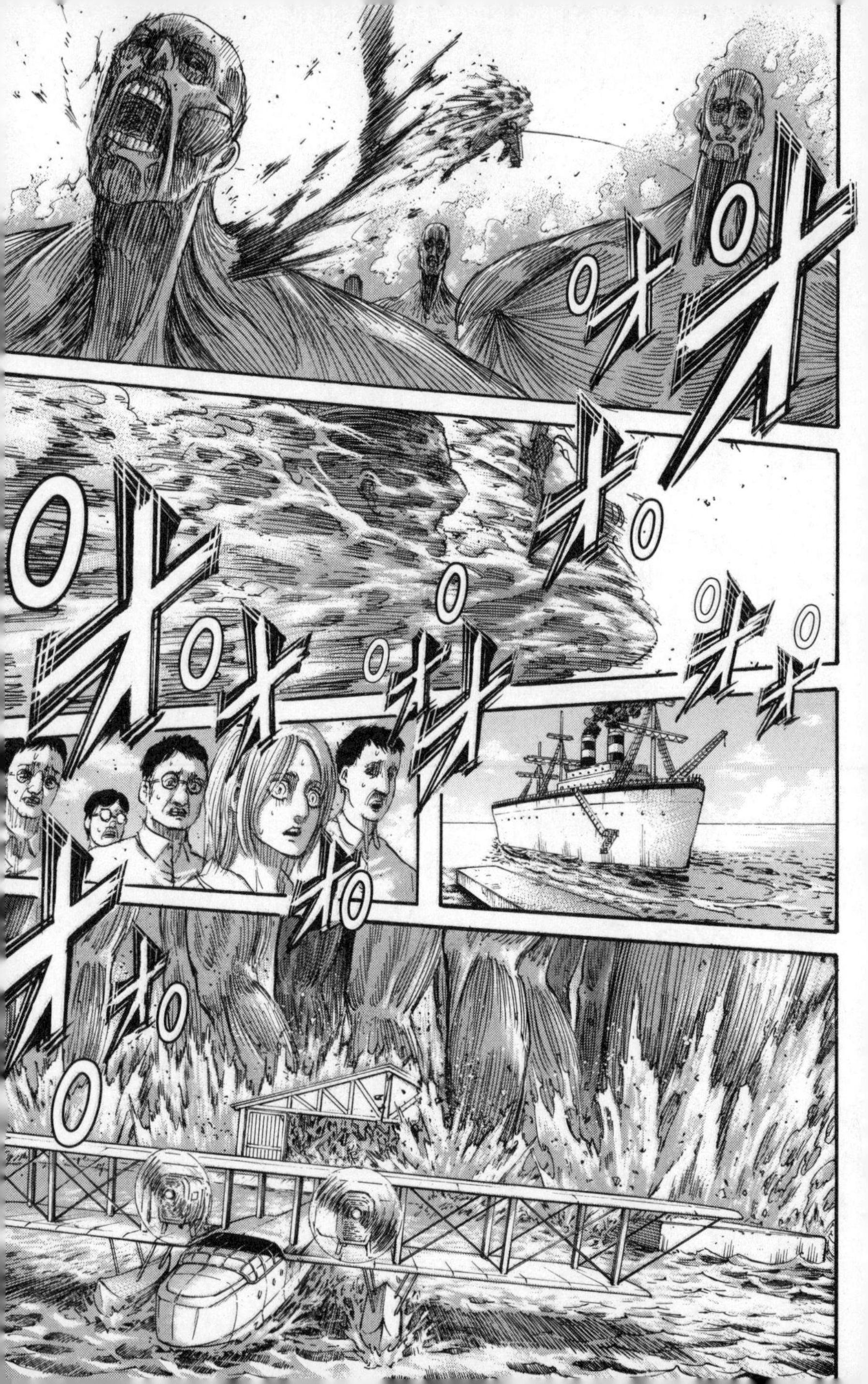

オオオオオオオオオオ

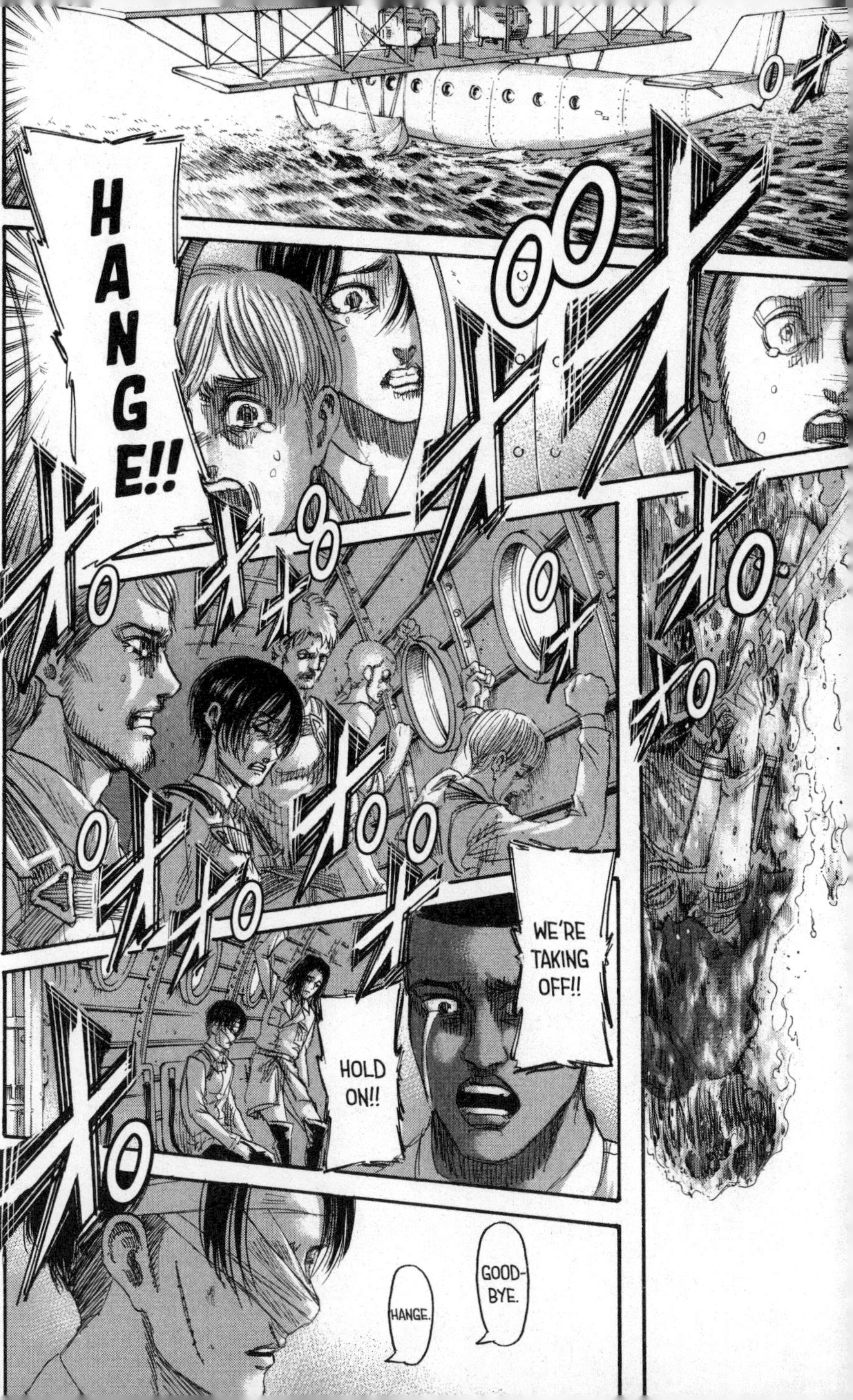
HANGE!!
WE'RE TAKING OFF!!
HOLD ON!!
GOOD-BYE.
HANGE.

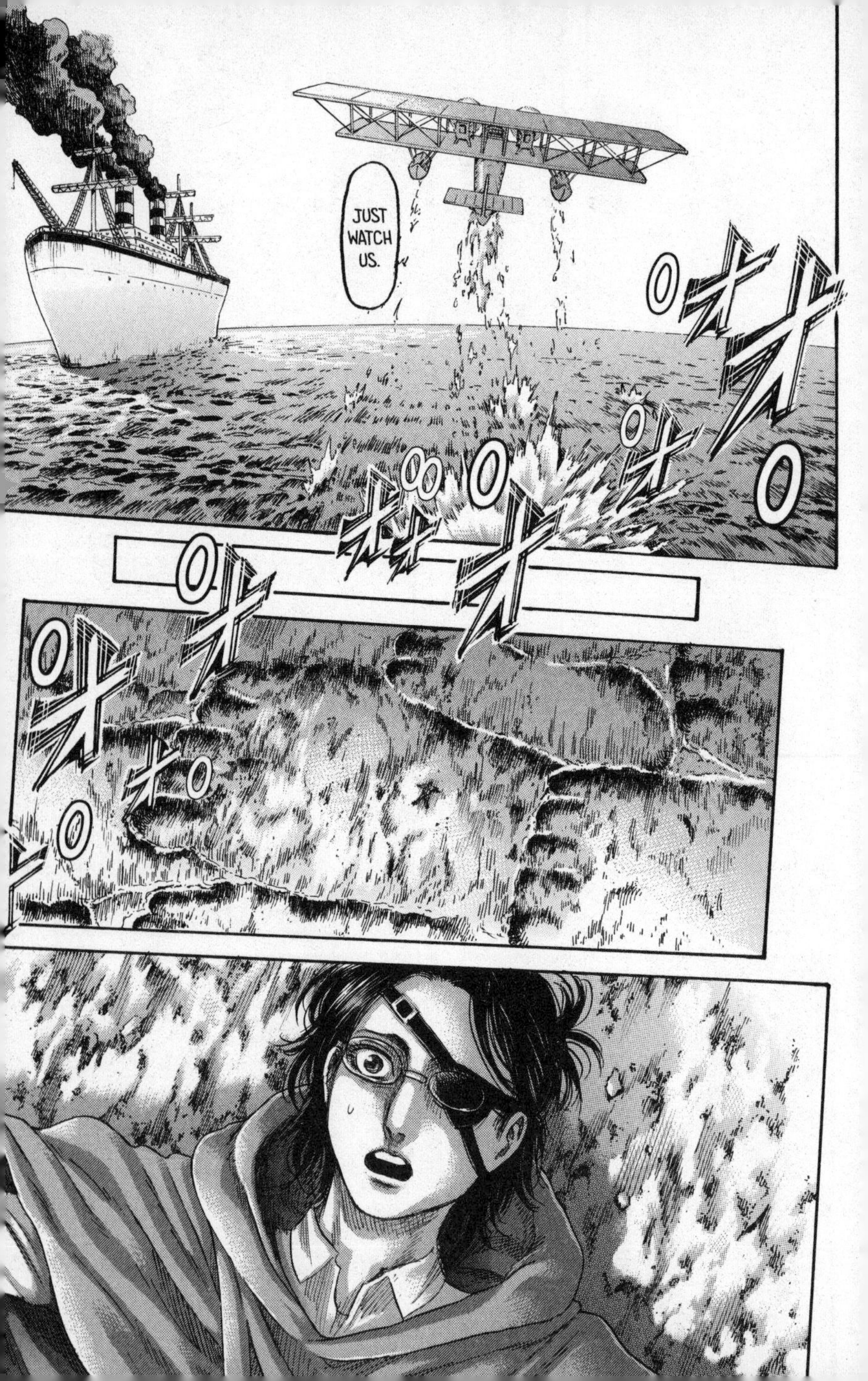
JUST WATCH US.

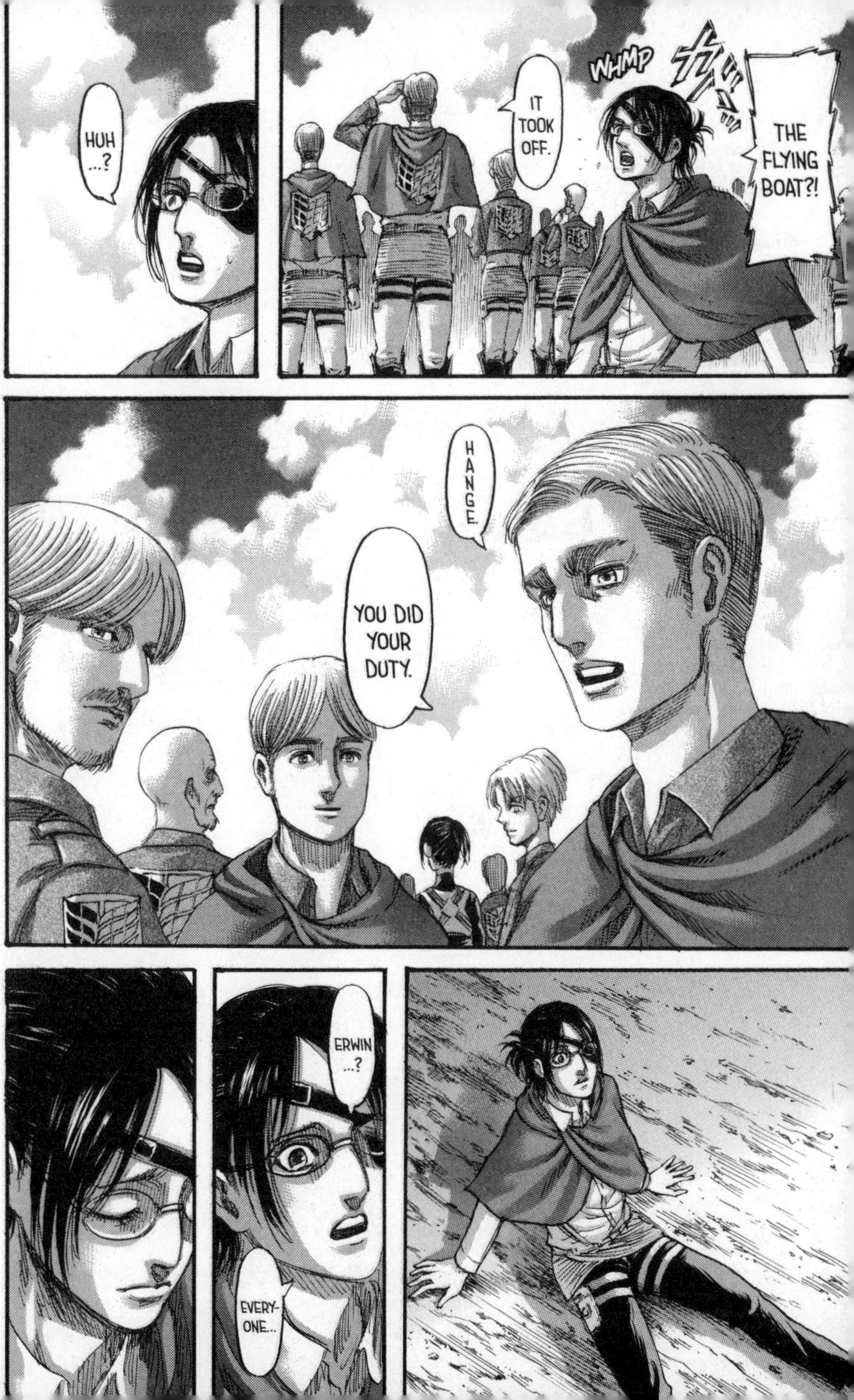
WHMP
THE FLYING BOAT?!
IT TOOK OFF.
HUH ...?
HANGE.
YOU DID YOUR DUTY.
ERWIN ...?
EVERY-ONE...

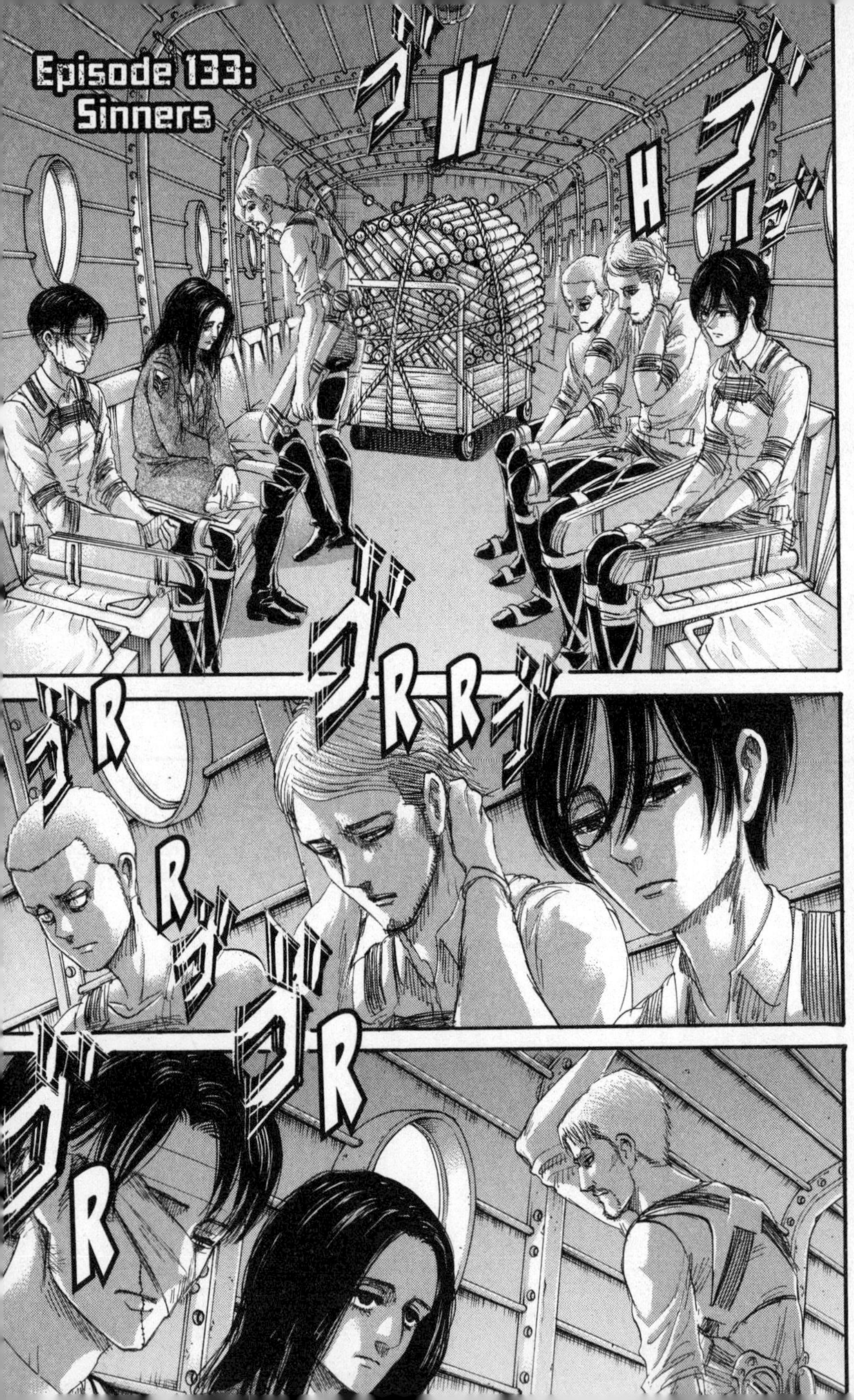
Episode 133:
Sinners
ゴW
ゴHゴ
ゴRRゴ
ゴR
Rゴ
ゴR
ゴR

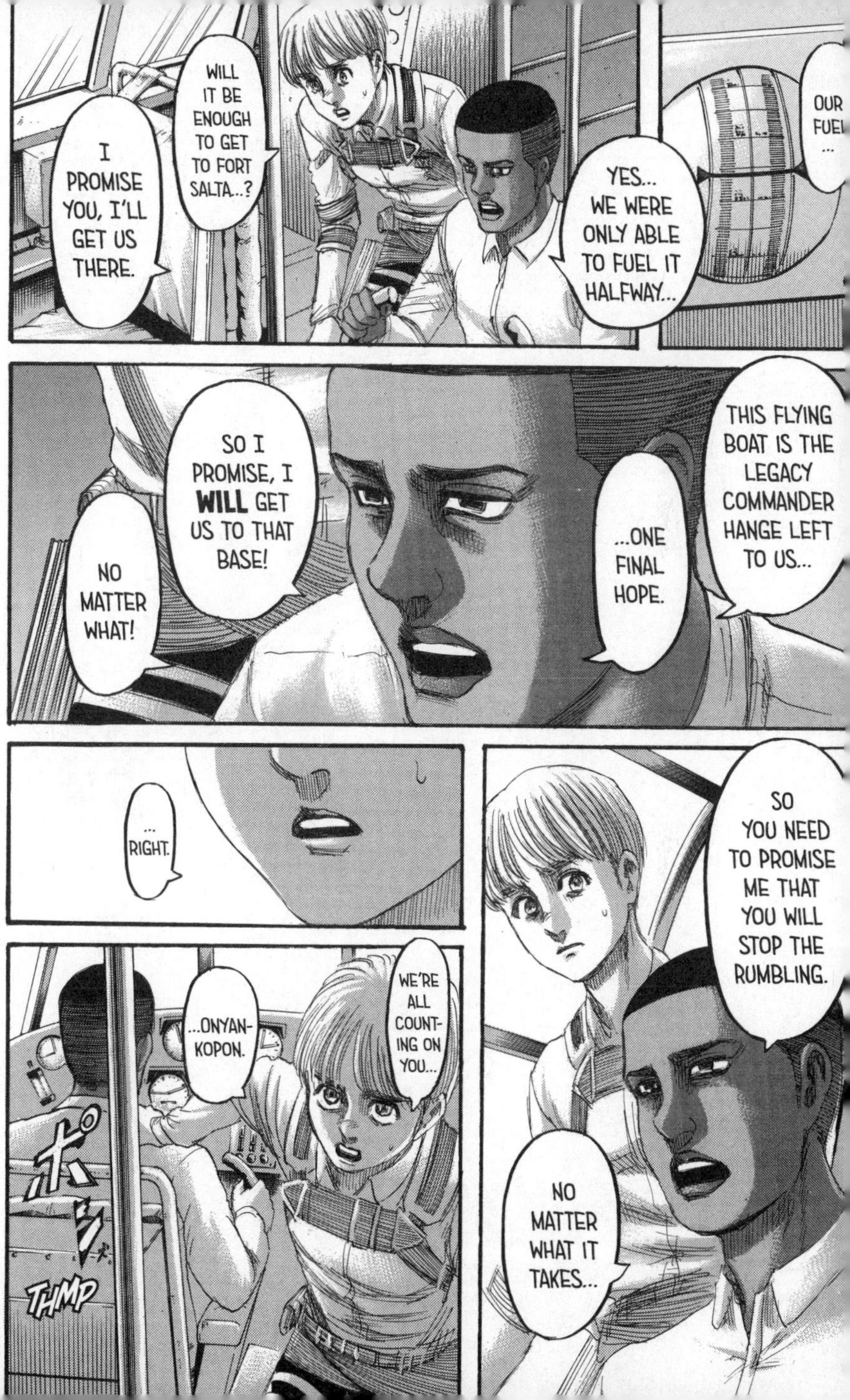
OUR FUEL...
YES... WE WERE ONLY ABLE TO FUEL IT HALFWAY...
WILL IT BE ENOUGH TO GET TO FORT SALTA...?
I PROMISE YOU, I'LL GET US THERE.
THIS FLYING BOAT IS THE LEGACY COMMANDER HANGE LEFT TO US...
...ONE FINAL HOPE.
SO I PROMISE, I **WILL** GET US TO THAT BASE!
NO MATTER WHAT!
SO YOU NEED TO PROMISE ME THAT YOU WILL STOP THE RUMBLING.
NO MATTER WHAT IT TAKES...
...RIGHT.
WE'RE ALL COUNTING ON YOU...
...ONYANKOPON.
THMP

ATTACK on TITAN

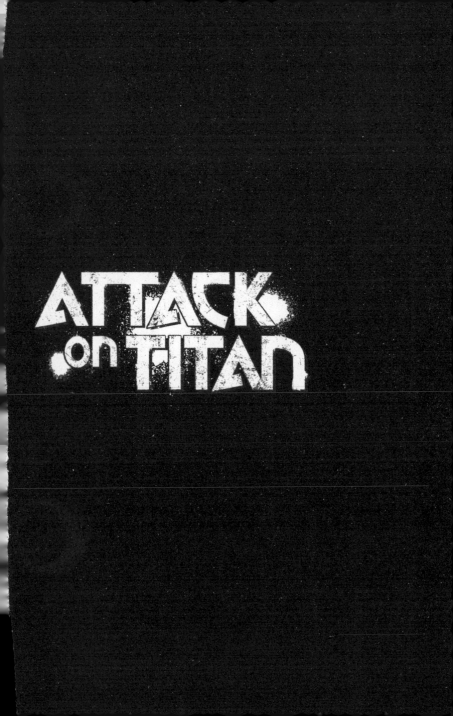

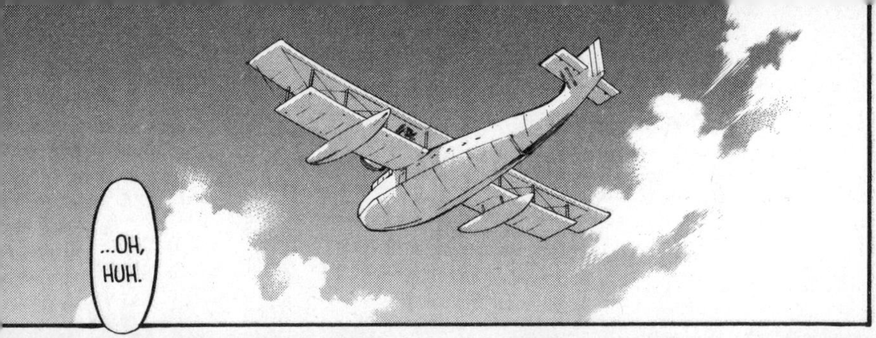
...OH, HUH.

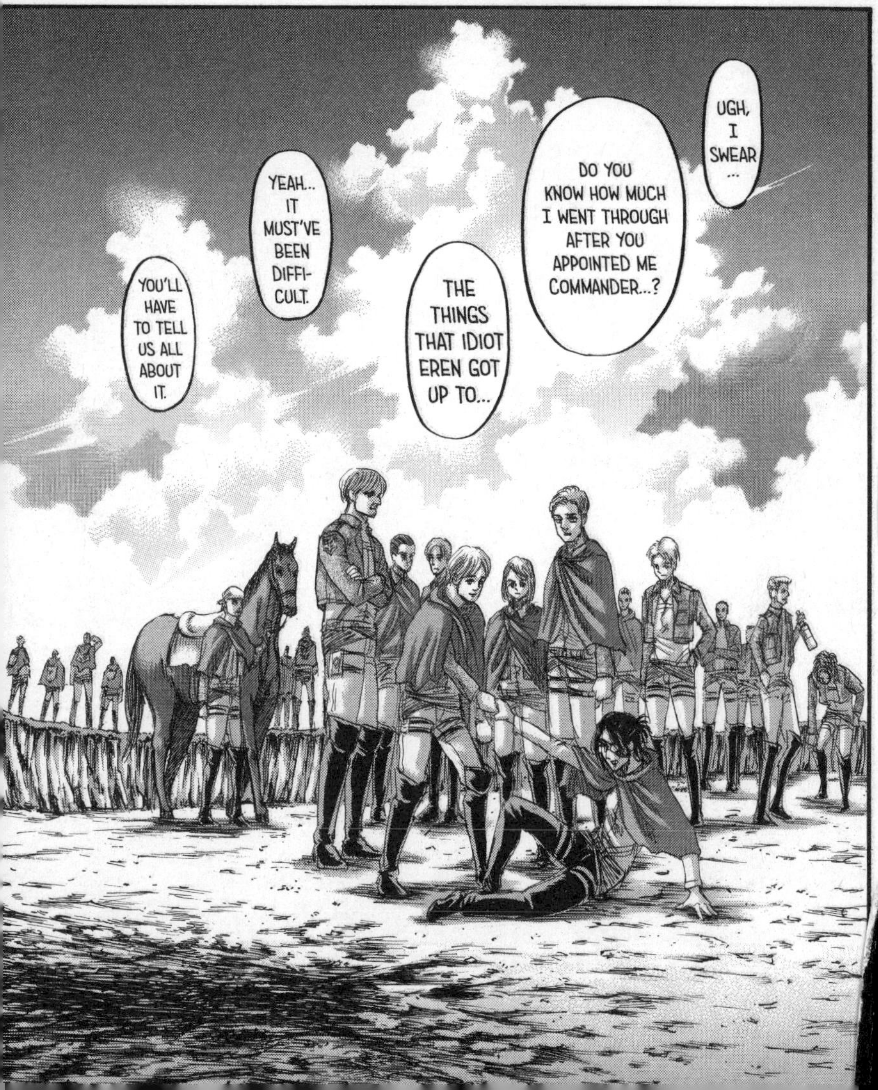
UGH, I SWEAR...
DO YOU KNOW HOW MUCH I WENT THROUGH AFTER YOU APPOINTED ME COMMANDER...?
THE THINGS THAT IDIOT EREN GOT UP TO...
YEAH... IT MUST'VE BEEN DIFFI-CULT.
YOU'LL HAVE TO TELL US ALL ABOUT IT.

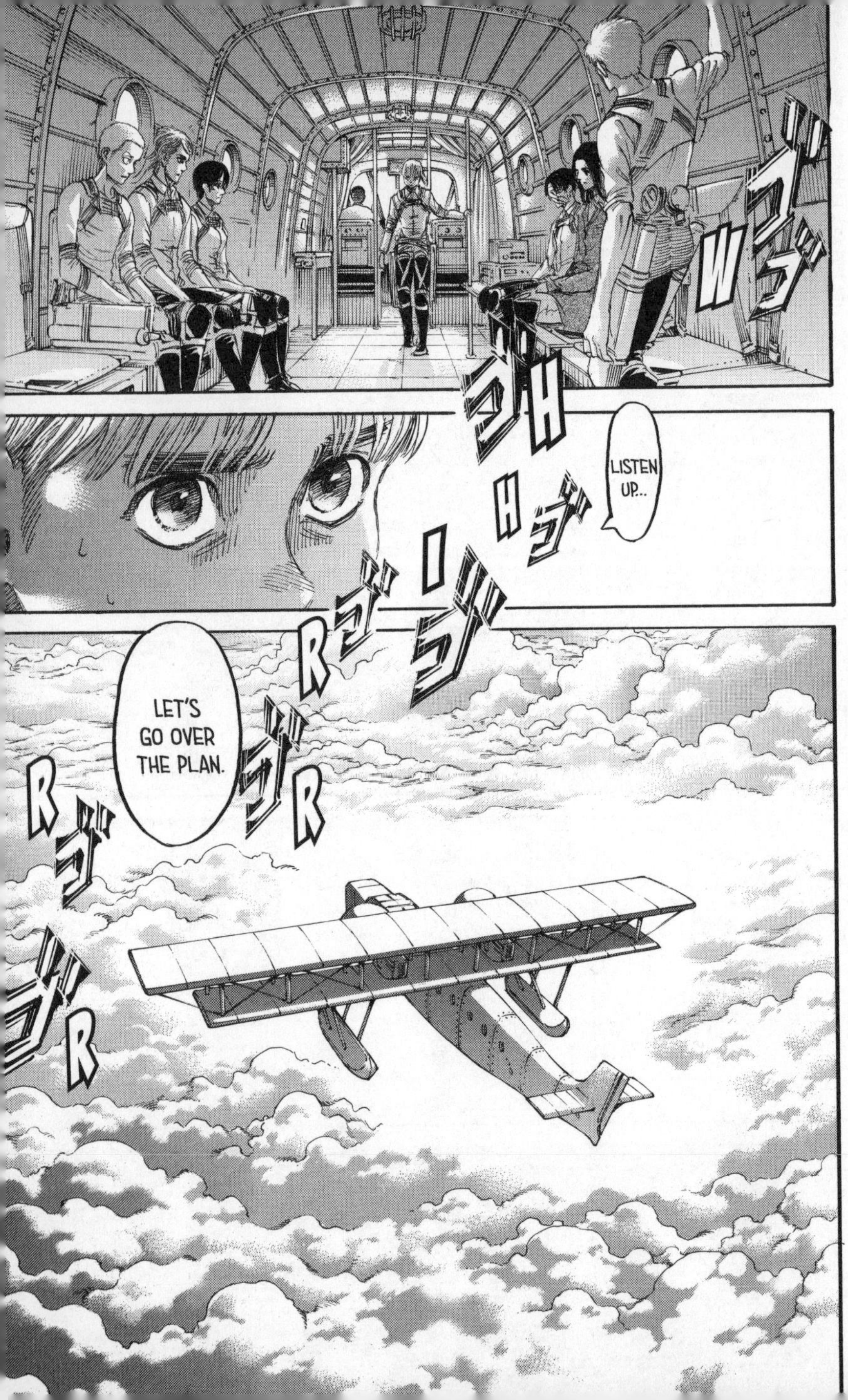
WHHIRRR
LISTEN UP...
LET'S GO OVER THE PLAN.

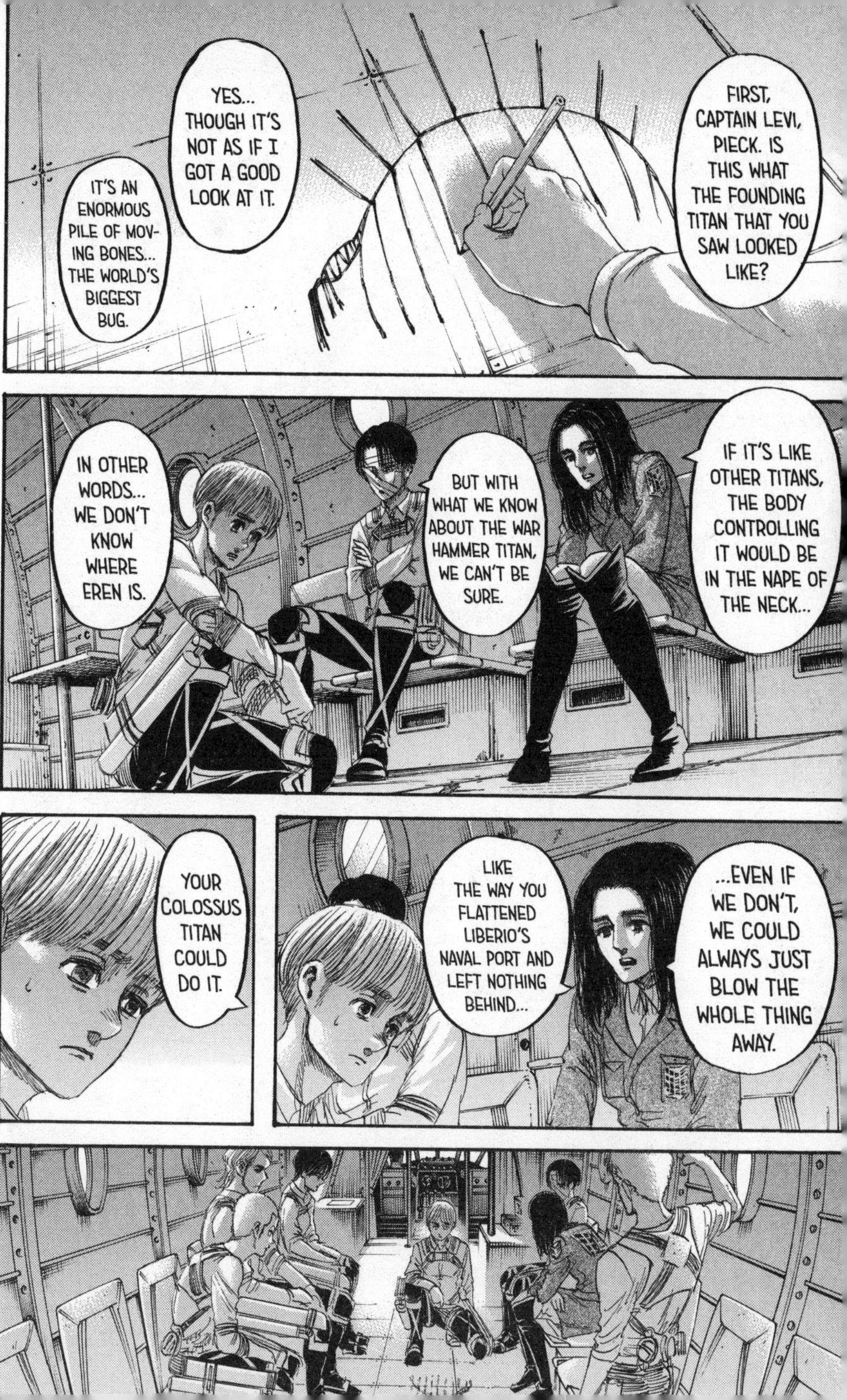
FIRST, CAPTAIN LEVI, PIECK. IS THIS WHAT THE FOUNDING TITAN THAT YOU SAW LOOKED LIKE?
YES... THOUGH IT'S NOT AS IF I GOT A GOOD LOOK AT IT.
IT'S AN ENORMOUS PILE OF MOV-ING BONES... THE WORLD'S BIGGEST BUG.
IF IT'S LIKE OTHER TITANS, THE BODY CONTROLLING IT WOULD BE IN THE NAPE OF THE NECK...
BUT WITH WHAT WE KNOW ABOUT THE WAR HAMMER TITAN, WE CAN'T BE SURE.
IN OTHER WORDS... WE DON'T KNOW WHERE EREN IS.
...EVEN IF WE DON'T, WE COULD ALWAYS JUST BLOW THE WHOLE THING AWAY.
LIKE THE WAY YOU FLATTENED LIBERIO'S NAVAL PORT AND LEFT NOTHING BEHIND...
YOUR COLOSSUS TITAN COULD DO IT.

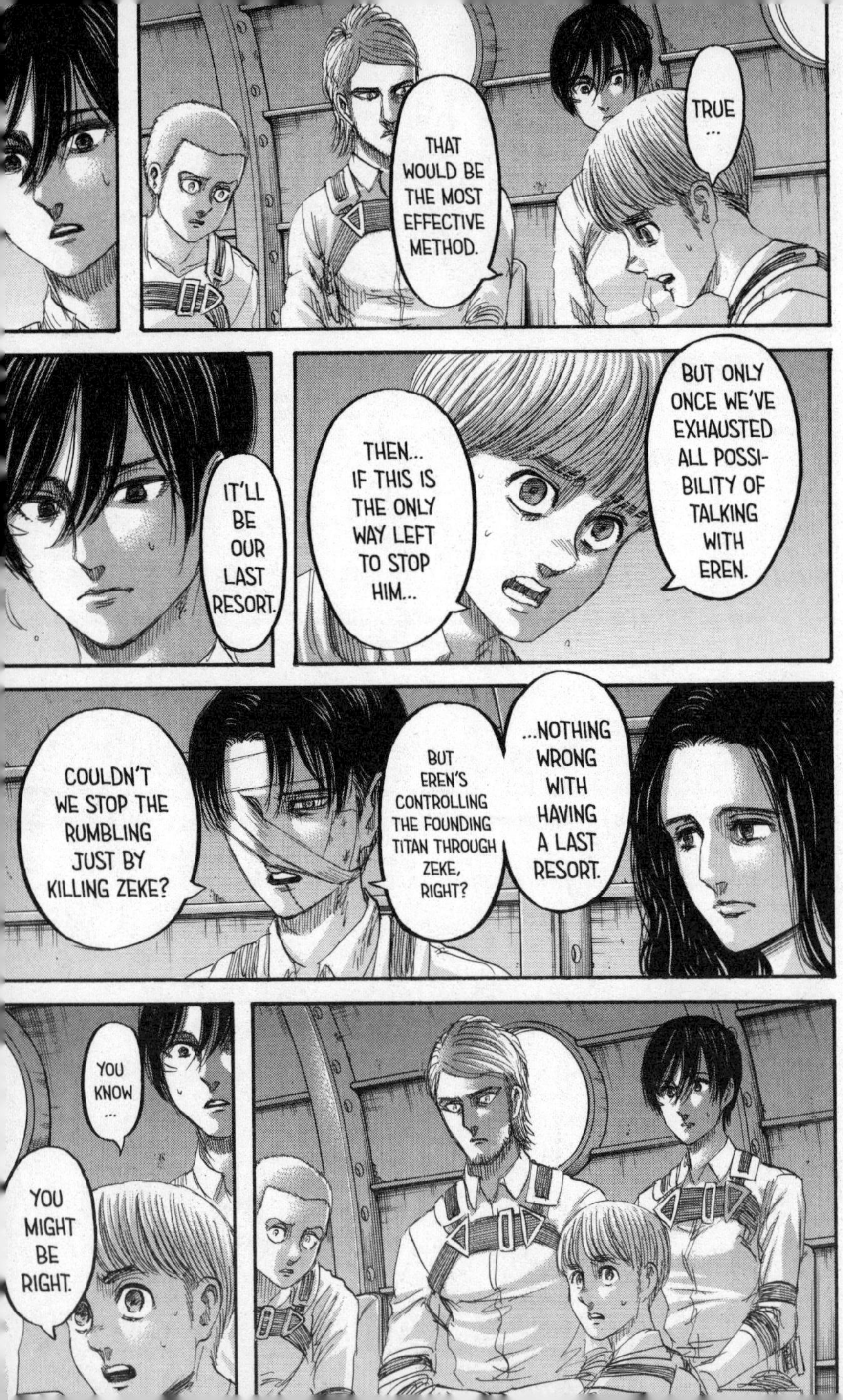
TRUE ...
THAT WOULD BE THE MOST EFFECTIVE METHOD.
BUT ONLY ONCE WE'VE EXHAUSTED ALL POSSI- BILITY OF TALKING WITH EREN.
THEN... IF THIS IS THE ONLY WAY LEFT TO STOP HIM...
IT'LL BE OUR LAST RESORT.
...NOTHING WRONG WITH HAVING A LAST RESORT.
BUT EREN'S CONTROLLING THE FOUNDING TITAN THROUGH ZEKE, RIGHT?
COULDN'T WE STOP THE RUMBLING JUST BY KILLING ZEKE?
YOU KNOW ...
YOU MIGHT BE RIGHT.

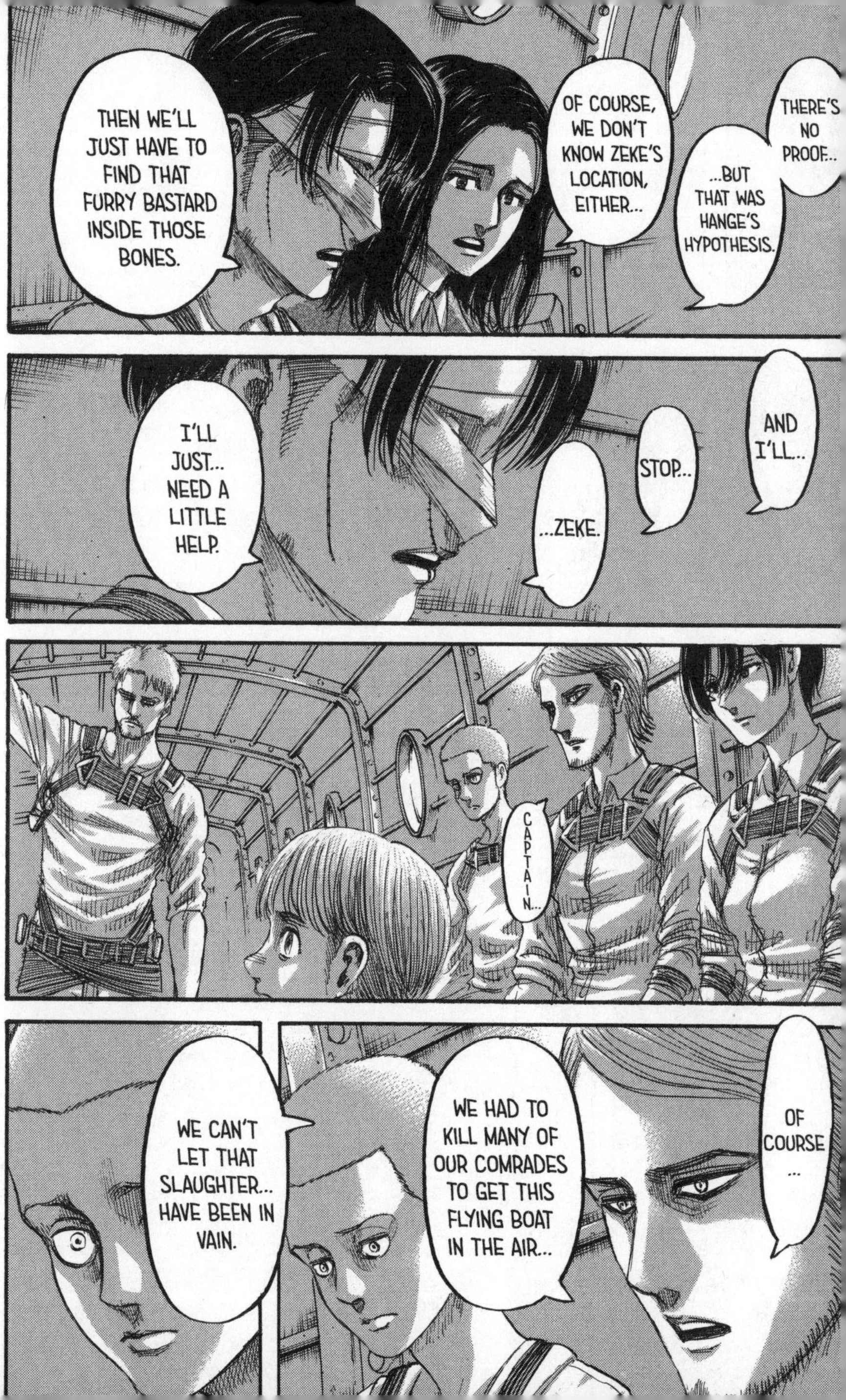
THERE'S NO PROOF...
...BUT THAT WAS HANGE'S HYPOTHESIS.
OF COURSE, WE DON'T KNOW ZEKE'S LOCATION, EITHER...
THEN WE'LL JUST HAVE TO FIND THAT FURRY BASTARD INSIDE THOSE BONES.
AND I'LL...
STOP...
...ZEKE.
I'LL JUST... NEED A LITTLE HELP.
CAPTAIN...
OF COURSE...
WE HAD TO KILL MANY OF OUR COMRADES TO GET THIS FLYING BOAT IN THE AIR...
WE CAN'T LET THAT SLAUGHTER... HAVE BEEN IN VAIN.

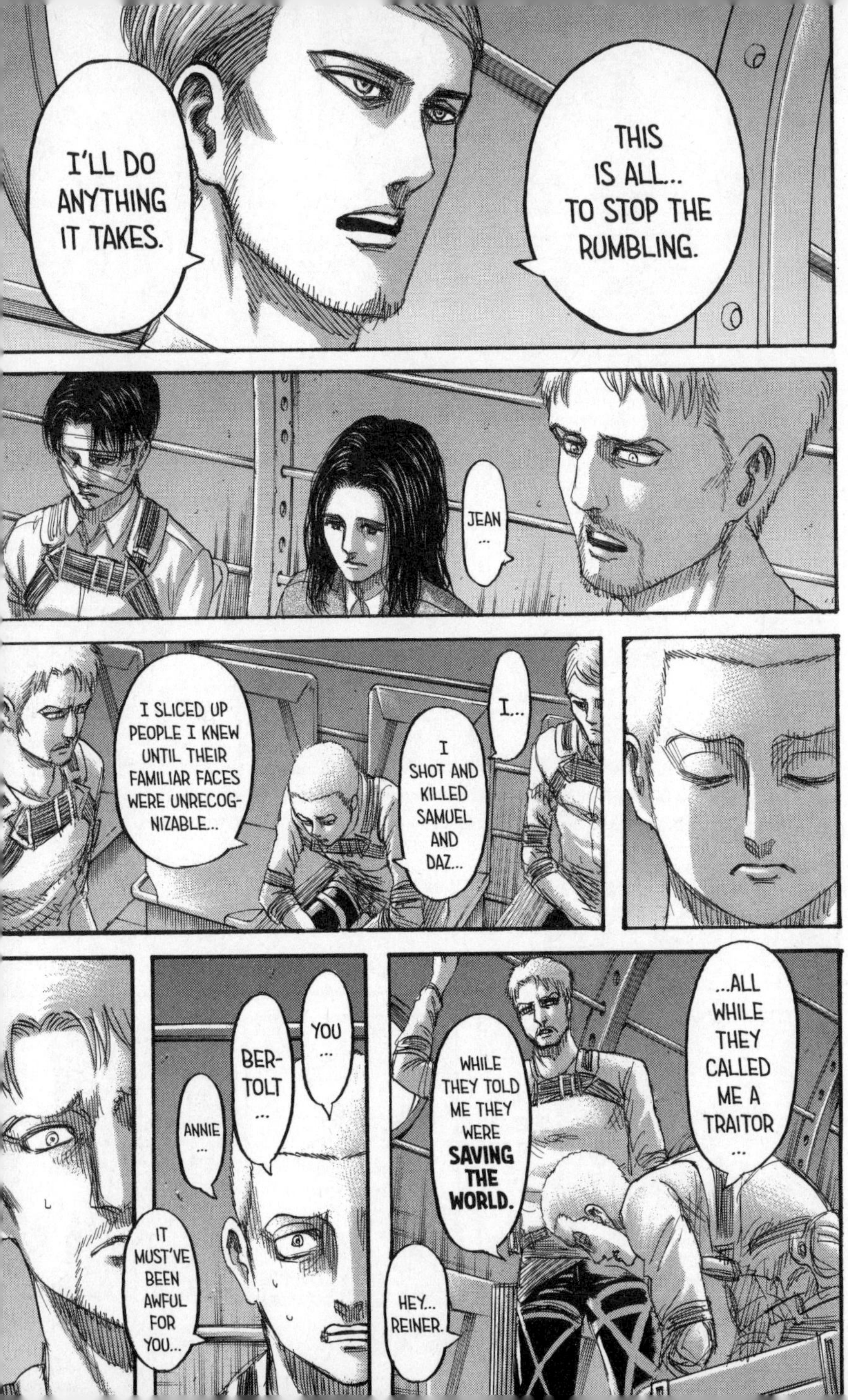

THIS IS ALL... TO STOP THE RUMBLING.
I'LL DO ANYTHING IT TAKES.
JEAN ...
I...
I SHOT AND KILLED SAMUEL AND DAZ...
I SLICED UP PEOPLE I KNEW UNTIL THEIR FAMILIAR FACES WERE UNRECOG-NIZABLE...
...ALL WHILE THEY CALLED ME A TRAITOR ...
WHILE THEY TOLD ME THEY WERE **SAVING THE WORLD.**
HEY... REINER.
YOU ...
BER-TOLT ...
ANNIE ...
IT MUST'VE BEEN AWFUL FOR YOU...

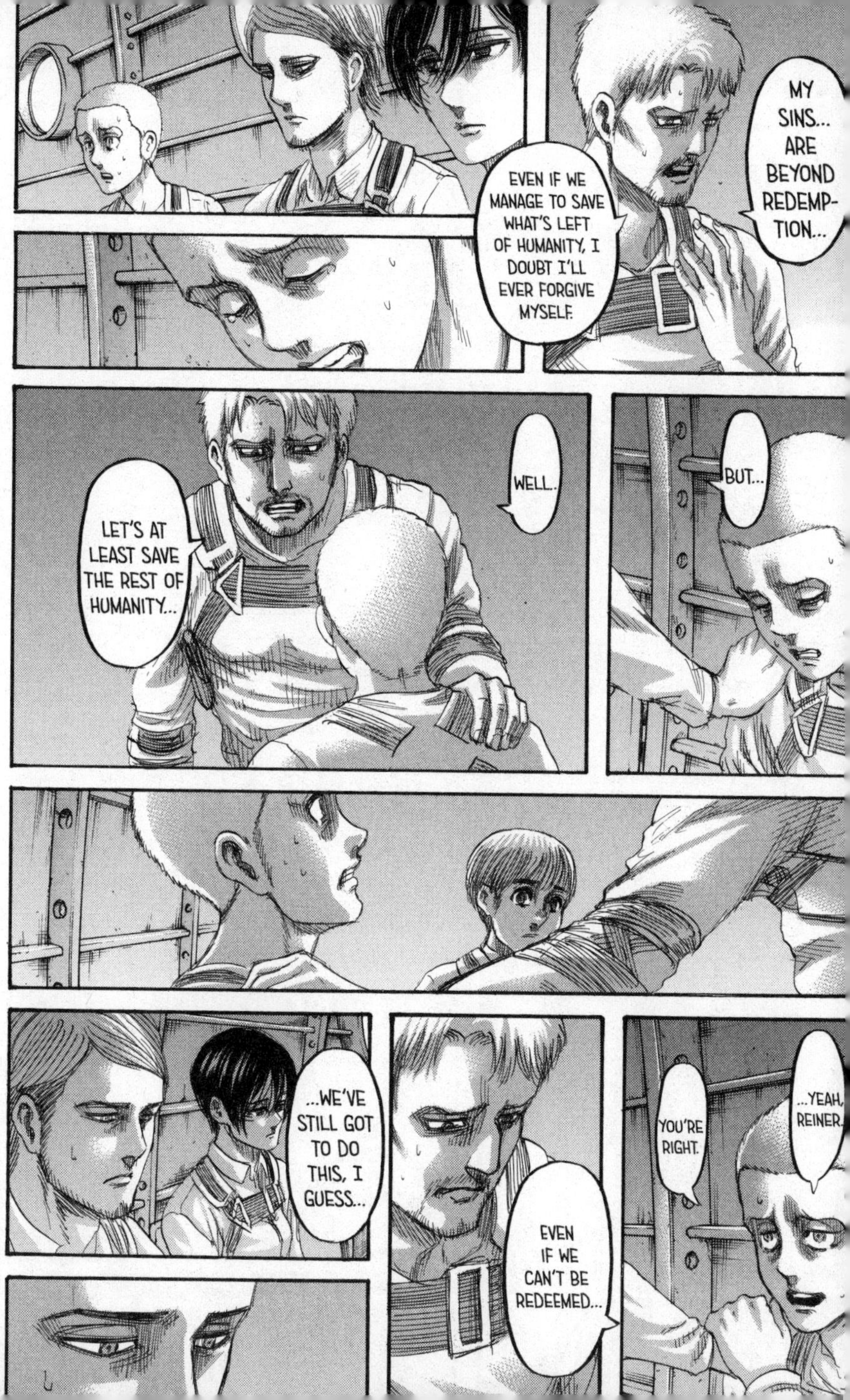
MY SINS... ARE BEYOND REDEMPTION...
EVEN IF WE MANAGE TO SAVE WHAT'S LEFT OF HUMANITY, I DOUBT I'LL EVER FORGIVE MYSELF.
BUT...
WELL..
LET'S AT LEAST SAVE THE REST OF HUMANITY...
...YEAH, REINER.
YOU'RE RIGHT.
EVEN IF WE CAN'T BE REDEEMED...
...WE'VE STILL GOT TO DO THIS, I GUESS...

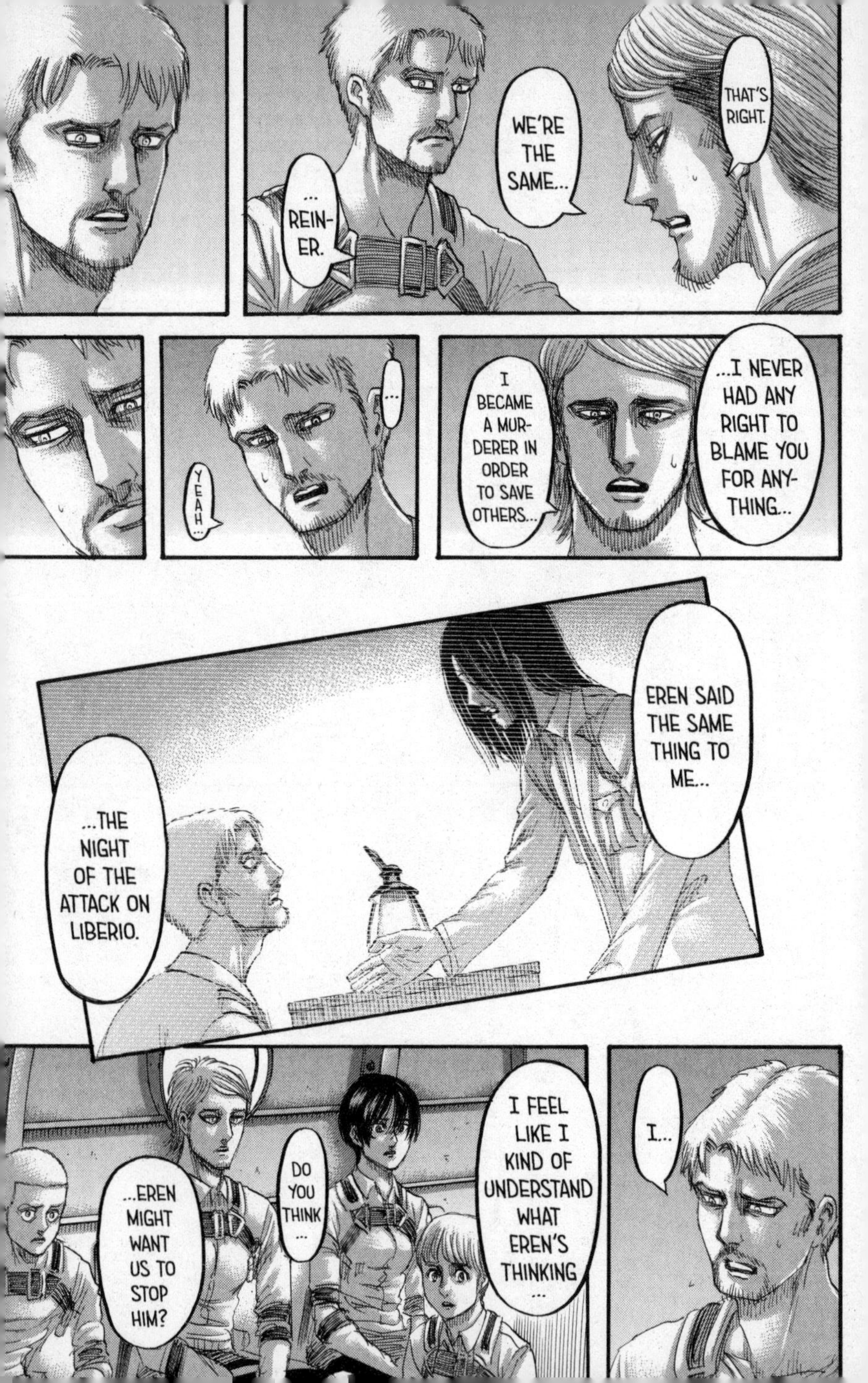
THAT'S RIGHT.
WE'RE THE SAME...
...REINER.
...I NEVER HAD ANY RIGHT TO BLAME YOU FOR ANYTHING...
I BECAME A MURDERER IN ORDER TO SAVE OTHERS...
...
YEAH...
EREN SAID THE SAME THING TO ME...
...THE NIGHT OF THE ATTACK ON LIBERIO.
I...
I FEEL LIKE I KIND OF UNDERSTAND WHAT EREN'S THINKING...
DO YOU THINK...
...EREN MIGHT WANT US TO STOP HIM?

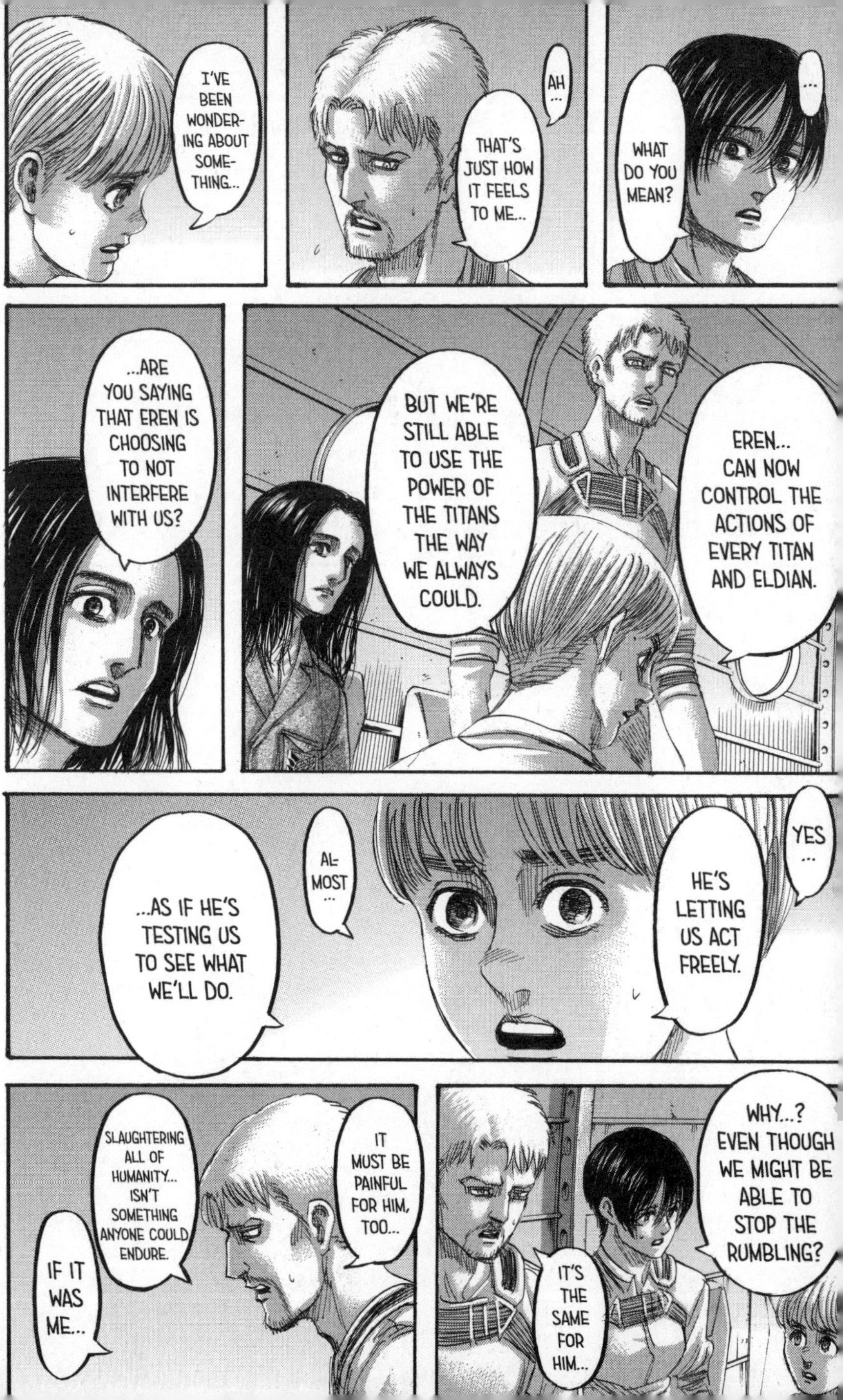
...
WHAT DO YOU MEAN?
AH...
THAT'S JUST HOW IT FEELS TO ME...
I'VE BEEN WONDERING ABOUT SOMETHING...
EREN... CAN NOW CONTROL THE ACTIONS OF EVERY TITAN AND ELDIAN.
BUT WE'RE STILL ABLE TO USE THE POWER OF THE TITANS THE WAY WE ALWAYS COULD.
...ARE YOU SAYING THAT EREN IS CHOOSING TO NOT INTERFERE WITH US?
YES...
HE'S LETTING US ACT FREELY.
ALMOST...
...AS IF HE'S TESTING US TO SEE WHAT WE'LL DO.
WHY...? EVEN THOUGH WE MIGHT BE ABLE TO STOP THE RUMBLING?
IT'S THE SAME FOR HIM...
IT MUST BE PAINFUL FOR HIM, TOO...
SLAUGHTERING ALL OF HUMANITY... ISN'T SOMETHING ANYONE COULD ENDURE.
IF IT WAS ME...

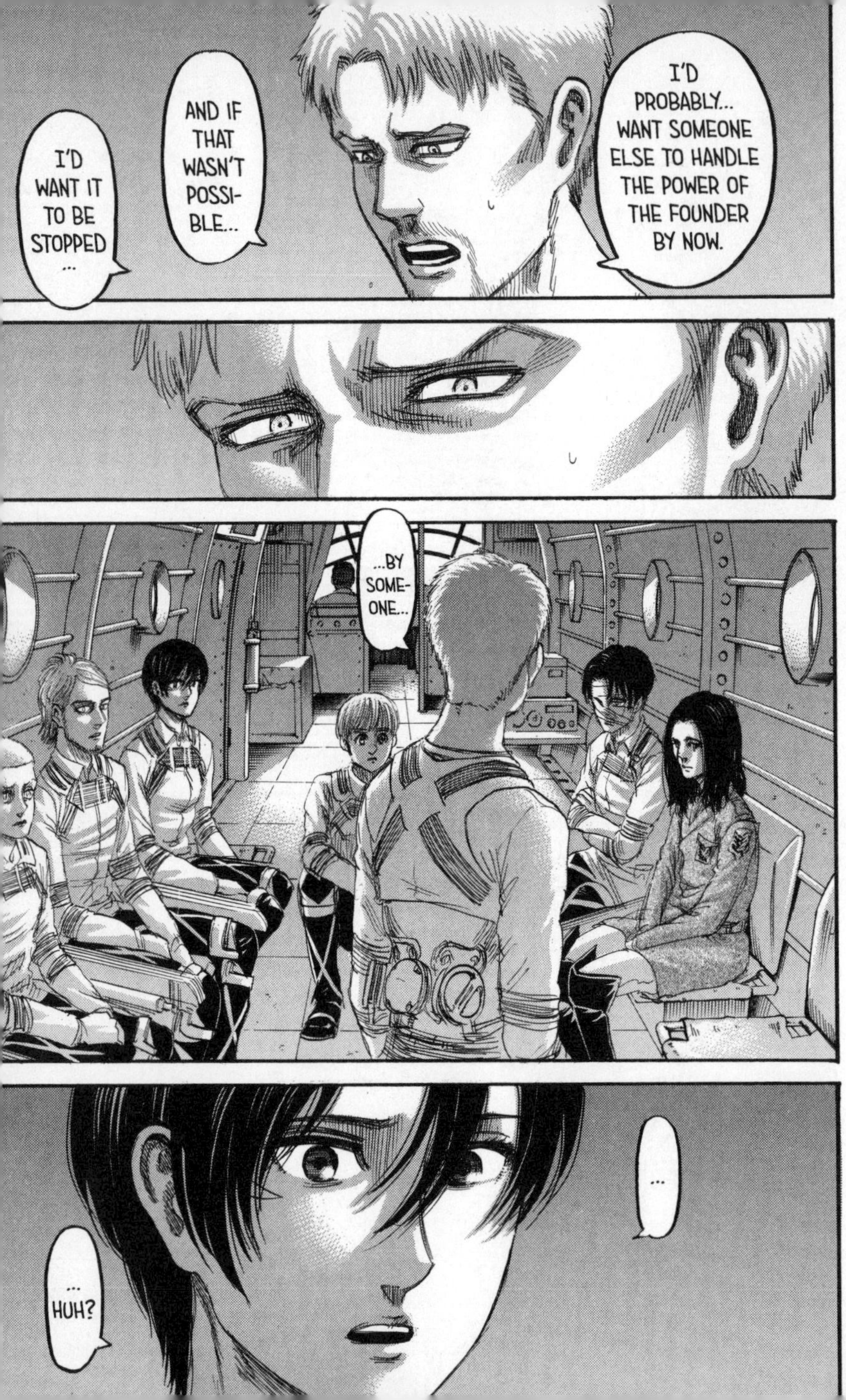
I'D PROBABLY... WANT SOMEONE ELSE TO HANDLE THE POWER OF THE FOUNDER BY NOW.
AND IF THAT WASN'T POSSI-BLE...
I'D WANT IT TO BE STOPPED ...
...BY SOME-ONE...
...
... HUH?

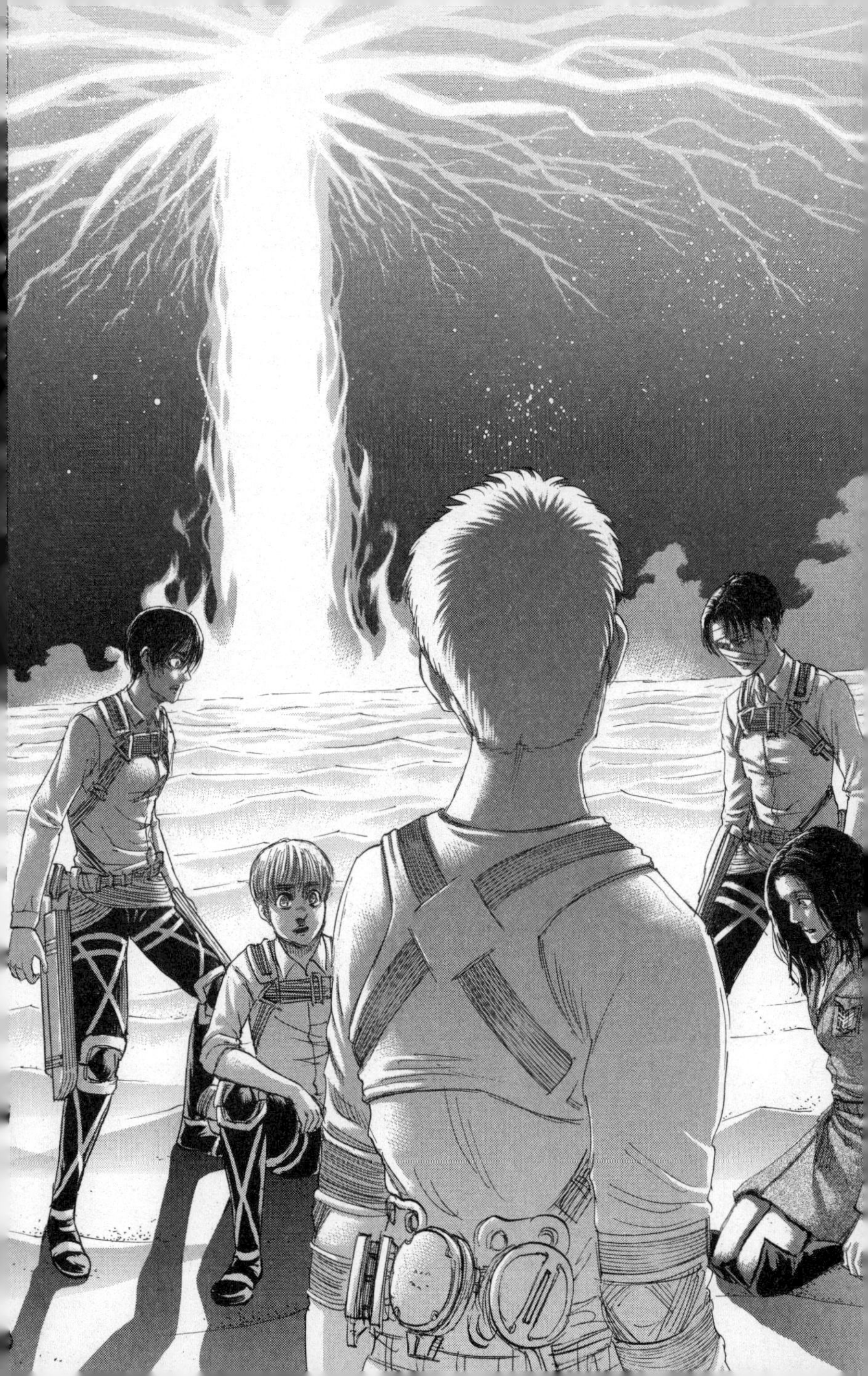

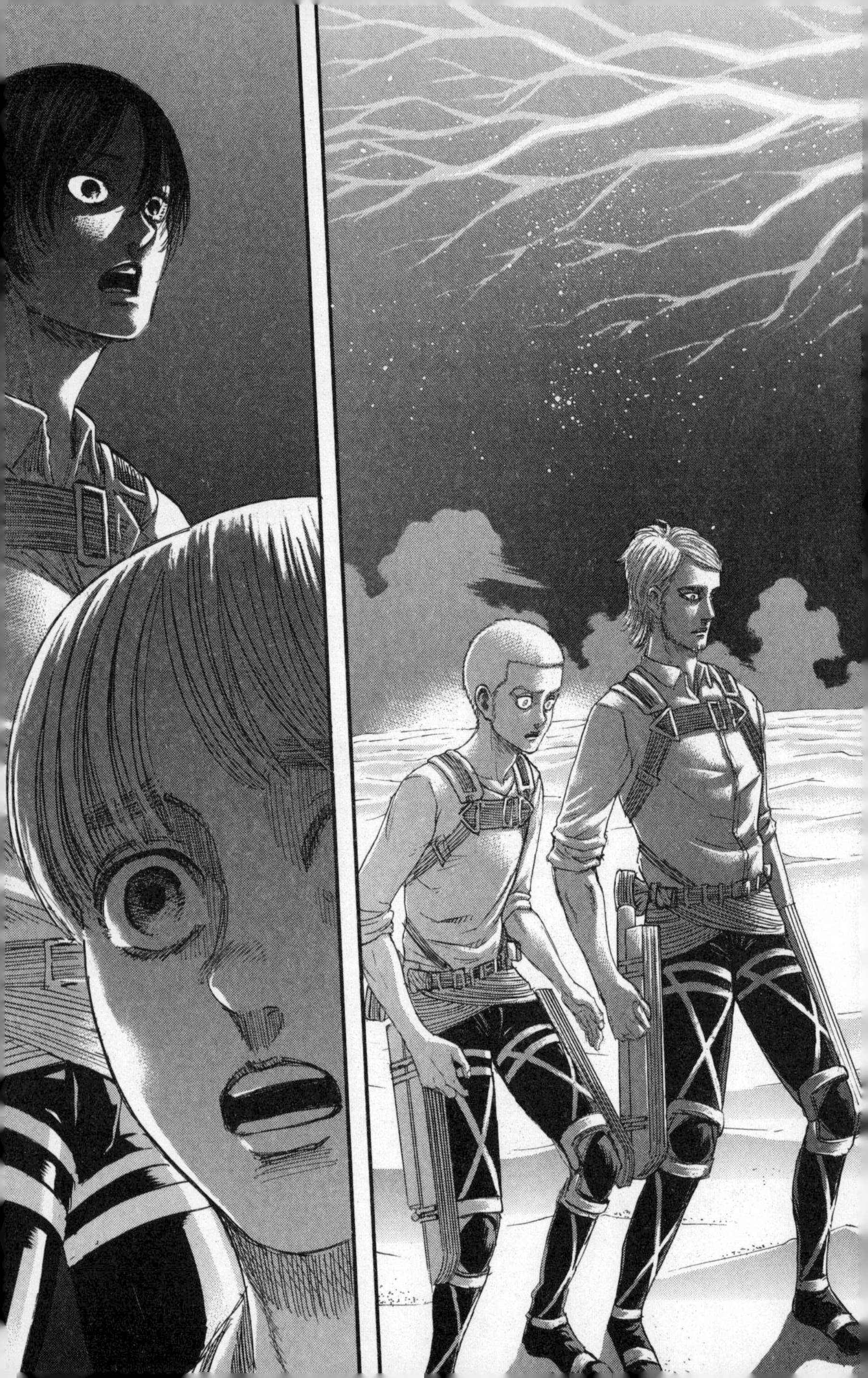

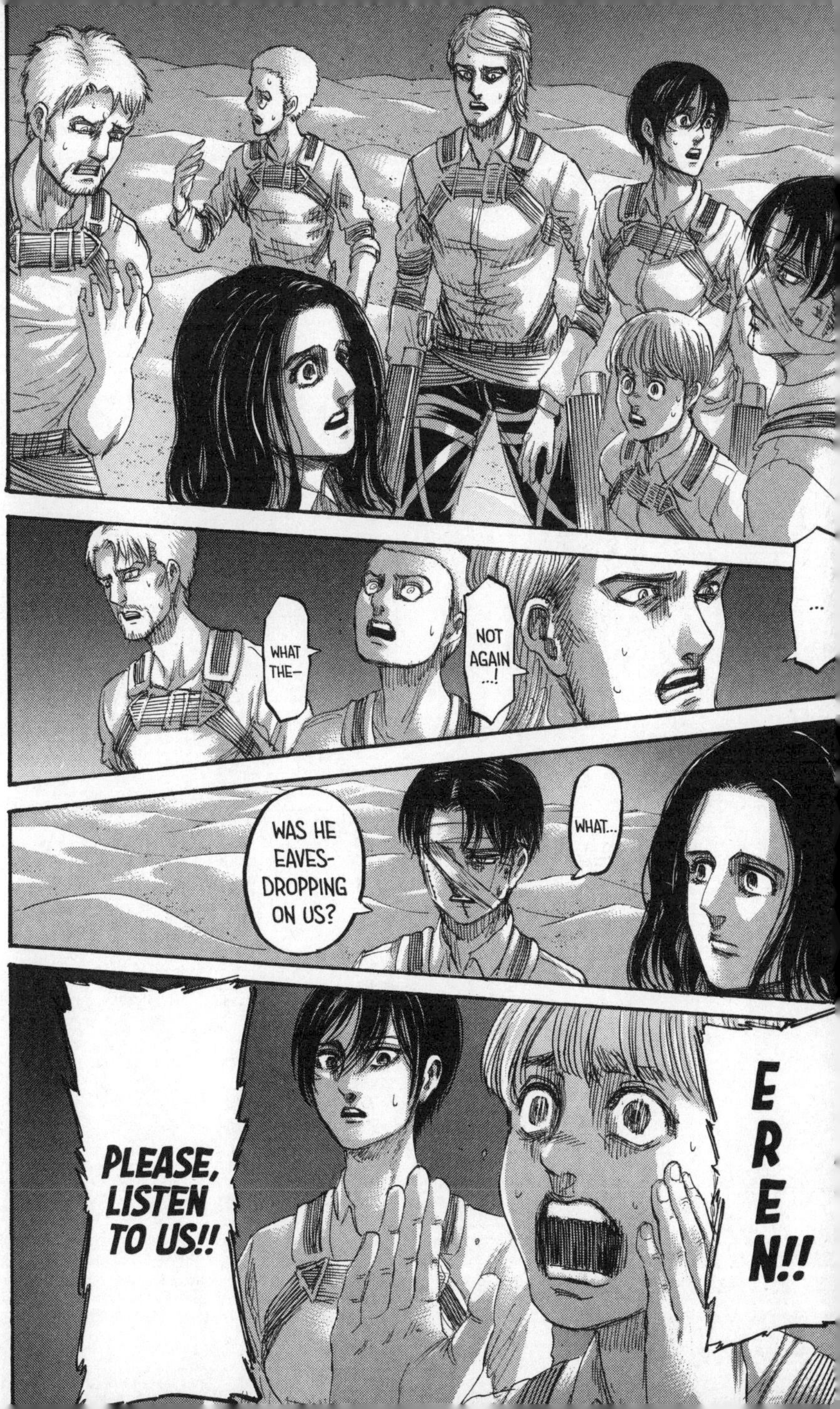
...
NOT AGAIN ...!
WHAT THE—
WHAT...
WAS HE EAVES-DROPPING ON US?
EREN!!
PLEASE, LISTEN TO US!!

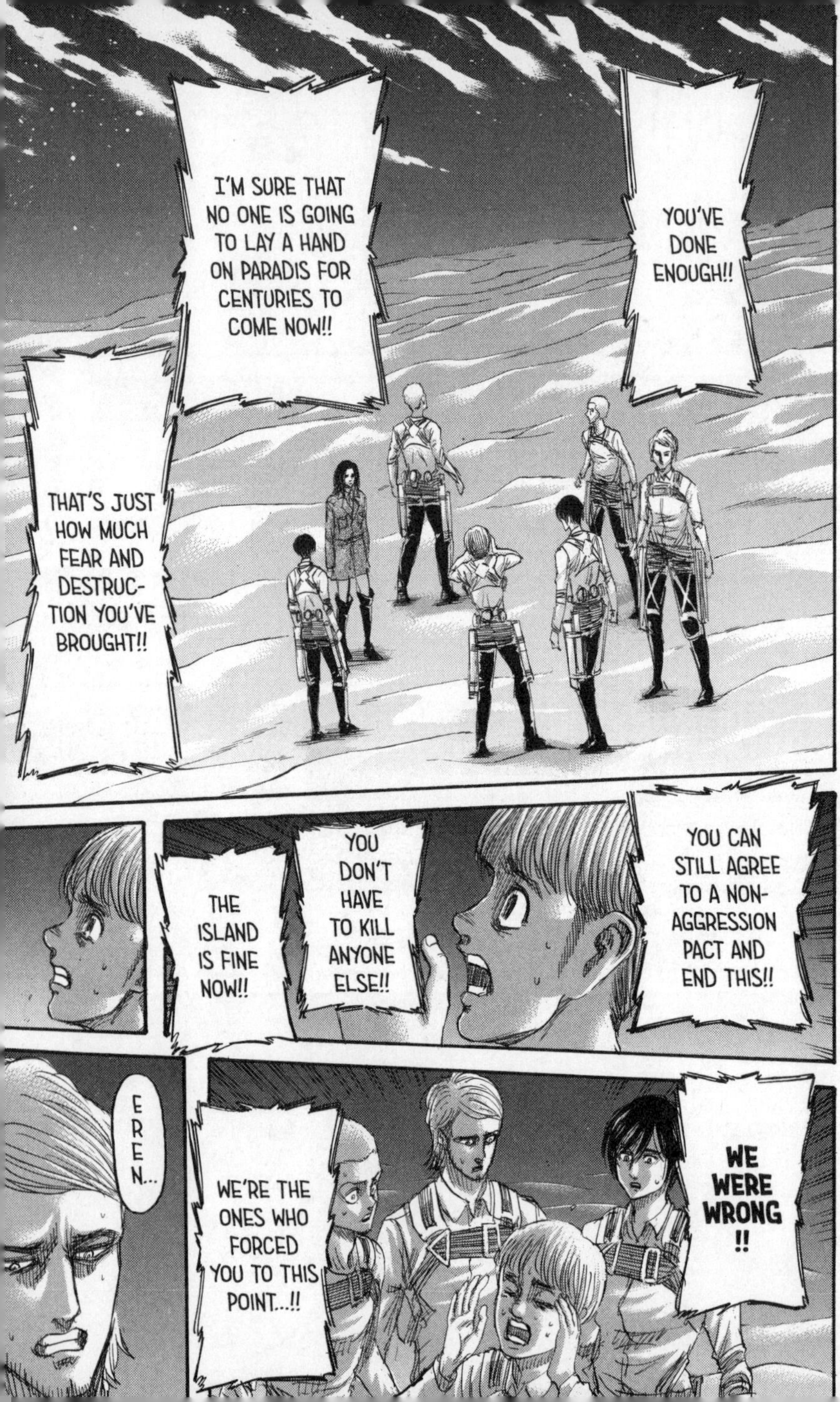
YOU'VE DONE ENOUGH!!
I'M SURE THAT NO ONE IS GOING TO LAY A HAND ON PARADIS FOR CENTURIES TO COME NOW!!
THAT'S JUST HOW MUCH FEAR AND DESTRUCTION YOU'VE BROUGHT!!
YOU CAN STILL AGREE TO A NON-AGGRESSION PACT AND END THIS!!
YOU DON'T HAVE TO KILL ANYONE ELSE!!
THE ISLAND IS FINE NOW!!
WE WERE WRONG!!
WE'RE THE ONES WHO FORCED YOU TO THIS POINT...!!
EREN...

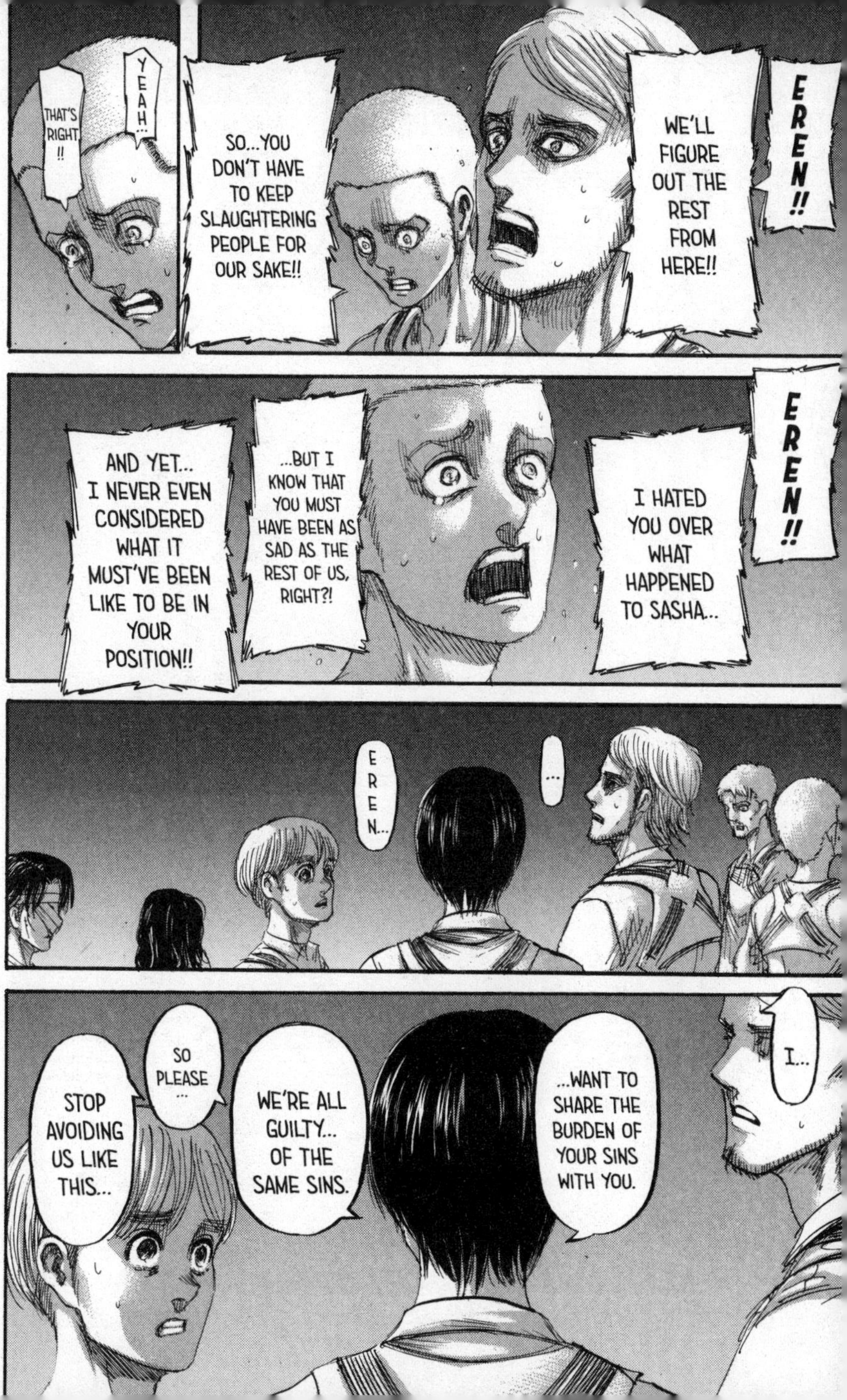
EREN!!
WE'LL FIGURE OUT THE REST FROM HERE!!
SO...YOU DON'T HAVE TO KEEP SLAUGHTERING PEOPLE FOR OUR SAKE!!
YEAH...
THAT'S RIGHT!!
EREN!!
I HATED YOU OVER WHAT HAPPENED TO SASHA...
...BUT I KNOW THAT YOU MUST HAVE BEEN AS SAD AS THE REST OF US, RIGHT?!
AND YET... I NEVER EVEN CONSIDERED WHAT IT MUST'VE BEEN LIKE TO BE IN YOUR POSITION!!
...
EREN...
I...
...WANT TO SHARE THE BURDEN OF YOUR SINS WITH YOU.
WE'RE ALL GUILTY... OF THE SAME SINS.
SO PLEASE...
STOP AVOIDING US LIKE THIS...

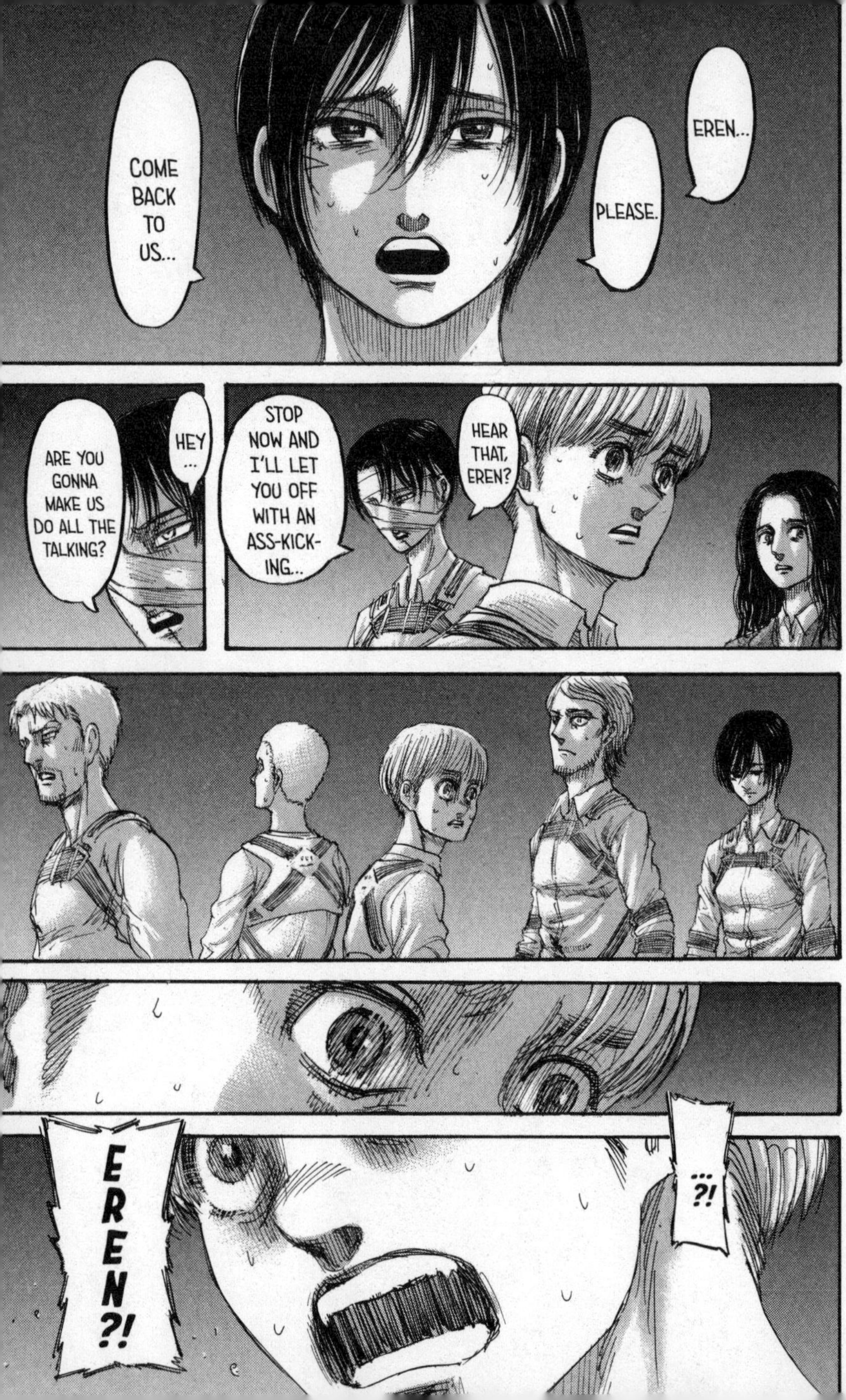
EREN...
PLEASE.
COME BACK TO US...
HEAR THAT, EREN?
STOP NOW AND I'LL LET YOU OFF WITH AN ASS-KICKING...
HEY ...
ARE YOU GONNA MAKE US DO ALL THE TALKING?
...?!
EREN?!

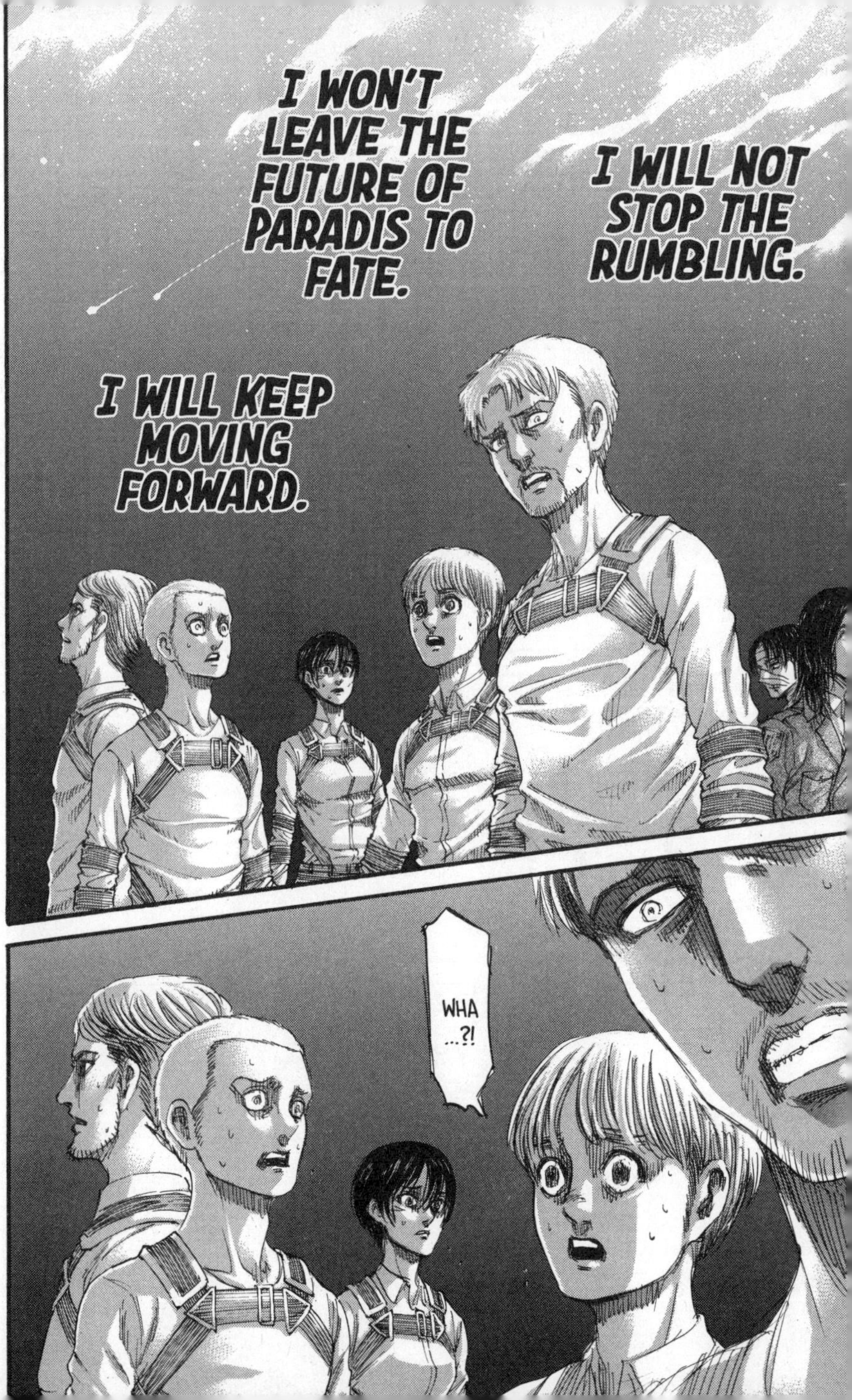
I WILL NOT STOP THE RUMBLING.
I WON'T LEAVE THE FUTURE OF PARADIS TO FATE.
I WILL KEEP MOVING FORWARD.
WHA ...?!

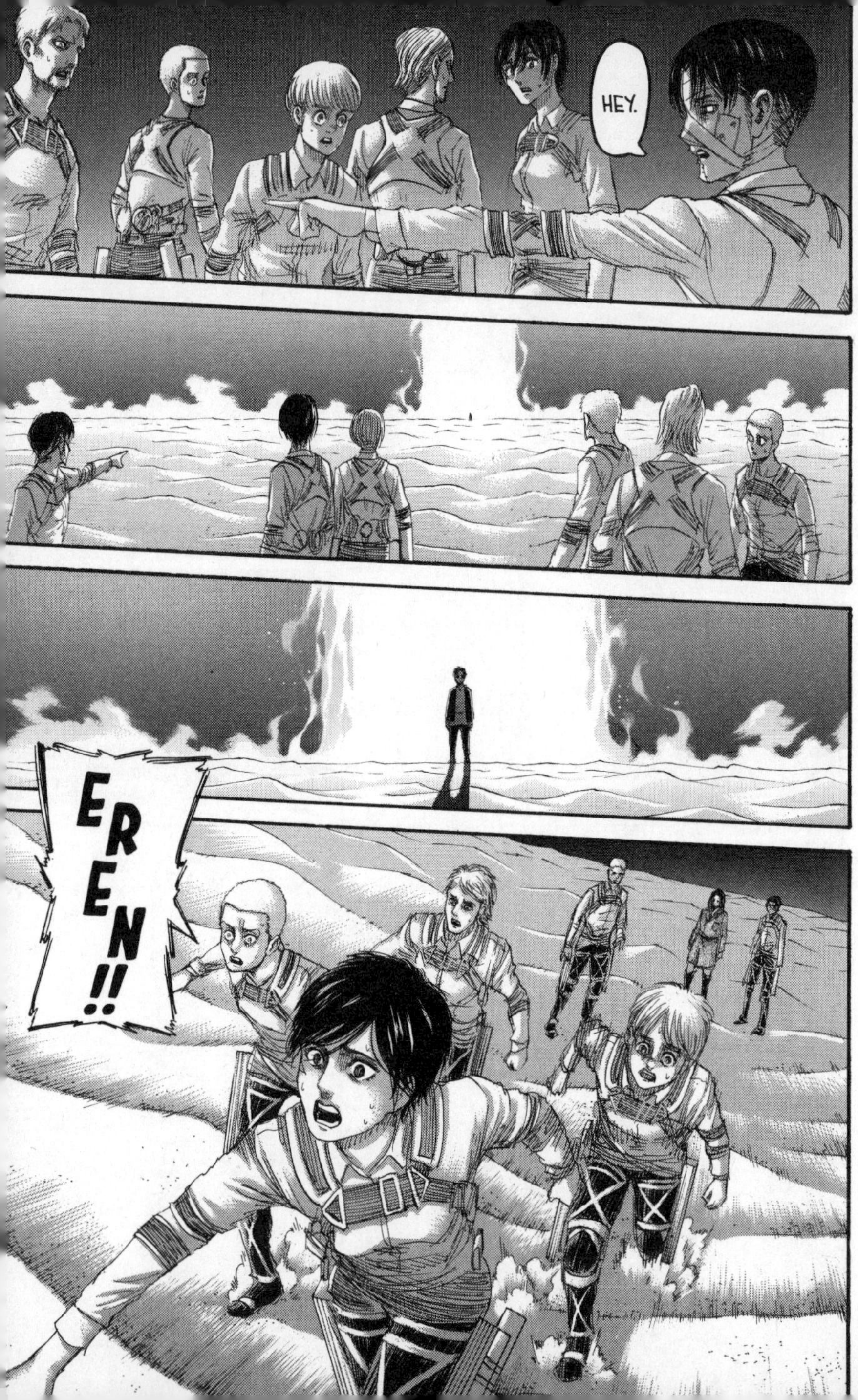
HEY.
EREN!!

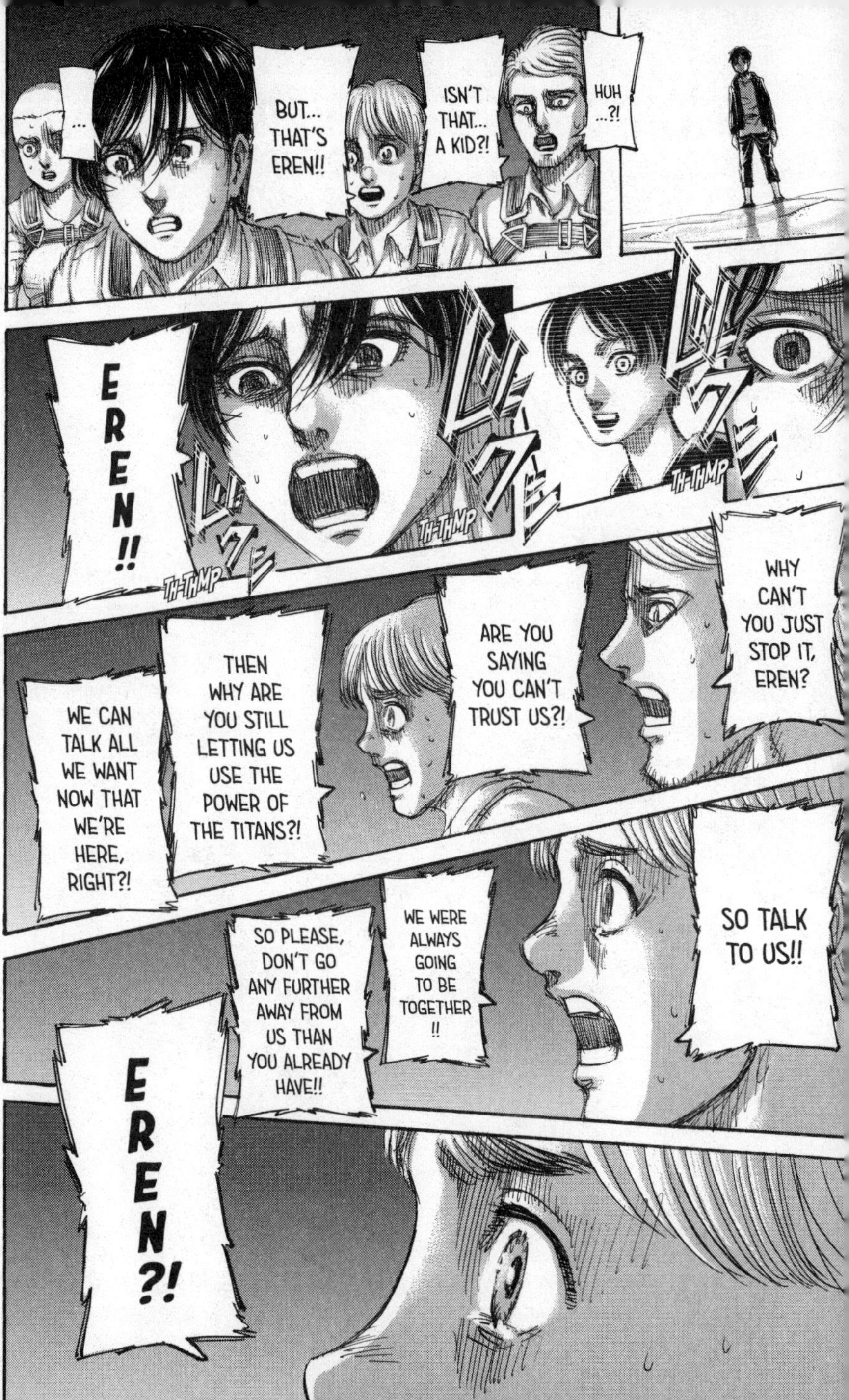
HUH ...?!
ISN'T THAT... A KID?!
BUT... THAT'S EREN!!
...
TH-THMP
TH-THMP
EREN!!
TH-THMP
WHY CAN'T YOU JUST STOP IT, EREN?
ARE YOU SAYING YOU CAN'T TRUST US?!
THEN WHY ARE YOU STILL LETTING US USE THE POWER OF THE TITANS?!
WE CAN TALK ALL WE WANT NOW THAT WE'RE HERE, RIGHT?!
SO TALK TO US!!
WE WERE ALWAYS GOING TO BE TOGETHER!!
SO PLEASE, DON'T GO ANY FURTHER AWAY FROM US THAN YOU ALREADY HAVE!!
EREN?!

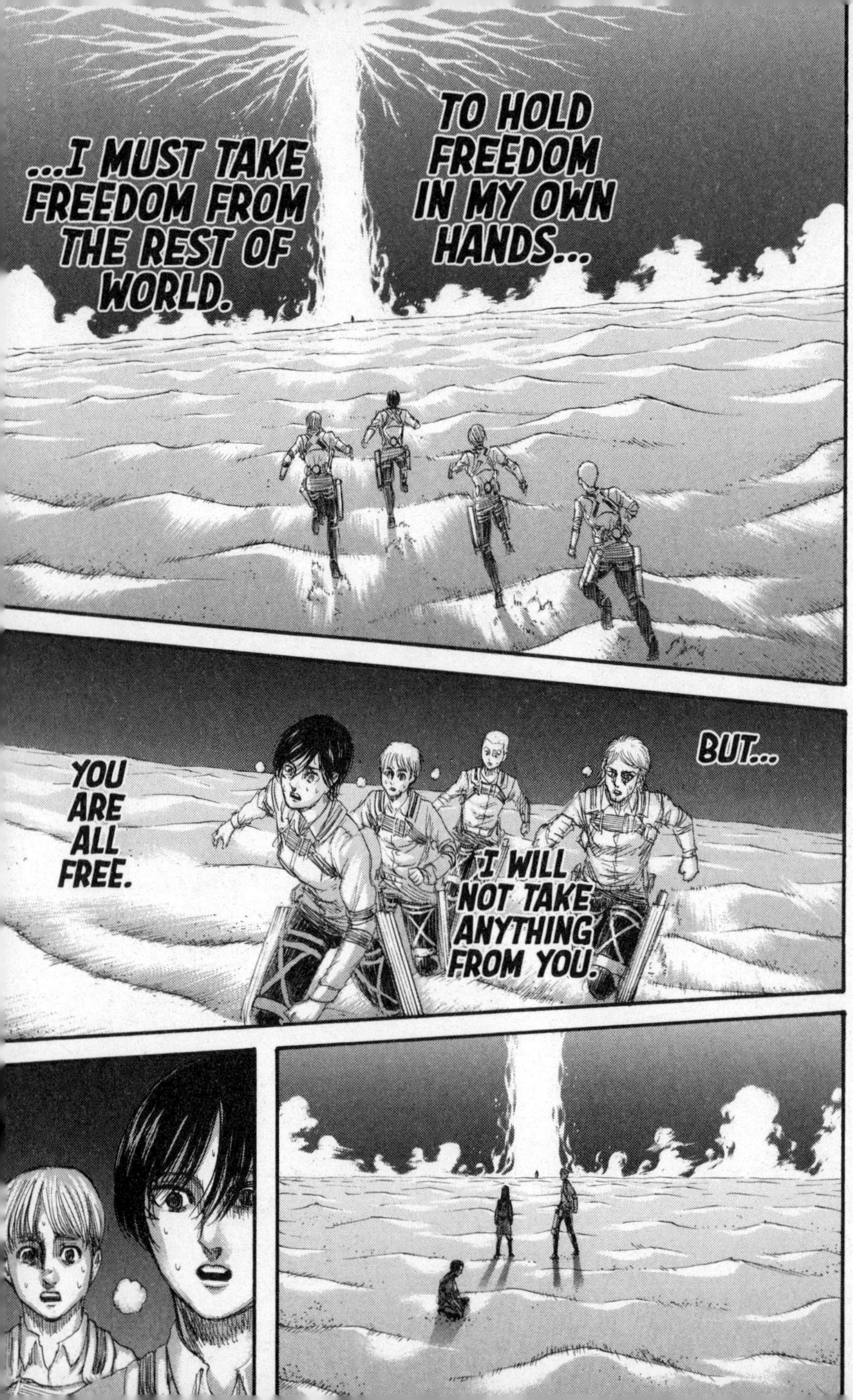
TO HOLD FREEDOM IN MY OWN HANDS...
...I MUST TAKE FREEDOM FROM THE REST OF WORLD.
BUT...
I WILL NOT TAKE ANYTHING FROM YOU.
YOU ARE ALL FREE.

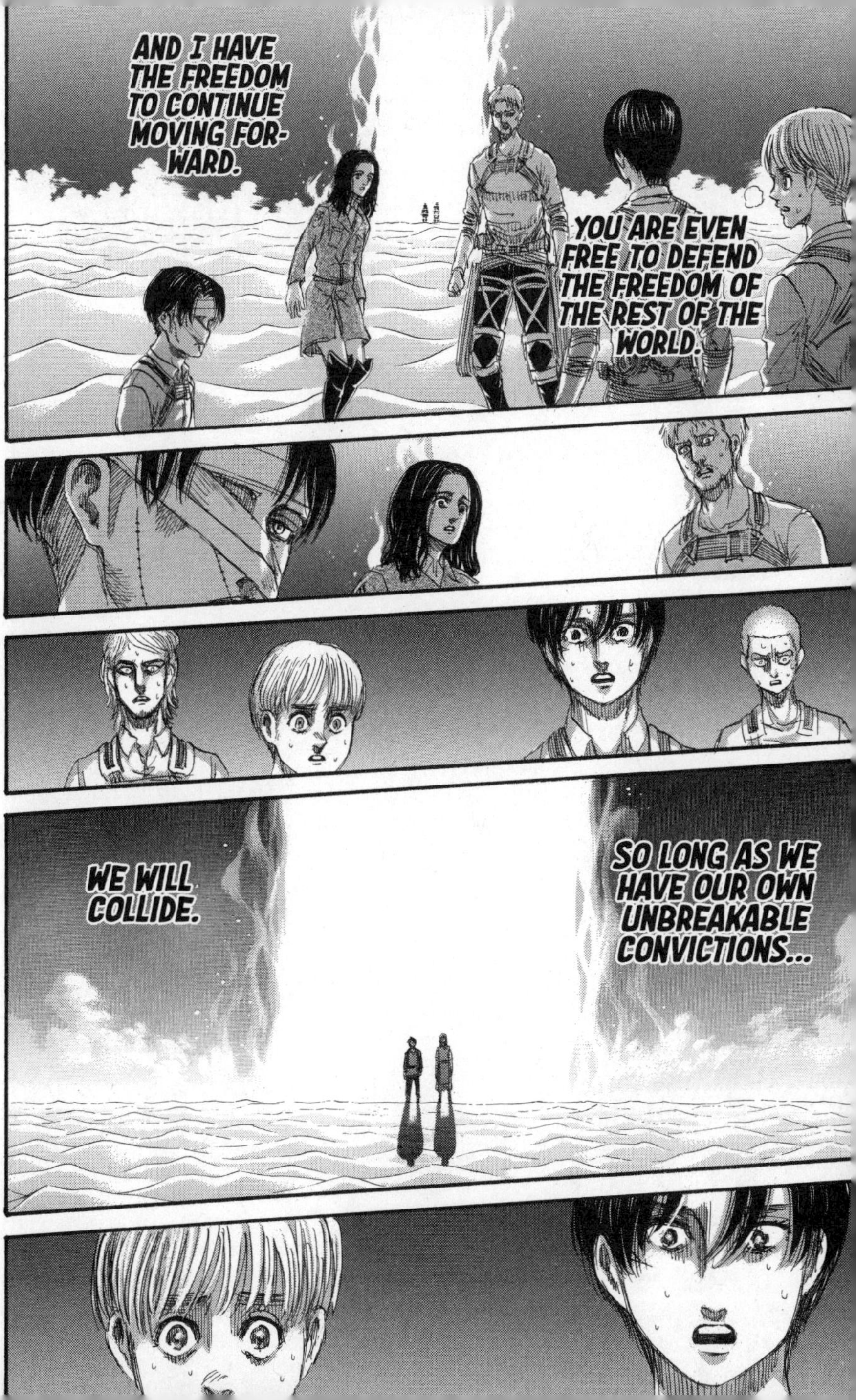
YOU ARE EVEN FREE TO DEFEND THE FREEDOM OF THE REST OF THE WORLD.
AND I HAVE THE FREEDOM TO CONTINUE MOVING FOR-WARD.
SO LONG AS WE HAVE OUR OWN UNBREAKABLE CONVICTIONS...
WE WILL COLLIDE.

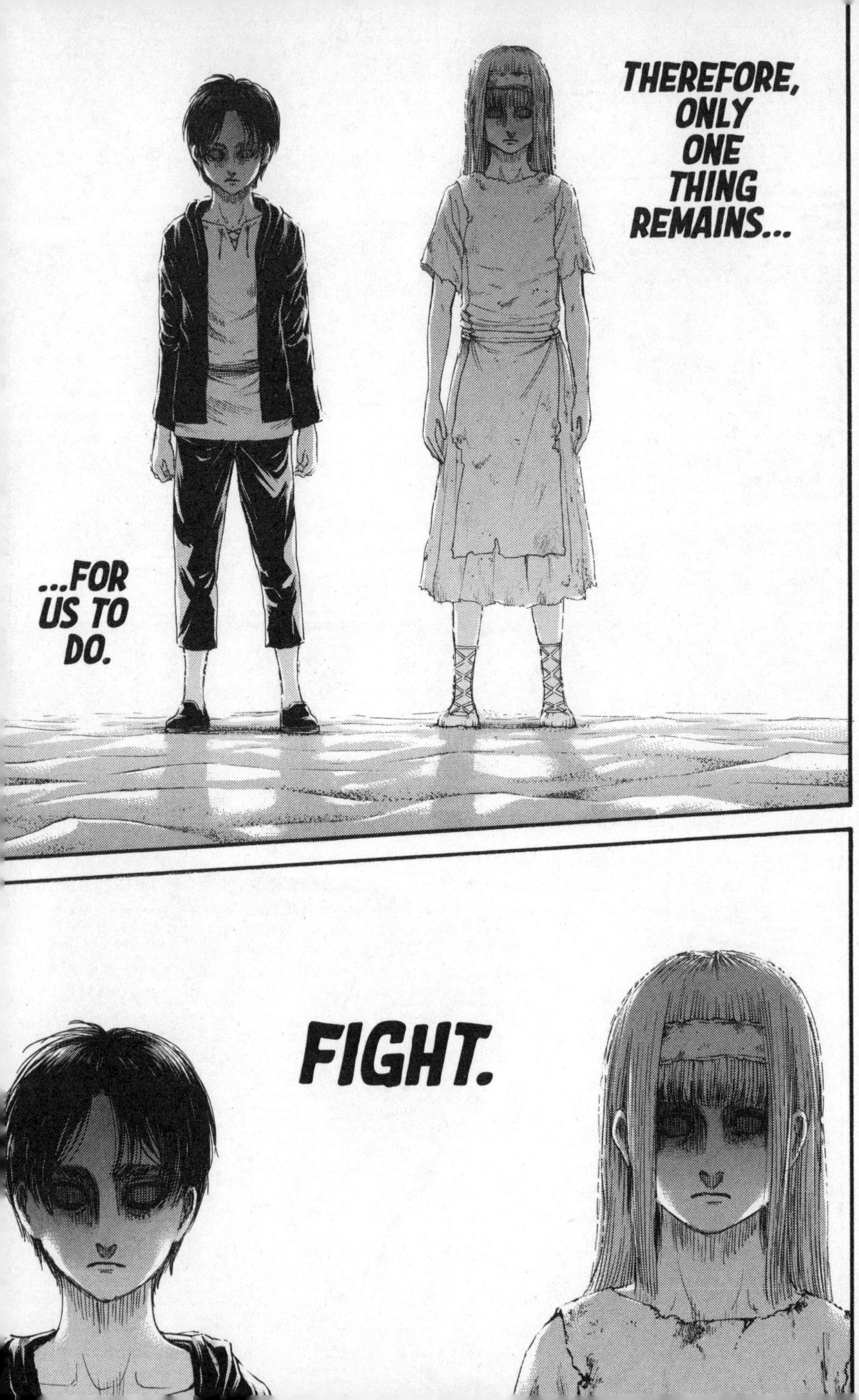
THEREFORE, ONLY ONE THING REMAINS...
...FOR US TO DO.
FIGHT.

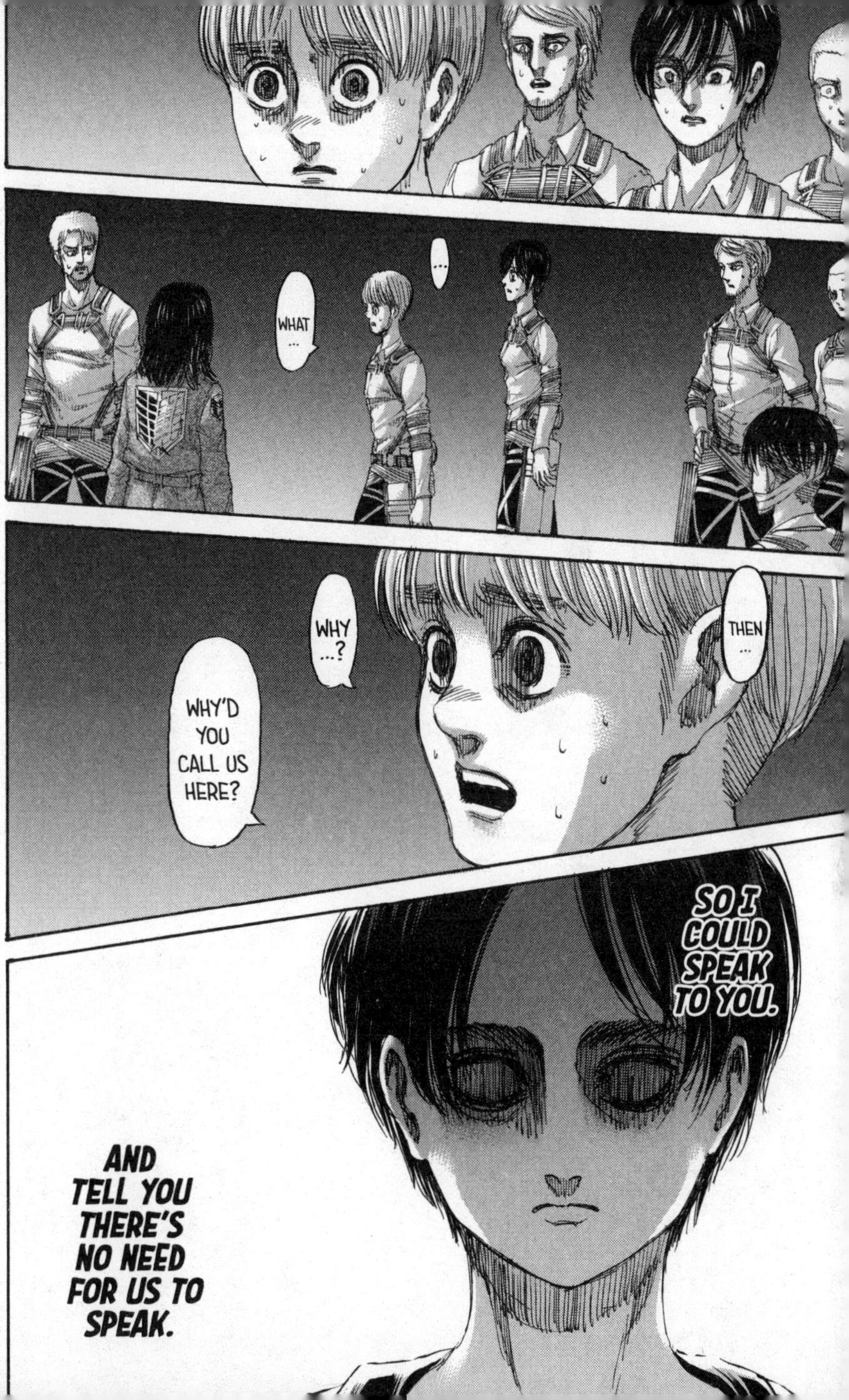
...
WHAT ...
THEN ...
WHY ...?
WHY'D YOU CALL US HERE?
SO I COULD SPEAK TO YOU.
AND TELL YOU THERE'S NO NEED FOR US TO SPEAK.

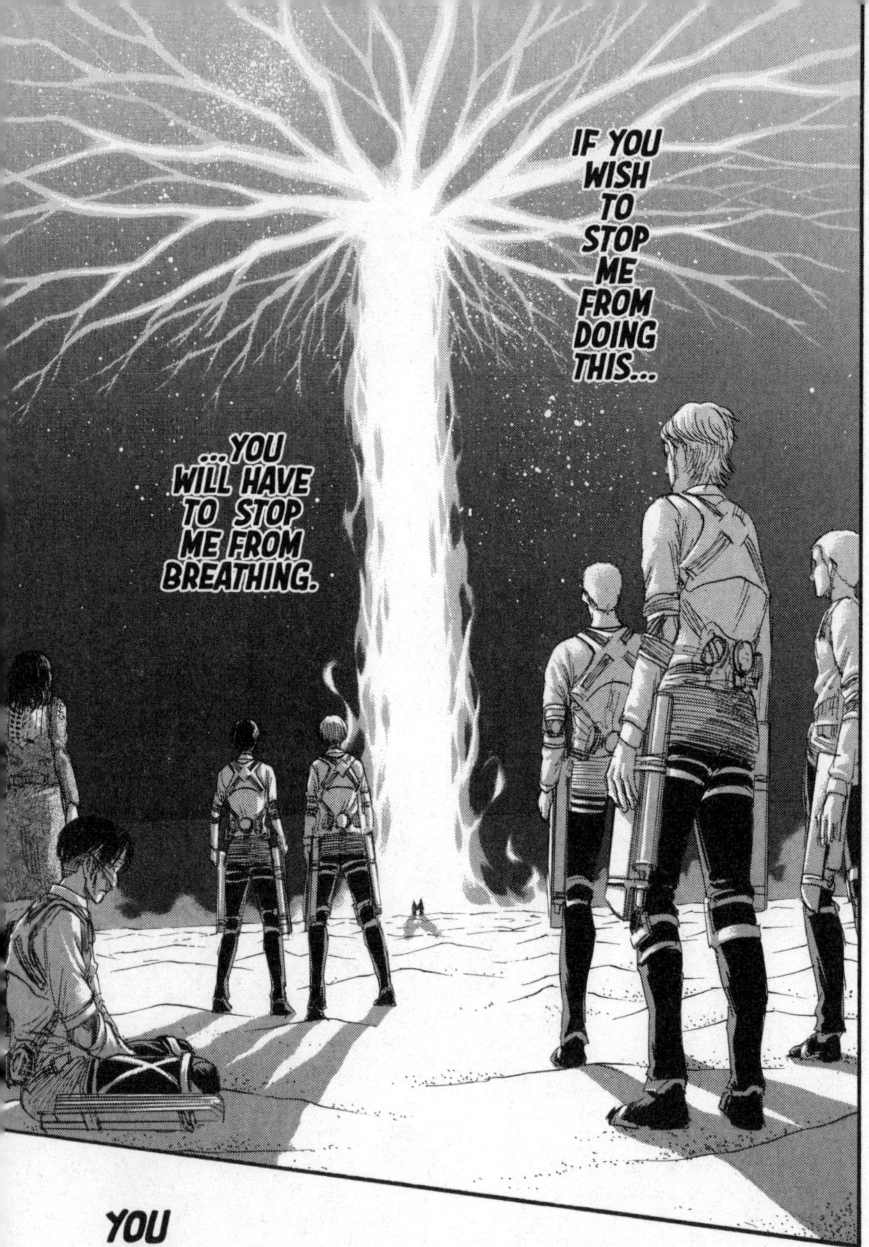
IF YOU WISH TO STOP ME FROM DOING THIS...
...YOU WILL HAVE TO STOP ME FROM BREATHING.

YOU ARE FREE TO TRY.

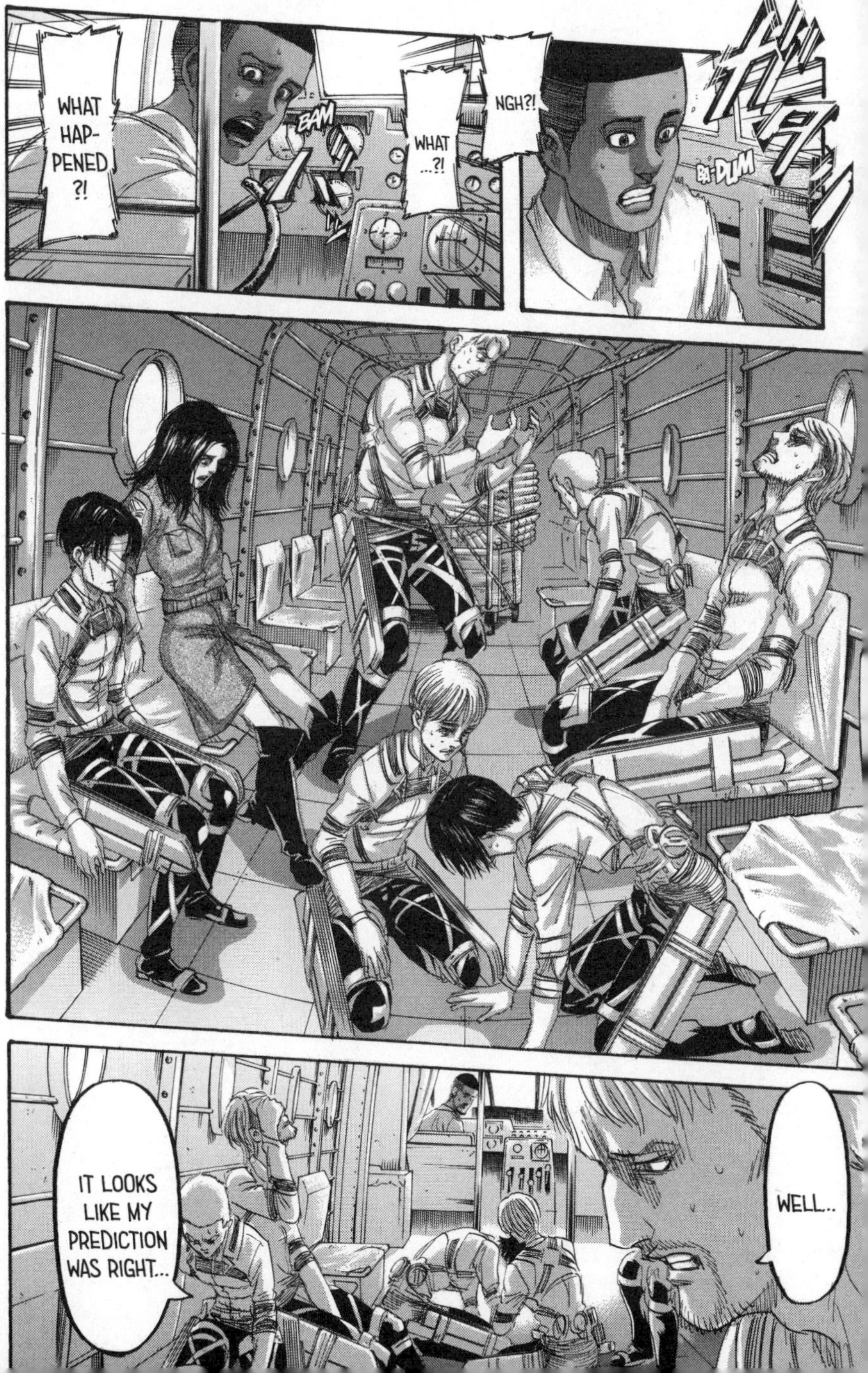
NGH?!
BA-DUM
WHAT ...?!
WHAT HAP-PENED ?!
BAM
WELL..
IT LOOKS LIKE MY PREDICTION WAS RIGHT...

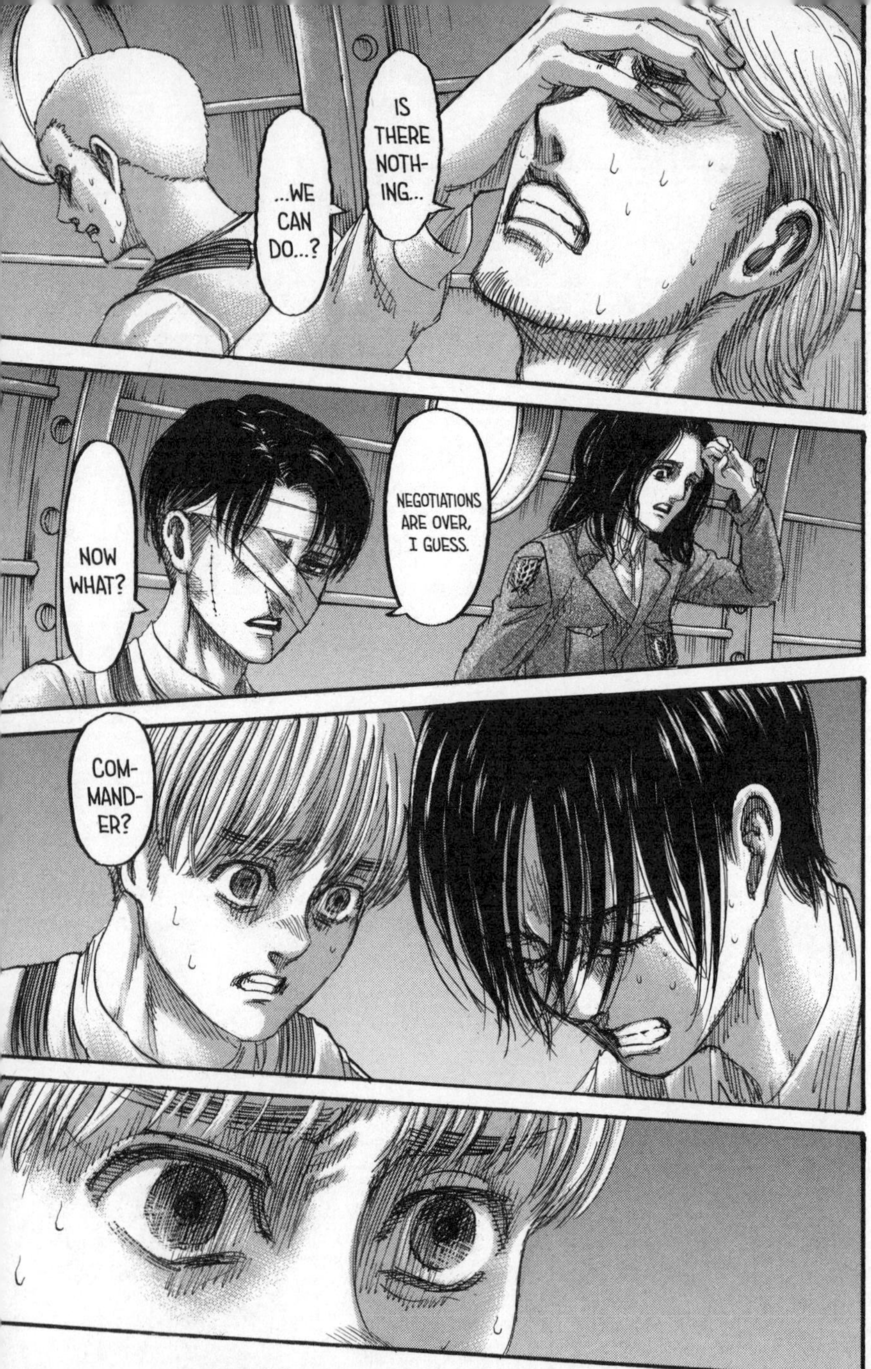
IS THERE NOTHING-ING...
...WE CAN DO...?
NEGOTIATIONS ARE OVER, I GUESS.
NOW WHAT?
COM-MAND-ER?

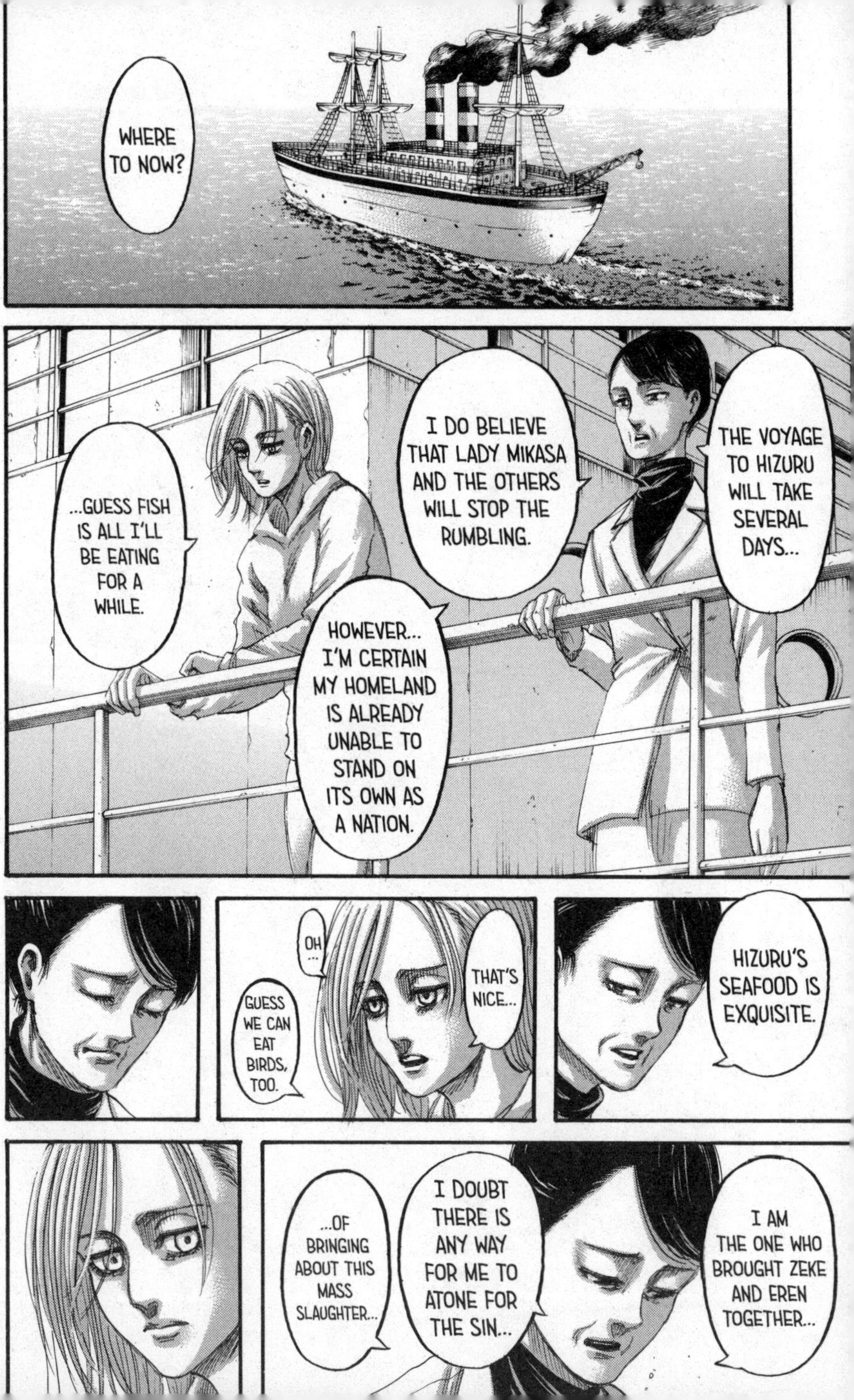
WHERE TO NOW?
THE VOYAGE TO HIZURU WILL TAKE SEVERAL DAYS...
I DO BELIEVE THAT LADY MIKASA AND THE OTHERS WILL STOP THE RUMBLING.
HOWEVER... I'M CERTAIN MY HOMELAND IS ALREADY UNABLE TO STAND ON ITS OWN AS A NATION.
...GUESS FISH IS ALL I'LL BE EATING FOR A WHILE.
HIZURU'S SEAFOOD IS EXQUISITE.
THAT'S NICE...
OH...
GUESS WE CAN EAT BIRDS, TOO.
I AM THE ONE WHO BROUGHT ZEKE AND EREN TOGETHER...
I DOUBT THERE IS ANY WAY FOR ME TO ATONE FOR THE SIN...
...OF BRINGING ABOUT THIS MASS SLAUGHTER...

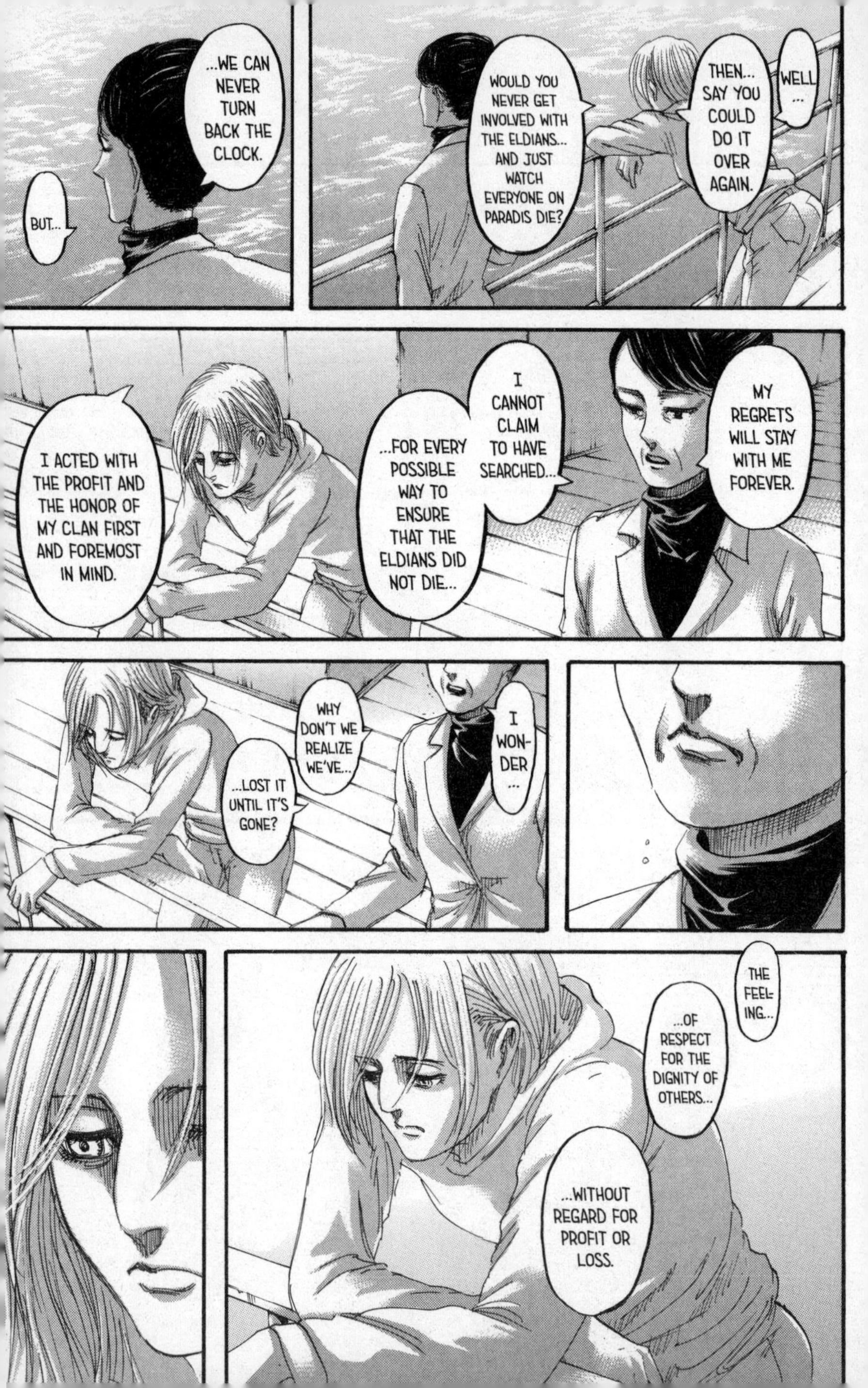
...WELL...
THEN... SAY YOU COULD DO IT OVER AGAIN.
WOULD YOU NEVER GET INVOLVED WITH THE ELDIANS... AND JUST WATCH EVERYONE ON PARADIS DIE?
...WE CAN NEVER TURN BACK THE CLOCK.
BUT...
MY REGRETS WILL STAY WITH ME FOREVER.
I CANNOT CLAIM TO HAVE SEARCHED...
...FOR EVERY POSSIBLE WAY TO ENSURE THAT THE ELDIANS DID NOT DIE...
I ACTED WITH THE PROFIT AND THE HONOR OF MY CLAN FIRST AND FOREMOST IN MIND.
I WONDER...
WHY DON'T WE REALIZE WE'VE...
...LOST IT UNTIL IT'S GONE?
THE FEELING...
...OF RESPECT FOR THE DIGNITY OF OTHERS...
...WITHOUT REGARD FOR PROFIT OR LOSS.

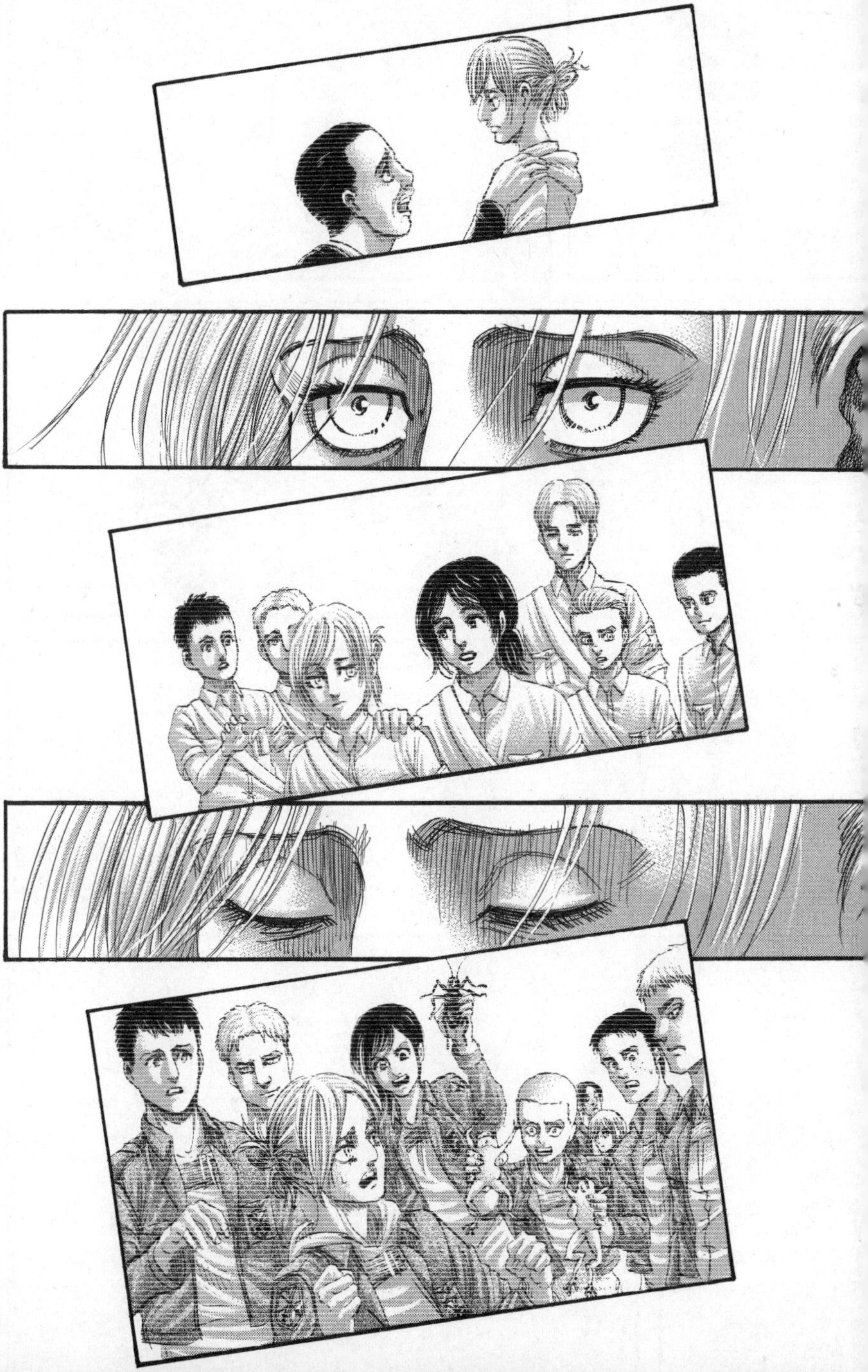

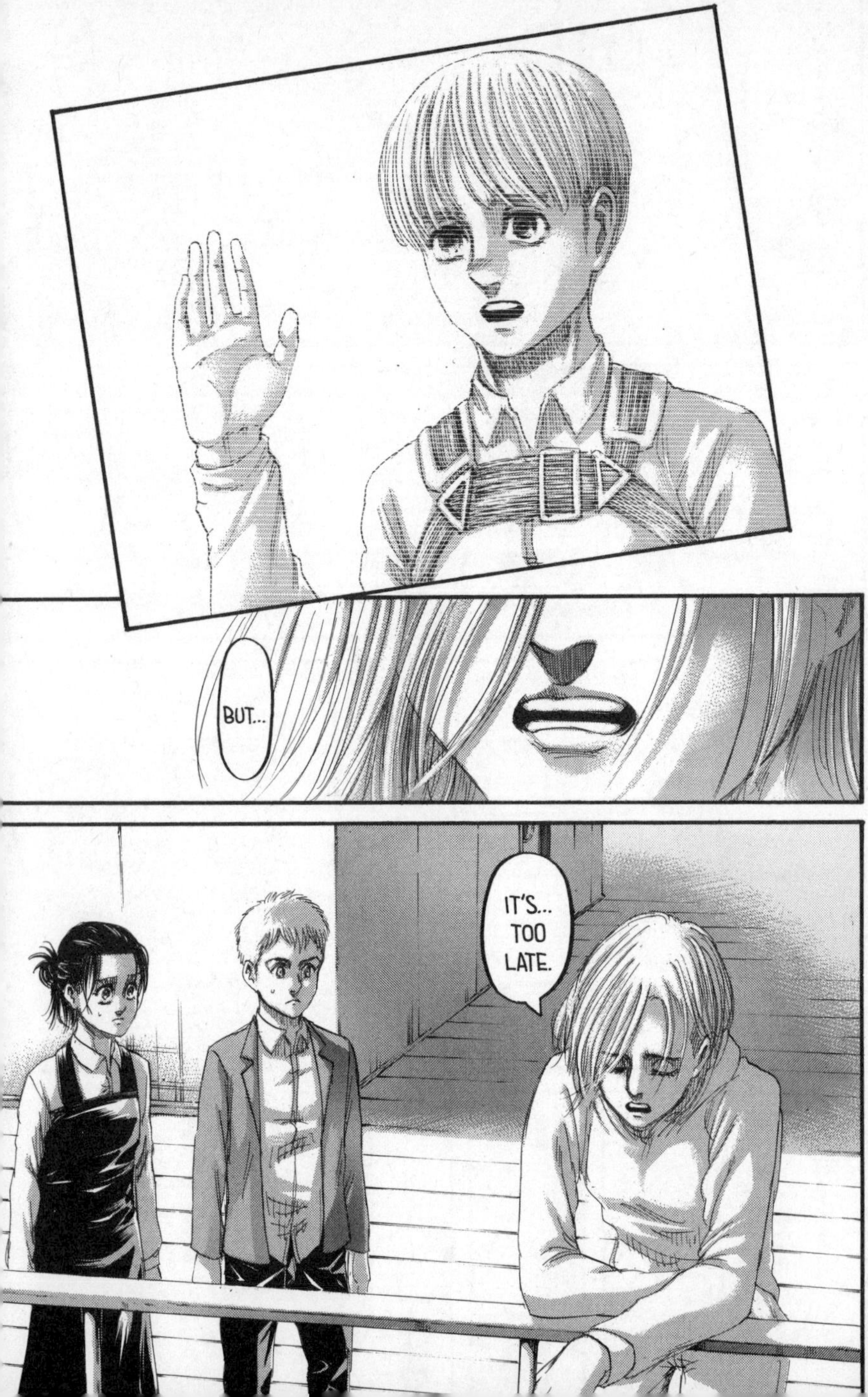
BUT...
IT'S... TOO LATE.

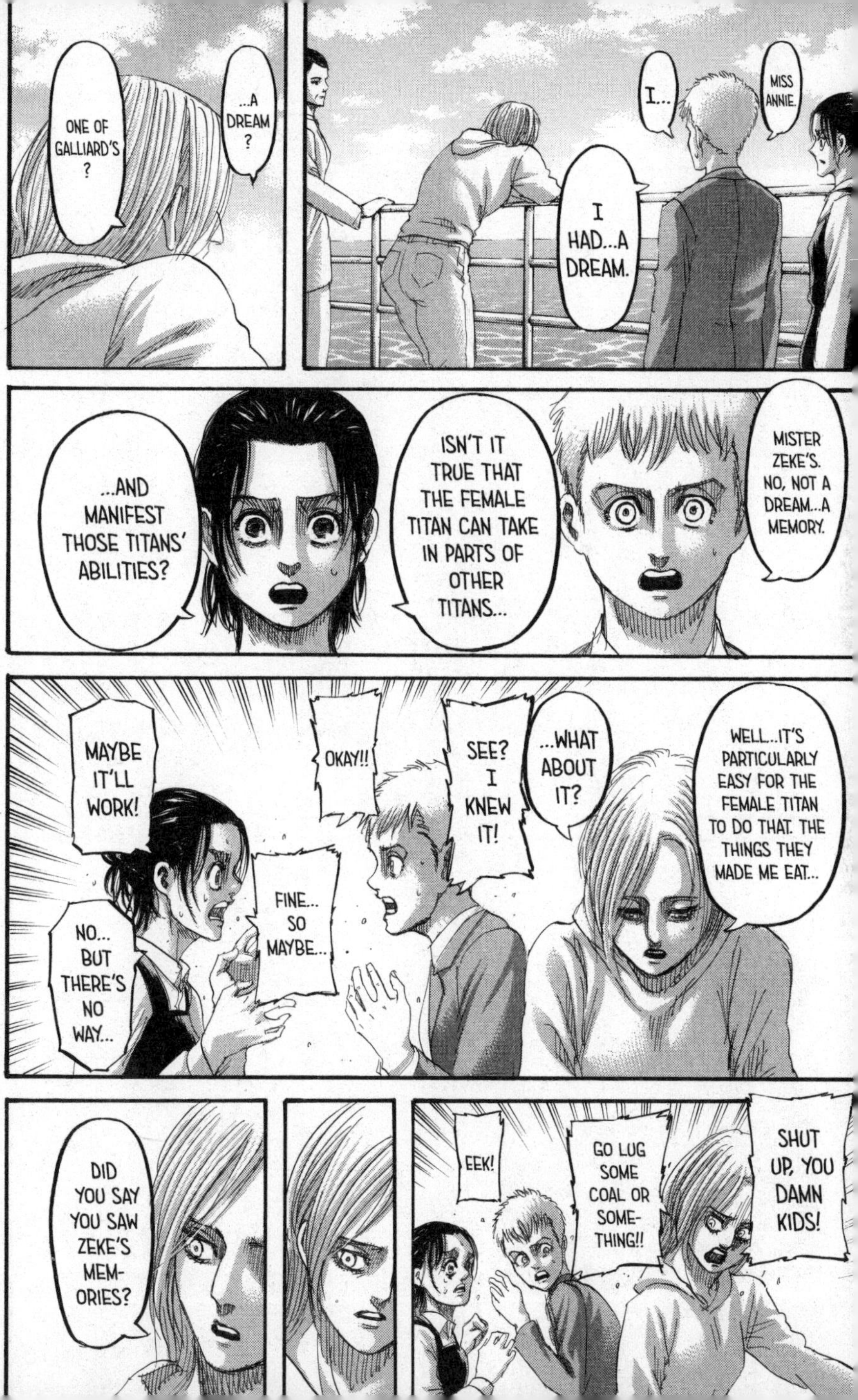
MISS ANNIE.
I...
I HAD...A DREAM.
...A DREAM?
ONE OF GALLIARD'S?
MISTER ZEKE'S. NO, NOT A DREAM...A MEMORY.
ISN'T IT TRUE THAT THE FEMALE TITAN CAN TAKE IN PARTS OF OTHER TITANS...
...AND MANIFEST THOSE TITANS' ABILITIES?
WELL...IT'S PARTICULARLY EASY FOR THE FEMALE TITAN TO DO THAT. THE THINGS THEY MADE ME EAT...
...WHAT ABOUT IT?
SEE? I KNEW IT!
OKAY!!
MAYBE IT'LL WORK!
FINE... SO MAYBE...
NO... BUT THERE'S NO WAY...
SHUT UP, YOU DAMN KIDS!
GO LUG SOME COAL OR SOME-THING!!
EEK!
DID YOU SAY YOU SAW ZEKE'S MEM-ORIES?

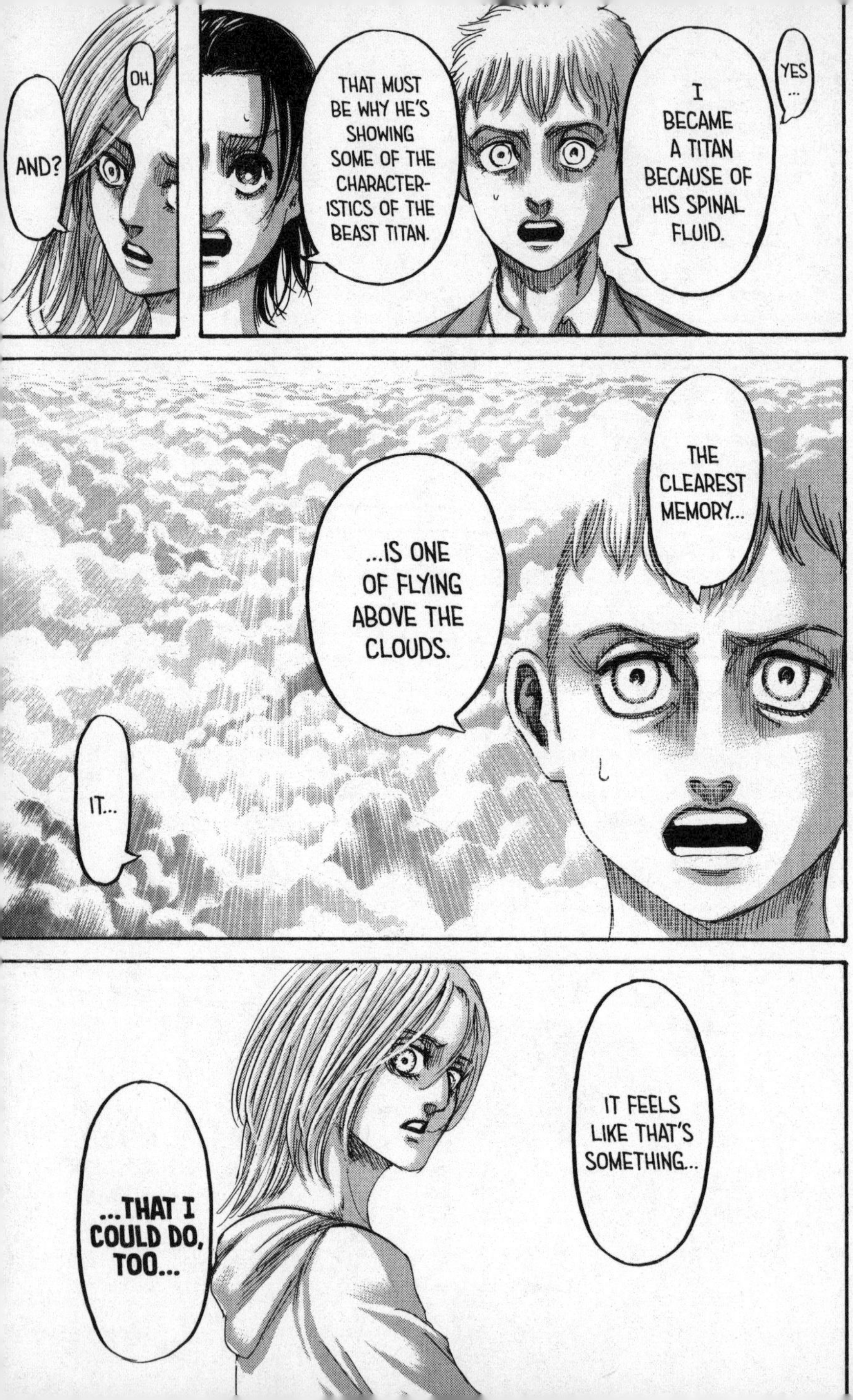
YES...
I BECAME A TITAN BECAUSE OF HIS SPINAL FLUID.
THAT MUST BE WHY HE'S SHOWING SOME OF THE CHARACTER-ISTICS OF THE BEAST TITAN.
OH.
AND?
THE CLEAREST MEMORY...
...IS ONE OF FLYING ABOVE THE CLOUDS.
IT...
IT FEELS LIKE THAT'S SOMETHING...
...THAT I COULD DO, TOO...

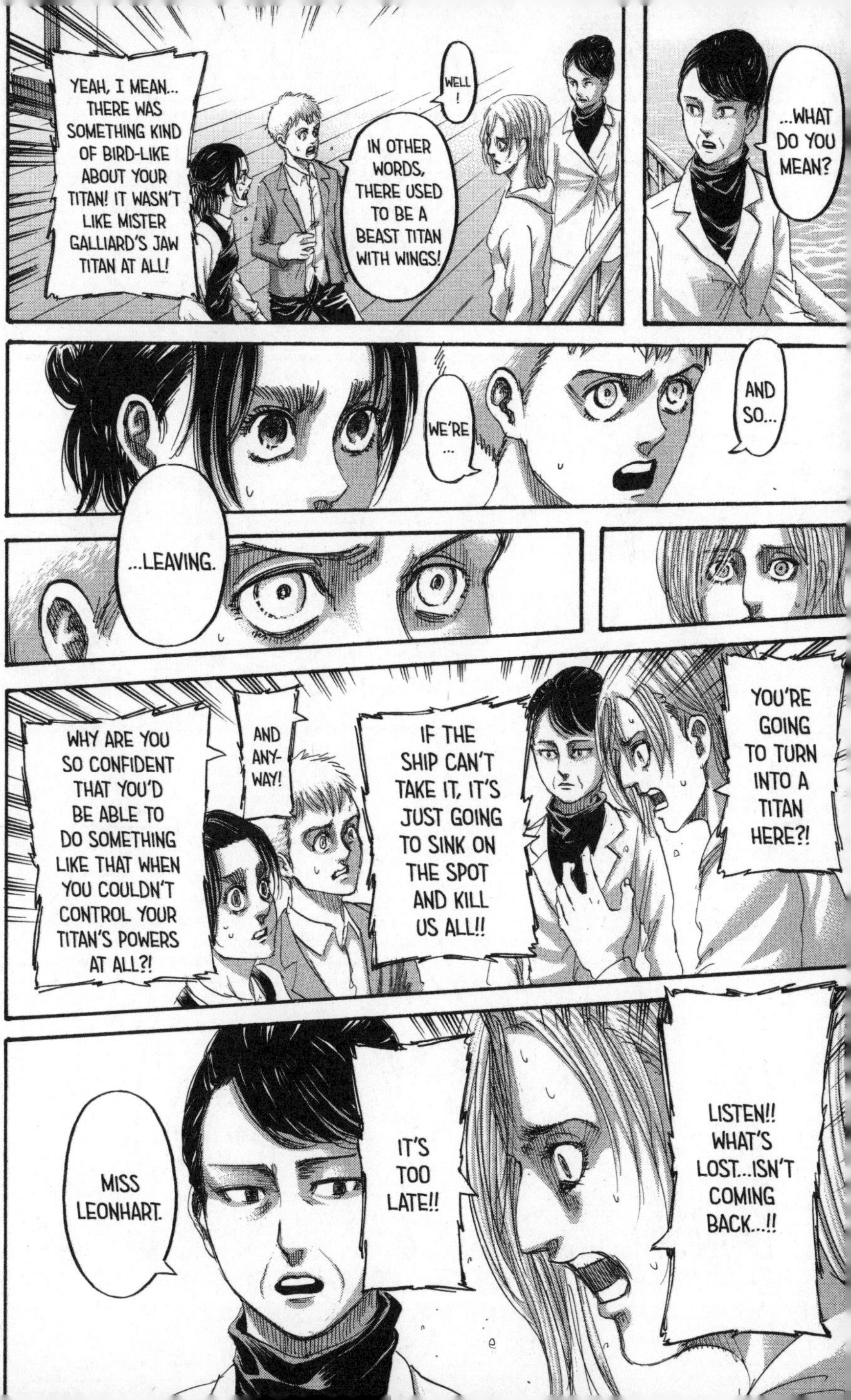
...WHAT DO YOU MEAN?
WELL!
IN OTHER WORDS, THERE USED TO BE A BEAST TITAN WITH WINGS!
YEAH, I MEAN... THERE WAS SOMETHING KIND OF BIRD-LIKE ABOUT YOUR TITAN! IT WASN'T LIKE MISTER GALLIARD'S JAW TITAN AT ALL!
AND SO...
WE'RE ...
...LEAVING.
YOU'RE GOING TO TURN INTO A TITAN HERE?!
IF THE SHIP CAN'T TAKE IT, IT'S JUST GOING TO SINK ON THE SPOT AND KILL US ALL!!
AND ANY-WAY!
WHY ARE YOU SO CONFIDENT THAT YOU'D BE ABLE TO DO SOMETHING LIKE THAT WHEN YOU COULDN'T CONTROL YOUR TITAN'S POWERS AT ALL?!
LISTEN!! WHAT'S LOST...ISN'T COMING BACK...!!
IT'S TOO LATE!!
MISS LEONHART.

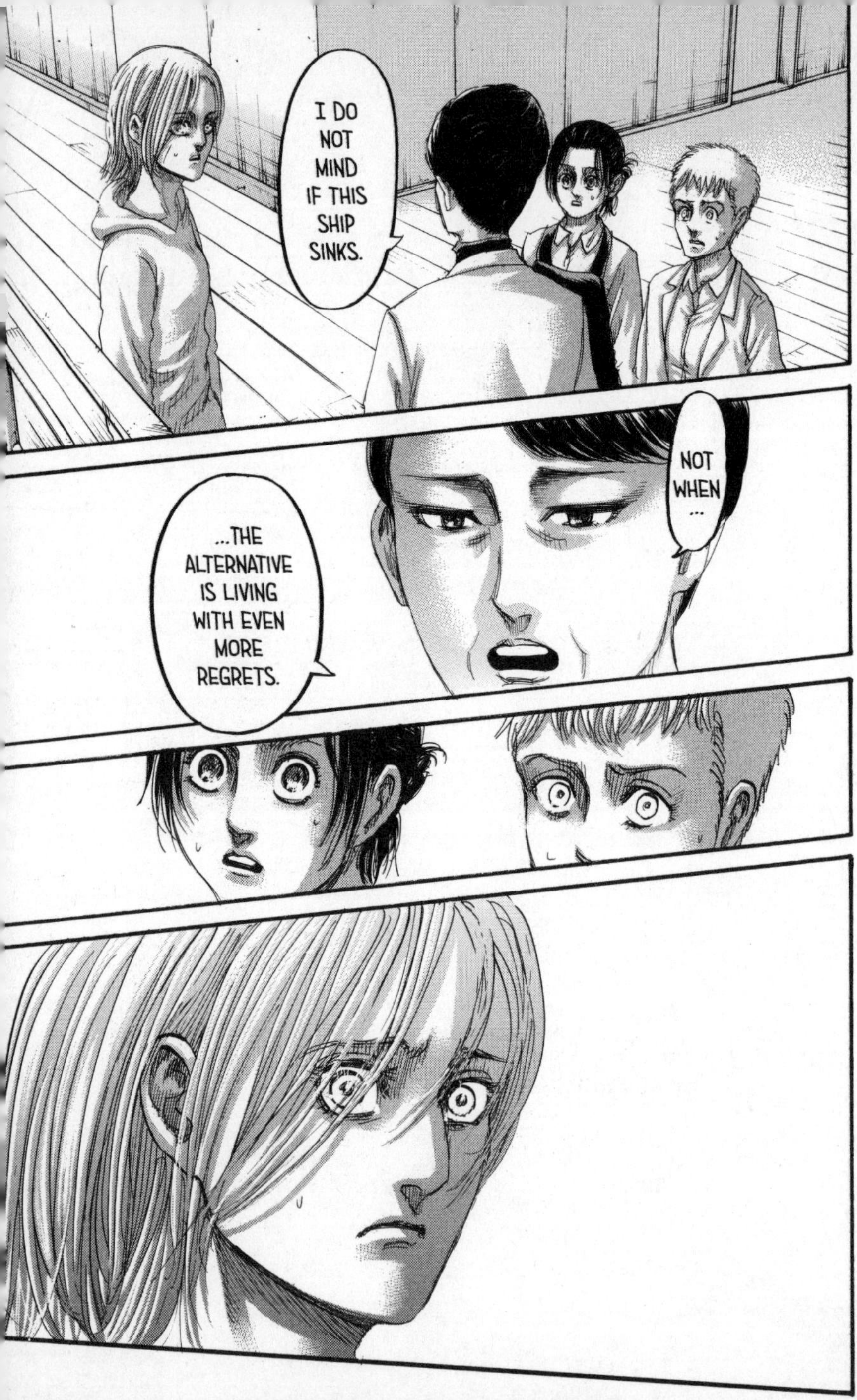
I DO NOT MIND IF THIS SHIP SINKS.
NOT WHEN ...
...THE ALTERNATIVE IS LIVING WITH EVEN MORE REGRETS.

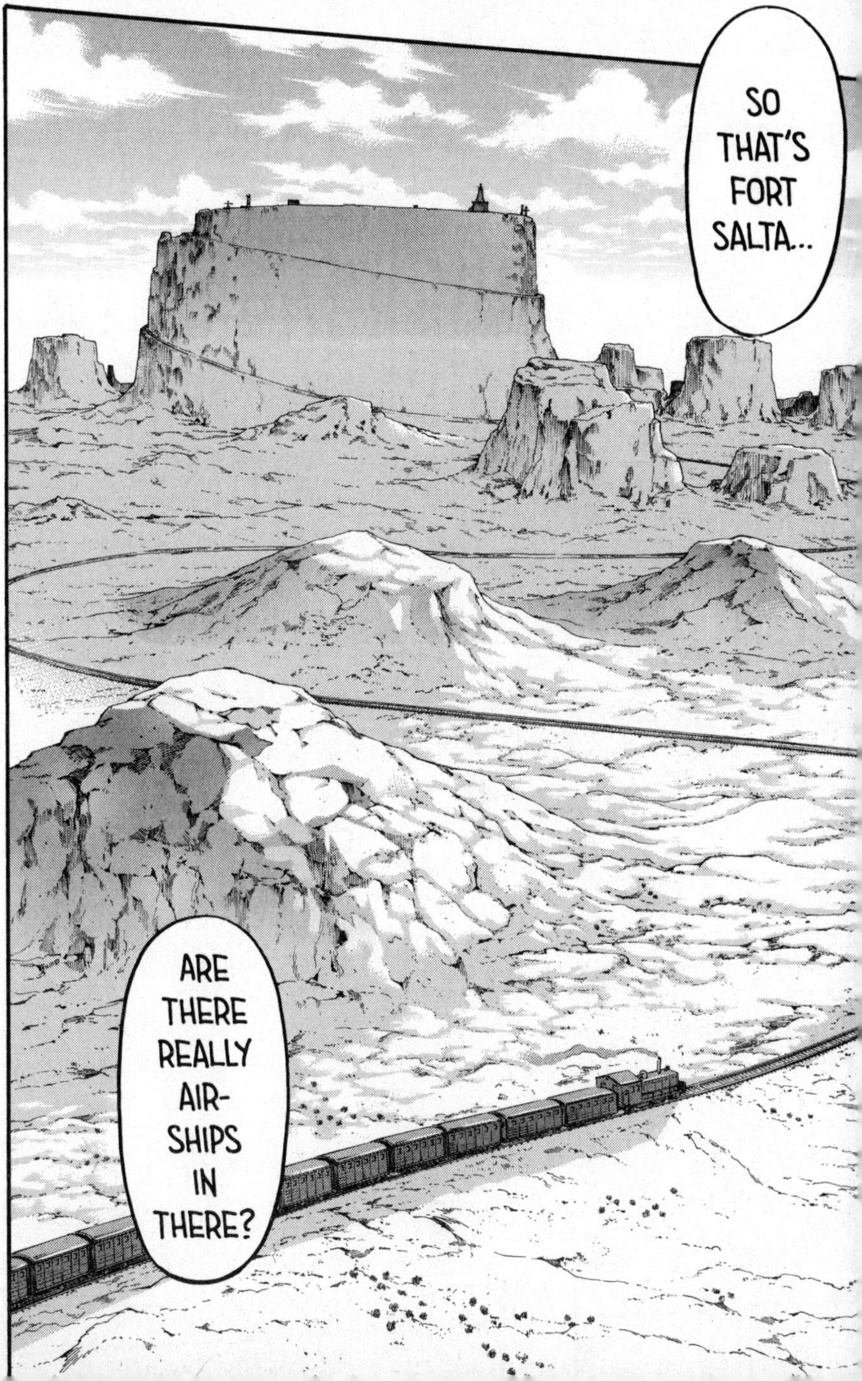
SO THAT'S FORT SALTA...
ARE THERE REALLY AIR-SHIPS IN THERE?

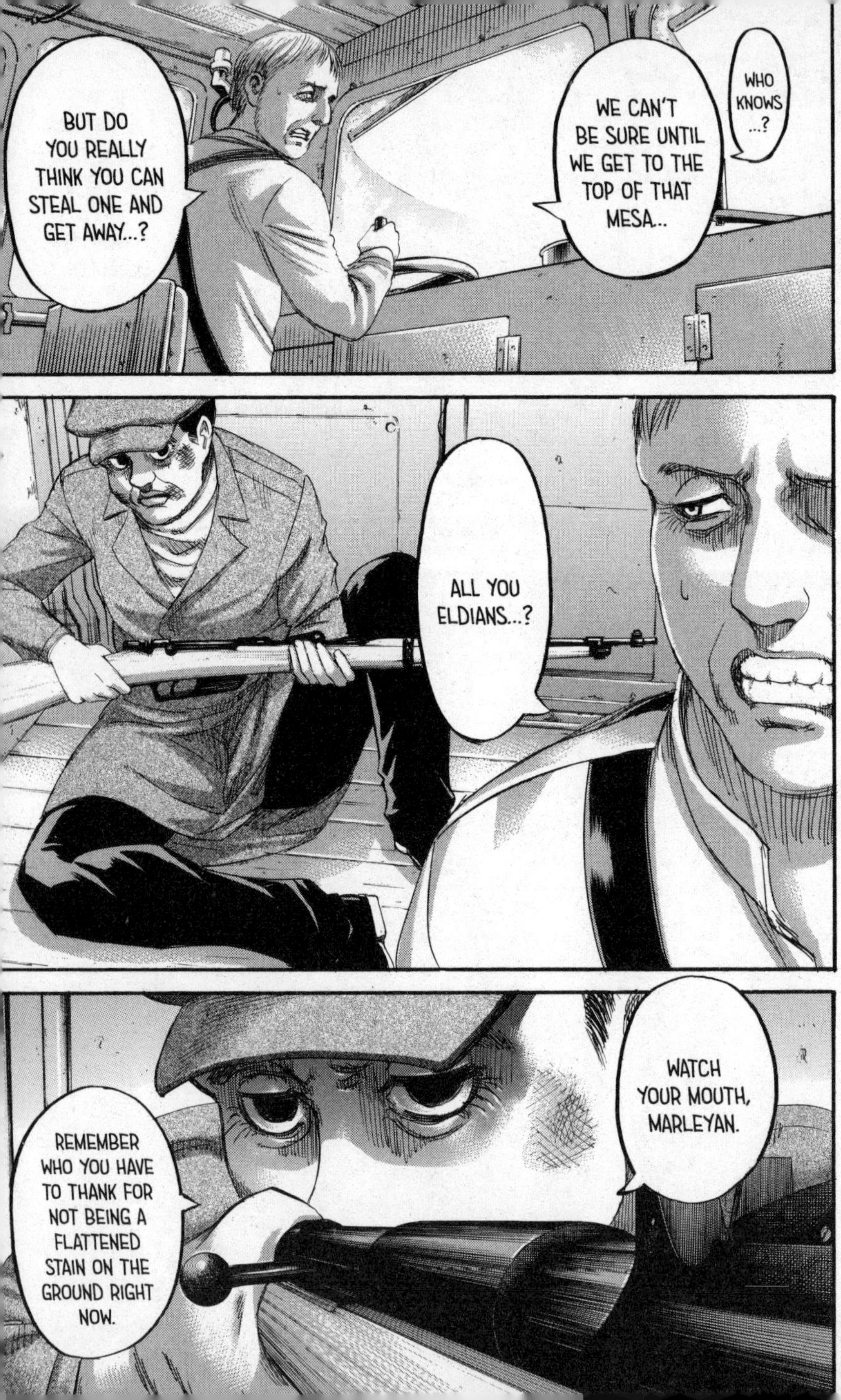
WHO KNOWS ...?
WE CAN'T BE SURE UNTIL WE GET TO THE TOP OF THAT MESA...
BUT DO YOU REALLY THINK YOU CAN STEAL ONE AND GET AWAY...?
ALL YOU ELDIANS...?
WATCH YOUR MOUTH, MARLEYAN.
REMEMBER WHO YOU HAVE TO THANK FOR NOT BEING A FLATTENED STAIN ON THE GROUND RIGHT NOW.

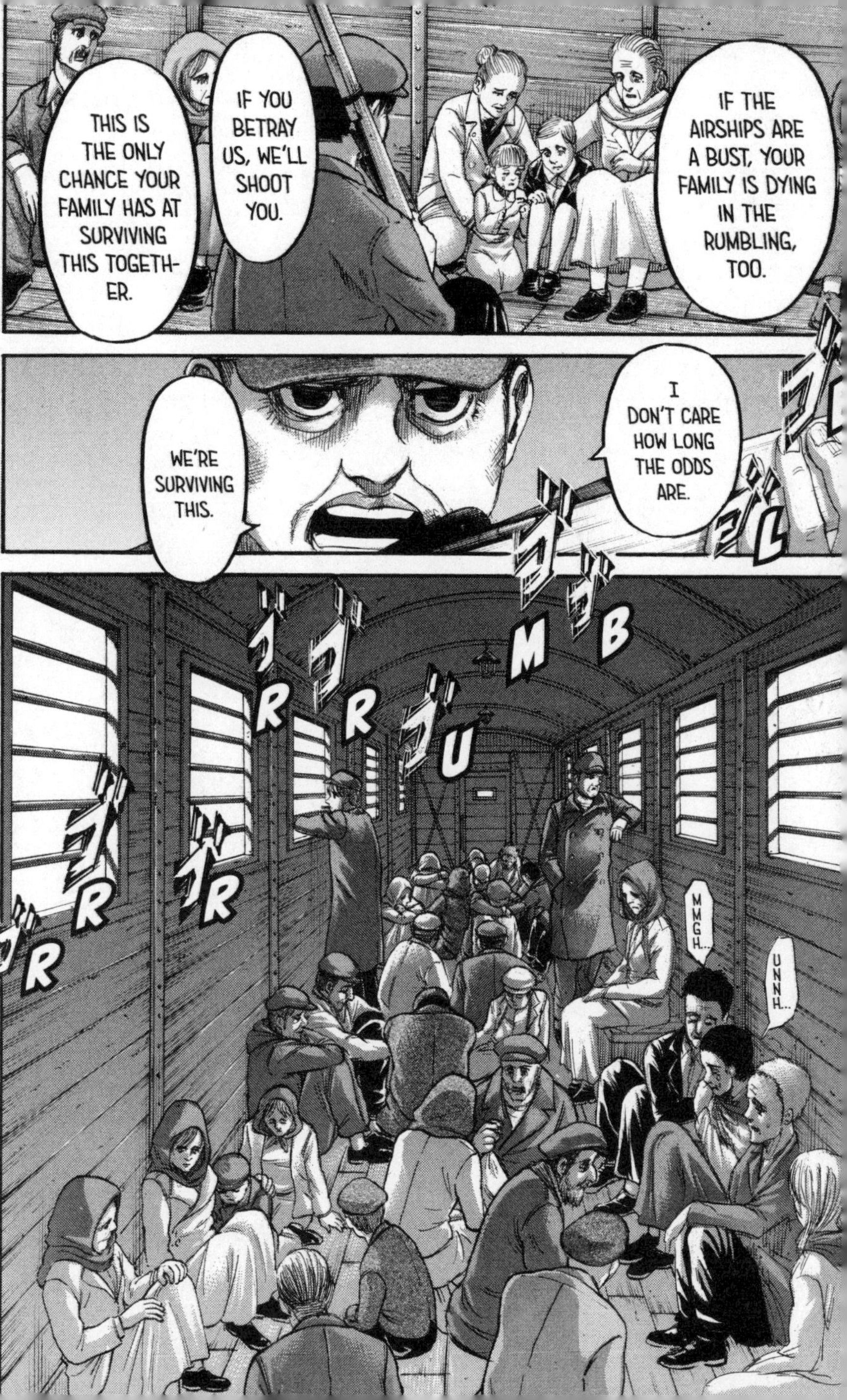
IF THE AIRSHIPS ARE A BUST, YOUR FAMILY IS DYING IN THE RUMBLING, TOO.
IF YOU BETRAY US, WE'LL SHOOT YOU.
THIS IS THE ONLY CHANCE YOUR FAMILY HAS AT SURVIVING THIS TOGETH-ER.
I DON'T CARE HOW LONG THE ODDS ARE.
WE'RE SURVIVING THIS.
RRUMBL
RRRR
UNNH...
MMGH...

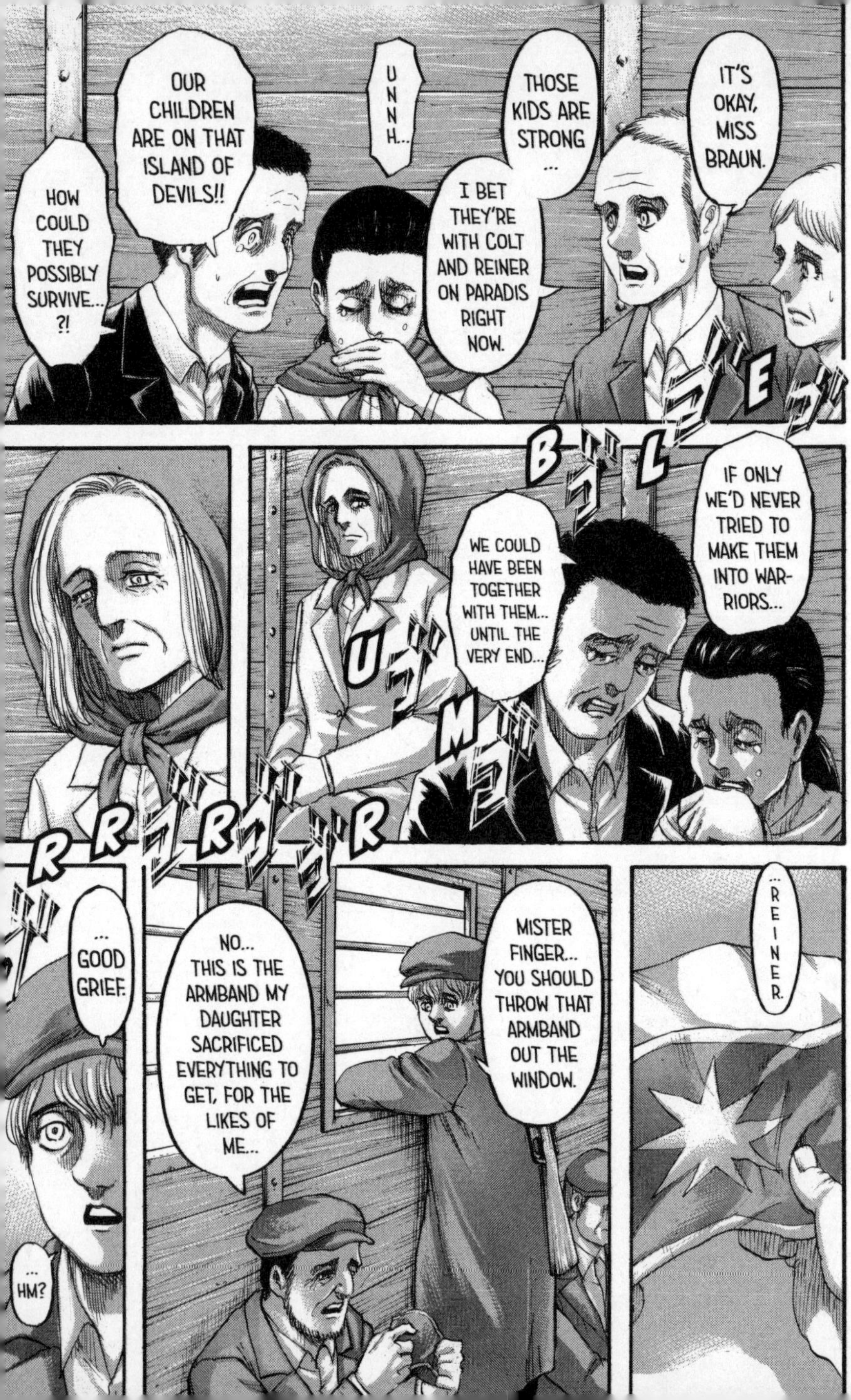
IT'S OKAY, MISS BRAUN.
THOSE KIDS ARE STRONG...
I BET THEY'RE WITH COLT AND REINER ON PARADIS RIGHT NOW.
UNNH...
OUR CHILDREN ARE ON THAT ISLAND OF DEVILS!!
HOW COULD THEY POSSIBLY SURVIVE...?!
IF ONLY WE'D NEVER TRIED TO MAKE THEM INTO WAR-RIORS...
WE COULD HAVE BEEN TOGETHER WITH THEM... UNTIL THE VERY END...
RRRRUMBLE
...REINER.
MISTER FINGER... YOU SHOULD THROW THAT ARMBAND OUT THE WINDOW.
NO... THIS IS THE ARMBAND MY DAUGHTER SACRIFICED EVERYTHING TO GET, FOR THE LIKES OF ME...
...GOOD GRIEF.
...HM?

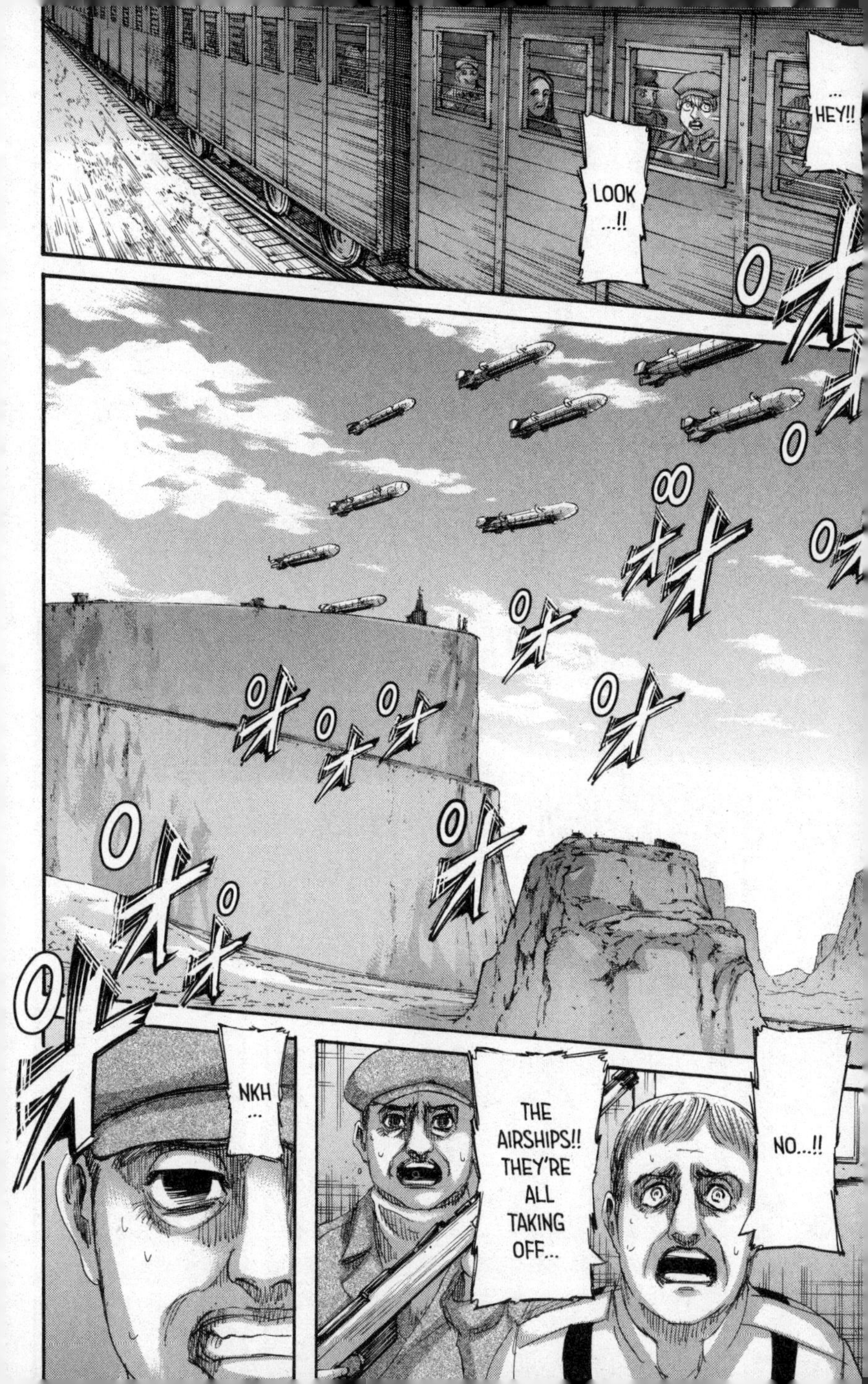
... HEY!!
LOOK ...!!
NO...!!
THE AIRSHIPS!! THEY'RE ALL TAKING OFF...
NKH ...

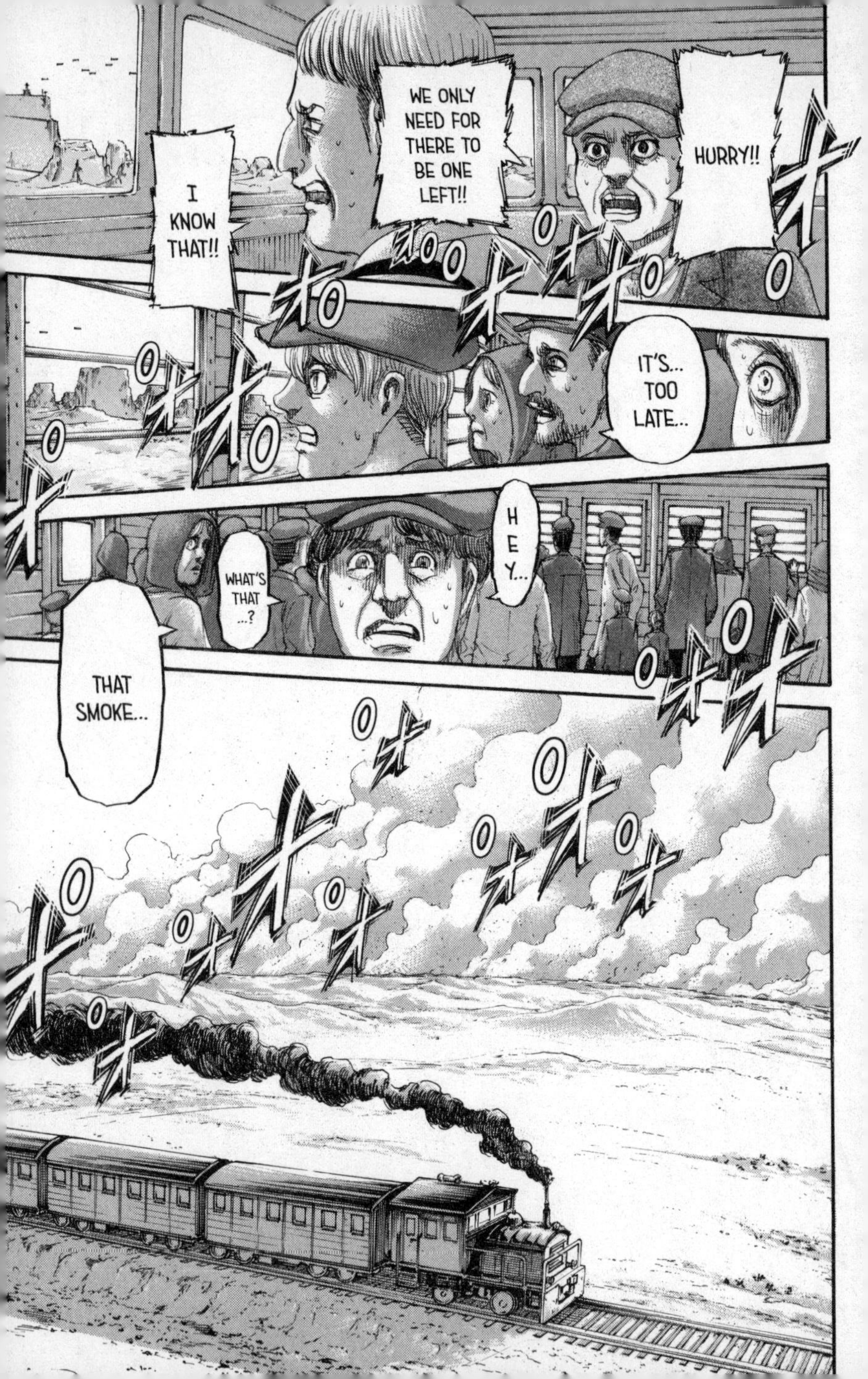
HURRY!!
WE ONLY NEED FOR THERE TO BE ONE LEFT!!
I KNOW THAT!!
IT'S... TOO LATE...
HEY...
WHAT'S THAT ...?
THAT SMOKE...

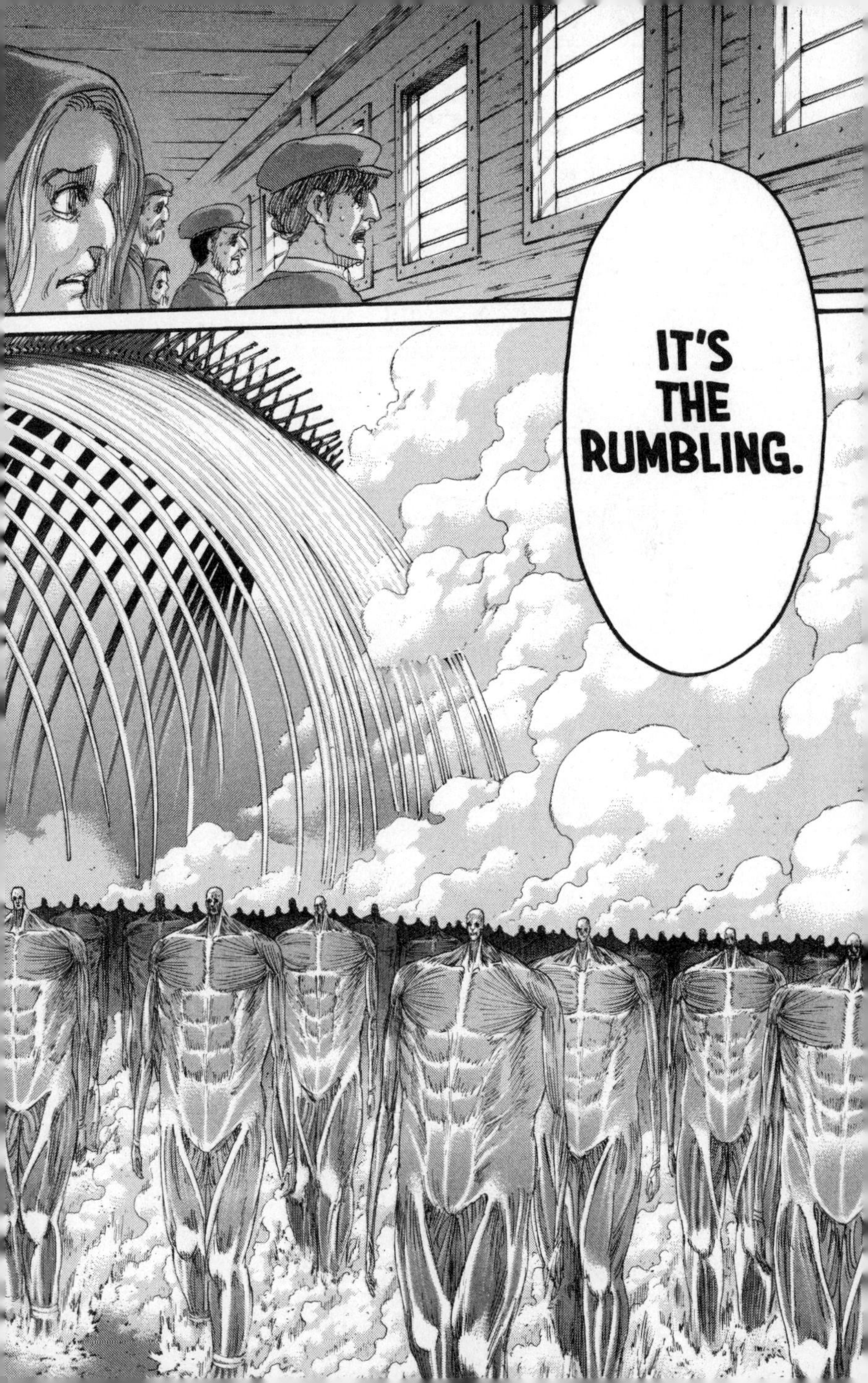
IT'S THE RUMBLING.

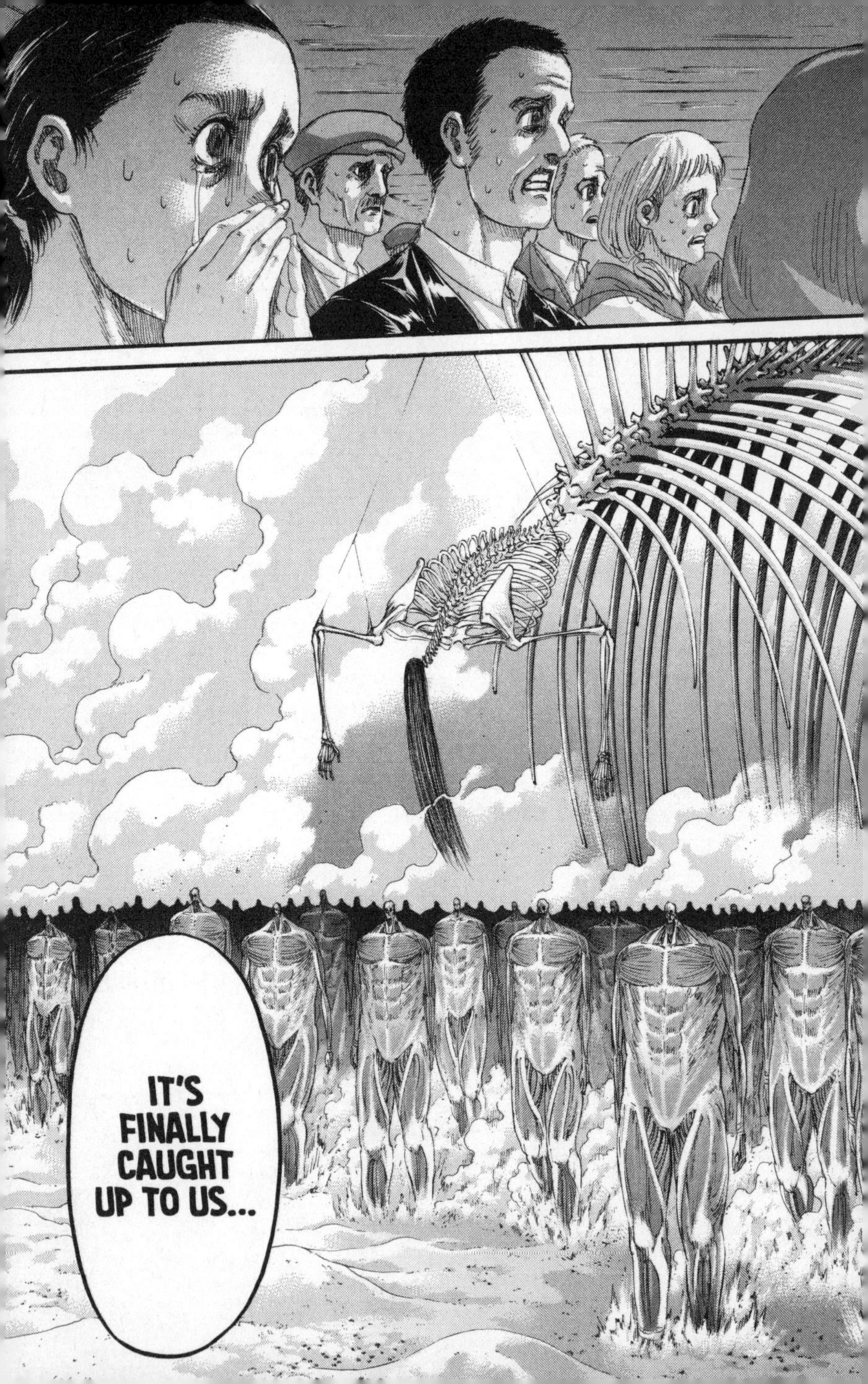
IT'S FINALLY CAUGHT UP TO US...

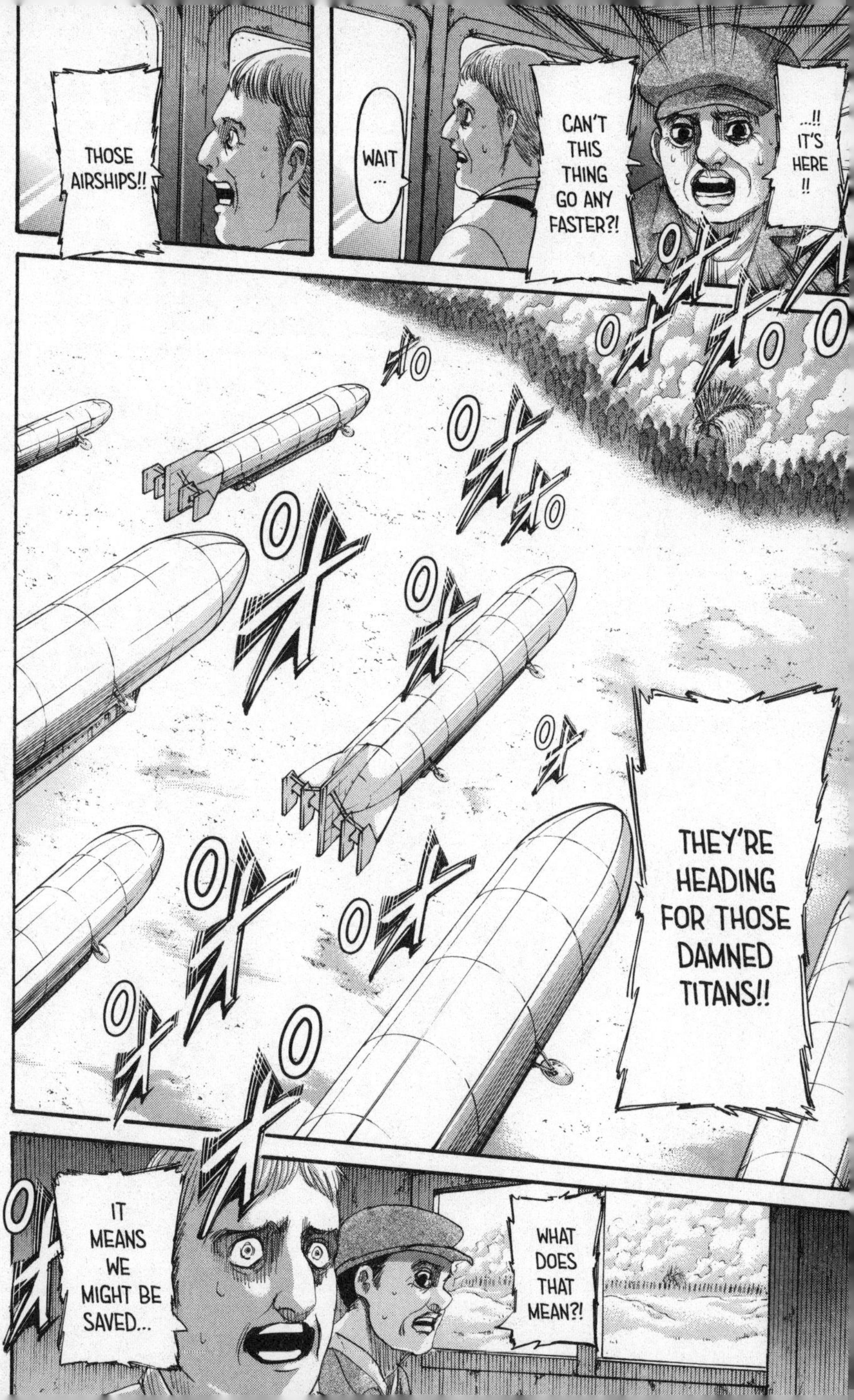
...!! IT'S HERE !!
CAN'T THIS THING GO ANY FASTER?!
WAIT ...
THOSE AIRSHIPS!!
THEY'RE HEADING FOR THOSE DAMNED TITANS!!
WHAT DOES THAT MEAN?!
IT MEANS WE MIGHT BE SAVED...

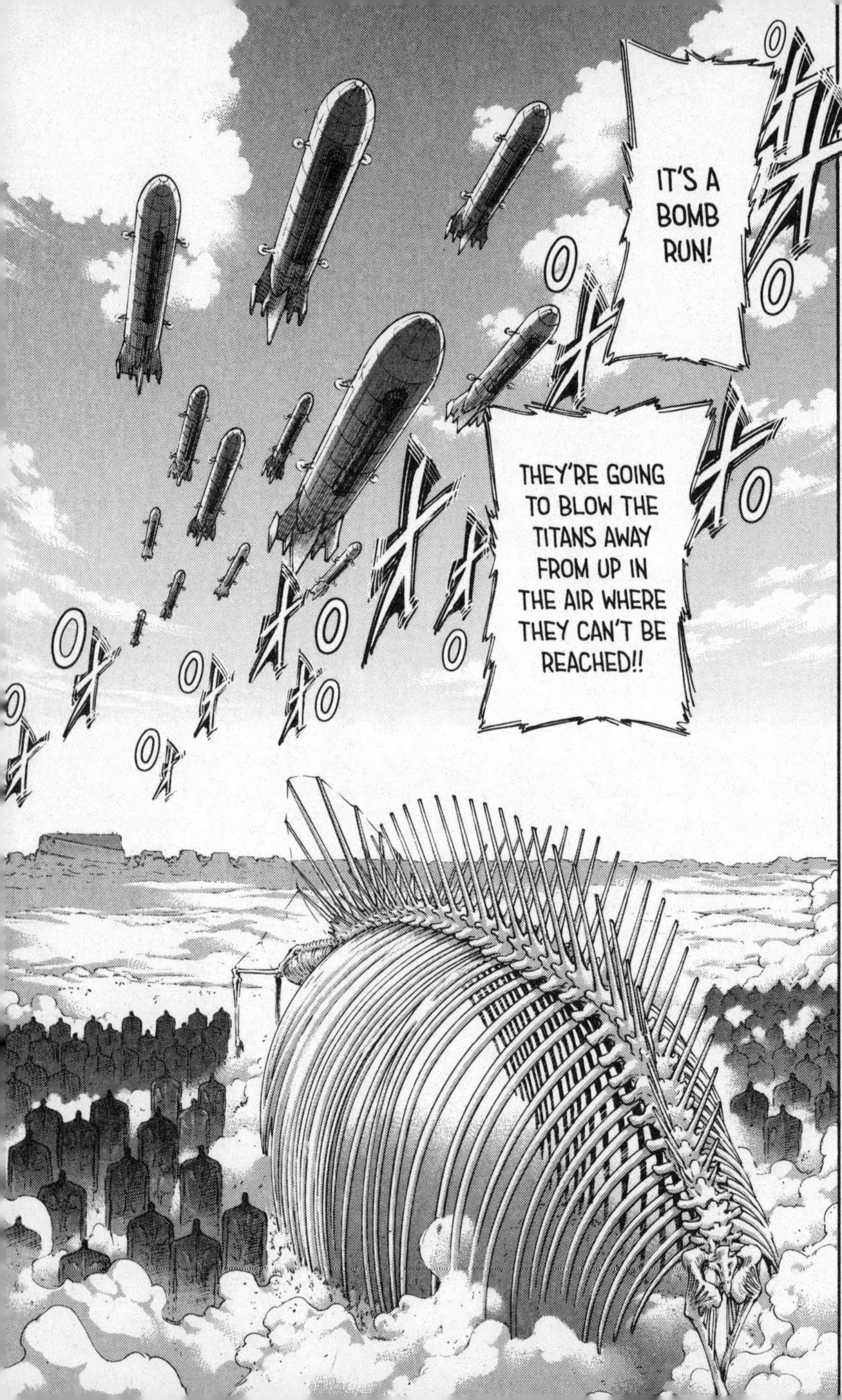
IT'S A BOMB RUN!
THEY'RE GOING TO BLOW THE TITANS AWAY FROM UP IN THE AIR WHERE THEY CAN'T BE REACHED!!

ATTACK on TITAN

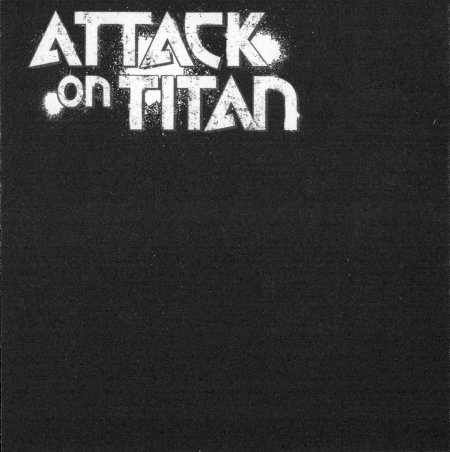

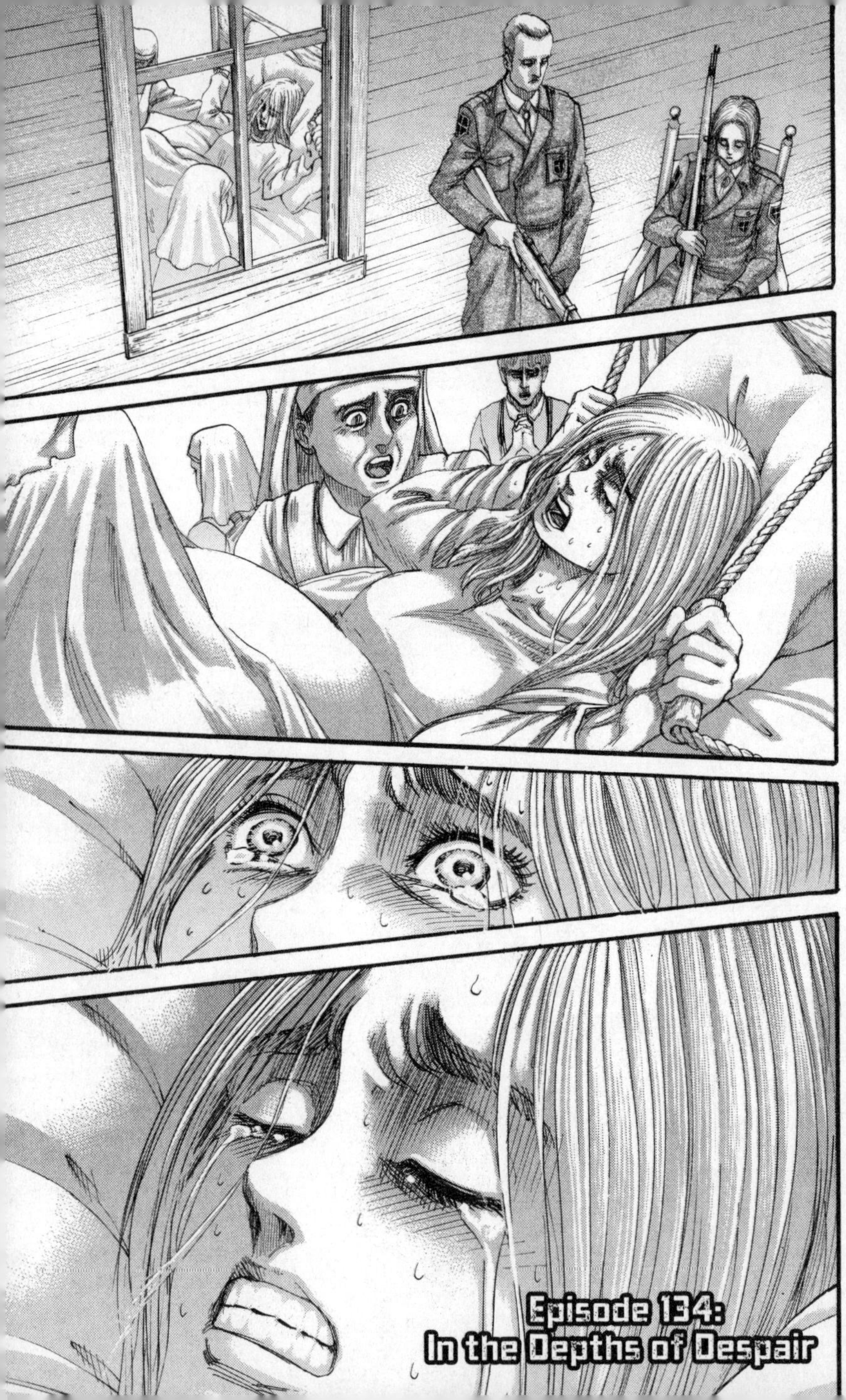
Episode 134:
In the Depths of Despair

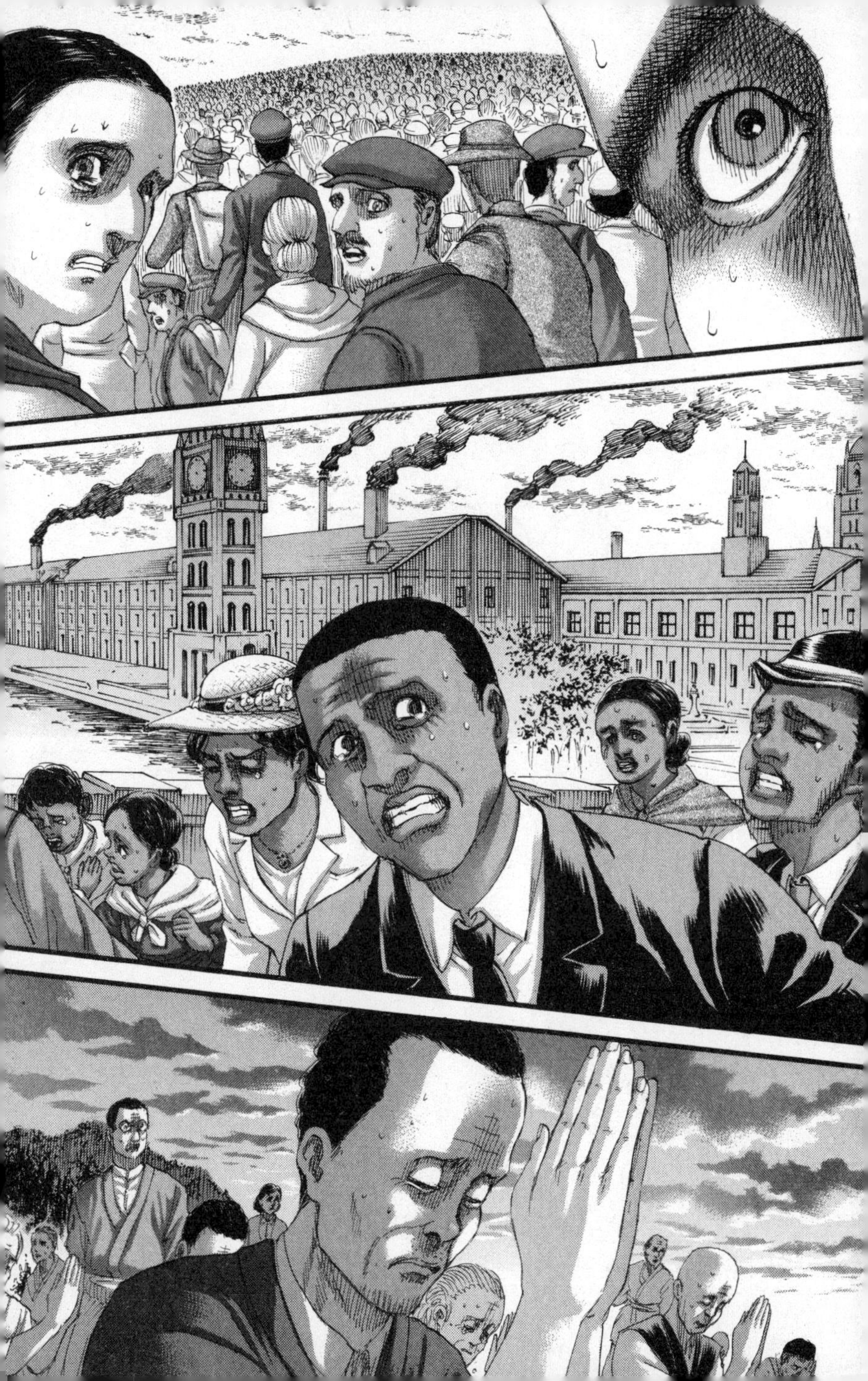

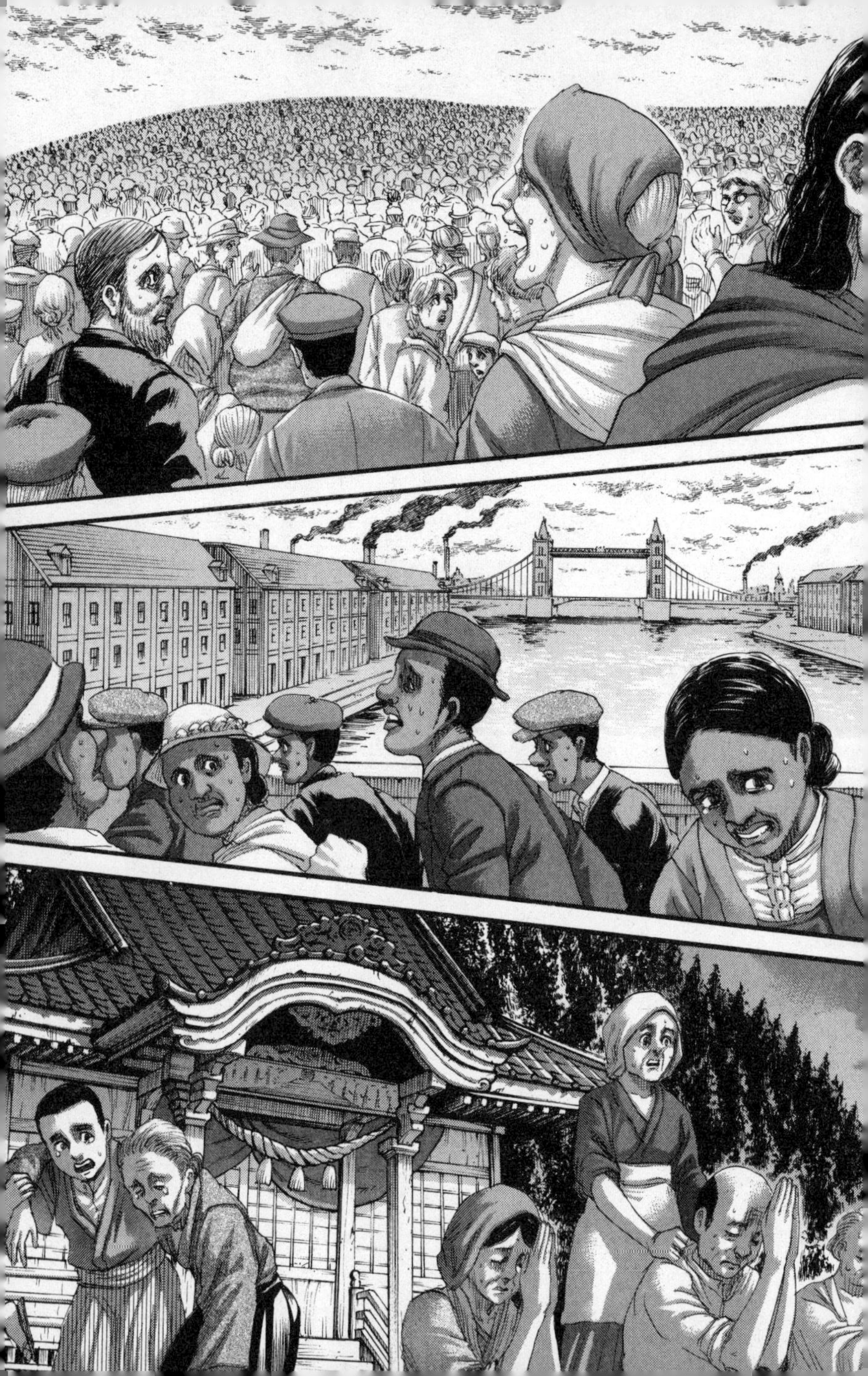

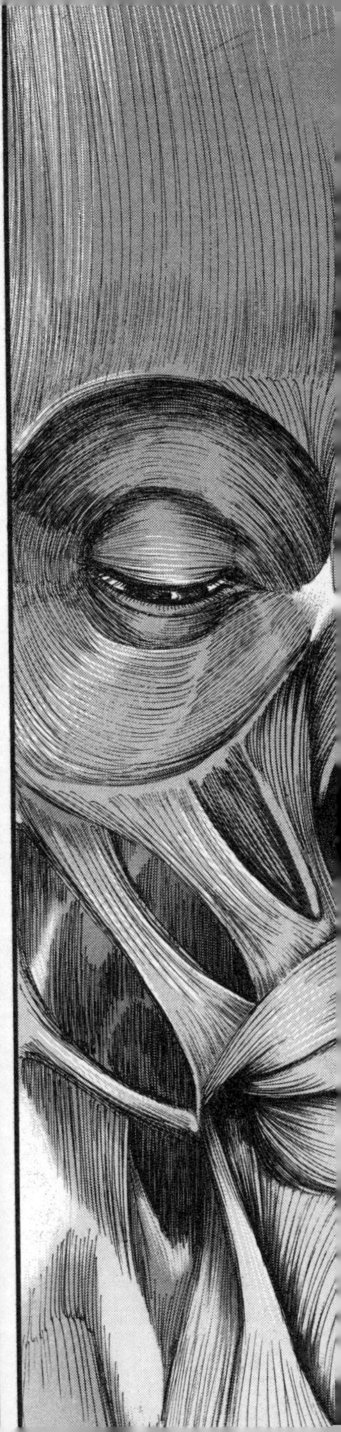
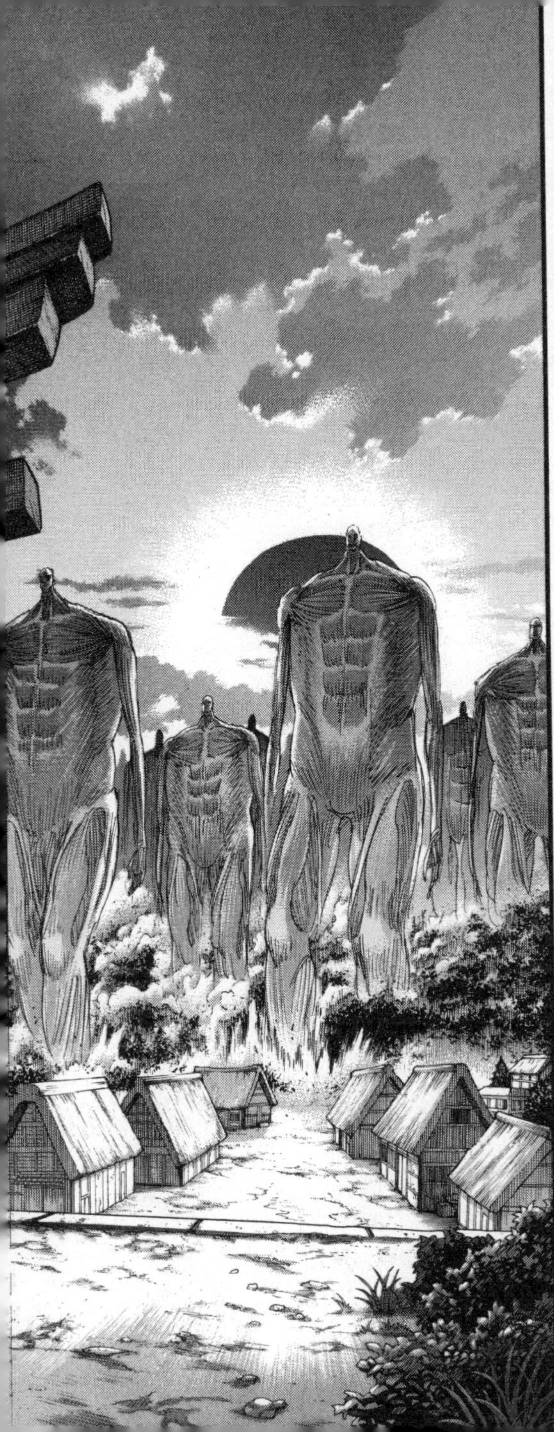

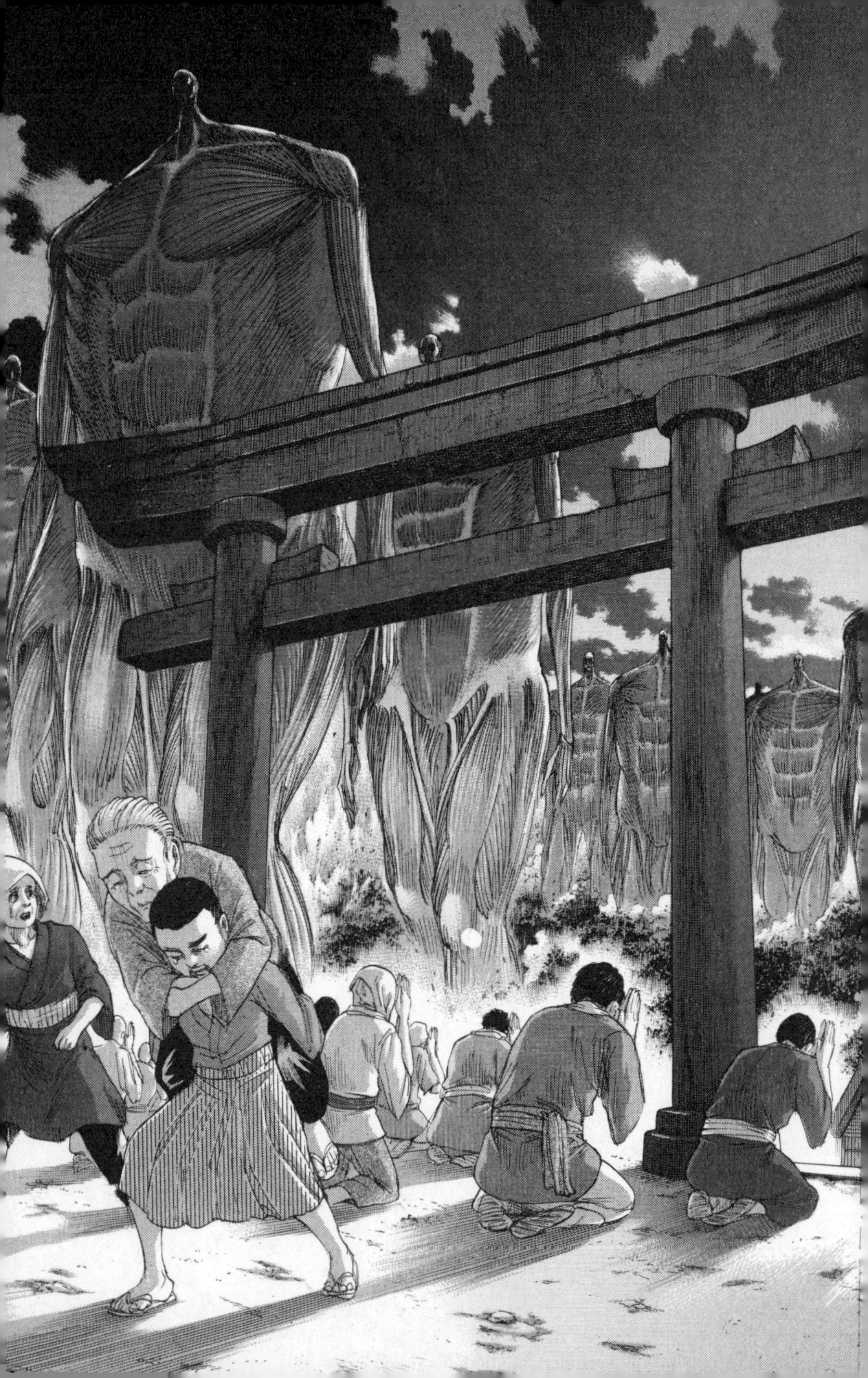

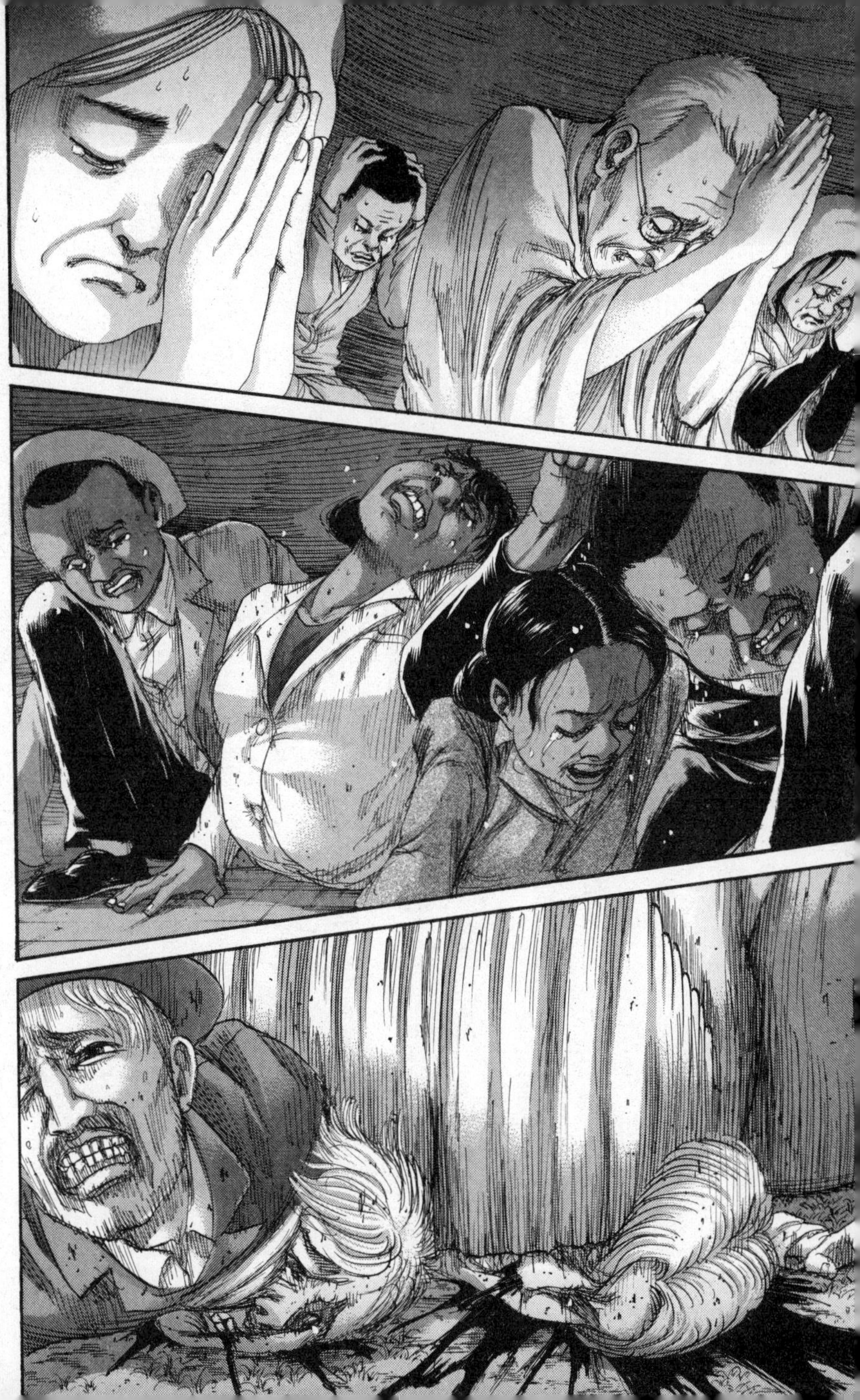

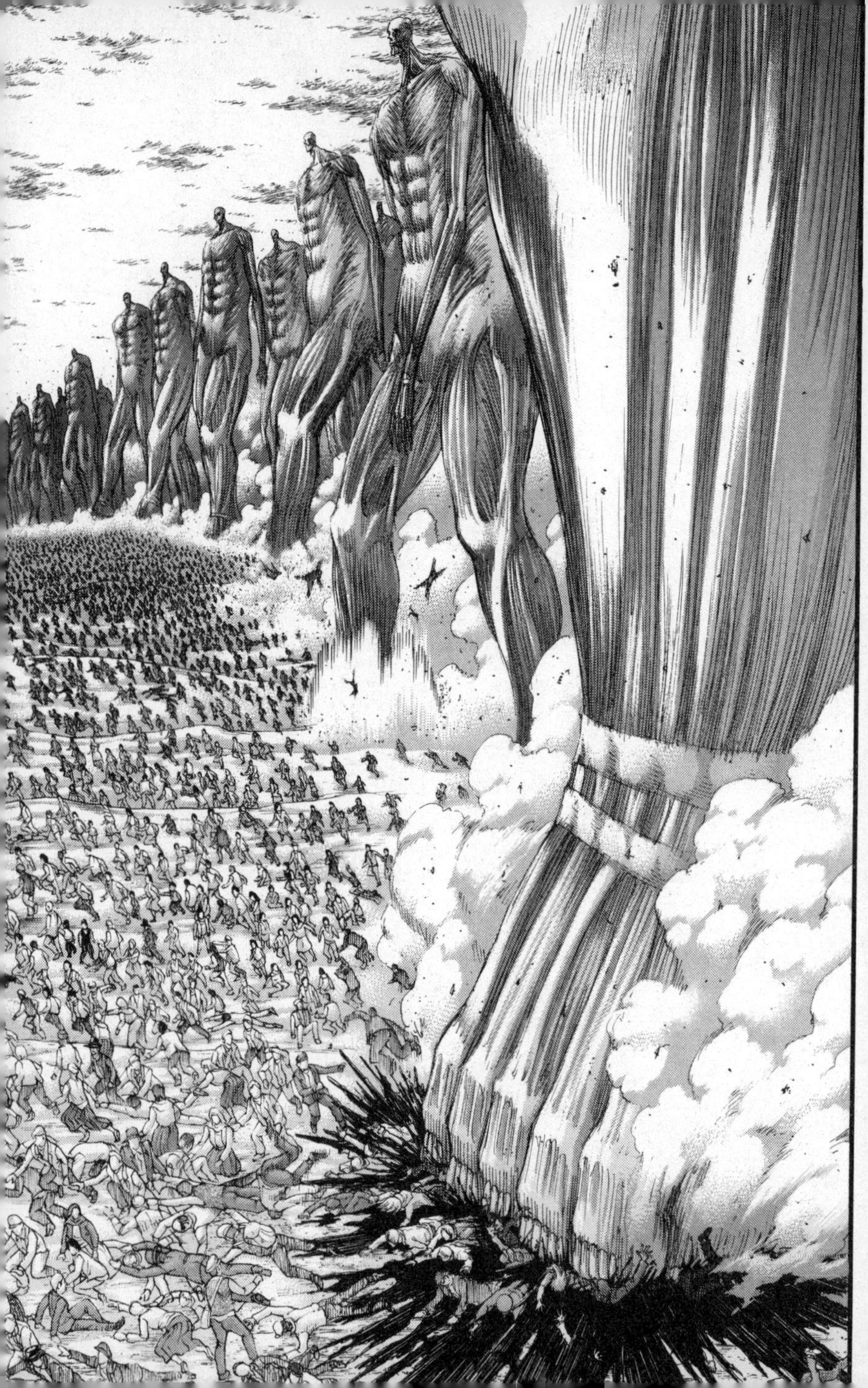

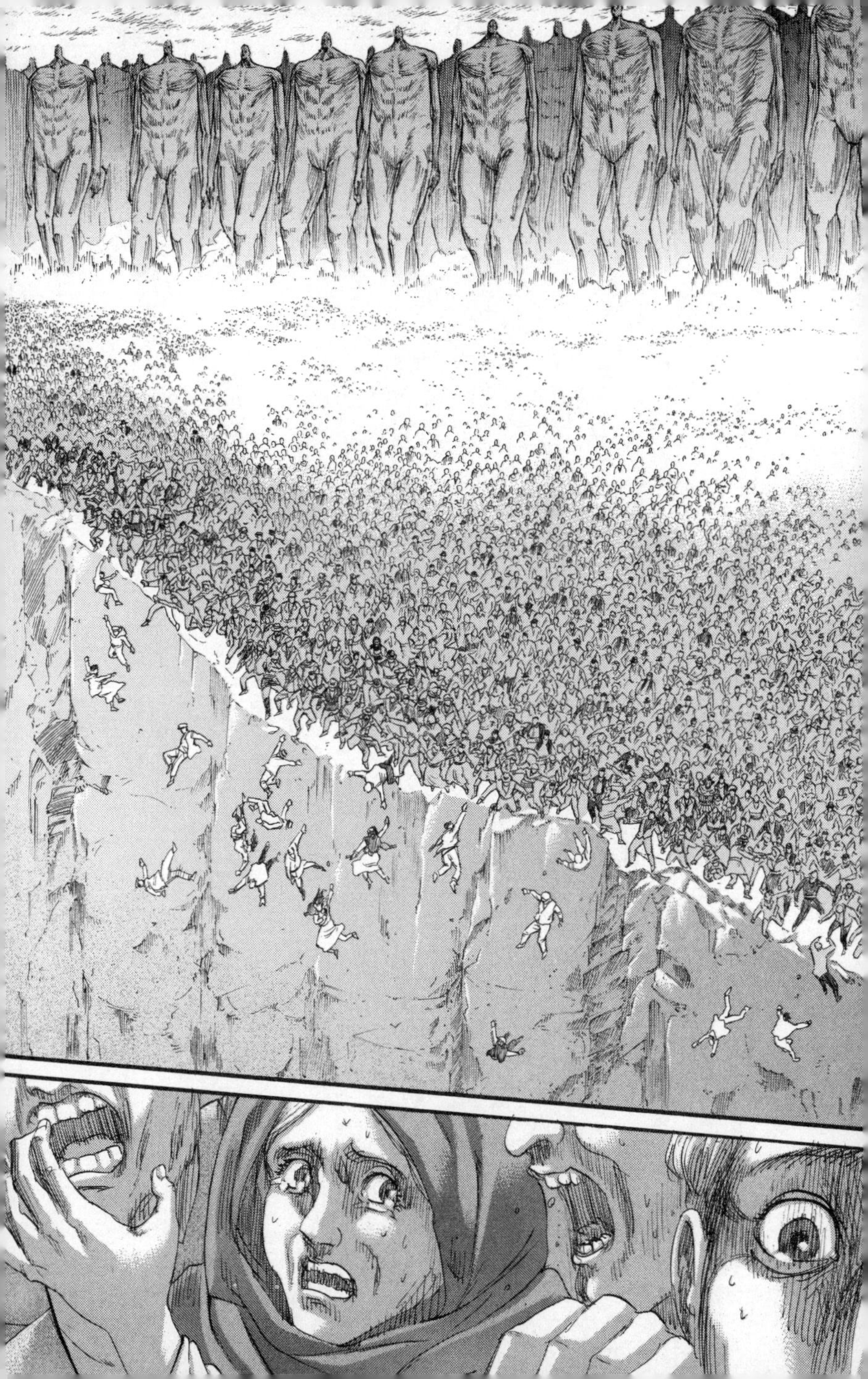

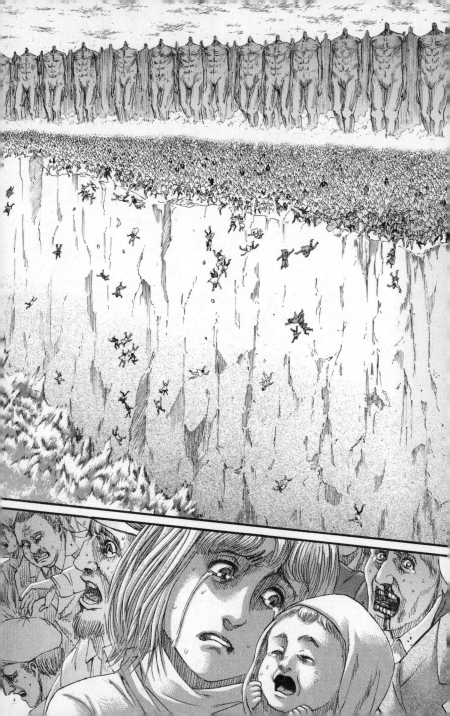

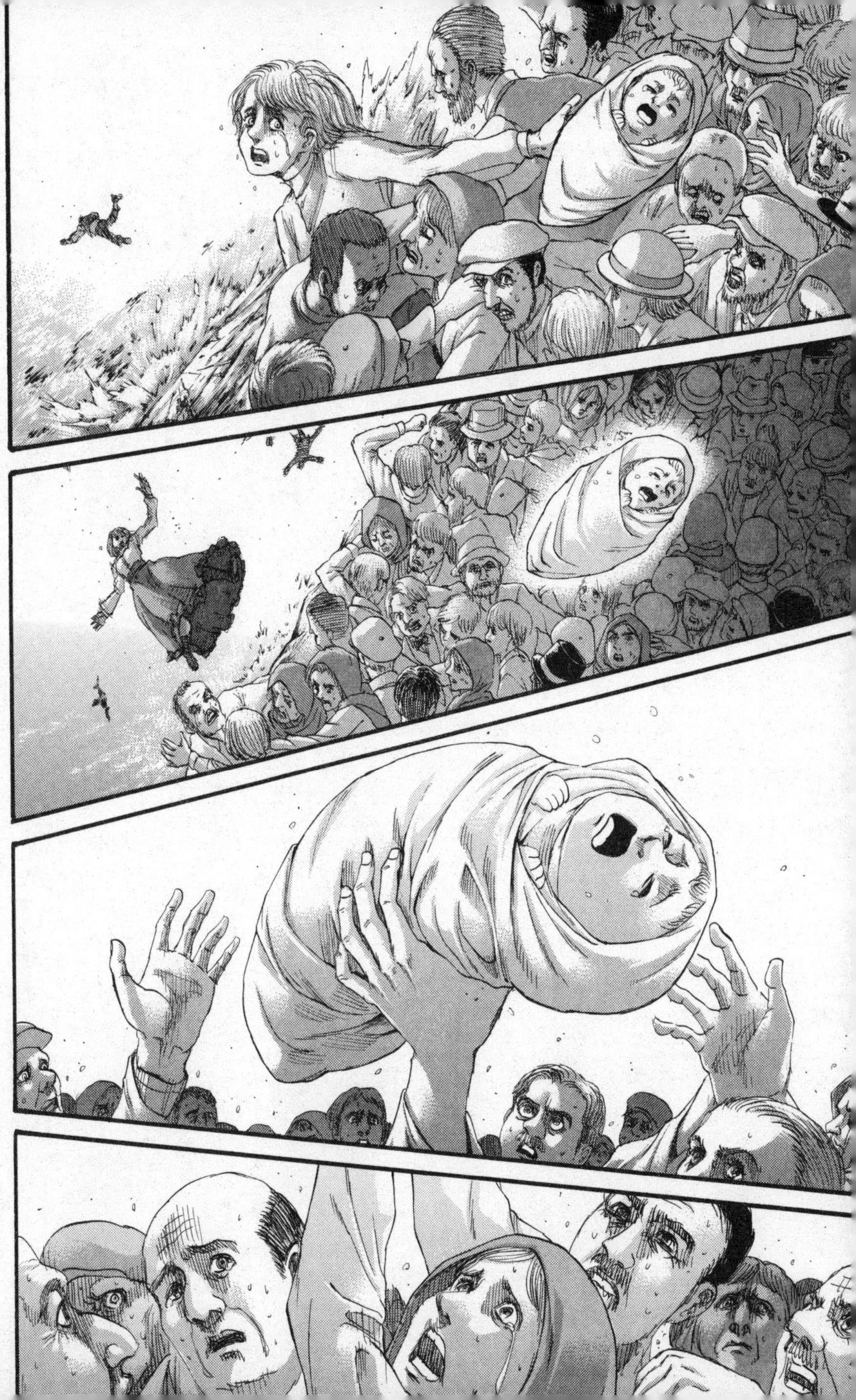

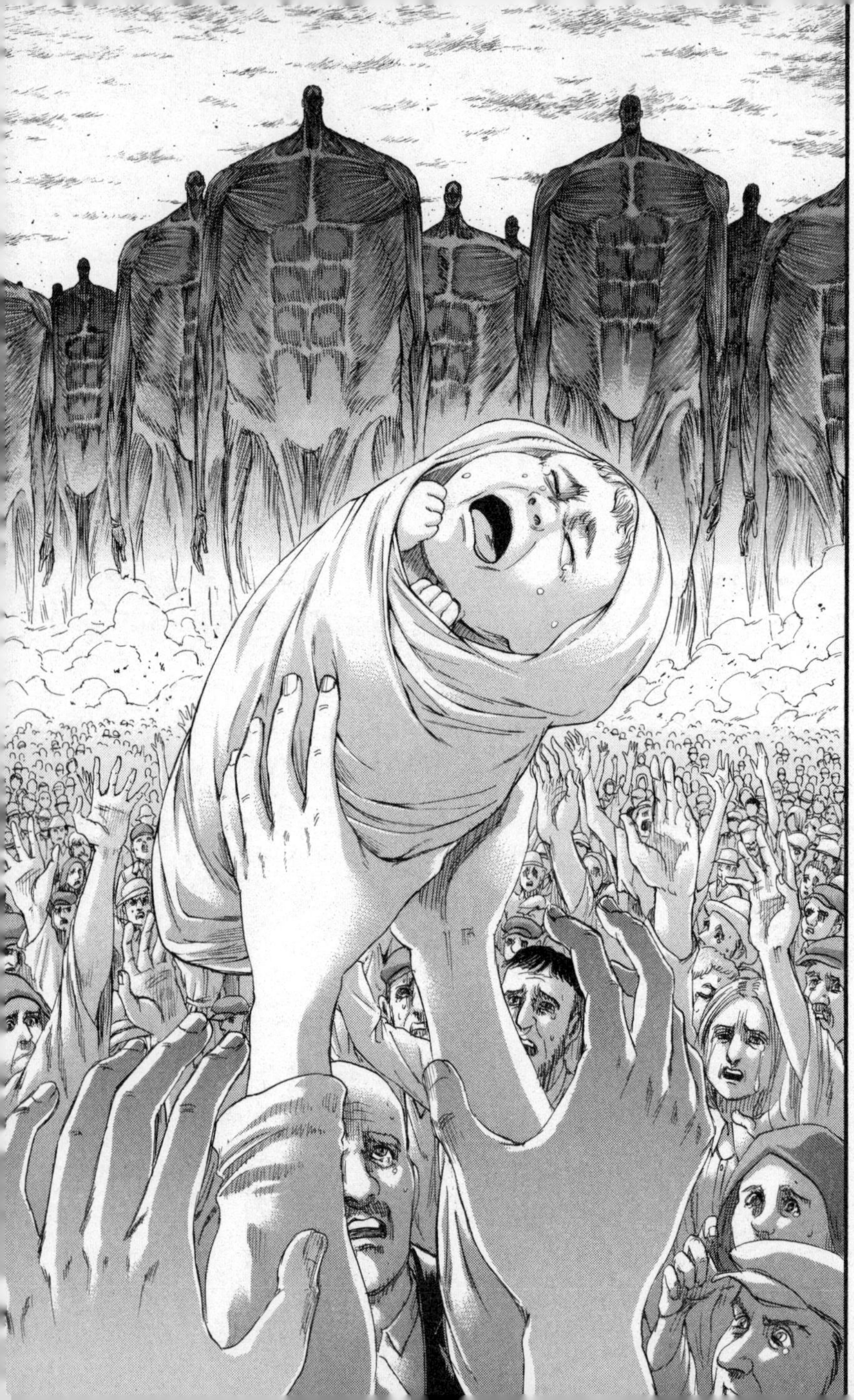

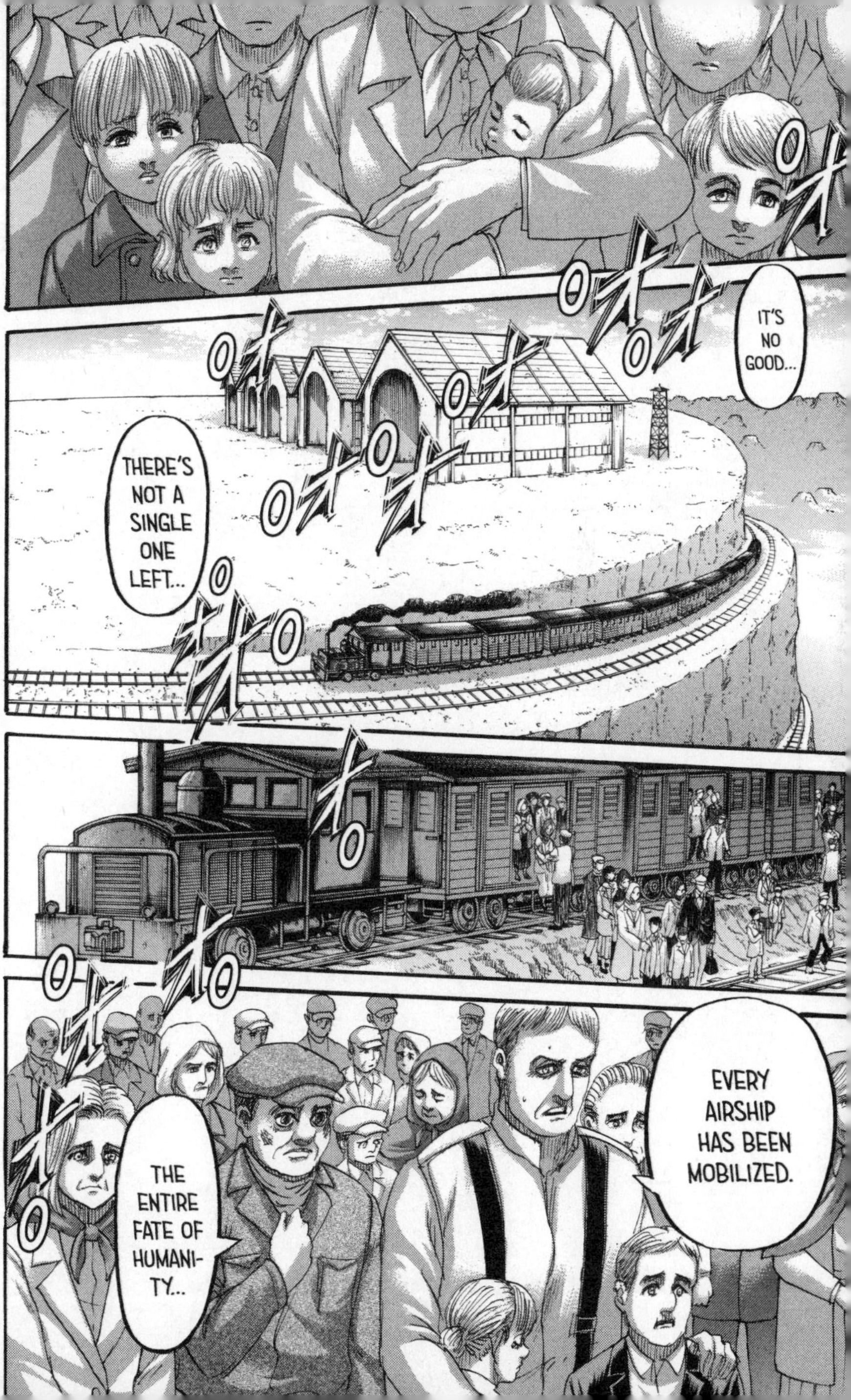
IT'S NO GOOD...
THERE'S NOT A SINGLE ONE LEFT...
EVERY AIRSHIP HAS BEEN MOBILIZED.
THE ENTIRE FATE OF HUMANI-TY...

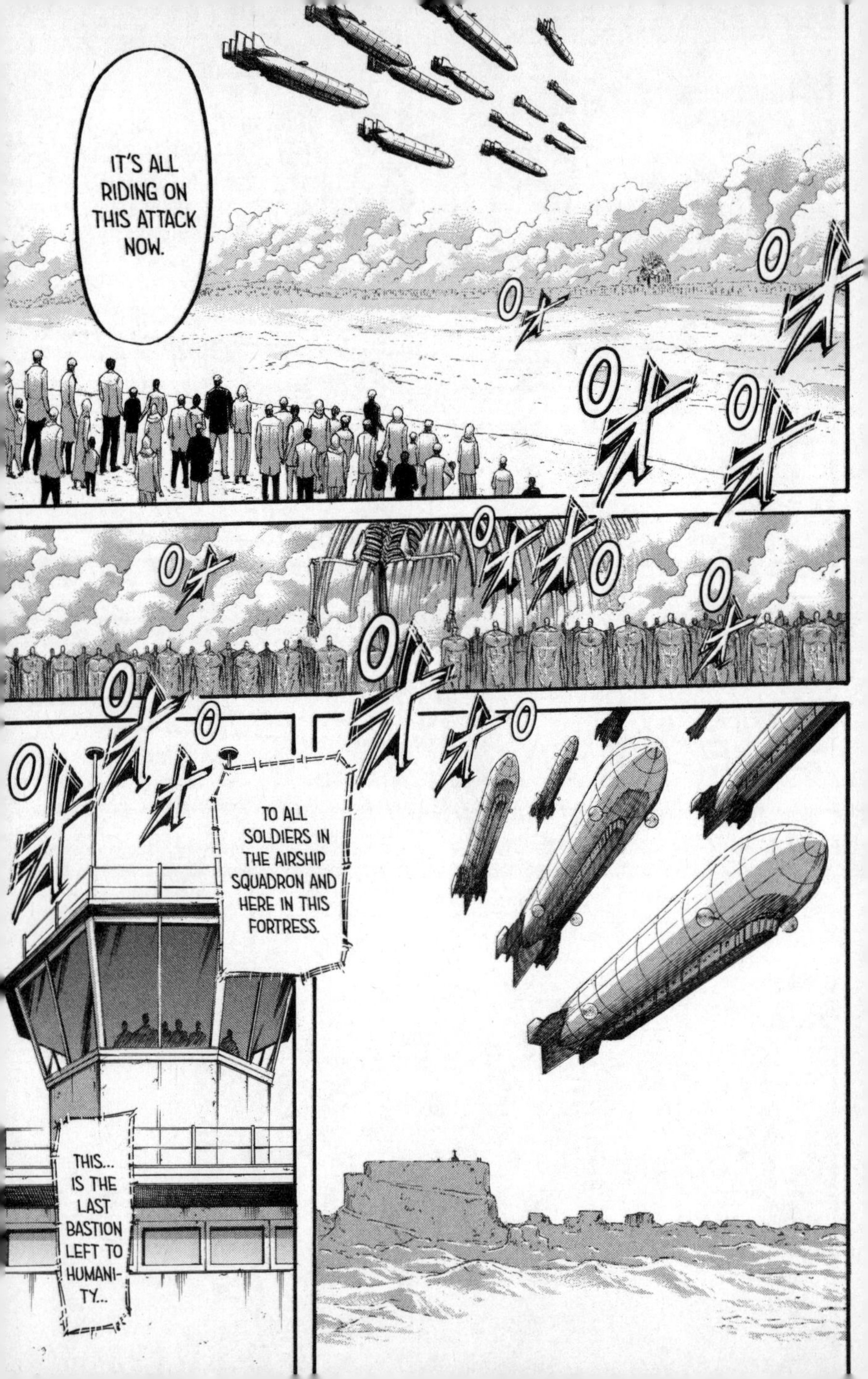
IT'S ALL RIDING ON THIS ATTACK NOW.
TO ALL SOLDIERS IN THE AIRSHIP SQUADRON AND HERE IN THIS FORTRESS.
THIS... IS THE LAST BASTION LEFT TO HUMANITY...

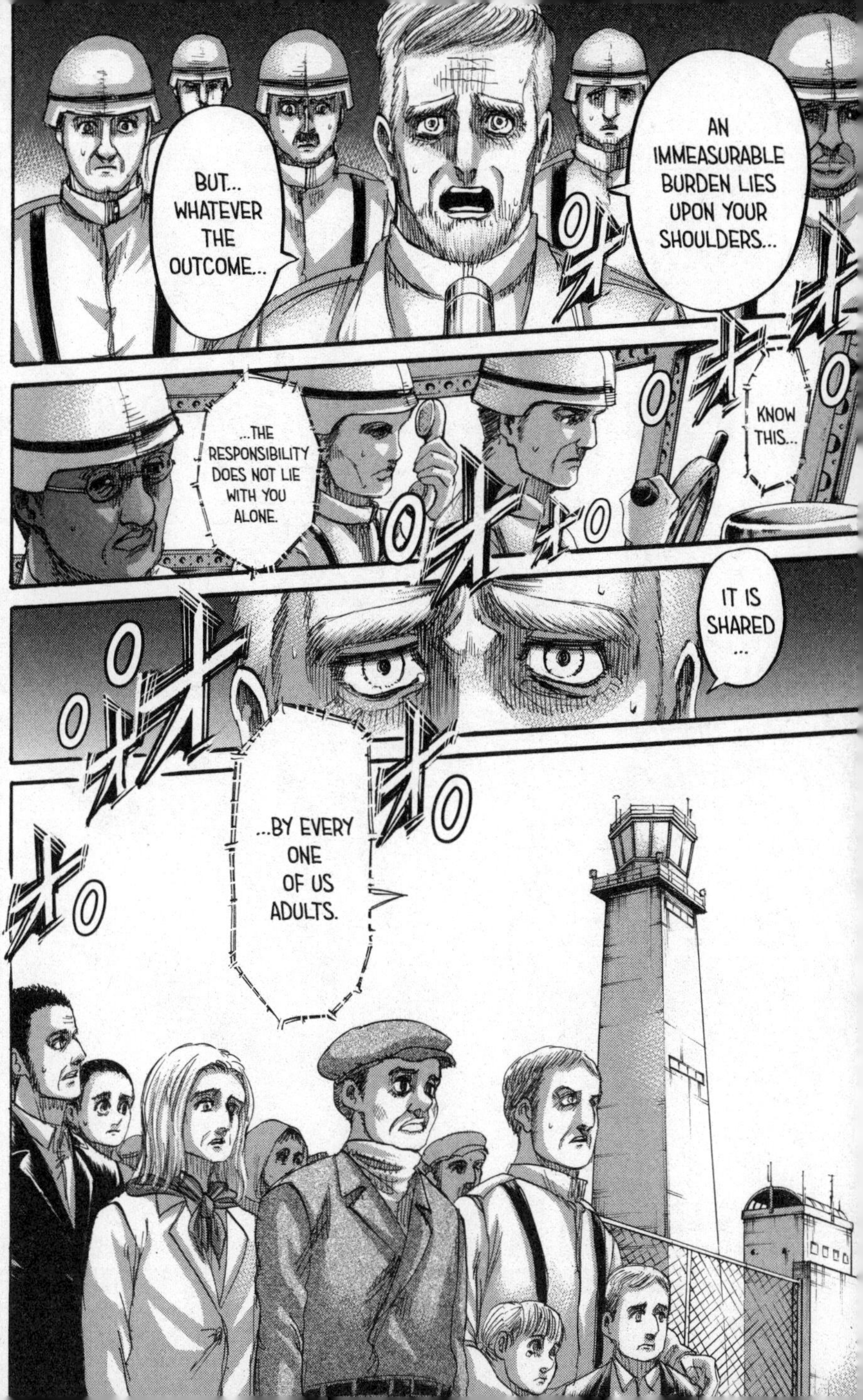
AN IMMEASURABLE BURDEN LIES UPON YOUR SHOULDERS...
BUT... WHATEVER THE OUTCOME...
KNOW THIS...
...THE RESPONSIBILITY DOES NOT LIE WITH YOU ALONE.
IT IS SHARED ...
...BY EVERY ONE OF US ADULTS.

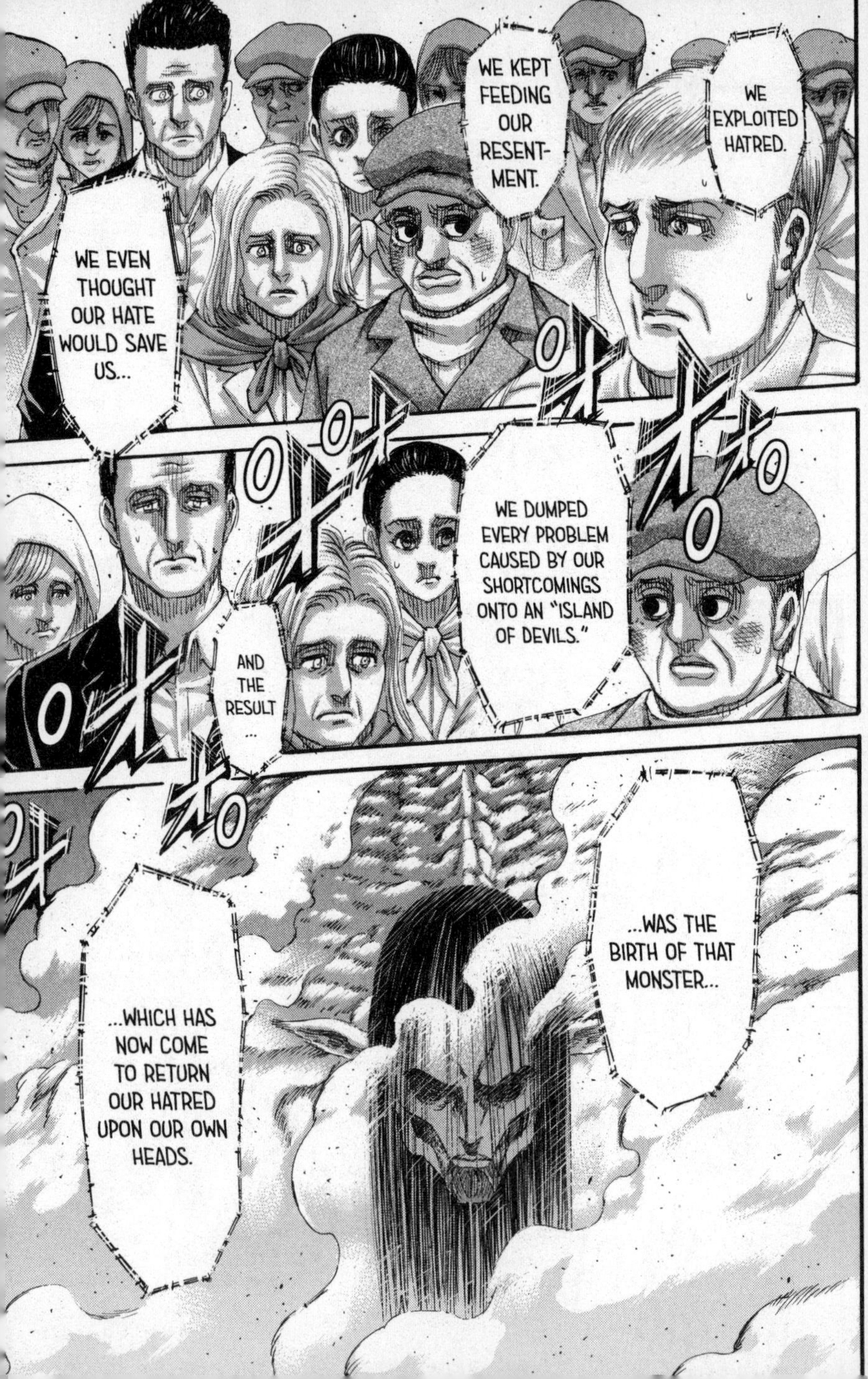
WE EXPLOITED HATRED.
WE KEPT FEEDING OUR RESENT-MENT.
WE EVEN THOUGHT OUR HATE WOULD SAVE US...
WE DUMPED EVERY PROBLEM CAUSED BY OUR SHORTCOMINGS ONTO AN "ISLAND OF DEVILS."
AND THE RESULT ...
...WAS THE BIRTH OF THAT MONSTER...
...WHICH HAS NOW COME TO RETURN OUR HATRED UPON OUR OWN HEADS.

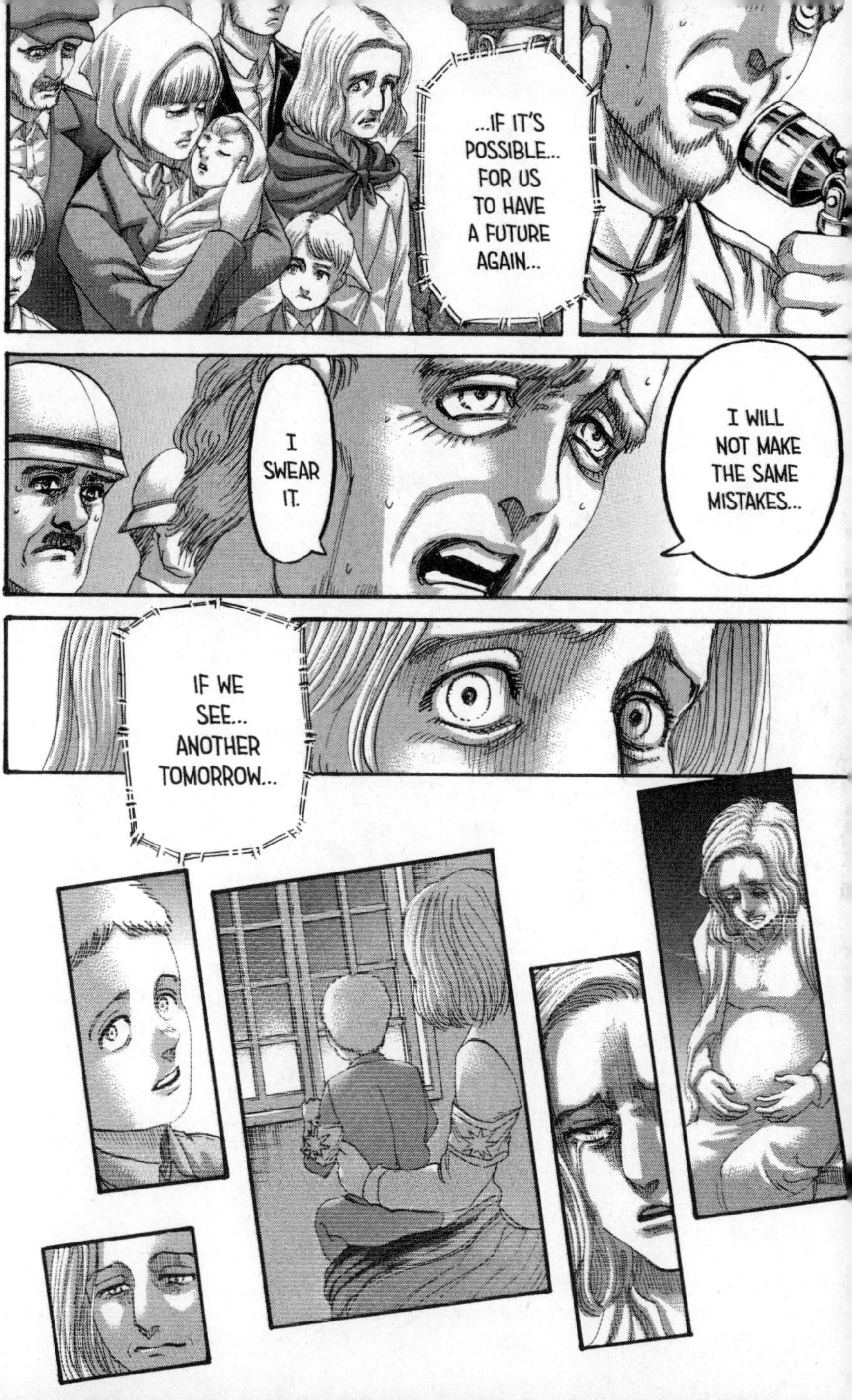
...IF IT'S POSSIBLE... FOR US TO HAVE A FUTURE AGAIN...
I WILL NOT MAKE THE SAME MISTAKES...
I SWEAR IT.
IF WE SEE... ANOTHER TOMORROW...

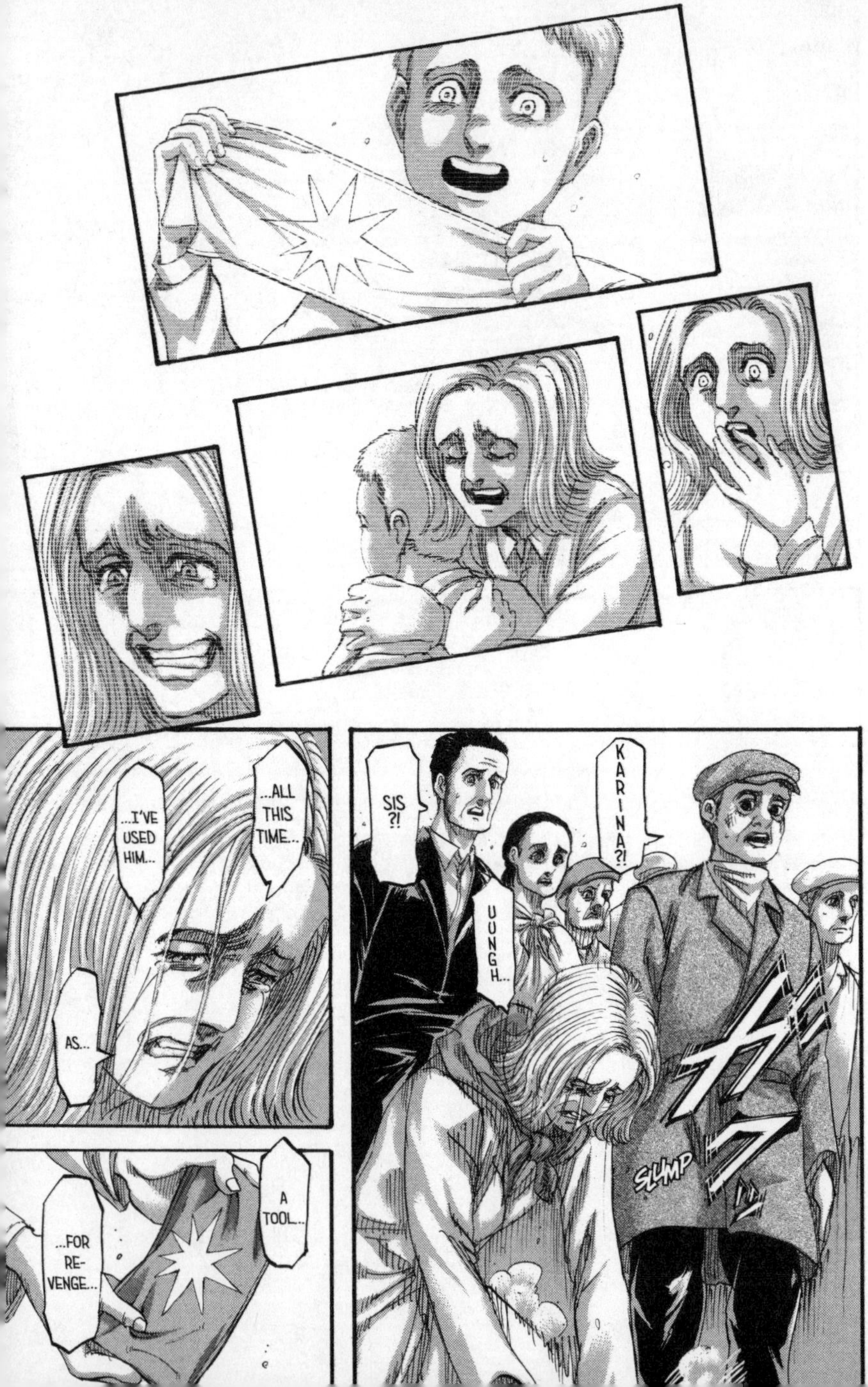
KARINA?!
SIS ?!
UUNGH...
SLUMP
...ALL THIS TIME...
...I'VE USED HIM...
AS...
A TOOL...
...FOR RE-VENGE...

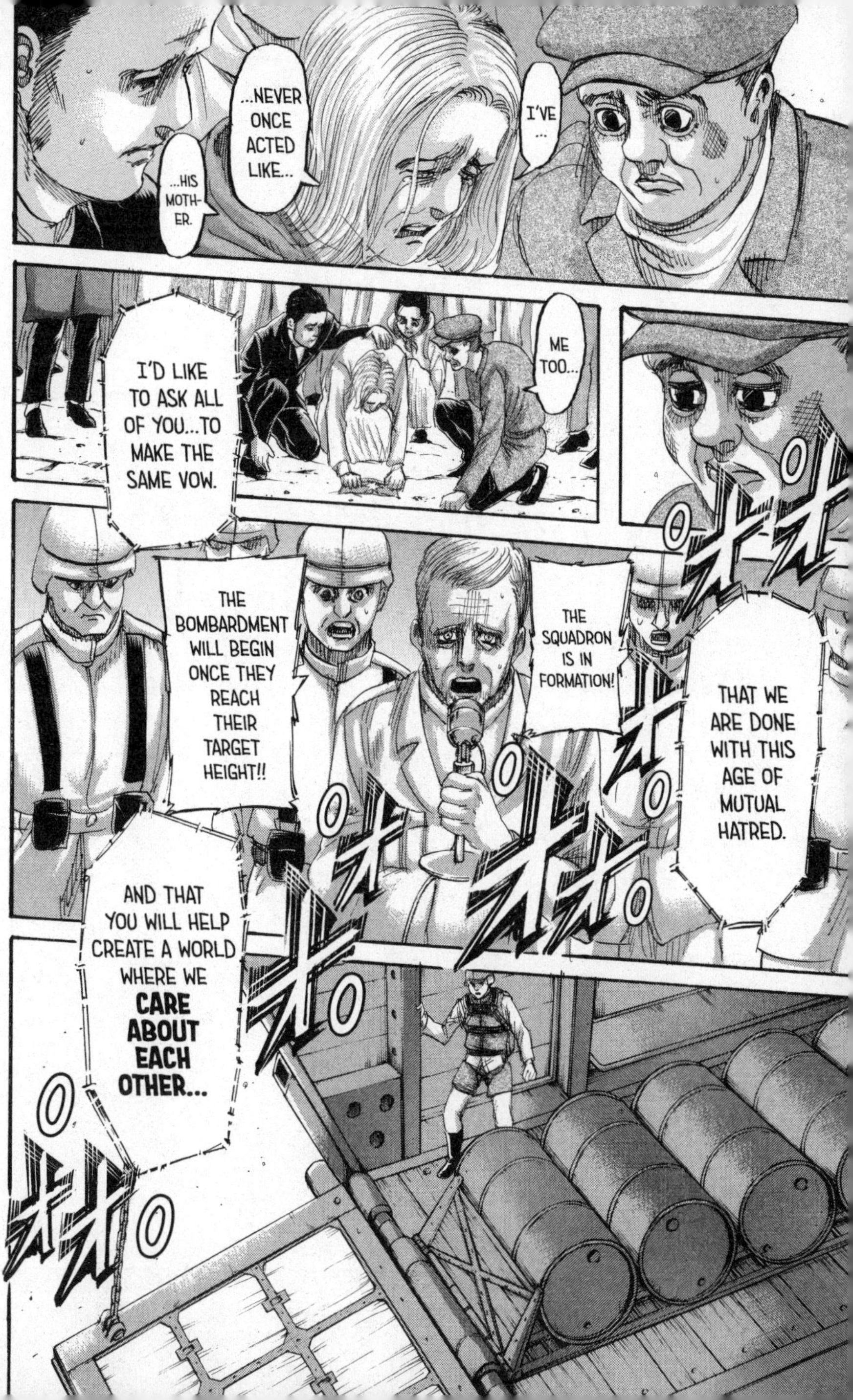
I'VE ...
...NEVER ONCE ACTED LIKE...
...HIS MOTH-ER.
ME TOO...
I'D LIKE TO ASK ALL OF YOU...TO MAKE THE SAME VOW.
THAT WE ARE DONE WITH THIS AGE OF MUTUAL HATRED.
THE SQUADRON IS IN FORMATION!
THE BOMBARDMENT WILL BEGIN ONCE THEY REACH THEIR TARGET HEIGHT!!
AND THAT YOU WILL HELP CREATE A WORLD WHERE WE **CARE ABOUT EACH OTHER...**

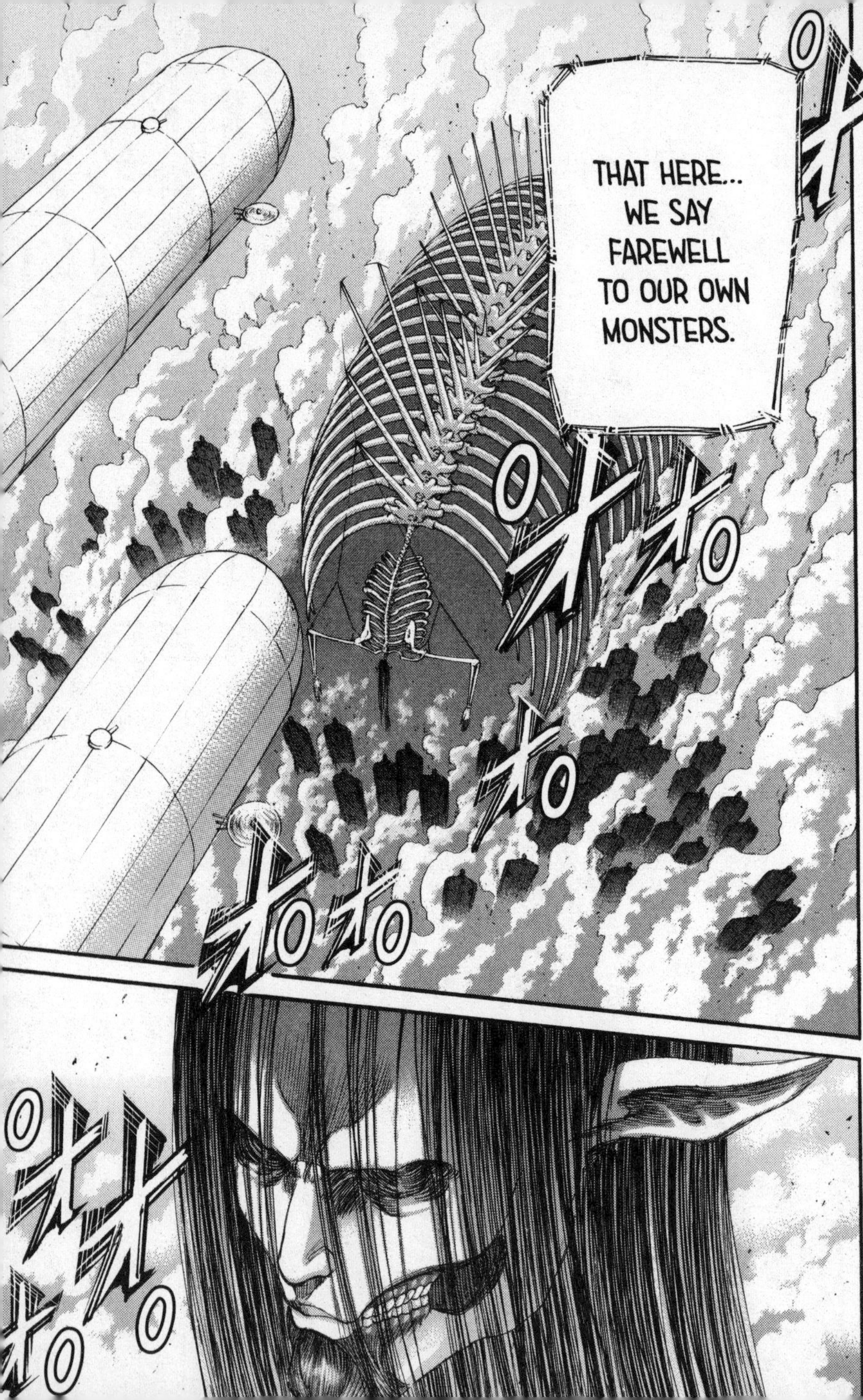
THAT HERE... WE SAY FAREWELL TO OUR OWN MONSTERS.

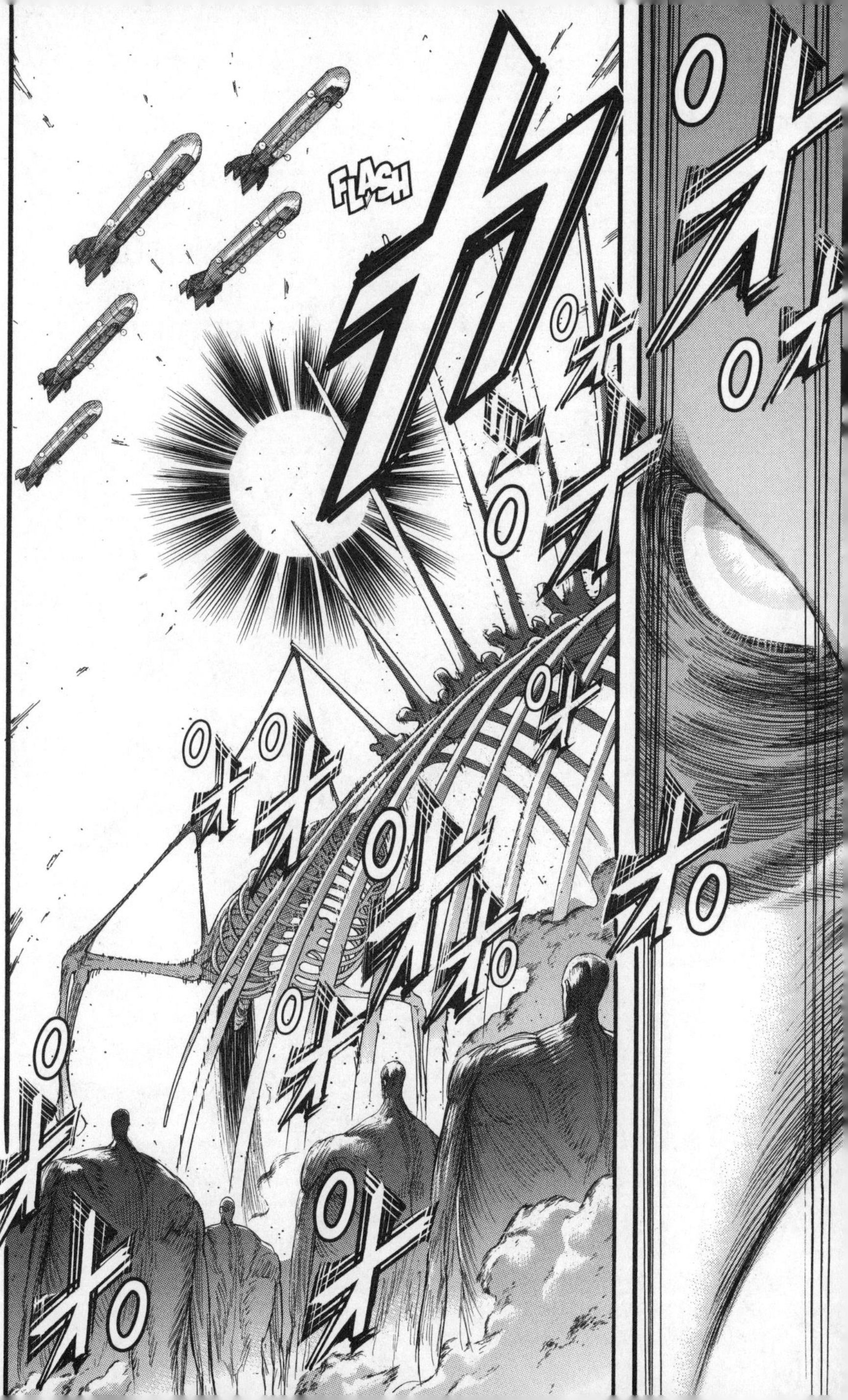
FLASH

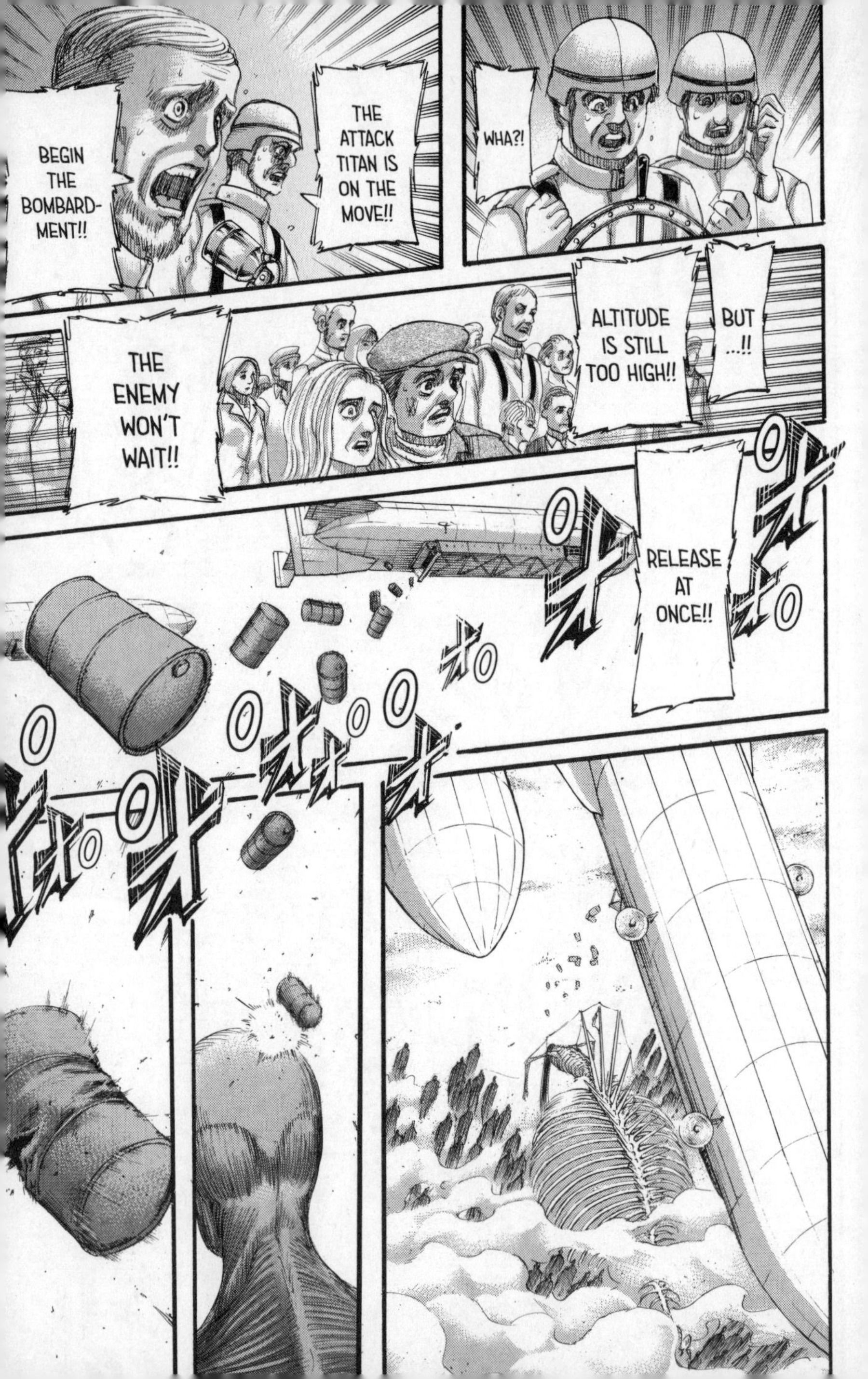
WHA?!
THE ATTACK TITAN IS ON THE MOVE!!
BEGIN THE BOMBARD-MENT!!
BUT ...!!
ALTITUDE IS STILL TOO HIGH!!
THE ENEMY WON'T WAIT!!
RELEASE AT ONCE!!

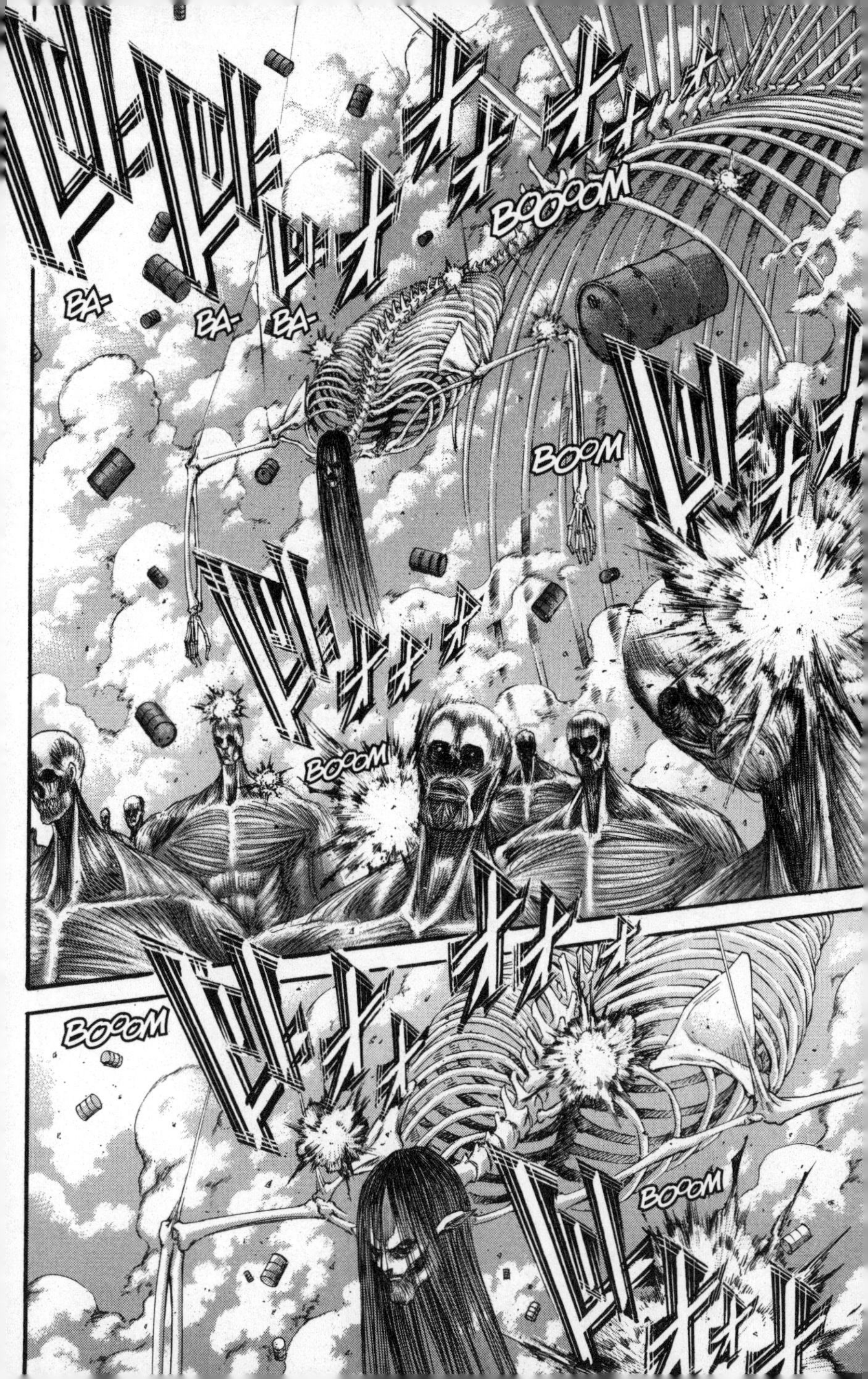
BOOOOM
BA-
BA-
BA-
BOOM
BOOOM
BOOOM
BOOOM

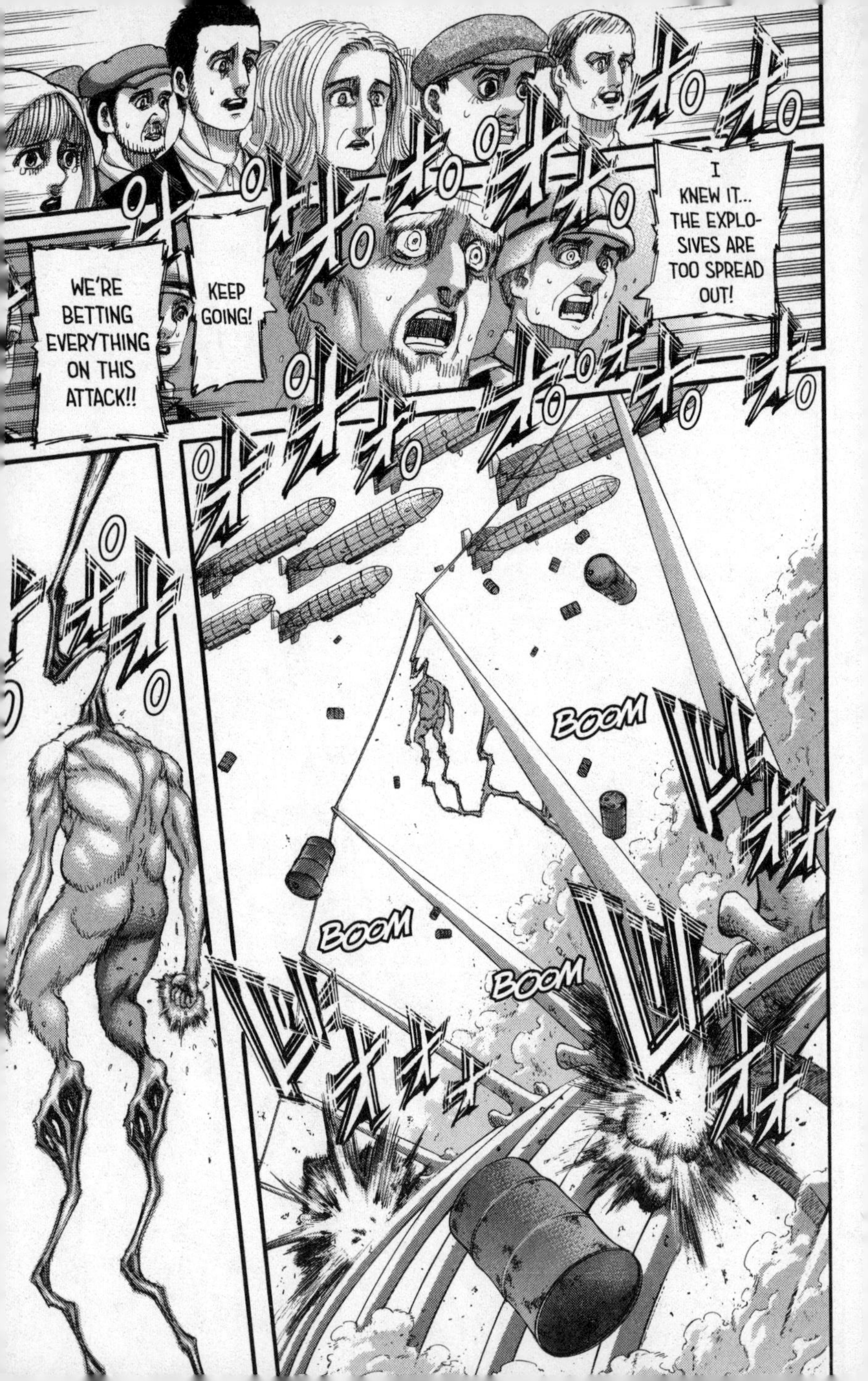
I KNEW IT... THE EXPLOSIVES ARE TOO SPREAD OUT!
KEEP GOING!
WE'RE BETTING EVERYTHING ON THIS ATTACK!!
BOOM
BOOM
BOOM

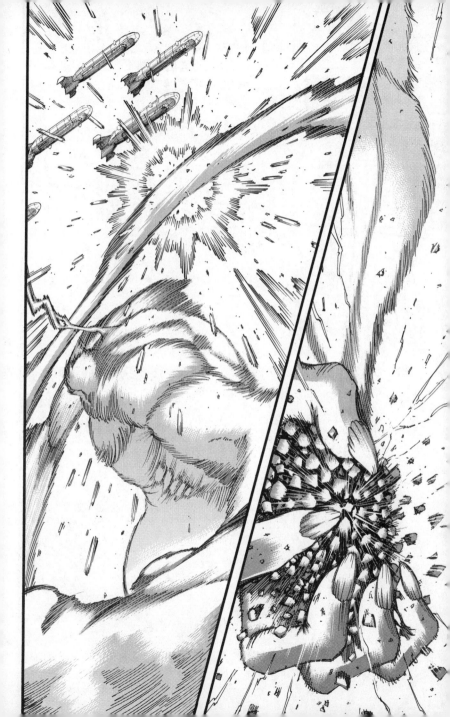

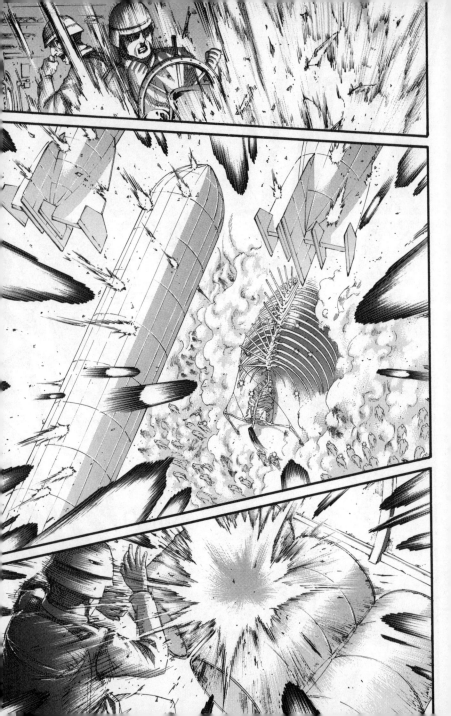

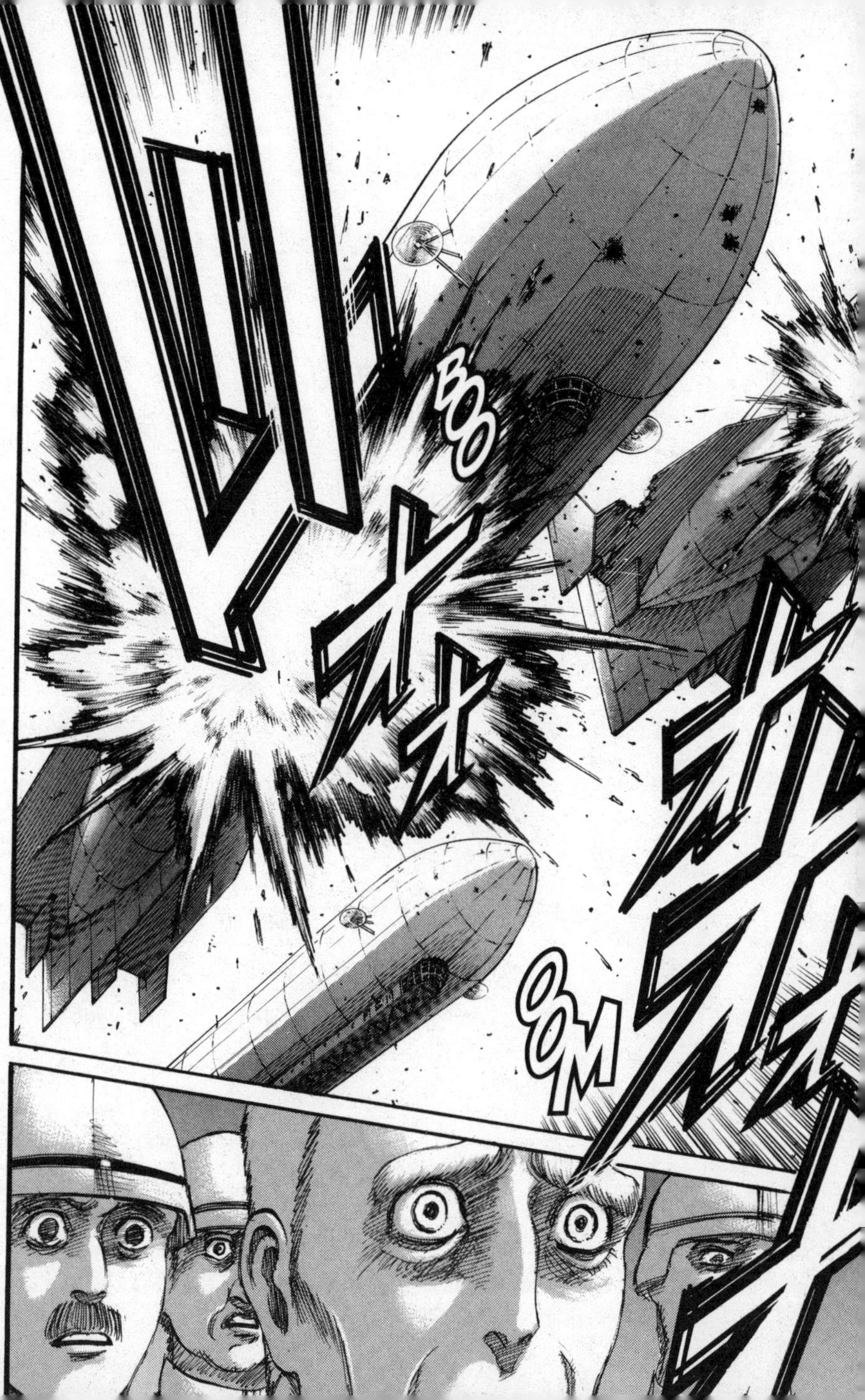
BOO
OOM

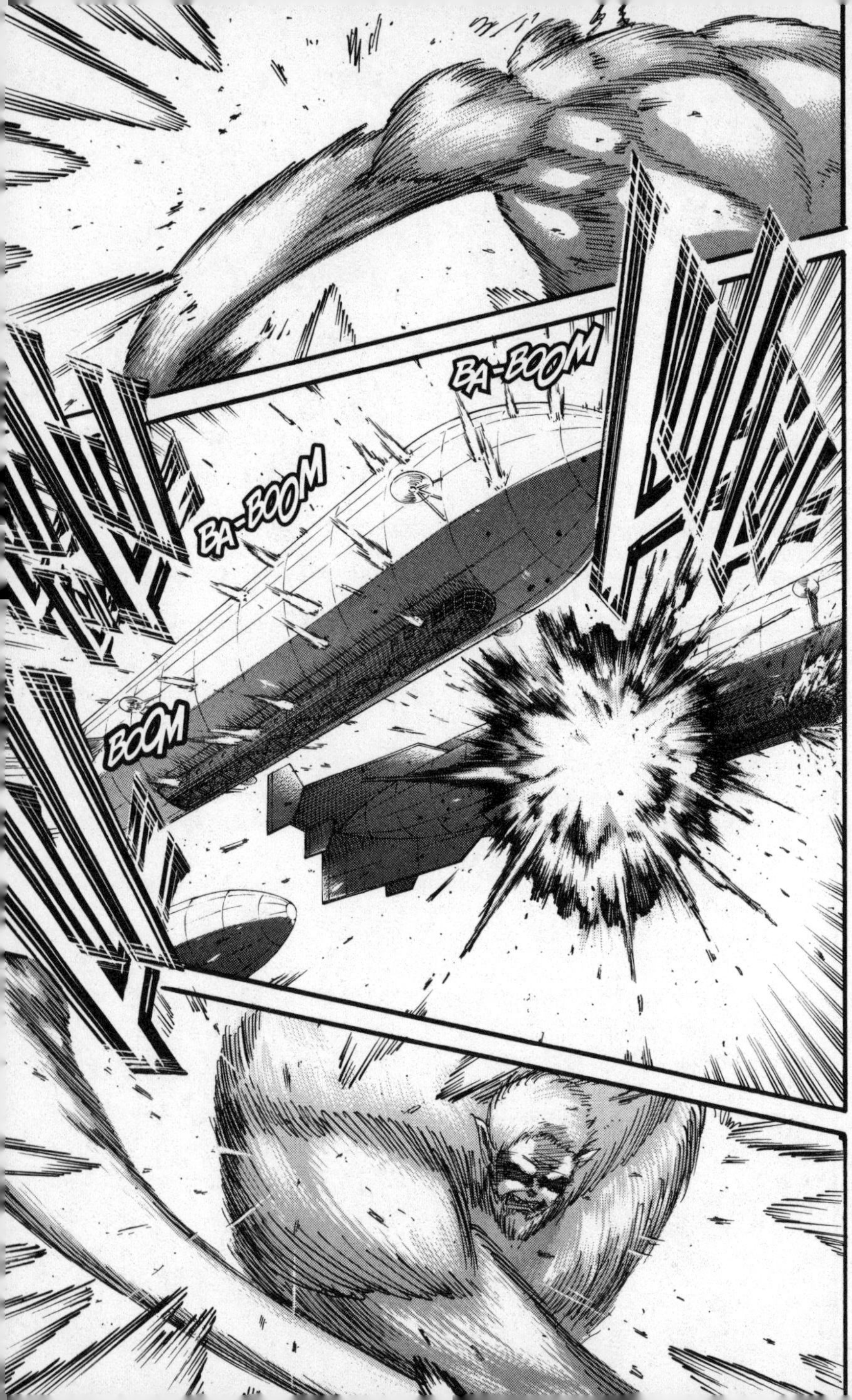
BA-BOOM
BA-BOOM
BOOM

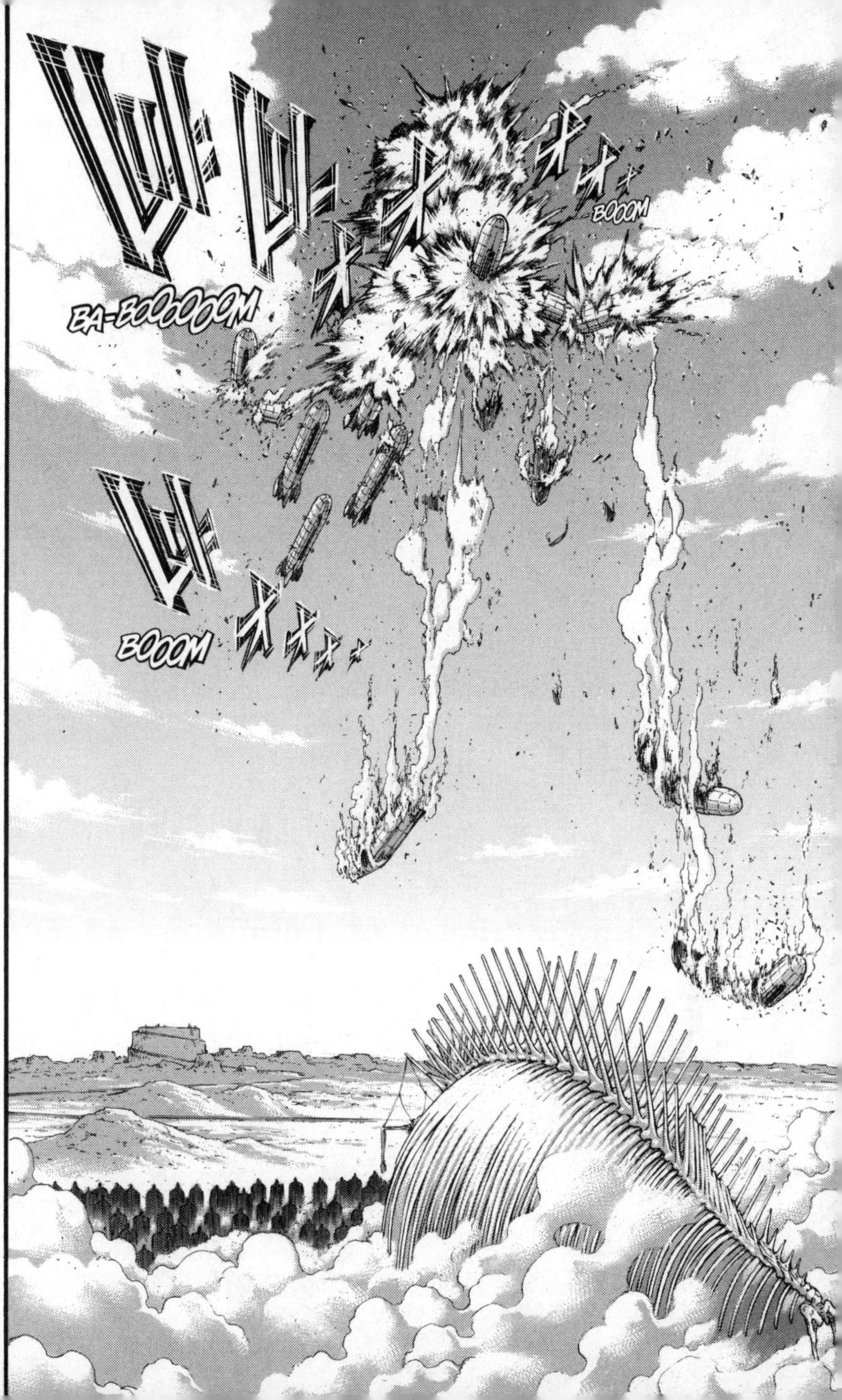
BOOOM
BA-BOOOOOOM
BOOOM

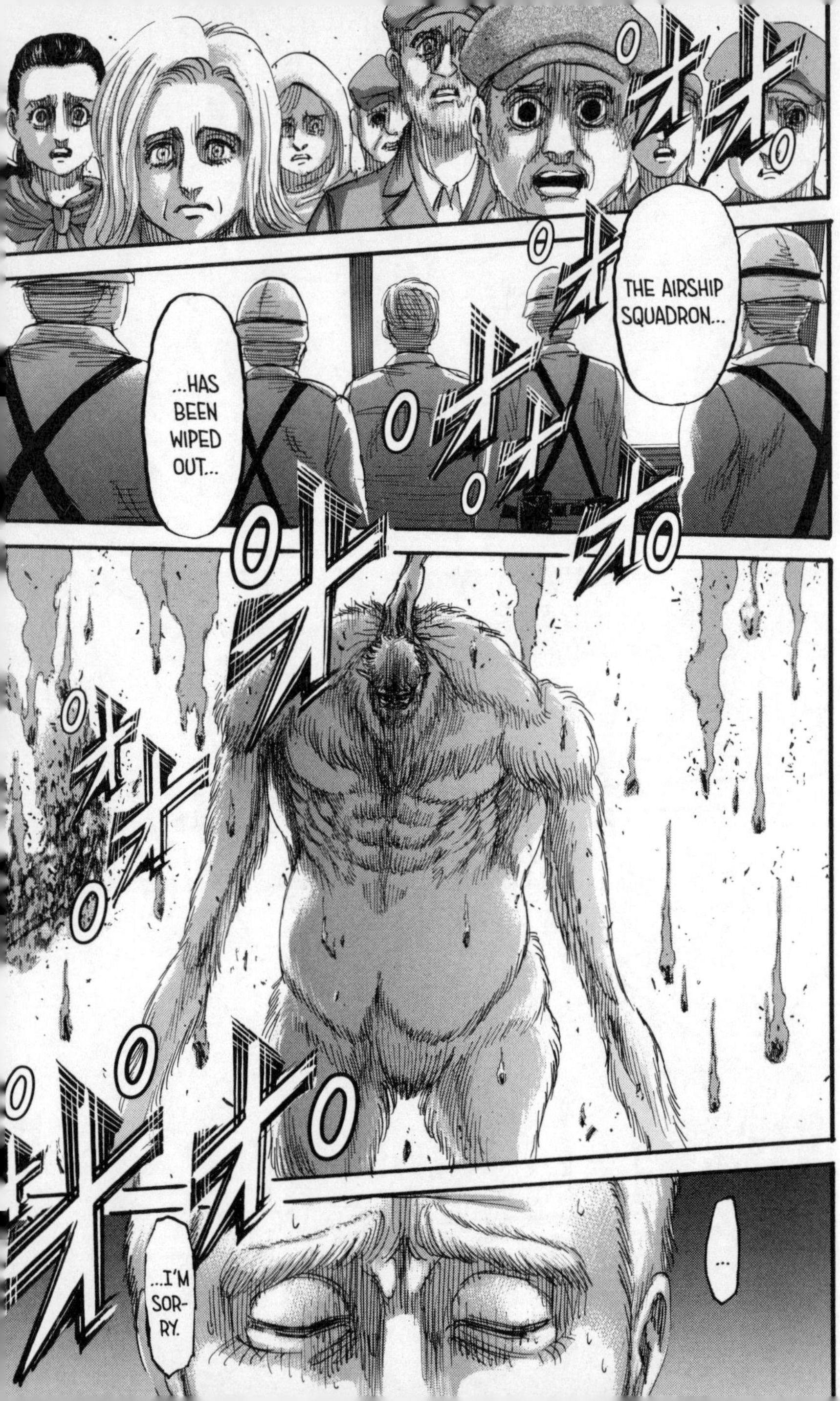
THE AIRSHIP SQUADRON...
...HAS BEEN WIPED OUT...
...
...I'M SOR-RY.

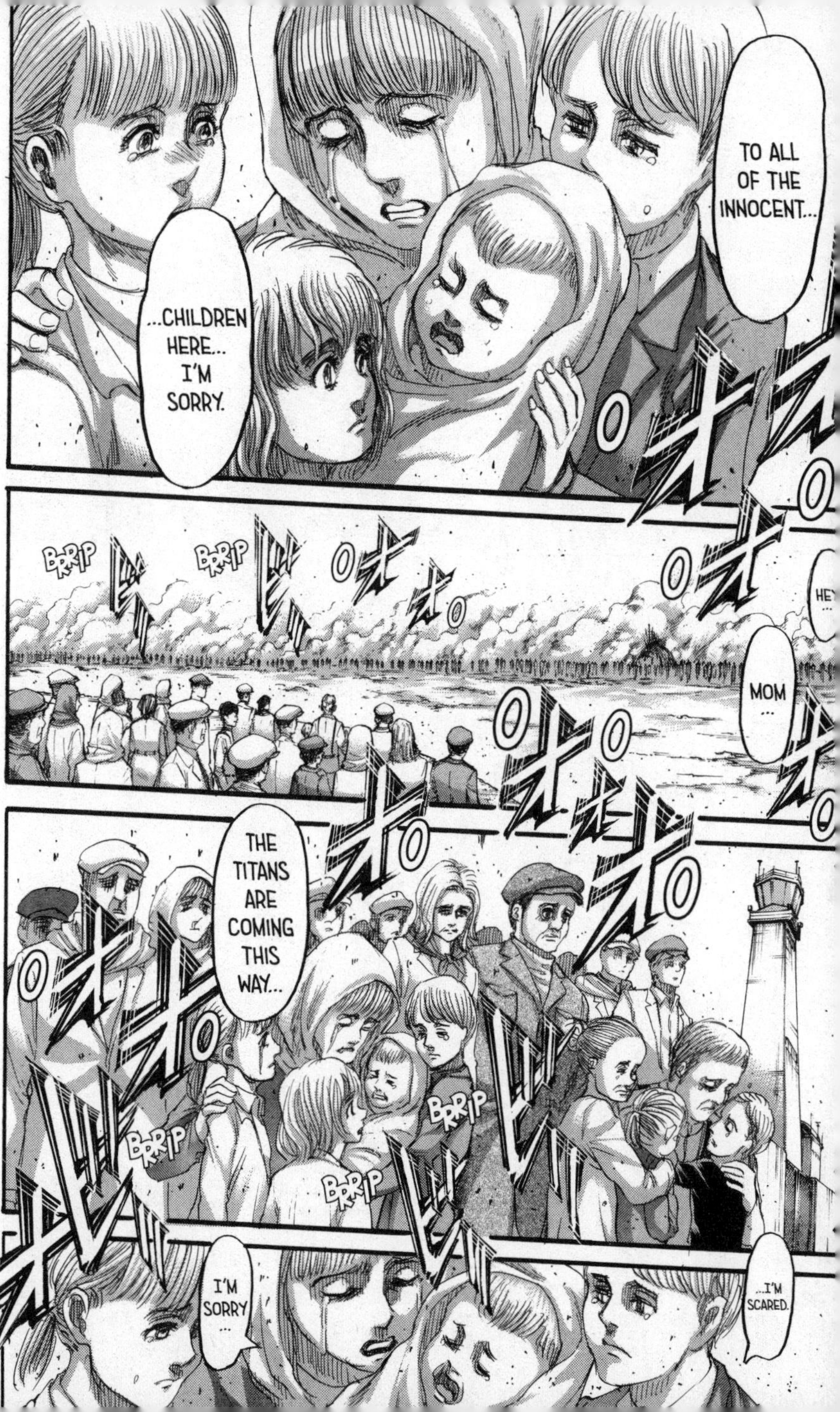
TO ALL OF THE INNOCENT...
...CHILDREN HERE... I'M SORRY.
MOM...
BRRIP
BRRIP
THE TITANS ARE COMING THIS WAY...
BRRIP
BRRIP
BRRIP
...I'M SCARED.
I'M SORRY...

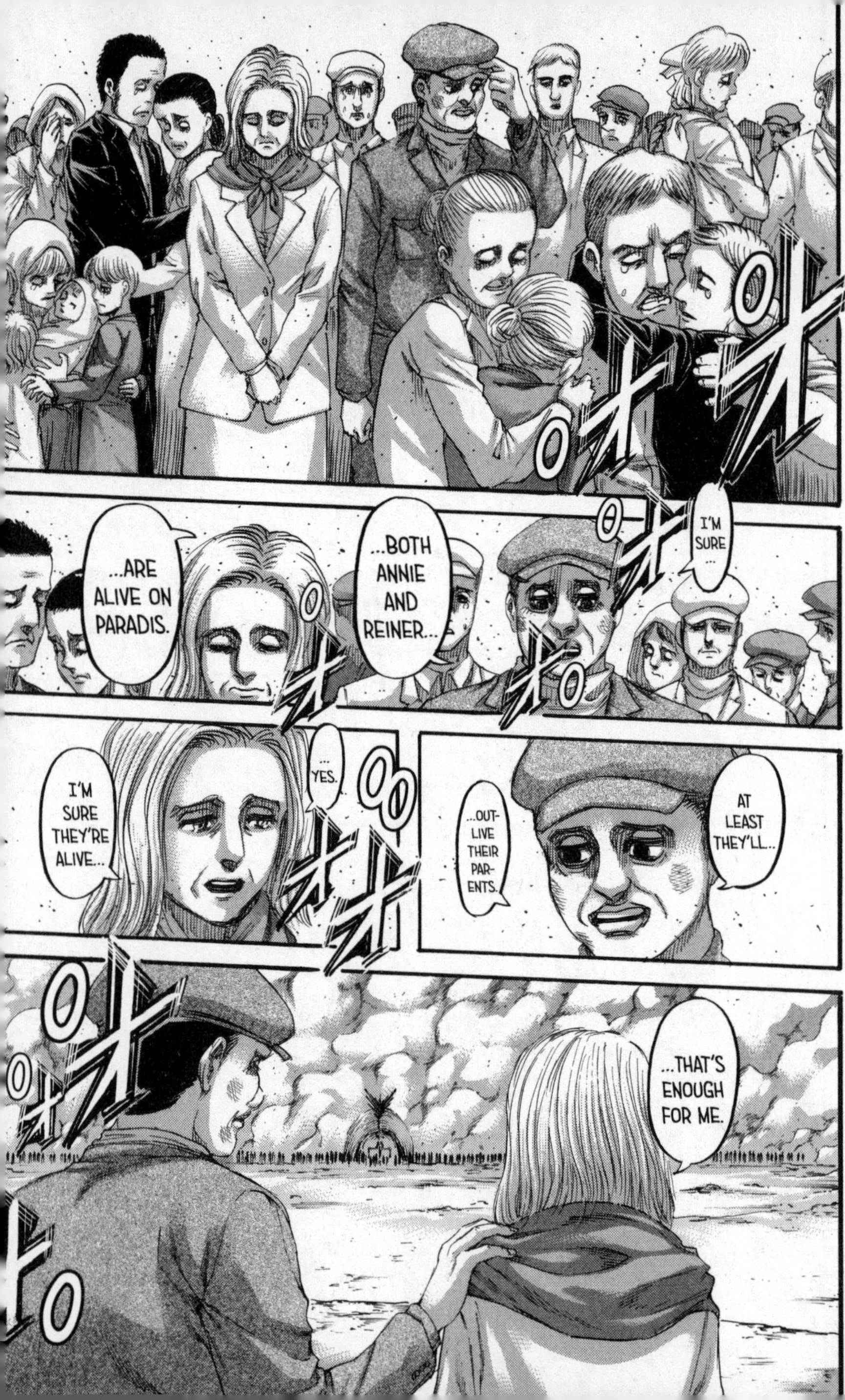
I'M SURE...
...BOTH ANNIE AND REINER...
...ARE ALIVE ON PARADIS.
AT LEAST THEY'LL...
...OUT-LIVE THEIR PAR-ENTS.
...YES.
I'M SURE THEY'RE ALIVE...
...THAT'S ENOUGH FOR ME.

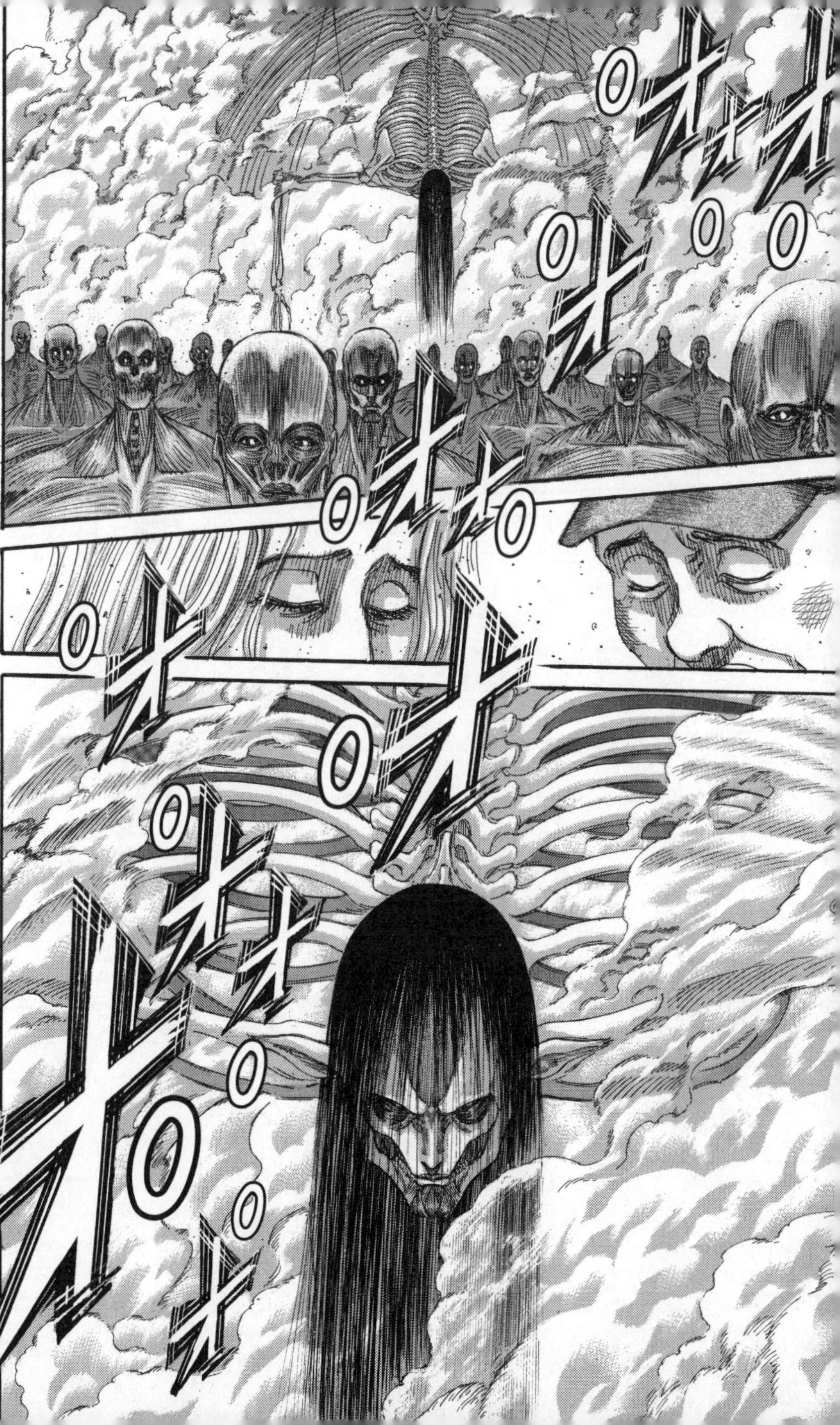
ォォオ
オ
オォ
オ
ォオ
ォォ
ォ

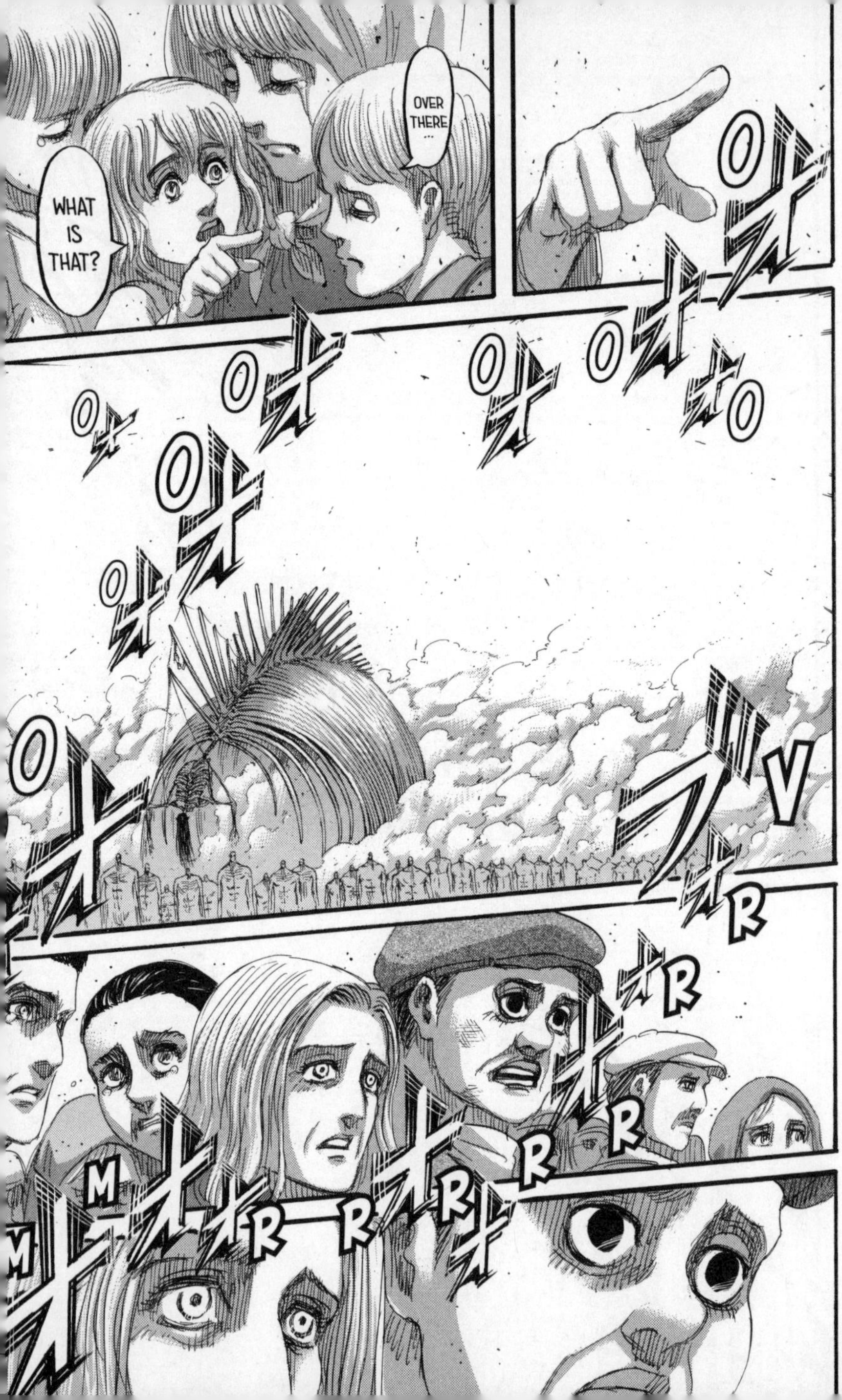
O
OVER THERE ...
WHAT IS THAT?
O O O O O O O O
V
R R R R R R R R R
M M

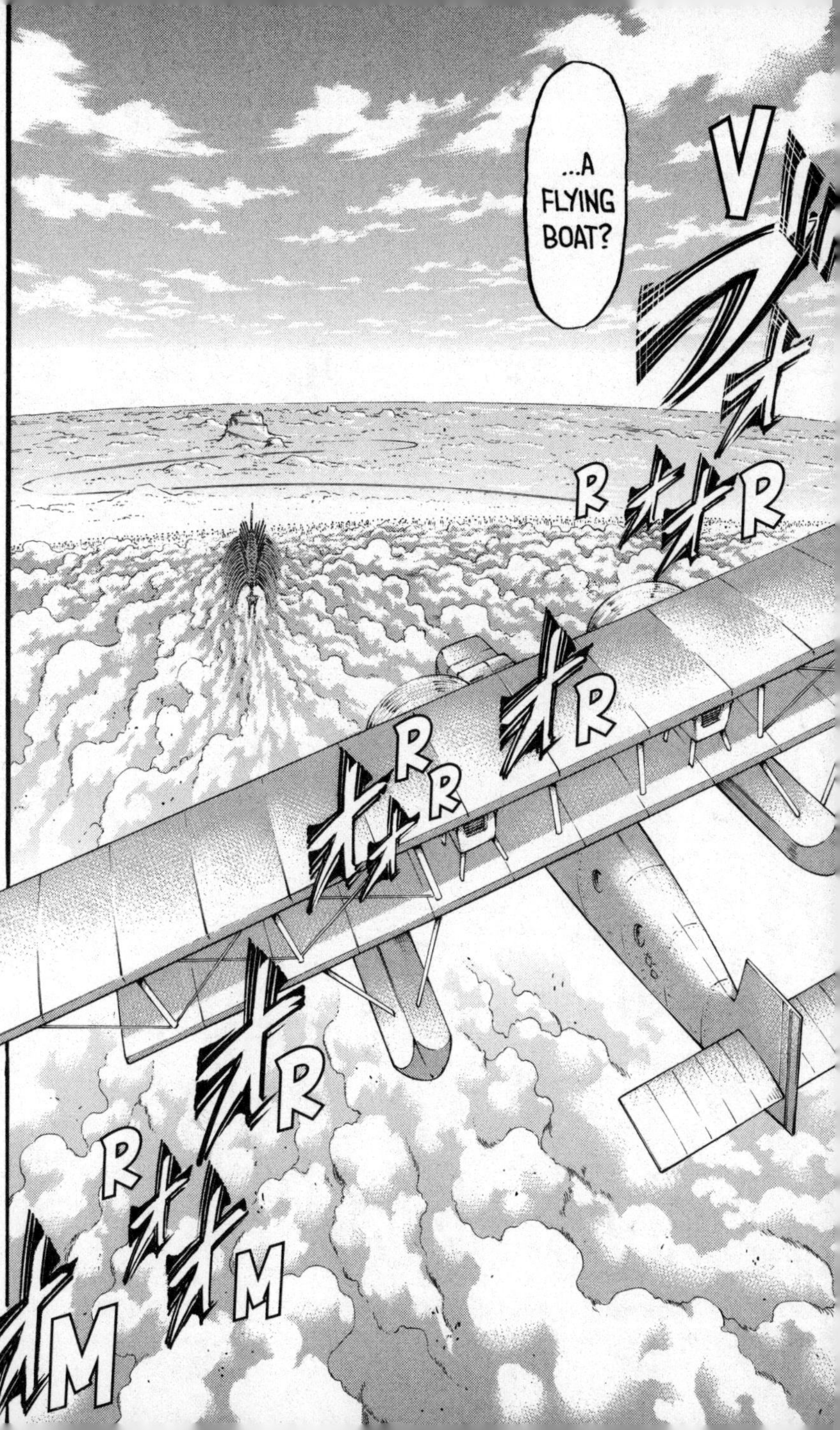
...A FLYING BOAT?
VRRRRRRRMM

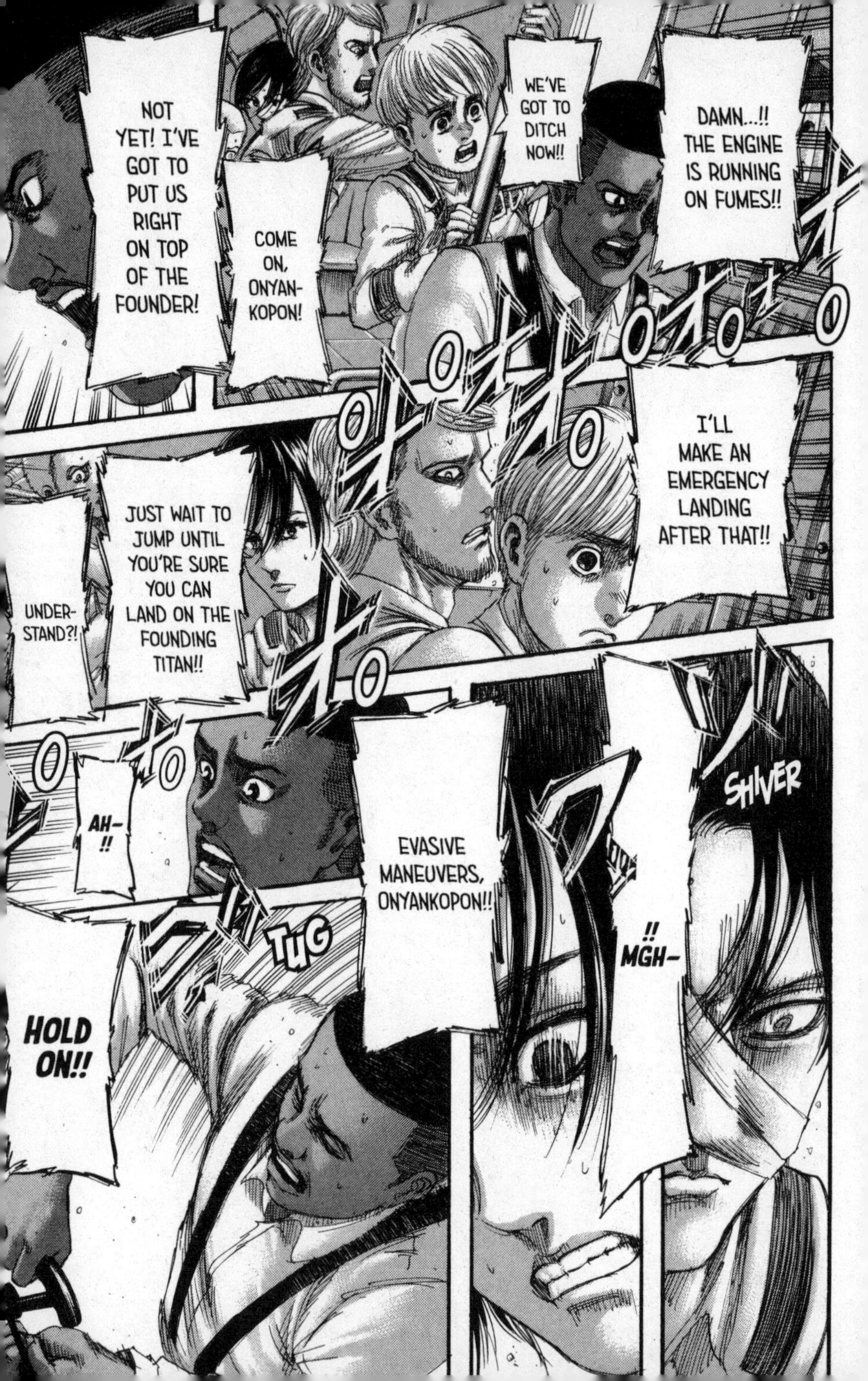
DAMN...!! THE ENGINE IS RUNNING ON FUMES!!
WE'VE GOT TO DITCH NOW!!
COME ON, ONYANKOPON!
NOT YET! I'VE GOT TO PUT US RIGHT ON TOP OF THE FOUNDER!
I'LL MAKE AN EMERGENCY LANDING AFTER THAT!!
JUST WAIT TO JUMP UNTIL YOU'RE SURE YOU CAN LAND ON THE FOUNDING TITAN!!
UNDER-STAND?!
SHIVER
!! MGH-
EVASIVE MANEUVERS, ONYANKOPON!!
AH-!!
TUG
HOLD ON!!

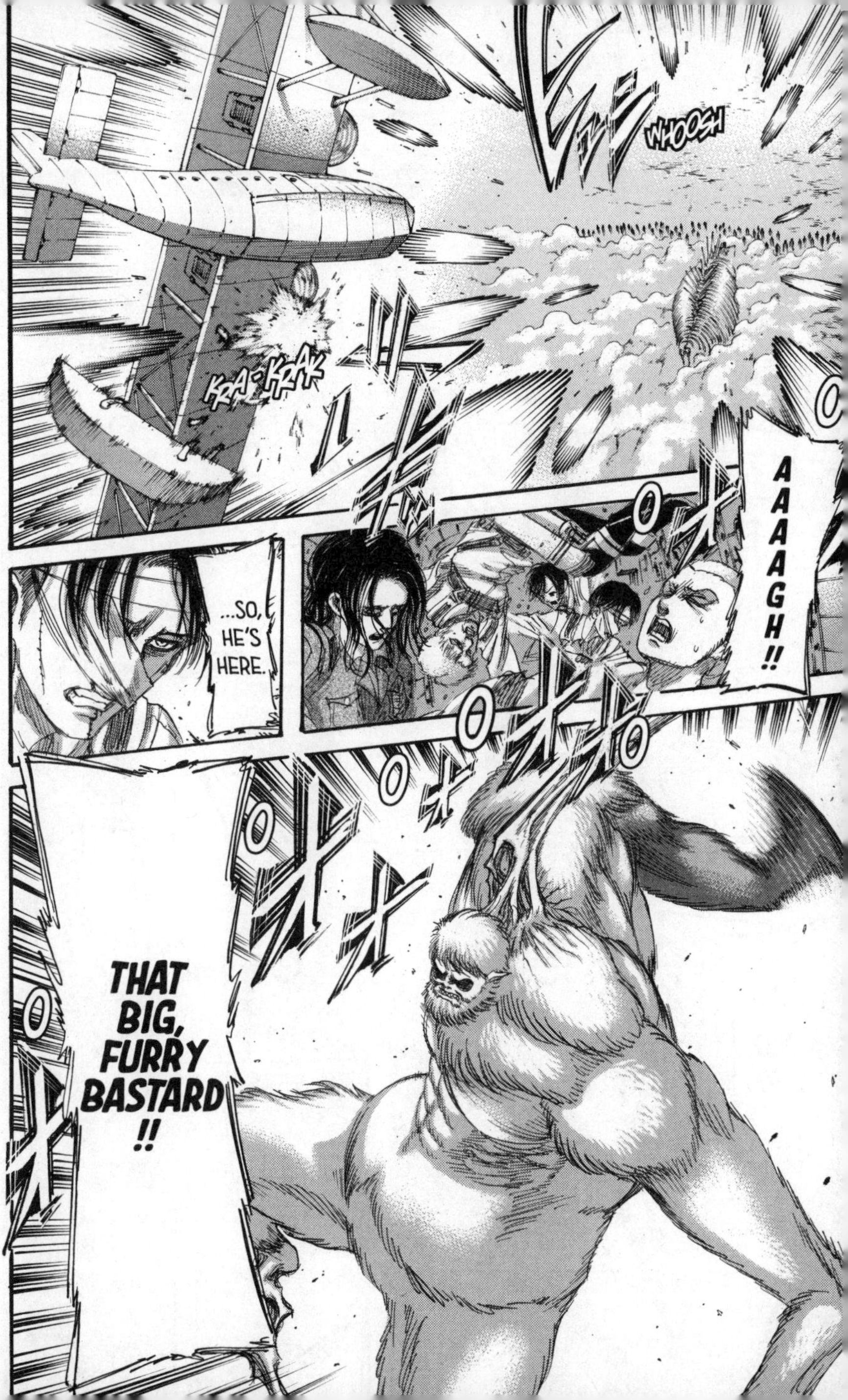
WHOOSH
KRA-KRAK
AAAAAGH!!
...SO, HE'S HERE.
THAT BIG, FURRY BASTARD!!

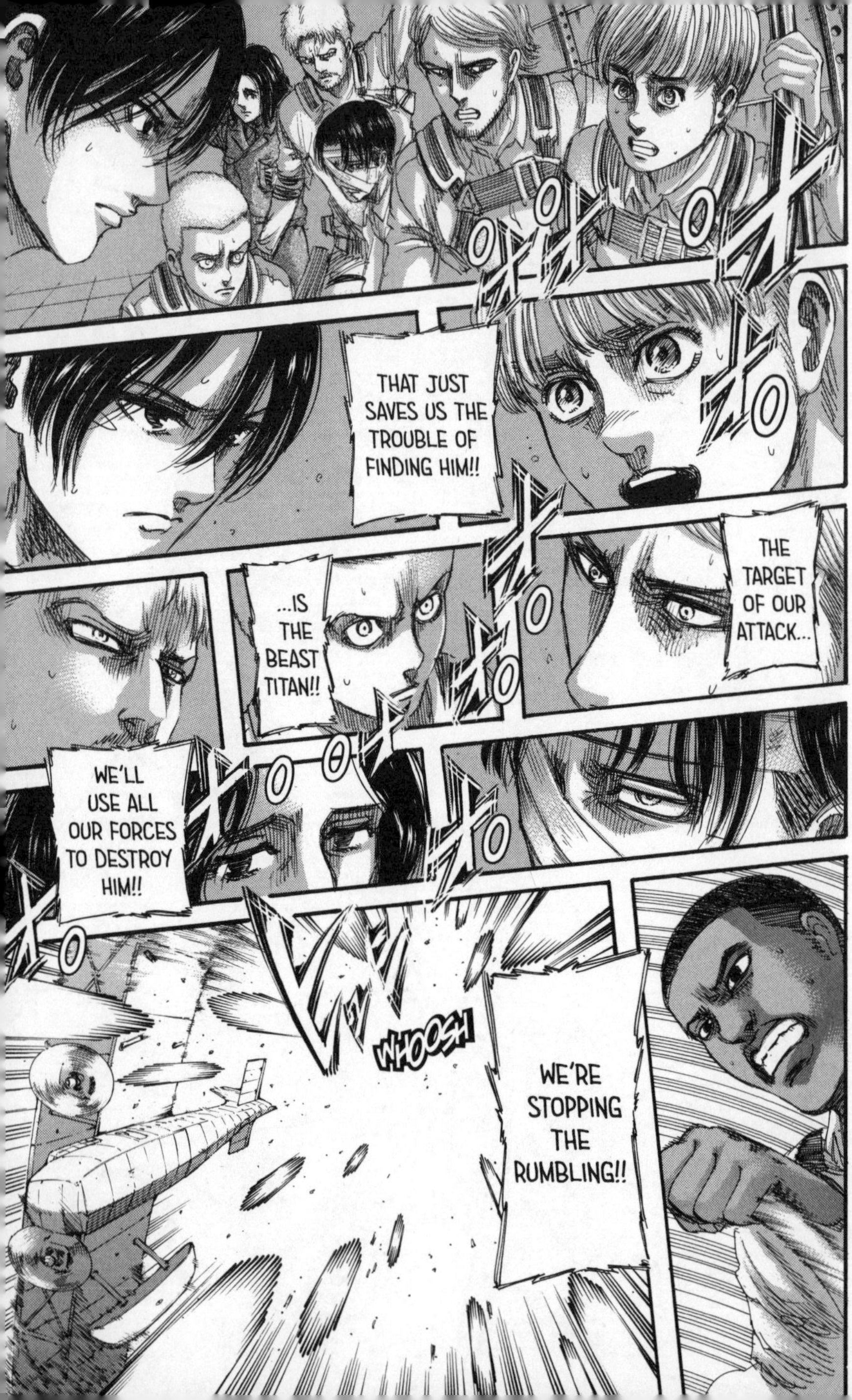
THAT JUST SAVES US THE TROUBLE OF FINDING HIM!!
THE TARGET OF OUR ATTACK...
...IS THE BEAST TITAN!!
WE'LL USE ALL OUR FORCES TO DESTROY HIM!!
WE'RE STOPPING THE RUMBLING!!
WHOOSH

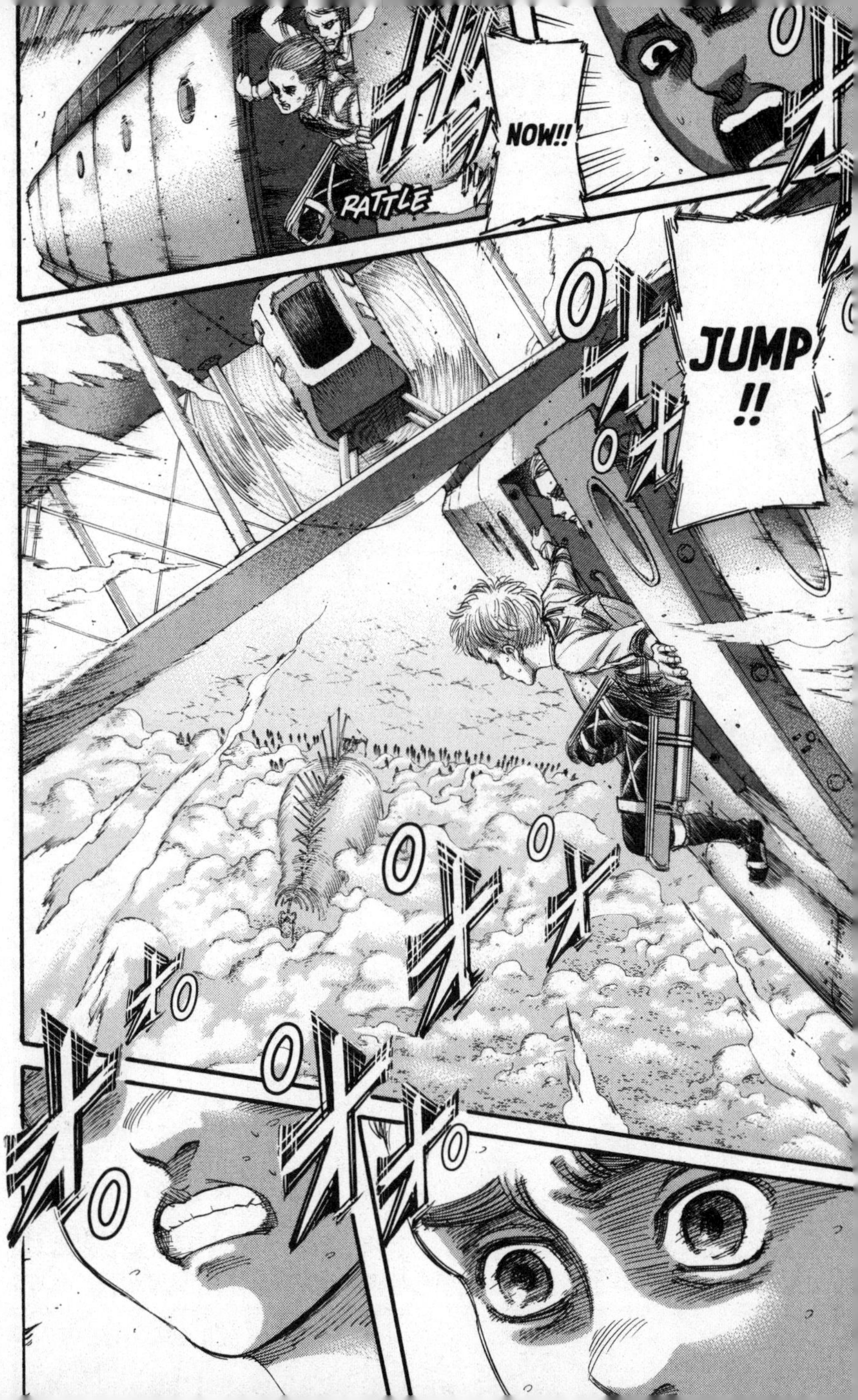
NOW!!
RATTLE
JUMP !!

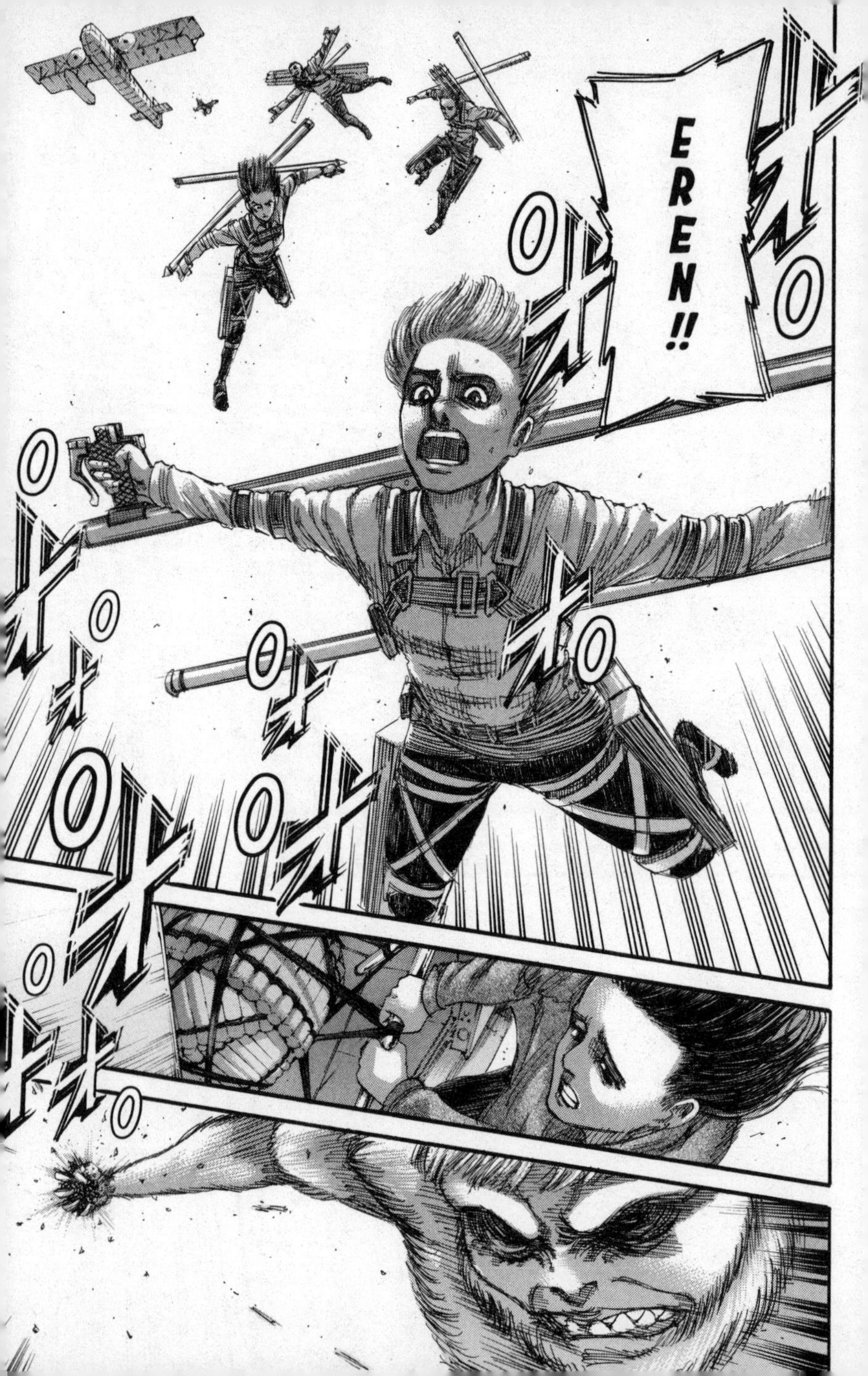
EREN!!

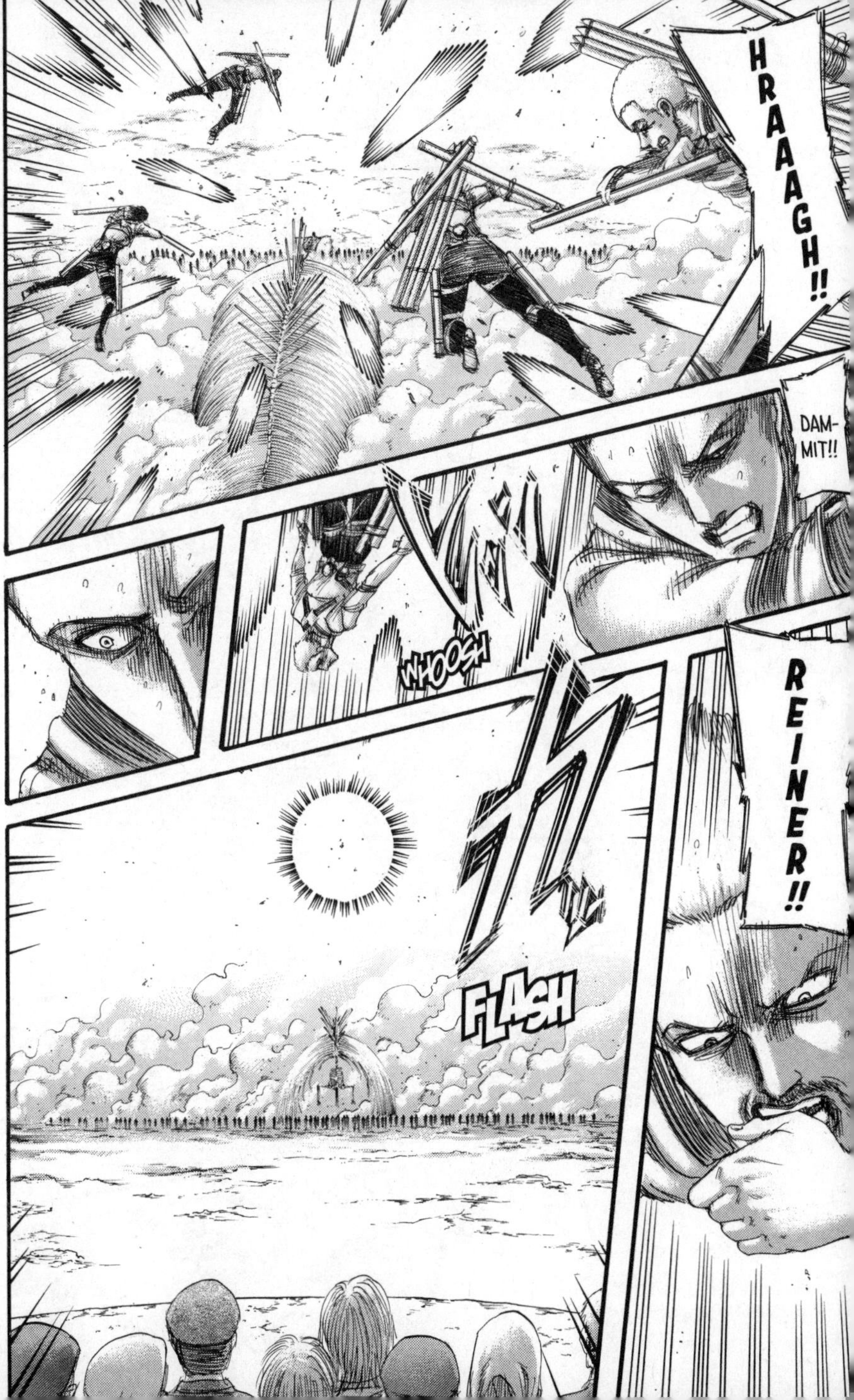
HRAAAGH!!
DAM-MIT!!
WHOOSH
REINER!!
FLASH

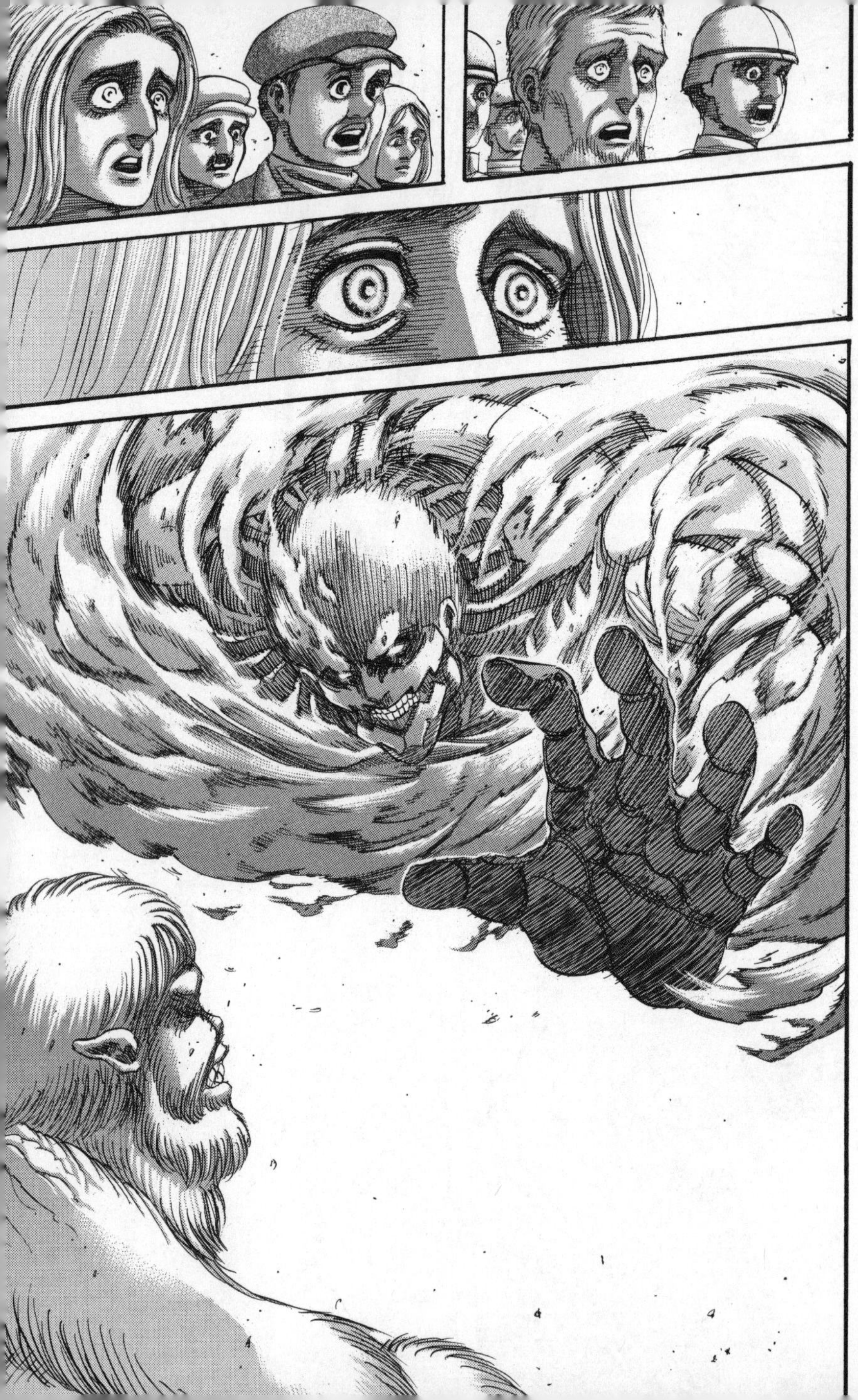

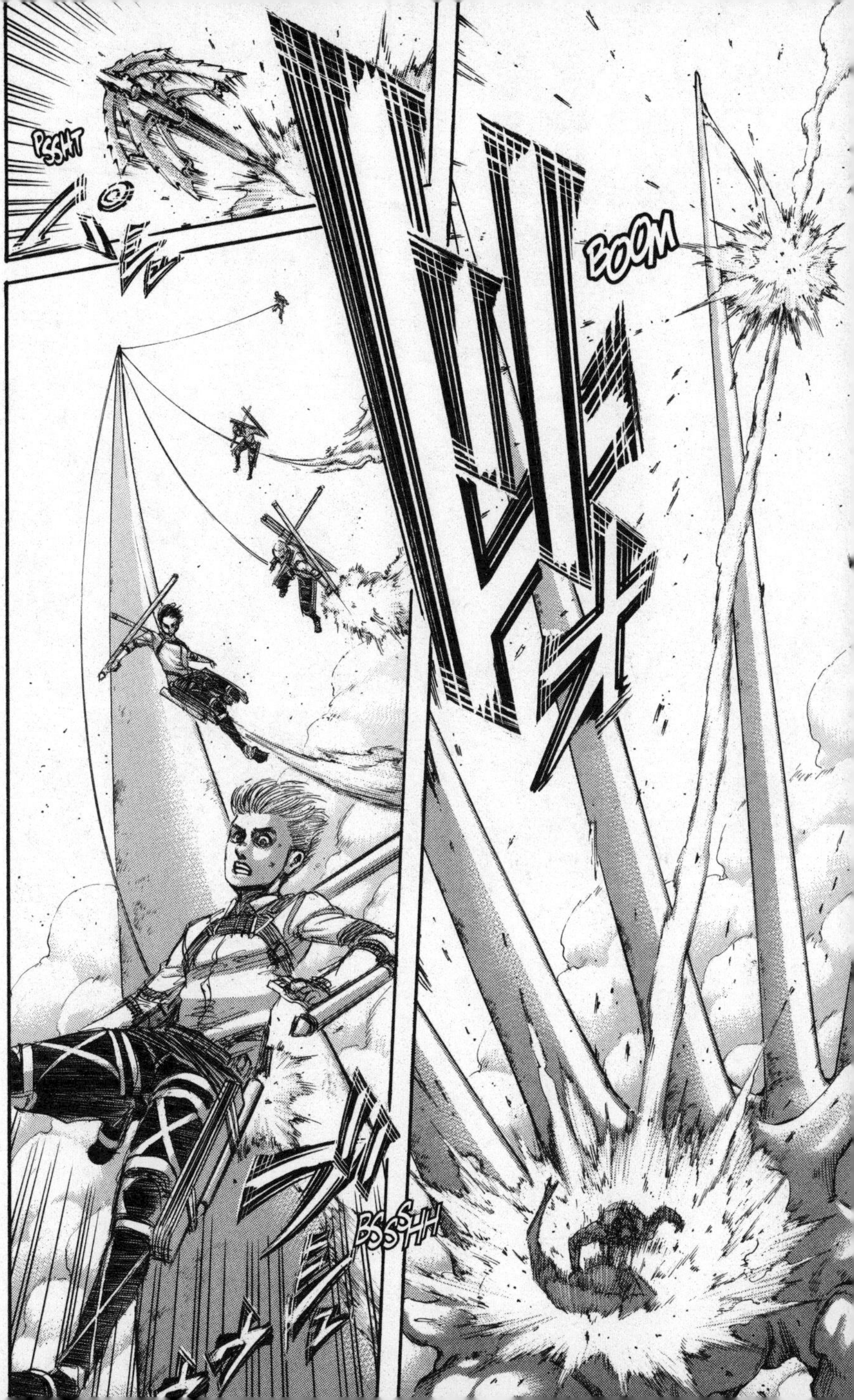
PSSHT
BOOM
BSSSHH

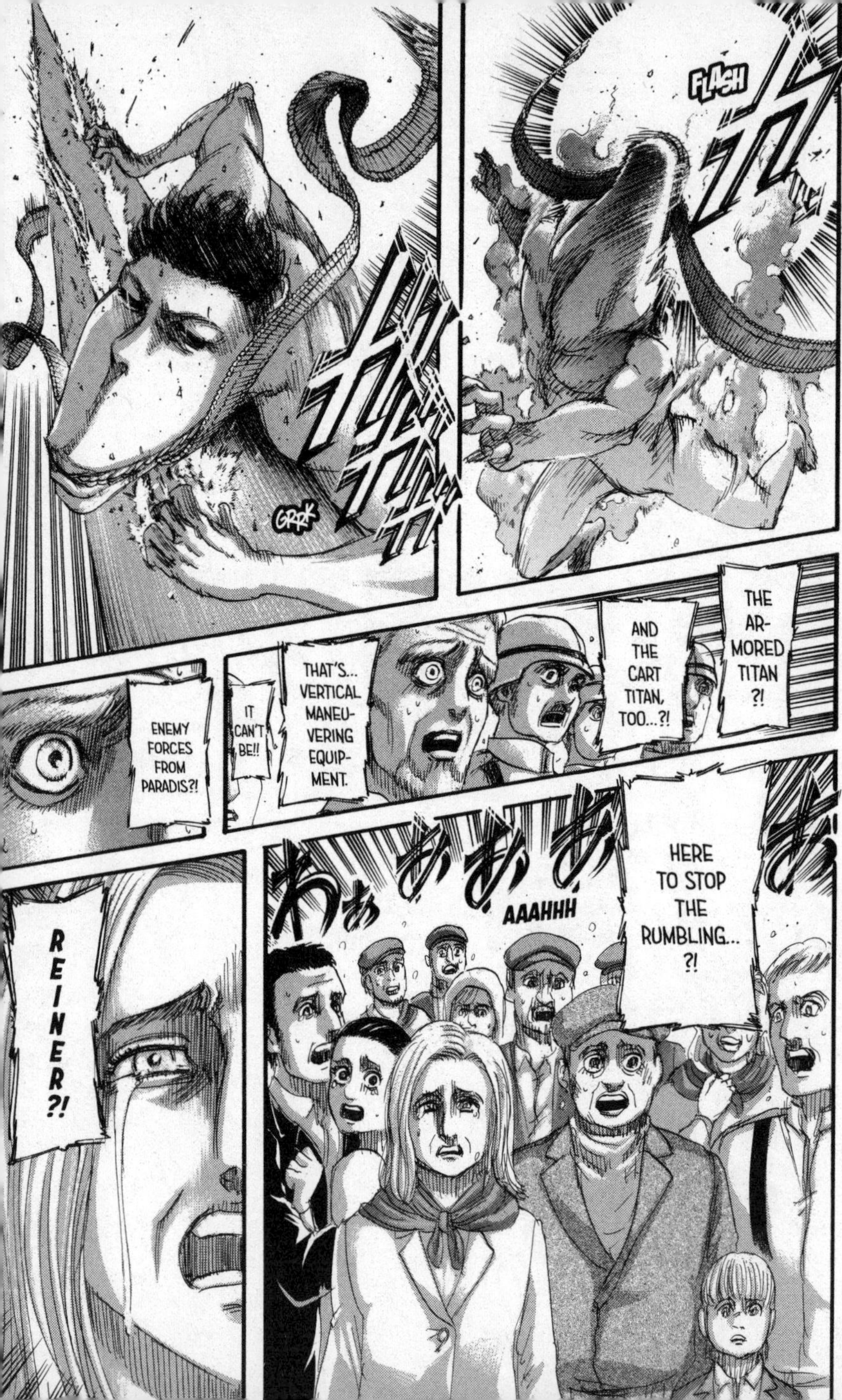
FLASH
GRRK
THE ARMORED TITAN?!
AND THE CART TITAN, TOO...?!
THAT'S... VERTICAL MANEUVERING EQUIPMENT.
IT CAN'T BE!!
ENEMY FORCES FROM PARADIS?!
HERE TO STOP THE RUMBLING...?!
AAAHHH
REINER?!

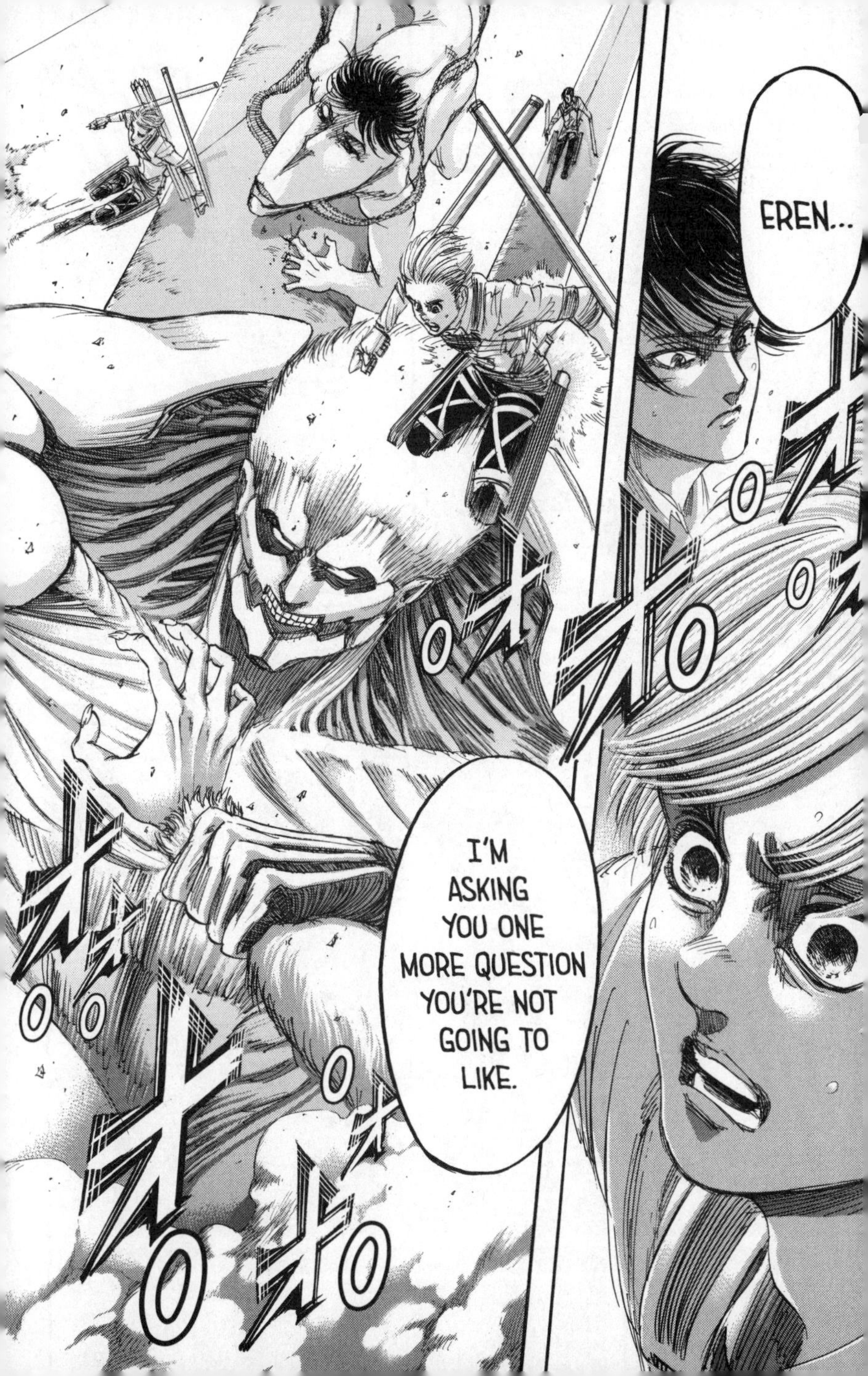
EREN...
I'M ASKING YOU ONE MORE QUESTION YOU'RE NOT GOING TO LIKE.

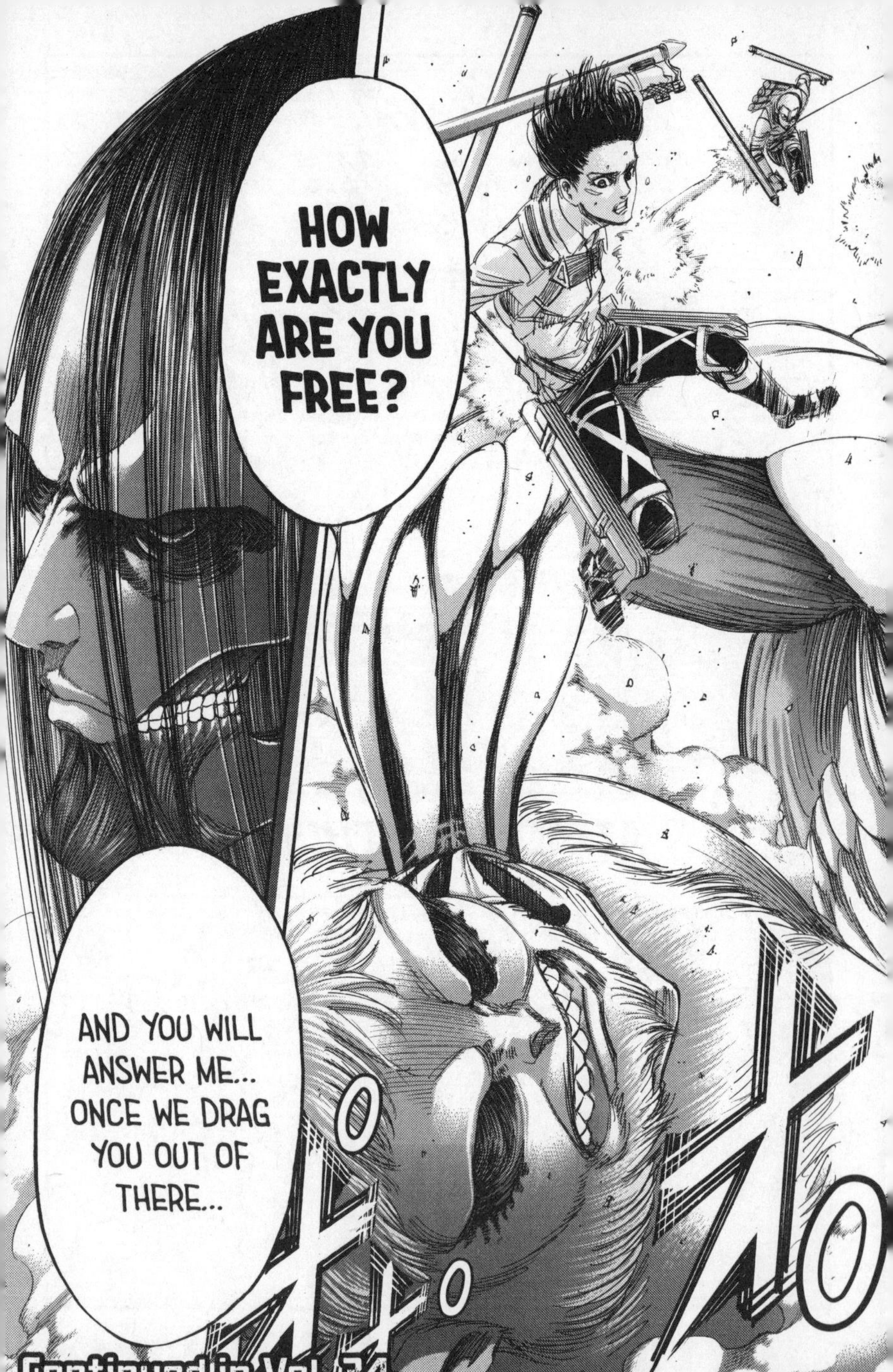
HOW EXACTLY ARE YOU FREE?
AND YOU WILL ANSWER ME... ONCE WE DRAG YOU OUT OF THERE...

Continued in Vol. 34

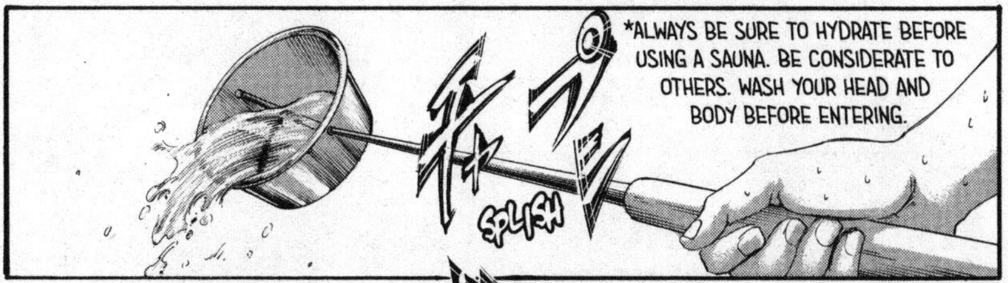
*ALWAYS BE SURE TO HYDRATE BEFORE USING A SAUNA. BE CONSIDERATE TO OTHERS. WASH YOUR HEAD AND BODY BEFORE ENTERING.
SPLISH

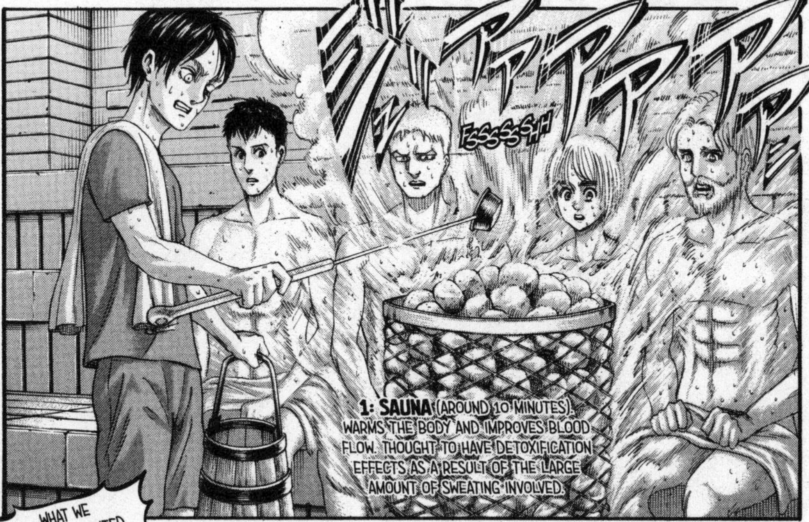
FSSSSSSH
1: SAUNA (AROUND 10 MINUTES). WARMS THE BODY AND IMPROVES BLOOD FLOW. THOUGHT TO HAVE DETOXIFICATION EFFECTS AS A RESULT OF THE LARGE AMOUNT OF SWEATING INVOLVED.

WHAT WE ULTIMATELY WANTED TO CONVEY IN THESE BONUS PAGES!

ATTACK ON SCHOOL CASTES

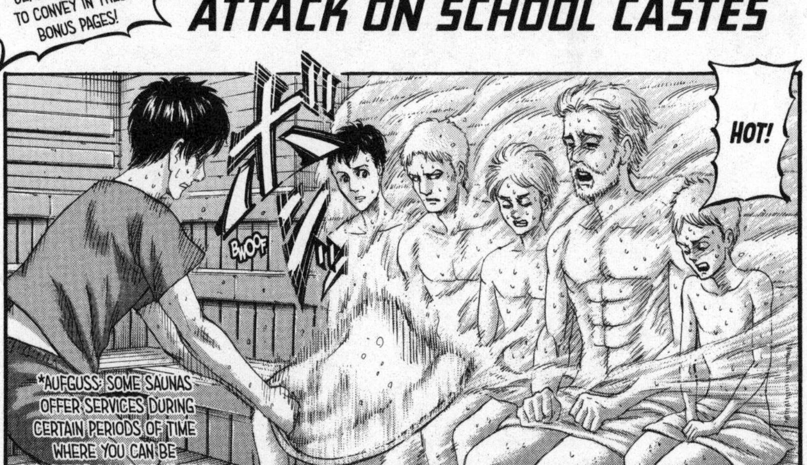
HOT!
BWOOF
*AUFGUSS: SOME SAUNAS OFFER SERVICES DURING CERTAIN PERIODS OF TIME WHERE YOU CAN BE SUBJECTED TO WAVES OF HEAT.

COMING FALL 2021!

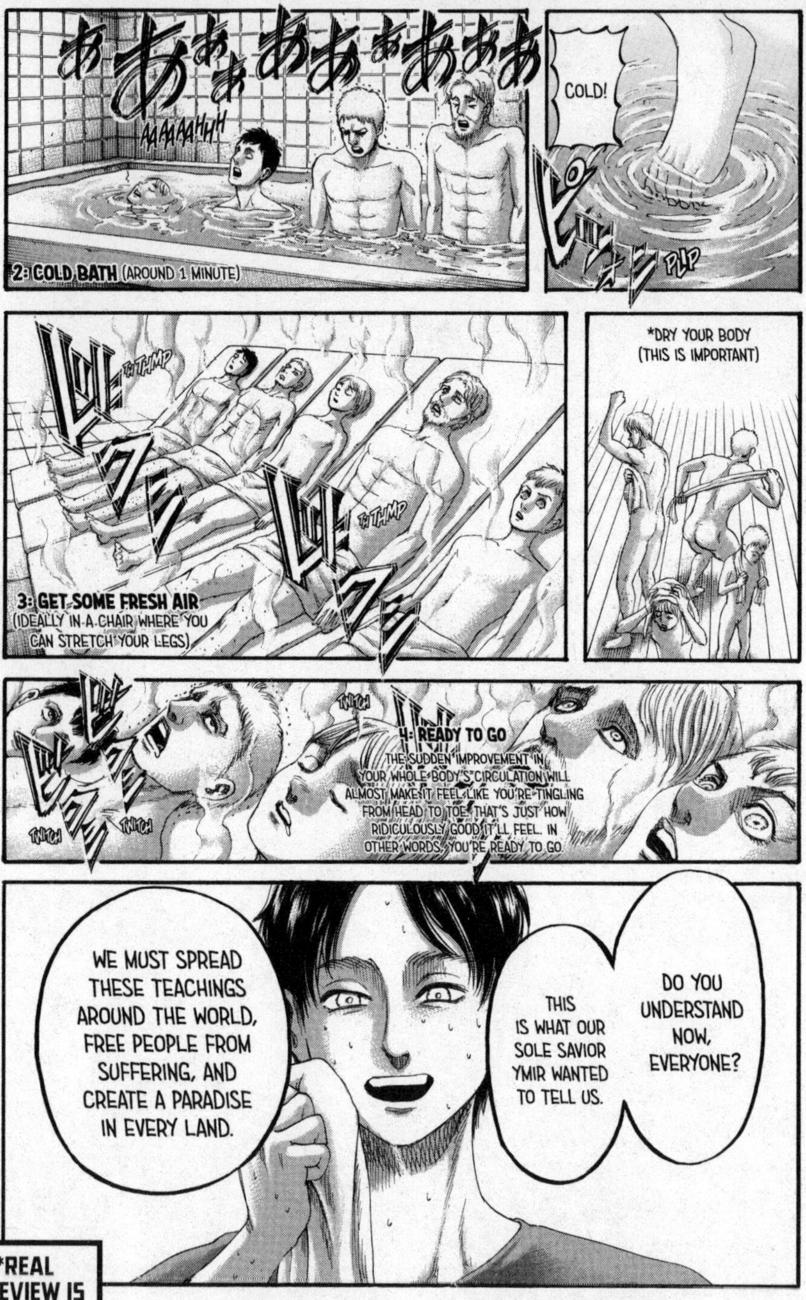
COLD!
PLIP
AAAAAAHHH
2: COLD BATH (AROUND 1 MINUTE)
*DRY YOUR BODY (THIS IS IMPORTANT)
TH-THMP
TH-THMP
3: GET SOME FRESH AIR
(IDEALLY IN A CHAIR WHERE YOU CAN STRETCH YOUR LEGS)
TWITCH
4: READY TO GO
THE SUDDEN IMPROVEMENT IN YOUR WHOLE BODY'S CIRCULATION WILL ALMOST MAKE IT FEEL LIKE YOU'RE TINGLING FROM HEAD TO TOE. THAT'S JUST HOW RIDICULOUSLY GOOD IT'LL FEEL. IN OTHER WORDS, YOU'RE READY TO GO.
TWITCH
TWITCH
DO YOU UNDERSTAND NOW, EVERYONE?
THIS IS WHAT OUR SOLE SAVIOR YMIR WANTED TO TELL US.
WE MUST SPREAD THESE TEACHINGS AROUND THE WORLD, FREE PEOPLE FROM SUFFERING, AND CREATE A PARADISE IN EVERY LAND.

*REAL PREVIEW IS ON THE FOLLOWING PAGE!

FINAL VOLUME

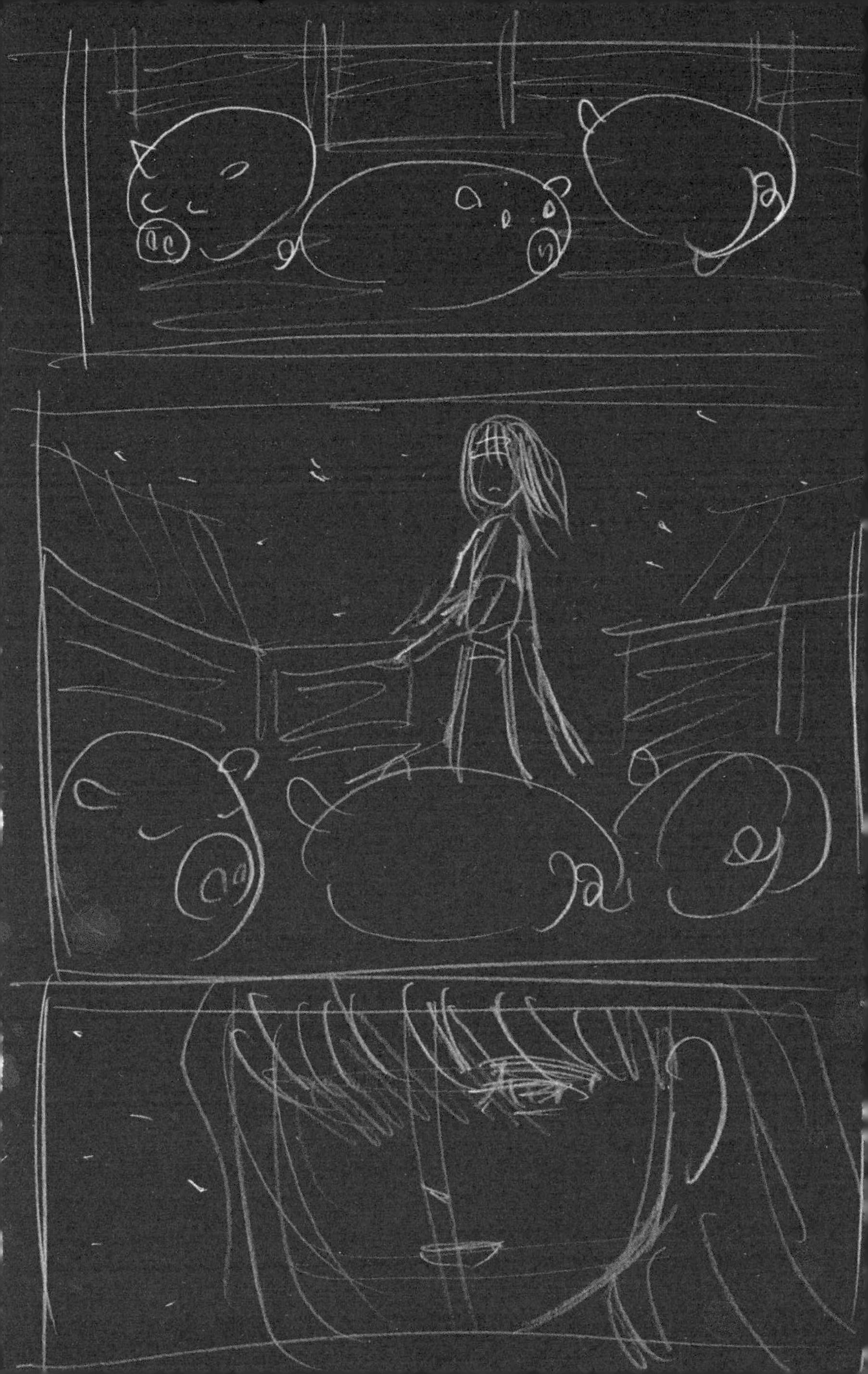